Disaster Risk, Resilience, Reconstruction and Recovery

Series Editors
Helen James, Australian National University, Canberra, ACT, Australia
Anna Lukasiewicz, Disaster Risk Science Institute, Australian National University, Canberra, ACT, Australia

This Palgrave Macmillan book series takes an interdisciplinary integrated approach to disaster risk, resilience and reconstruction. It brings together the multi-disciplinary expertise in the physical sciences and social sciences necessary for effective disaster risk reduction and recovery. With a broad focus on disaster risk science and sustainability, the series affords significant attention to those areas of the world which experience large scale societal and economic losses from disaster events. It includes disasters arising from climate change impacts and those from geological processes and tectonic movements, poor governance and emergency management practices. It takes into account both rural and urban environments in developing and developed countries and the ecological impacts of disasters.

By taking an integrated approach to the four research communities – poverty alleviation, development, climate change and disasters – this series brings new perspectives to the global disaster policy and practice communities. The series connects people and technology and examines the roles and contributions of multiple stakeholders across scale and their interactions with policy development and implementation. It provides significant inclusion of and acknowledgment of the importance of indigenous knowledge and cultural practices in shaping disaster risk reduction from numerous countries. By bringing together the multiple facets of disaster preparedness, response, recovery and reconstruction, the series opens new vistas on achieving reduced societal and economic losses from disasters around the world.

The series was founded by Prof. Helen James of the Disaster Risk Science Institute, at the Australian National University.

More information about this series at
https://link.springer.com/bookseries/16455

Helen James · Rajib Shaw · Vinod Sharma · Anna Lukasiewicz
Editors

Disaster Risk Reduction in Asia Pacific

Governance, Education and Capacity

Editors
Helen James
Disaster Risk Science Institute
Australian National University
Canberra, ACT, Australia

Vinod Sharma
Indian Institute of Public Administration
New Delhi, Delhi, India

Rajib Shaw
Graduate School of Media & Governance
Keio University
Fujisawa, Japan

Anna Lukasiewicz
Institute for Climate, Energy & Disaster Solutions
Australian National University
Canberra, ACT, Australia

ISSN 2662-5660　　　　　ISSN 2662-5679　(electronic)
Disaster Risk, Resilience, Reconstruction and Recovery
ISBN 978-981-16-4810-6　　ISBN 978-981-16-4811-3　(eBook)
https://doi.org/10.1007/978-981-16-4811-3

© The Editor(s) (if applicable) and The Author(s), under exclusive license to Springer Nature Singapore Pte Ltd. 2022
This work is subject to copyright. All rights are solely and exclusively licensed by the Publisher, whether the whole or part of the material is concerned, specifically the rights of translation, reprinting, reuse of illustrations, recitation, broadcasting, reproduction on microfilms or in any other physical way, and transmission or information storage and retrieval, electronic adaptation, computer software, or by similar or dissimilar methodology now known or hereafter developed.
The use of general descriptive names, registered names, trademarks, service marks, etc. in this publication does not imply, even in the absence of a specific statement, that such names are exempt from the relevant protective laws and regulations and therefore free for general use.
The publisher, the authors and the editors are safe to assume that the advice and information in this book are believed to be true and accurate at the date of publication. Neither the publisher nor the authors or the editors give a warranty, expressed or implied, with respect to the material contained herein or for any errors or omissions that may have been made. The publisher remains neutral with regard to jurisdictional claims in published maps and institutional affiliations.

Cover illustration: @FC_Italy/Alamy Stock Photo

This Palgrave Macmillan imprint is published by the registered company Springer Nature Singapore Pte Ltd.
The registered company address is: 152 Beach Road, #21-01/04 Gateway East, Singapore 189721, Singapore

Series Dedication

The *Disaster Risk, Resilience, Reconstruction and Recovery* book series is dedicated to the late Prof Helen James, who is its founding editor. Helen was an internationally ranked expert on Southeast Asia, especially Thailand and Myanmar. She was a true polymath, blending knowledge from a wide range of disciplines and always seeking practical solutions. She believed that collaboration—between disciplines, nationalities and institutions was the only way to advance knowledge and she built an international community of scholars and practitioners who are dedicated to preventing and mitigating disasters.

Prof. Helen James (1947–2020)

This series takes an interdisciplinary, integrated approach to disaster risk, resilience and reconstruction. It brings together the multi-disciplinary expertise in the physical sciences and social sciences necessary for effective disaster recovery. With a broad focus on disaster risk science and sustainability, the series is global in scope and includes disasters arising from climate change impacts and those from geological processes and tectonic movements, poor governance and emergency management practices. It provides significant inclusion of and acknowledgment of the importance of Indigenous knowledge and cultural practices in shaping disaster risk reduction from numerous countries. By bringing together the multiple facets of disaster preparedness response, recovery and reconstruction, the series will open new vistas on achieving reduced societal and economic losses from disasters around the world.

Contents

1 Disaster Risk Reduction and Resilience: Practices and Challenges in Asia Pacific   1
Rajib Shaw, Helen James, Vinod Sharma, and Anna Lukasiewicz

Part I   Governance

2 Policy Learning for Disaster Risk Reduction   19
Stephen Dovers

3 Na Ara Ahurea: Envisioning Collaborative Governance in Disaster Risk Reduction in Aotearoa   37
Christine M. Kenney

4 Improving Multi-Agency Governance Arrangements for Preparedness Planning and Response: Implementing the *Integrated Approach* in Australia   55
Alan Ryan

5   'Blackfella Way, Our Way of Managing Fires
     and Disasters Bin Ignored but "Im Still Here"':
     Australian Aboriginal Governance Structures
     for Emergency Management   71
     Bevlyne Sithole, David Campbell, and Steve Sutton with
     contributions from O. Campion, C. Brown, G. Daniels,
     A. Daniels, C. Brian, J. Campion, D. Yibarbuk,
     E. Phillips, G. Daniels, K. Daniels, B. Hedley,
     M. Radford, A. Campion, H. Hunter-Xenie, I. Sutton,
     and S. Pickering

Part II   Education and Capacity

6   Facilitating Effective DRR Education and Human
     Survival: Intentionally Engaging the Transformative
     Education-Paradigm Shift Spiral   97
     Petra Buergelt and Douglas Paton

7   All Singing from the Same Song Sheet: DRR
     and the Visual and Performing Arts   123
     Douglas Paton, Petra Buergelt, Etan Pavavalung,
     Kirby Clark, Li-Ju Jang, and Grace Kuo

8   High Expectations, Low Recognition: The Role
     of Principals and Teachers in Disaster Response
     and Recovery in the Asia–Pacific   147
     Carol Mutch

9   Planning and Capability Requirements
     for Catastrophic and Cascading Events   175
     Andrew Gissing, Michael Eburn, and John McAneney

10   Development and Implementation of Disaster Risk
     Management Specialization Program: Philippine
     School of Business Administration-Manila
     and Quezon City Government Collaboration Towards
     Sustainable Development Solutions   187
     Tabassam Raza, Jose F. Peralta, Thess Khaz S. Raza,
     and Carmelita R. E. U. Liwag

Part III Science Technology, Risk Assessment, Communities

11 Vulnerability and Resilience Science: Concepts, Tools, and Practice   213
    Susan L. Cutter

12 Flood Hazards and Disciplinary Silos   233
    Robert J. Wasson and Daryl Lam

13 Theorizing Disaster Communitas   251
    Steve Matthewman and Shinya Uekusa

14 Use of Scientific Knowledge and Public Participation in Disaster Risk Reduction and Response in the State of Sikkim, India   271
    Vinod Sharma

Part IV Recovery

15 Post-Disaster Recoveries in Indonesia and Japan: Building Back Better   291
    Minako Sakai

16 Housing Continuum: Key Determinants Linking Post-Disaster Reconstruction to Resilience in the Long Term   323
    Mittul Vahanvati

17 Disaster Risk Reduction and Recovery in Samoa   347
    Tautala Mauala

18 Towards a Resilient Asia Pacific Region   369
    Vinod Sharma, Helen James, Rajib Shaw, and Anna Lukasiewicz

Index   377

Notes on Contributors

Assist. Prof. Petra Buergelt is a transdisciplinary social scientist. For over 15 years, she has been qualitatively exploring holistically, in-depth and cross-culturally the nexus between disaster risk reduction; Indigenous worldviews, knowledges and practices; and transformation to contribute to a paradigm shift.

David Campbell is an emergency management and educational specialist working extensively across the public and private sectors. He works on a range of projects and delivers programs that focus on building individual, team and community disaster and organizational resilience capabilities.

Kirby Clark completed her honours thesis on the relationship between song lyrics, disaster risk reduction and disaster recovery. She is now working as an organizational psychologist in Australia.

Prof. Susan L. Cutter has authored or edited 15 books, 150+ plus peer-reviewed articles and book chapters, and mentored more than 60 masters and doctoral candidates. Her research focuses on vulnerability and resilience science with specific reference to methods, models, and metrics.

Em Prof. Stephen Dovers focuses on the generic policy and institutional dimensions of sustainable development, disasters and climate adaptation, combining contemporary and historical perspectives, across a diverse range of sectors and issues including climate adaptation, emergency management and disasters, biodiversity, water, urban studies, forests, coastal management and others.

Hon Assoc. Prof. Michael Eburn is the leading researcher in the area of emergency services, emergency management, and the law. He is the author or co-author of three books and has made over 80 other contributions as book chapters, journal articles, professional publications, and conference and professional development presentations. His blog, Australian Emergency Law, is widely read and respected throughout the sector.

Dr. Andrew Gissing is a Director of Risk Frontiers. He is an emergency and risk management expert. Andrew has performed senior executive roles in the emergency management and social services sectors, including as the Deputy Chief Officer of the Victoria State Emergency Service. He is an Adjunct Fellow of Macquarie University.

Dr. Li-Ju Jang is a professor of social work. She specializes in disaster social work. She has researched social impact and recovery following large scale disasters in Taiwan, including the 921 earthquake and Typhoon Morakot. She advises government and NGO agencies on DRR practices.

Professor Helen James was a specialist in Mainland Southeast Asia, especially Thailand and Myanmar (Burma). She has held academic appointments in a number of universities including the University of Pittsburgh, Thammasat and Chulalongkorn Universities, Bangkok, as well as the University of Canberra, the Australian Catholic University and The Australian National University.

Assoc. Prof. Christine M. Kenney is a Māori social scientist and researcher in disaster governance, risk reduction, recovery and resilience. She chairs the joint UNDRR/ISC/IRDR Indigenous science caucus and has expertise in research with Indigenous peoples and governments in Canada, Australia and New Zealand. Christine is also a contributing author to the GAR, and an expert advisor to the Warsaw International Mechanism for Loss and Damage.

Grace Kuo works develop and manage art exhibitions. She was involved in developing artworks covering disaster recovery in Linali Village in Taiwan and curating exhibitions of artworks addressing disaster recovery and environmental reintegration in displaced populations.

Dr. Daryl Lam is a waterway scientist who works with companies, academics and policy makers to address environmental concerns. Daryl specialized in locating and analyzing fluvial sedimentary evidence of palaeofloods but has worked across various environmental research and consultancy projects including urban hydrology, coastal processes, fluvial geomorphology, and flood management.

Prof. Carmelita R. E. U. Liwag is an Assistant Professor in the School of Urban and Regional Planning, University of the Philippines and an Adjunct Professor of PSBA, Manila. She has more than 20 years of local and international consultancy work experience in the field of Environmental Planning. She has locally and internationally published a substantial number of researches.

Dr. Anna Lukasiewicz researches issues at the interface of justice and natural resource management. This includes: working on concepts of social justice (resource distribution, decision-making processes, the environment as a stakeholder, and stakeholder-decision-maker interactions); as well as disaster justice (disaster management policy and disaster preparedness, mitigation, response and recovery).

Assoc. Prof. Steve Matthewman is an associate professor in Sociology at the University of Auckland. His current research focuses on the rebuilding of Christchurch following the 2010 and 2011 earthquakes. He is particularly interested in how a city gets put back together and what the barriers to building back better.

Tautala Mauala better known as Tala, has been the Secretary General for Samoa Red Cross Society (SRCS) for the past 20 years. She represents the SRCS on Samoa's Disaster Advisory Committee (DAC), Health Programs Advisory Council (HPAC) and the Steering Committee for Samoa's Water and Sanitation Sector.

Professor John McAneney is a Non-executive Director of Risk Frontiers, a company that models and prices natural catastrophe risks for the insurance and government sectors and advises on the management of such risks including adaptation to Global Climate Change. John was formerly the Managing Director of Risk Frontiers and oversaw its spin out from Macquarie University in 2017. His academic background is in physics and mathematics and has published over 100 peer-reviewed articles on different aspects of natural hazard risks and environmental physics. John is also a novelist; you can find his books at https://www.amazon.com/John-McAneney/e/B008D2ZKUC/ref=aufs_dp_mata_dsk.

Prof. Carol Mutch is a professor of Critical Studies in Education in the Faculty of Education and Social Work. She is also the Education Commissioner for UNESCO New Zealand. Dr. Mutch came to The University of Auckland following many years as a primary teacher, teacher educator and policy advisor.

Prof. Douglas Paton researched cross-cultural theories of disaster readiness, response and recovery based on research mostly in the Asia Pacific region. The findings are used to develop community engagement and professional training programs for communities and for social services and emergency professions.

Etan Pavavalung is a Taiwanese aboriginal of Paiwan ethnicity. His artistic creations are diverse as he works with cloth, poetry, prose, graphic design, painting, carving, installation art and video recording. In terms of visual art, Etan has decided to use "line laying carving" as his personal style of expression.

Jose F. Peralta is President, CEO, CAO, and Dean of Undergraduate Studies and Graduate School of Business, PSBA-Manila. He has served the Rotary Club of San Juan District 3800 as Past District Governor. President Peralta has written books on accounting and done substantial researches. He has more than 50 years experience of Academic leadership.

Dr. Tabassam Raza is Dean (External Education) of Graduate School of Business (GSB) and Director of Disaster Risk Management Unit, GSB, PSBA- Manila, Philippines. He is also a Professor in UP-SURP and has more than 25 years of experience working internationally and locally as Government Adviser, Senior Director, Associate Dean, and Technical Director.

Thess Khaz S. Raza is an Environmental Management Specialist II, under Task Force on Solid Waste Management, Environmental Protection and Waste Management Department, Quezon City Government, Philippines. She has published a substantial number of Disaster Risk Reduction and Climate Change Adaptation research papers locally and internationally.

Dr. Alan Ryan is the Executive Director of the Australian Civil-Military Centre. He was previously the Principal of the Centre for Defence and Strategic Studies at the Australian Defence College. Prior to this appointment he was the Senior Adviser to the Minister for Defence.

Dr. Minako Sakai is an Associate Professor at the School of Humanities and Social Sciences, the University of New South Wales (UNSW) Canberra. Her research interests include just and fair development, disaster relief, gender, Islamic economy with a focus on Indonesia. She has co-edited Disaster Relief in Asia Pacific (Routledge).

Prof. Vinod Sharma is the First Professor of Disaster Management in India and one of the pioneers of DRR in South Asia. He is the Founder Coordinator of the National Centre of Disaster Management (now National Institute of Disaster Management). He was founder Chairman of SEEDS India from 1995 to 2020. He is a member of the National Science Technology and Innovation Policy 2020. He is also the Vice-Chair of the Sikkim State Disaster Management Authority.

Prof. Rajib Shaw apart from being a professor in Keio University, is also a Senior Fellow of the Institute of Global Environmental Strategies (IGES) Japan, and the Chairperson of SEEDS Asia and CWS Japan, two Japanese NGOs. He is also co-founder of a Delhi (India) based social entrepreneur startup Resilience Innovation Knowledge Academy (RIKA). His expertise includes disaster risk governance, technology and innovation, community-based disaster risk management, climate change adaptation, urban risk management, and risk communication.

Dr. Bevlyne Sithole is a social scientist and experienced participatory research practitioner who has worked in community development and action research for over 20 years. Her broader professional experience is informed by leadership roles key indigenous research and evaluation products undertaken with the Aboriginal Research Practitioners' Network (ARPNet) which she founded in 2007.

Steve Sutton is a Ph.D. candidate at Charles Darwin University and directs a research project with the Bushfire and Natural Hazards CRC. His research focuses on enablers and barriers to effective preparation for natural hazard events, particularly in remote communities with limited service delivery from centralized government agencies.

Dr. Shinya Uekusa is an assistant professor in global studies at Aarhus University. His main research interests are in the sociology of disasters, particularly social vulnerability and resilience to disasters and climate change, focussing on the socially disadvantaged groups such as (im)migrants, refugees and linguistic minorities.

Dr. Mittul Vahanvati has done research which focuses on the theory and practice of resilience, both, after the disaster, through housing reconstruction projects, or pre-disaster, through resilience action planning and resilient public space design. She adopts community-led or co-production approaches. Her field of research sits at the intersection of built environment, human geography and sustainable design.

Prof. Robert J. Wasson is a geomorphologist with a Ph.D. from Macquarie University, and has held positions at the University of Auckland, the Australian National University (ANU), Charles Darwin University and the National University of Singapore. He has done research in Australia, New Zealand, Singapore, Indonesia, Timor-Leste, Malaysia, India, Nepal, Pakistan, China, Myanmar and Thailand.

List of Figures

Fig. 3.1	Potential framework for Iwi engagement with CDEM regional disaster governance structures (*Source* Adapted from Resource Legislation Amendment Act, 2017)	44
Fig. 3.2	Draft Māori emergency management governance model showing potential relationships with other stakeholders (© This figure is not to be used or reproduced without the permission of the author Dr C. Kenney)	51
Fig. 5.1	Aboriginal leadership and decision-making structure	80
Fig. 5.2	Essential Aboriginal leadership skills	81
Fig. 5.3	Components identified as key knowledge areas for decision-making pathways	82
Fig. 7.1	A depiction of traditional Taiwanese beliefs regarding the cause of earthquakes (**a**) and a painting of depicting the relationship between traditional beliefs and an activity used to mitigate risk (**b**) (*Source* Douglas Paton)	132
Fig. 7.2	The wind on the slope is very fragrant (*Source* Etan Pavavalung, 2014)	136
Fig. 7.3	Labored breathing at another foothill (*Source* Etan Pavavalung, 2013)	137
Fig. 10.1	Ranking results of the candidate cities (*Source* Raza, 2015)	196
Fig. 10.2	Location of the Quezon City selected as pilot urban area (*Source* Raza, 2015)	196
Fig. 10.3	Institutional Coping Capacity of QCG Barangays, QCG and NGOs	197
Fig. 10.4	Institutional Adaptive Capacity	198

Fig. 10.5	Personnel Coping Capacity Level of QCG Barangays, QCG and NGOs	199
Fig. 10.6	Personnel Adaptive Capacity Level of QCG Barangays, QCG and NGOs	199
Fig. 10.7	Framework for Developing Formal Education Program (*Source* PSBA, 2017)	202
Fig. 11.1	SoVI® for the U.S. using 2010–2014 data by census tract (top) using a three-class categorization, and by county (bottom) using a five-class categorization	220
Fig. 11.2	SoVI® coupled with FEMA verified loss counts tells the story of where resources are needed to support flood recovery in the aftermath of the 2015 flooding in South Carolina (*Source* South Carolina Disaster Recovery Office [SCDRO], South Carolina Action Plan for Disaster Recovery [Columbia: South Carolina Department of Commerce, 2016, p. 18], https://www.sccommerce.com/sites/default/files/hud_submittal_action_plan_1 60719.pdf)	225
Fig. 14.1	Map of Sikkim	272
Fig. 14.2	Ruins of a house in 2011 earthquake	275
Fig. 14.3	Options for the post-disaster reconstruction in Sikkim of residential housing	276
Fig. 14.4	Layout of a typical house	278
Fig. 14.5	Earthquake-resistant features	280
Fig. 15.1	Map of case study sites	300
Fig. 15.2	Foundation Stone, an example funded by the Dompet Dhuafa Foundation in the Merapi Slopes, listing the projects sponsored by the foundation	303
Fig. 15.3	Banner of a new snack (*keripik*) business placed along a major roadside	306
Fig. 15.4	Kesennuma City Mascot, Hoya Boya the Ocean Boy	310
Fig. 16.1	Detailed conceptual framework for post-disaster reconstruction and recovery projects in a spatial and temporal systems' context, with feedback (and feed-forward), loops between past experiences and future expectations. (*Source* Vahanvati 2017)	332

List of Tables

Table 2.1	Policy learning: who learns what and to what effect	23
Table 8.1	The role of schools in disaster preparedness, response and recovery	151
Table 8.2	Participants, settings and disaster types across the study	153
Table 10.1	Verbal interpretation of level of expertise	194
Table 11.1	Selected BRIC Scores by Capital and Change from 2010 to 2015	223
Table 16.1	Various meanings of the resilience concept—from the narrow to an integrated socio-ecological systems' interpretation	327
Table 16.2	Characteristics and dimensions of disaster resilience from a socio-ecological systems (SES) perspective	328
Table 16.3	A summary of multi-scalar reconstruction efforts post-2001 and 2008 disasters	335
Table 16.4	Short-term outcomes post-2001 and 2008 reconstruction efforts	337
Table 16.5	Long-term impacts of post-disaster reconstruction projects after 2001 and 2008 disasters, from SES resilience perspective	338
Table 16.6	A novel framework for ODHR projects to enhance the disaster resilience of communities in the long term	339
Table 17.1	Stakeholders' roles in prevention and preparedness	353
Table 17.2	Stakeholders' roles in response and recovery	357

CHAPTER 1

Disaster Risk Reduction and Resilience: Practices and Challenges in Asia Pacific

Rajib Shaw, Helen James, Vinod Sharma, and Anna Lukasiewicz

Introduction

The concept of disaster risk reduction has evolved over years. Back in 1990, when we had the first International Decade of Natural Disaster Reduction (IDNDR: 1990–1999), it was proposed as "international decade on hazard reduction" (as appeared in the proposal of Frank Press, then President of the National Academy of Sciences of USA, who proposed the decade). Also, the decade name was "natural disaster". Two

R. Shaw
Keio University, Tokyo, Japan
e-mail: shaw@sfc.keio.ac.jp

H. James · A. Lukasiewicz (✉)
Australian National University, Canberra, ACT, Australia
e-mail: anna.lukasiewicz@anu.edu.au

V. Sharma
Indian Institute of Public Administration, New Delhi, India

© The Author(s), under exclusive license to Springer Nature Singapore Pte Ltd. 2022
H. James et al. (eds.), *Disaster Risk Reduction in Asia Pacific*, Disaster Risk, Resilience, Reconstruction and Recovery,
https://doi.org/10.1007/978-981-16-4811-3_1

concepts have been changed significantly: we do not reduce the hazard, rather, we reduce the risks or vulnerability. And, there is no "natural" disaster, we call it a natural hazard, and the consequence is a disaster. Also, the "disaster reduction" concept has evolved to disaster "risk" reduction, and gradually to resilience building. From one disaster, we now talk about systemic risks and cascading disasters, which is happening in different parts of the world. NATECH (natural hazards induced technological disaster) is also observed recently. Thus, the whole disaster risk reduction issues are becoming complex with climate change adaptation as well as biological hazards like the global pandemic COVID-19.

The Asia Pacific region always bears the maximum brunt of the disasters due to its higher population exposures as well as occurrences of different types of hazards. Urbanization rate in Asia Pacific is the highest in the world, and migration from rural and urban areas is very prominent. This adds to the already vulnerable and fragile urban ecosystem putting pressure on the system. Thus, while we talk about urban resilience, we need to think of urban rural collective resilience and ensure sustainable resource flow, be it food, water, energy, or human resources and livelihood supports.

This introductory chapter covers four parts which the book is divided into. Those are: disaster risk governance, education and capacity, science technology, and disaster recovery. These are four major pillars of different types of interventions in the Asia Pacific region.

Disaster Risk Governance

Disaster risk governance is one of the four Sendai priorities. At the national, regional, and global levels, it is very crucial for prevention, mitigation, preparedness, response, recovery, and rehabilitation. It also fosters collaboration and partnership. Risk governance depends on the legal and institutional aspects (Djalante et al., 2017; Pal & Shaw, 2017).

At the regional level, proper risk governance is quite challenging. It needs inter-governmental processes. Possibly two classic examples are that of ASEAN (Association of South East Asian Nations) and EU (European Union). All ten ASEAN Member States have law and policy frameworks for national disaster preparedness and response. However, there are varying types of disaster response systems in ASEAN Member States. It has been an important goal of ASEAN to share implementation of the ASEAN Agreement on Disaster Management and Emergency

Response (AADMER) though identifying and analyzing them individually and regionally in order to jointly respond to disasters. The adoption and implementation of AADMER has facilitated the enhancement of regional mechanisms on preparedness and response. "One ASEAN, One Response" was developed to build upon AADMER in order to have a collective strength of all stakeholders in ASEAN collaborating together during a natural disaster. Similarly, The EU Civil Protection Mechanism brings together a total of 34 countries: 27 EU Member States, 6 Participating States (Norway, Iceland, Montenegro, North Macedonia, Serbia, and Turkey), and the UK during the transition period. This European Civil Protection "family" shares operational challenges and similar approaches to managing disaster, while the structure and composition of emergency services in the 33 countries varies considerably from country to country.

In the national level, disaster management law/regulation is the key pillar of disaster risk governance. After the 2004 Indian Ocean Tsunami, most countries of the Asia Pacific region have introduced their national disaster management law/ legislation at the national level. Disaster Response fund has been set up in many countries. This is also related to the resource allocation, especially for the pre-disaster mitigation aspects. Philippines is a classic example where 5% off the budget from national to local can be used as calamity fund, which is usually post disasters, but can also be used for pre-disaster preparedness measures. Science-based decision making is another aspect of good risk governance. In different countries, there exist a science policy forum in the form of advisory group (Shaw, 2020).

At the local level, risk governance becomes critical, and there often exists a strong gap between the national and local level governance. Resources at the local government level becomes critical. As mentioned above, the Philippines is a great example of uniform local level resource distribution. Even in case of Japan, local governments, especially in the small cities and towns are resources constrained. Thus, the Japanese government has started a national resilience program, which enhances the capacities of the local governments through allocation of resources (DeWit et al., 2020). Capacity and trained professionals at the local governance is also a challenging issue. As per the Indonesian disaster management law, each local government needs to have a disaster risk reduction office, however availability of required numbers of trained professional is a challenge.

In the community level, community governance becomes an important issue (Shaw, 2014). Trust in the community, local leadership, participation of communities in different events become critical factors to enhance community governance. Indigenous or local governance does exist in different communities and become effective in case of disaster response as well as recovery.

EDUCATION AND CAPACITY

Disaster risk reduction education is a two-way learning process. For effective risk communication, there needs to be a balance of expert knowledge and local knowledge (Kikkawa, 1999). The end product is enhanced knowledge at both levels. The role of facilitators is also quite critical. Shiwaku et al. (2016) argued for experiential learning, and it is found that school community and home linkage is very important for disaster risk reduction education. Shaw and Oikawa et al. (2014) argued that education for sustainable development (ESD) and DRR education have lots of overlap, and both these concepts are linked to school community linkages. This has been also demonstrated in two cities namely Kesennuma and Kamaishi, where ESD and DRR education were implemented. Both these cities were affected by the Great East Japan Earthquake Tsunami of 2011, and no casualties in the schools were observed.

Disaster education (2009) discussed a model called KIDA (Knowledge Interest Desire Action) as a part of the disaster education model, where it is argued that the education is more as a process than a product, and DRR education can be a lifelong learning. In Japan, three types of help are considered important for DRR: self-help, mutual help, and public help. There is another help, called network help with links these three types of helps and make it workable for DRR actions. DRR education enhances these types of helps. Edutainment (education with entertainment) can also be used effectively to disaster education, which can be linked to songs, fold art, drama, music etc.

Higher education is another area which needs to be focused. Izumi et al. (2020) in a recent survey have highlighted the importance of higher education management, SOPs (standard operation procedures) and campus safety are important pillars of education continuity in case of the disaster. Campus safety programs help the students and teachers from different disciplines to enhance their understanding and perception on disaster risks and can facilitate risk reduction actions.

Capacity building or training for enhancing DRR skills is an integral part of education programs. There are several regional, national and local specialized agencies for capacity enhancement. Capacity enhancement needs for government officials, non-government professionals as well as corporate sector members. Community volunteers often play vital role before, during, and after disasters. Examples include local urban volunteers in many cities, fire volunteers, first aid and rescue volunteers, flood/forest volunteers etc. Enhancing the capacities of community volunteers is very critical.

SCIENCE TECHNOLOGY AND DISASTER RISK REDUCTION

Science and technology have been the core of DRR over many years. Shaw (2020) did a review of the evolution of science and technology in DRR over last thirty years. The year 2020 marks thirty years from the formal international disaster decade in 1990. Thus, it is argued that thirty year is a good number of years for a disciplinary evolution of the subject "disaster management".

At the global, regional, and national level there exists advisory groups, which provide expert advices to the countries for evidence-based decision making. At the global level, the Science Technology Advisory Group (STAG) provides critical advices to the UN and other global bodies. At the regional level similar regional STAGs exist, and there are regional science technology conferences held with the presence of science technology and other related stallholders, including governments, UN agencies, media, non-government agencies, and private sectors. At the global level, in 2019, a Science and Technology Roadmap to Support the Implementation of the Sendai Framework for Disaster Risk Reduction 2015–2030 was evolved, which includes four expected outcomes and 58 actions under four Priorities of Sendai Framework. There are specific governance-related actions which are linked to: (1) assessing and updating data and knowledge, (2) dissemination, (3) monitoring and review, and (4) capacity building. All these four outcomes become crucial elements of disaster risk governance, which is linked to enabling environment of technology development and its implementation.

At the national level, as mentioned in the governance section, national science technology advisory group exist. Malaysia is a classic example where the national disaster management agency is advised by a science technology group at the apex level. In the Philippines, national government, academia, and private sectors form national resilience council. However, the key challenge is science technology advices in the local level, where the local governments and local research institutes/ university or specialized agency partnership is critical. Thus, for effective application of science and technology, a techno-legal regime is very much required (Shaw et al., 2017).

The role of new and emerging technologies is DRR is often discussed. Both the emerging and disruptive technologies play an important role. Japan put forward a vision of human centric technology-based society called "Society 5.0", where the technology divide can be minimized through different types of disruptive technology usages (Mavrodieva & Shaw, 2020). Social innovation in disaster risk reduction is an area which needs additional support (SIOH, 2020). Several countries are supporting innovation or start-up ecosystem; however, these start-ups are mainly implemented in technology or education or health-based areas. DRR start-ups are still few in numbers, and they need proper supporting ecosystem with links to funding agencies, mentorship, market opening, etc. That would lead to new innovations in the field of disaster risk reduction.

Post Disaster Recovery

While there has been extensive work to focus on pre-disaster mitigation and preparedness activities, post disaster recovery is the time, when significant attention is gained. Also, resources pour in after the disasters, new innovations happen, and new partnership is emerged. Thus, the recovery process becomes a pillar to future risk reduction activities, and disaster is often termed as a used or misused development opportunity (Shaw, 2013).

The key question is: even though lots of effort is put into disaster recovery programs, why have some communities carried out faster (in terms of time frame) and more satisfying (in terms of holistic and participatory) recovery programs while others have not? Where do such differences come from? There is possibly no straightforward answer, since it is a complex mixture of social, economic, religious, political, and other issues. Disaster recovery is thus, often characterized based on cultural aspects. People plays an important role in the recovery process, and it is community participation and ownership of the people which makes it a sustainable recovery. Social capital plays an important role in disaster recovery. Nakagawa and Shaw (2004) in their landmark paper, compared two communities in Kobe and urged that the one with higher social capital, especially in terms of both bridging and bonding capital can be evolved as a better recovered community. Aldrich (2012) with empirical data from disasters showed that regardless of the quality of governance, different neighborhoods under the same leadership come back at different rates over the medium to a longer time.

During the negotiation period for the Sendai Framework, the concept of "Build Back Better" was proposed by the Japanese delegation as a holistic concept which states: "The principle of 'Build Back Better' is generally understood to use the disaster as a trigger to create more resilient nations and societies than before. This was through the implementation of well-balanced disaster risk reduction measures, including physical restoration of infrastructure, revitalization of livelihood and economy/industry, and the restoration of local culture and environment". The concept was fully agreed as one of the most important concepts among each state's delegates and embedded into the Sendai Framework. Thus, the focus on recovery has now become widely recognized as one of the four Sendai priorities.

There are different arguments on sustainable recovery or ecosystem-based recovery. In a recent intervention, Mukherjee et al. (2020) argued for an eco-centric recovery from COVID-19, and suggested ten principles under people, process, facility, and technologies. Cluster concept, graduated adoption, and scalability are suggested as three key pillars of eco-centric recovery.

Local governance plays the most critical role in recovery. It is the direct interface with the communities to incorporate their view and priorities. Often, local government officials themselves are the victims of the disasters, and often bear the brunt while supporting affected people. Capacity of local governments in post disaster scenarios often becomes a challenging issue. Local governments are also the focal points of media attention and have additional pressure to cope with the complex technical, social, political processes.

GLOBAL PANDEMIC AND RESILIENCE BUILDING

The global pandemic (COVID-19) has shaken the whole world from early 2020, with its deep impacts on every aspects of the society, impacting all of the SDG (sustainable development goals). The Sendai Framework for Disaster Risk Reduction 2015–2030 reinforced the scope of disaster risk management by including biological hazards such as outbreaks, epidemics, and pandemics in addition to natural, technological and other hazards as a key area of focus for disaster risk management. The Sendai Framework (UN, 2015) also places a strong emphasis on resilient health systems through the integration of disaster risk management into health care provision at all levels. In particular, it aims "to enhance cooperation between health authorities and other relevant stakeholders to strengthen country capacity for disaster risk management for health."

The Health Emergency and Disaster Risk Management (HEDRM) Framework of the World Health Organization (WHO, 2019) aims to provide a common language and a comprehensive approach that can be adapted and applied in health and other sectors for reducing health risks and consequences of emergencies and disasters. It is founded on the core principles of comprehensive emergency management, whole-of-health system, multi-sectoral and multi-disciplinary collaboration, people & community-centric, risk-based & all-hazards approach with due focus on ethical considerations. The International Conference on the Implementation of the Health Aspects of the Sendai Framework (held in Bangkok 2016) resulted in Bangkok Principles, which call for developing or revising multi-sectoral disaster risk reduction plans and policies to include the health sector. It also recommends greater participation of health sector representatives in disaster risk reduction platforms and committees at all levels.

Analysis of the past cases of pandemics and public health emergencies of international concern (PHEIC) and the experience of countries in managing COVID-19 point toward the need for evidence-based decision making supported by technology and innovations to develop early warning and risk assessment tools. The direct, indirect, and wider impacts of a health emergency are sector-specific and vary across economies. The COVID-19 pandemic will have a lasting impact on all aspects of development planning in the years to come. The pandemic brought into light the need for effective risk management to safeguard development and the implementation of the International Health Regulations (IHR), SDGs, the Sendai Framework, Paris Agreement, and New Urban Agenda as well as other global, regional, and national frameworks.

ABOUT THE BOOK

This book has nineteen chapters, including the introduction and conclusion, and the rest of the seventeen chapters are divided into four parts. Part 1 focuses on governance, Part 2 focuses on education and capacity, Part 3 on science technology, risk assessment, and community, and Part 4 on disaster recovery.

Part 1 has four chapters. Chapter 2 focuses on higher-order levels of policy making and general principles and approaches, rather than sub-national policies and local scale practice. However, national policies flow through or are translated into sub-national policies and therefore also to local governance and practice, so the topic of policy learning has implications for those finer scales. The chapter recognizes that although beyond scope of the chapter, but very important is the need to enable communication between scales of governance so that policy lessons are shared between scales of governance, and that such communication is two-way and not simply top down.

Chapter 3 addresses the challenges of disaster policy in New Zealand, creating the first comprehensive Māori disaster management theory and implementation framework. Research findings will innovate New Zealand's disaster management legislation and infrastructure through facilitating the development of a collaborative co-governance framework for managing disaster contexts. The proposed framework, the first partnership between a government and colonized Indigenous peoples to ensure effective disaster preparedness, management, and resilience throughout a nation state, will also be designed to align with core priorities outlined in the Sendai Framework for Disaster Risk Reduction.

Chapter 4 argues that the traditional hierarchical structure of the public sector, in Australia and elsewhere, was optimized for the circumstances of the Industrial Age and for a professional public service model that relied on the concentration of expertise in distinct departments of state. Contemporary pressures for multi-hazard risk reduction, resilience and crisis response require government, civil society, and private sector organizations to coordinate their efforts more effectively. Within the public sector, civilian, military, and police officers and officials must develop systems to build national preparedness, share information, and work across boundaries for both domestic and offshore contingencies. This chapter considers how the lessons of recent offshore operations are shaping the effort to introduce the concept of the *Integrated Approach* in Australia.

Chapter 5 illustrates Australian aboriginal governance structure and emergency management through conducting participatory workshops. One of the prevailing themes in the workshop was the effectiveness of current governance frameworks and the extent to which they integrate Aboriginal ways of managing fires and disasters. Drawing on the outcomes from these consultative workshops, this chapter challenges the mainstream to gain a deeper understanding of the Blackfella way and become more creative in finding ways to integrate it within the existing governance frameworks or to go further and reconfigure the current systems to recognize and value existing systems.

Part 2 has five chapters on education and capacity. Chapter 6 focuses on the western concept and belief of relationships between humans and nature, disease, and "natural" disasters. It then explores how Indigenous worldviews encompass fundamental beliefs that facilitate ensuring that people live in harmony with nature, thus creating a valuable framework for embedding within the culture and society educational strategies and practices that foster the development of enduring harmonious socio-environmental relationships required for DRR. Living in harmony with nature, self and others, in turn, supports the development and application of DRR outcomes as a result of its fundamental focus on empowering people. The chapter concludes with a discussion of transformative educational pathways that could be adopted to facilitate the adoption of the empowering thinking and action that is implicitly evident in Indigenous beliefs and practices.

Chapter 7 explores one possibility; the potential for the performing (song) and visual arts, prominent socio-cultural media for communication and engagement in all countries, to complement existing approaches to DRR. The chapter examines whether songs and artworks can represent social-environmental contexts which could be used to facilitate the development of DRR beliefs and actions (e.g., understanding warnings, preparedness etc.). Finding evidence of a relationship between arts and DRR outcome would afford opportunities to use arts as a medium to support or complement DRR strategies to foster people's understanding of their social-environmental-hazard relationships and facilitate their ability to make informed choices about preparing for and/or responding to environmental challenge and change.

Chapter 8 shared findings from across five different disaster settings in the Asia Pacific region, highlighting the role of principals and teachers in post-disaster contexts. Common themes arising across the five settings were that: (a) principals and teachers put their students first when they faced a disaster situation together; (b) principals and teachers returned to work despite often being victims themselves; (c) teachers focused on children's needs more than their own; (d) teachers tried to balance helping children to process their experiences safely with returning to normal school routines; (e) schools also needed to look after their school families and communities; (f) schools continued to provide the best education they could despite limited facilities, lack of resources and insufficient funds; (g) the stress of coping and trying to keep positive through a prolonged recovery period led to the decreased physical and mental wellbeing of teachers and principals; (h) bureaucratic decisions made by government agencies without consideration or consultation added to the stresses that schools were facing; and (i) little acknowledgment was given to principals and teachers of the heavy burden that they carry in post-disaster contexts.

Chapter 9 focuses on catastrophic events in Australia and the unique challenges it poses. Previous reviews have highlighted gaps in Australia's preparedness for catastrophic disasters. Australia has no recent experience of a catastrophe, with the Spanish Flu (1918–1919) and Cyclone Tracey (1974) being perhaps two historic examples that have overwhelmed systems of management. Catastrophic events require the adoption of a whole community, nationwide approach. However, this is challenged by existing frameworks, the culture of emergency services, and wider community apathy. This chapter provides insights into building increased preparedness to reduce the occurrence of catastrophic disasters based upon a review of the global literature and existing disaster plans. Implications for practitioners are discussed.

Chapter 10 talks about a MBA higher education program in the Philippines with focus on disaster risk management (DRM). The MBA specialization in DRM is a distinctive program in the Philippines. Its main objective is to combine the strengths of general MBA core competencies in the areas of economics, finance, project research and development, marketing, production and operations, strategic management, and accounting, along with the intensive exploration of risk management fields, altogether making up an effective DRM toward sustainable development solutions. The curriculum of MBA in DRM can be adopted and customized by other institutions to fill the demand of producing Planners and Decision Makers who can mainstream DRR and CCA in national and local planning.

Part 3 has four chapters focused on science technology, risk assessment, and communities. Chapter 11 explores the concepts of social vulnerability and community resilience, their measurement, and the practical application of social vulnerability and community resilience metrics in emergency preparedness and response with specific reference to the U.S. experience. The chapter poses five propositions: (1) vulnerability and resilience are linked but they are not the opposite of one another; (2) community resilience is multi-faceted and multi-hazard; (3) measurement is important in establishing the value proposition for community resilience; (4) vulnerability and resilience science must be translated into practice and resilience practice must inform science; and (5) acknowledgment of the limitations of science and practice is critical in disaster risk reduction. After initially exploring social vulnerability and community resilience concepts, the chapter moves to a detailed discussion of approaches to measurement as a foundational element in providing the evidentiary basis for disaster risk reduction policies and practices.

Chapter 12 focuses on flood risk reduction. As a contribution to flood disaster risk reduction, estimates of extreme flood magnitude and frequency are essential components. The standard method for making such estimates (statistically generated from gauging station discharge values) is often of questionable value but is embedded in the professional practice of engineers and engineering hydrologists in many countries. Alternatives and complementary approaches to this problem have been in existence for many decades, based on research in the earth sciences and history, but they have not been widely adopted. Reasons for this failure on the part of risk analysts to use a much wider range of information are explored and it is suggested that it is a result of disciplinary silos that prevent cross-referencing of information and approaches. While all of the available methods and approaches to flood risk assessment have limitations, it is essential that flood risk analysts honestly evaluate the risks in their ways of knowing and work to break down disciplinary silos so that productive collaborations are established to advance the value of the flood hazard component of disaster risk reduction.

Chapter 13 began by considering the three factors responsible for communitas' emergence: the public nature of disaster, the limitations of authorities, and the social nature of human beings. It then outlines the motivations for writing this chapter, which are: to respond constructively to the critique that disaster studies suffer from a paucity of theory, to critique "disaster mythology" in public discourse, to offset the focus on top-down disaster recovery, to demonstrate a way in which communities might be a party to their own recovery, and to reiterate the importance of social infrastructure (as discussions of recovery typically prioritise physical infrastructure). It finally concludes on how might "communitas" be enhanced.

Chapter 14 focuses on scientific knowledge and public participation in disaster risk reduction in Sikkim, one mountain state in India. The chapter deals with some of state policies, plans, and strategies for use of science, technology, and people's participation in developing resilient reconstruction and disaster risk reduction in the state. Sikkim state's reconstruction approach on the principle of "Build Back Better" is one of the success stories of resilient construction, as Priority 4 of the Sendai Framework 2015–2030.

Part 4 focuses on disaster recovery and consists of three chapters. Chapter 15 focuses on the learning of post disaster recovery in Indonesia and Japan. The first section of the chapter analyzes embedded cultures to show the different trajectories of giving and expected returns of funds. The second section analyzes two case studies of Indonesia and Japan to explore how such embedded giving has affected the ways people are mobilizing funds from the community for recovery projects.

Chapter 16 focuses on long-term impacts of reconstruction processes to substantiate what works or hinders. A qualitative case-study methodology was employed to investigate four good-practice reconstruction projects long (>7 years) after a disaster in the context of India. Findings based on empirical evidence prove that owner-driven process is a must but equally important is providing the community with freedom to choose and a political voice, agility in program development, flexibility in recovery timeframe, transdisciplinary shelter hub setup, and sustaining capacity building, if reconstruction were to serve building societal resilience long time into the future.

Chapter 17 focuses on disaster recovery in Samoa, after the tsunami of 29 September 2009. The tsunami took everyone unprepared. The loss of property and the unprecedented loss of life alerted many Samoans to the realization that such an event could happen in their own backyard. This tragedy also highlighted the critical need to assist communities to ready themselves for future events and to help them recognize the need to consciously reduce risks. The chapter focuses on Samoan disaster management arrangements and the experiences of the Samoa Red Cross Society.

Chapter 18 is the concluding chapter and highlights the key findings of the earlier chapters.

REFERENCES

Aldrich, D. (2012). *Building resilience: Social capital in post disaster recovery.* University of Chicago Press.

Disaster Education. (2009). 1-2-3 of disaster education. Retrieved 12 September 2020 from: https://www.preventionweb.net/files/12088_123sm.pdf

DeWit, A., Shaw R., & Djalante R. (2020). An integrated approach to sustainable development, national resilience and COVID-19 responses: The case of Japan, *International Journal of Disaster Risk Reduction,* 51, 101808.

Djalante, R., Garschagen, M., Thomalla, F., & Shaw, R. (2017). *Disaster risk reduction in Indonesia: Progress, challenges, and issues.* Springer.

Izumi, T., Sukhwani, V., Surjan, A., & Shaw, R. (2020). Managing and responding to pandemics in higher educational institutions: Initial learning from COVID-19. *International Journal of Disaster Resilience in the Built Environment.* https://doi.org/10.1108/IJDRBE-06-2020-0054

Kikkawa, T. (1999). *Risk communication: Aiming at mutual understanding and better decision making,* Fukumura Press, p. 197.

Mavrodieva A., & Shaw R. (2020). Disaster and climate change issues in Japan's Society 5.0. *Sustainability,* 12, 1893. https://doi.org/10.3390/su12051893.

Mukherjee M., Chatterjee R., Khanna B., Dhillon P., Kumar A., Bajwa S., Prakash A., & Shaw R. (2020). Ecosystem-centric business continuity planning (eco-centric BCP): A post COVID-19 new normal. *Progress in Disaster Science,* 7, 100117.

Nakagawa, Y., & Shaw, R. (2004). Social capital: A missing link to disaster recovery. *International Journal of Mass Emergency and Disaster,* 22(1), 5–34.

Pal I., & Shaw R. (2017). *Disaster risk governance in India and cross cutting issues.* Springer.

SIOH. (2020). Social innovation online hackathon final report. Retrieved 10 September 2020 from: https://www.kri.sfc.keio.ac.jp/en/wp/wp-content/uploads/2020/01/Final-report-SIOH.pdf

Shaw, R. (2013). *Disaster recovery: Used or mis-used development opportunities.* Springer.

Shaw, R. (2014). *Community practices for disaster risk reduction in Japan.* Springer.

Shaw, R. (2020). Thirty years of science and technology, and academia in disaster risk reduction and emerging responsibilities. *International Journal of Disaster Risk Science*. https://doi.org/10.1007/s13753-020-00264-z

Shaw R., & Oikawa Y. (2014). *Education for sustainable development and disaster risk reduction*. Springer.

Shaw R., Shiwaku K., & Izumi T. (2017). *Science and technology in disaster risk reduction: Potentials and challenges*. Elsevier Academic Press.

Shiwaku, K., Sakurai, A., & Shaw, R. (2016). *Disaster resilience of education systems: Experiences from Japan*. Springer.

UN. (2015). Sendai framework for disaster risk reduction 2015–2030. Retrieved 22 April 2020, from: https://www.preventionweb.net/files/43291_sendaifra meworkfordrren.pdf

World Health Organization. (2019). Health emergency and disaster risk management framework. Retrieved 23 April 2020, from: https://www.who. int/hac/techguidance/preparedness/health-emergency-and-disaster-risk-man agement-framework-eng.pdf?ua=1

PART I

Governance

CHAPTER 2

Policy Learning for Disaster Risk Reduction

Stephen Dovers

INTRODUCTION

In the field of disaster risk reduction (DRR), as in any other, we hope that government agencies, other organizations and communities learn from past events and from their policy and management experiences to become more knowledgeable and more capable in the future. This chapter addresses one aspect of this for DRR:' policy learning', where we learn from experience with our policy and institutional responses to disasters to develop better settings in future. It does so by drawing together insights and propositions from the disaster field, including work by the author and colleagues in recent years, with fundamental concepts and frameworks from the (older and larger) fields of public policy and policy learning. The focus is on learning at the level of higher-level policy and broader institutional settings, rather than more technical and operational lesson-drawing (discussed further below). The chapter draws particularly on the Australian context for illustrative situations, but the overall ideas and some

---

S. Dovers (✉)
Fenner School of Environment and Society, The Australian National University, Canberra, Australia
e-mail: stephen.dovers@anu.edu.au

more specific possibilities should be more widely relevant (with the caveat discussed below regarding the exercise of due caution with comparative policy analysis and transfer).

At the broadest level, the DRR sector has seen a slow but steady progression from a reactive approach to disasters, where they are seen as 'Acts of God' and responded to largely by agencies of the state, towards a more proactive approach that emphasizes vulnerability reduction, risk mitigation, and recovery that aids both of these in future, delivered through partnerships of government, communities, NGOs and the private sector. This shift is clearly articulated in the progression of and principles enunciated in the international policy platforms of the Hyogo and Sendai frameworks (see further below), and these are reflected in (albeit uneven and often imperfect) national and sub-national policy and practice. For example, in Australia and elsewhere, DRR and emergency management utilize a framework such as P(revention), (P)reparedness), R(esponse), R(ecovery): over time, far more attention has been paid to proactive reforms to enhance the first P(reparedness) and the second R(ecovery), and more actors engaged across the entire spectrum. The principles embedded in Sendai are similar to those in Australia's national policy platform (CoAG, 2011), as they are in those of many other countries.

A revision to Australia's national 'guiding' policy, the 2018 National Disaster Risk Reduction Framework (Commonwealth of Australia, 2018, p. 6) makes the international-national policy congruence explicit:

> [The Framework] guides national, whole-of-society efforts to proactively reduce disaster risk in order to minimize the loss and suffering caused by disasters…
>
> The Framework establishes a 2030 vision, goals and priorities broadly aligned to the Sendai Framework and the 2030 Sustainable Development Goals…

Relevant to the topic of this chapter, contemporary policy increasingly supports the role of information and knowledge generation to support disaster policy:

> STRATEGY F: Support long-term and solution-driven research, innovation and knowledge practices, and disaster risk education.
> **Greater policy-research connection and innovation is needed** to ensure necessary evidence bases are available to inform efforts to identify, prioritise and reduce disaster risks. A greater variety of knowledge practices,

including Indigenous knowledge practices, should also be better integrated in research and knowledge application. Diverse ways of understanding and reducing disaster risk are needed to address disaster risk in all of its components. (Commonwealth of Australia, 2018, p. 13, emphasis added)

At the international level, policy frameworks are explicit in recognizing the links between disasters, human development, sustainable development and climate change, expressed in the work of the Intergovernmental Panel on Climate Change and the UN Sustainable Development Goals:

- Hyogo Framework for Action: Building the Resilience of Nations and Communities to Disasters (2005–2012) http://www.unisdr.org/we/coordinate/hfa.
- Sendai Framework for Disaster Risk Reduction (2015–2030) http://www.unisdr.org/we/inform/publications/43291, and summary chart at http://www.preventionweb.net/english/professional/publications/v.php?id=44983.
- SREX (Special Report by the Intergovernmental Panel on Climate Change: Managing the Risks of Extreme Events and Disaster to Advance Climate Change Adaptation 2012) https://www.ipcc.ch/report/managing-the-risks-of-extreme-events-and-disasters-to-advance-climate-change-adaptation.
- The Future We Want (Rio + 20, 2012), Paragraphs 186–189, and for example Sustainable Development Goals (2015) 11.5, 11.b, 13.1, 13.3. http://rio20.net/wp-content/uploads/2012/06/N1238164.pdf. https://sustainabledevelopment.un.org/?menu=1300.

Being vulnerable to disasters damages human development and environmental sustainability, and is inextricably linked to climate change and climate impacts (and to increased vulnerability caused by population growth and settlement patterns). These increasingly recognized links emphasize the importance of disaster policy and establish a more coherent and important agenda, but make the challenge of policy learning and development even more challenging in creating a larger and more dynamic policy landscape.

Against this background, this chapter presents and explains frameworks and concepts to enhance our understanding of the prospects for policy learning in DRR, and to identify barriers to policy learning and some antidotes to those barriers. It scopes beyond the immediate disaster and emergency management sector to consider the prospects for policy learning across the broader policy and institutional system that either enables or constrains DRR, consistent with the broader canvas described above.

The chapter first considers some further detail under the simple and hopeful term of 'policy learning' to explore who might learn what and to what effect. It then poses the question is whether the disaster field is a particularly challenging learning environment. It proceeds to consider the crucial question of prospects for policy change in other policy sectors. The chapter concludes with some possible remedies to address the task of improving policy learning in DRR.

The focus of this short chapter is on higher-order levels of policy making and general principles and approaches, rather than sub-national policies and local scale practice. However, national policies flow through or are translated into sub-national policies and therefore also to local governance and practice, so the topic of policy learning has implications for those finer scales. Beyond scope here but very important is the need to enable communication between scales of governance so that policy lessons are shared between scales of governance, and that such communication is two-way and not simply top down.

Forms and Levels of Policy Learning

Behind the simple, enticing and universally supported term 'policy learning' there lies a large theoretical and practical literature, countless experiences in practice, and multiple meanings and detail. For the purpose here, it suffices to delve briefly into questions of *who*, in the relevant policy and institutional system, might learn *what* from policy experience and to *what effect*. Table 2.1 presents a simplified but sufficiently comprehensive typology of policy learning that distils distinctions commonly drawn in much relevant literature, and recognizable from policy practice, but perhaps less often addressed in a clear fashion. While the categorizations within such a tabulation to some degree hide linkages between forms and levels of learning, there are differences explicit in Table 2.1 that have significantly varied implications, including for the focus of this chapter. These are now briefly discussed.

First, it is proposed that the first two forms of policy learning—instrumental and operational, and government learning—are reasonably well-attended in DRR and emergency management. Emergency service

Table 2.1 Policy learning: who learns what and to what effect

Form	What is learned?	Who learns (example)?	Intended result (example)
Instrumental and operational	How policy instruments and implementation processes have performed relative to stated goals	Core members of policy network, especially government officials and close non-government partners responsible for policy implementation	Redesign of existing or better design of future policy instrument and detailed implementation procedures. *Same problem frame*
Government	How administrative structures and processes have contributed to or limited policy implementation	Members of the policy network, especially senior government officials and key stakeholders accountable for design and maintenance of policy process	Redesign of existing or better design of future administrative structures and processes. *Same problem frame*
Social	The relevance and usefulness of policies and policy and social goals	The broader policy community, including more and less closely engaged actors within and outside government	Reframed problems and goals, via altered understanding of cause-effect linkages or social preferences. *Reframe problem?*
Political	How to effectively engage with and influence political and policy processes	Actors wishing to enhance their ability to change policy agendas and outcomes or defend existing ones	Changes in problem definition, policy goals, membership of the policy network, power of particular groups. *Reframe problem?*

Source Handmer & Dovers, 2013, p. 142; adapted from Bennett & Howlett, 1992; May, 1992; Connor & Dovers, 2004

organizations and other responders constantly seek to learn from incidents, and are proactive in preparing capacities, via internal or external post-incident reviews (but see further below), professional development, promulgation of consistent procedures and doctrine, preparation exercises, and inter-agency communication. For example, in Australia, the peak sector body, a national council of fire and emergency services agencies, develops detailed doctrine and lessons sharing mechanisms (https://www.afac.com.au/), while a separate but collaborating agency is active is collecting, further developing and disseminating relevant lessons (https://www.aidr.org.au/programs/) including via a professional journal widely accessed in the sector (https://knowledge.aidr.org.au/collections/australian-journal-of-emergency-management/), and a substantial applied research facility links research and management agencies in line with a nationally agreed agenda of knowledge requirements (https://www.bnhcrc.com.au/home), Further, since 2009 in Australia there have been over 140 post-incident inquiries where the primary focus is on learning from experiences and improving operational capacity within the emergency management sector (Cole et al., 2018, see further below). This level of lesson-drawing capacity is reflected in many other jurisdictions—albeit less in some, more in others—and indicates that operational/instrumental learning and program ('government') learning is catered for reasonably well, even if it could doubtless always be improved or its implementation better resourced.

With respect to these two forms of learning, 'lessons management' is an increasingly common framework used in emergency management (e.g. Donahue & Tuohy, 2006; Kletz, 2001; Milton, 2010; Savoia et al., 2012), and provides considerable guidance and structure to the identification and deployment of lessons accrued from experience. An example is the guidance to the emergency management sector provided by the Australian Institute for Disaster Resilience (AIDR, 2013) in a lessons management handbook. However, lessons management approaches largely (and usefully) apply *within* a specific policy sector and often within a particular organization. Lessons management as generally practised focuses on operational learning, and perhaps to some degree government learning.

If the claim above that operational lessons are already prioritized by many if not most emergency service organizations—whether fully well or not—that invites more attention to the broader forms of learning in Table 2.1. A crucial difference highlighted in Table 2.1 is that instrumental and government learning largely operates within the *current framing of the policy problem* and thus policy style and approach to DRR, which although expanded in most jurisdictions consistent with the evolution of a larger policy problem expressed in Sendai (see Introduction above), still basically assesses whether we can 'do the same but better'.

In contrast, social and political learning open the prospect of recasting the framing of the problem, towards allowing consideration of more innovative and (possibly) more effective policy responses. A focus on social and political learning, then, invites more systemic reviews of experience, outside of the parameters of current practice and responsibilities. Such an approach may be justified in the face of increasing vulnerability and risk caused by demographic, settlement and climate change, and by the recognized need to embed DRR into economic, human development, climate and sustainability policies. Importantly, the participants in social and political learning come from a wider and arguably more potentially powerful catchment of policy and political actors, not from only within the immediate disaster and emergencies sector: NGOs, independent researchers, civil society, senior officials from other policy portfolios, and central agencies. While 'public policy' is often assumed to be mostly the work of governments, especially in these two broader forms of policy learning, these non-government actors are always present and at times may lead policy debate and reform. In some post-event inquiry formats, non-government actors including impacted community individuals have input. Processes which include a wide array of stakeholders in policy learning are thus essential to expand the input of different ideas and perspectives, and to ensure wide appreciations of any new policy approaches.

At this point, we can recognize different forms and purposes of policy learning for DRR, and advance the argument to spread attention to forms of learning other than the operational and program (government) learning that is more well-attended at present. However, there is a caution: not all 'policy learning' might be always judged as a positive phenomenon, a question to which we now turn.

Will Policy Learning Be Positive?

As with any other situation, information gained through policy learning may be constructively used, or it may be poorly understood, misinterpreted, poorly utilized, or even distorted to negative effect—not all students learn well! There are two aspects to this briefly explored here: where we seek to learn from, and more positive and negative uses of information in public policy.

In a dynamic field such as DRR, we can learn from our own experiences (an event, or across a series of events) or we can seek to learn from others, the latter being a commendable approach to expand the catchment of available experiences from which to draw. However, as per the comment regarding (2) in the list below, there are risks of transplanting ideas or policy options from one social, legal, physical and/or political context to another without care: they may not fit into their new environment. This is a warning common in the policy learning (e.g. May, 1992) and comparative policy analysis literatures (e.g. Rose, 2005): the object of learning should not be to copy or mimic, but to increase our understanding and intelligence which is then applied sensitively to the relevant context.

Policy learning that looks to other sectors, jurisdictions or organizations, can seek useable lessons relevant to different levels in the policy system (these can be related to the levels and forms of learning above). To add detail to this, consider four levels and their efficacy for policy learning (from Handmer & Dovers, 2013):

1. General *policy styles and institutional options*, where another sector or jurisdiction that has experimented with a quite different approach that allows comparison with one's own experience, for example, a collaborative *versus* a more coercive or regulatory policy style, or voluntary *versus* mandatory evacuation regimes. This allows consideration of different ideas and enriches policy debate, but without the presumption that simple transfer might be possible. This can be argued to be valuable, but rare, with that rarity attributable to the lack of attention to social and political forms of policy learning.
2. At the level of *policy program or organizational models*, with possible transfers of the 'blueprint' from one context to another, for example, a risk management framework to replace or supplement existing prescriptive standards, or the structure of an overview statutory office to coordinate disaster responses. This target of learning is in some ways easy, quick and commonly observed, but it involves the risk of unthinking transfer identified above.
3. *Detailed sub-components* of the policy programs and organizational models in (2) above, such as communication strategies within a program, aspects of regulatory design, or cross-agency coordination mechanisms. A whole program or organizational model may be non-transferable, but there is a greater likelihood that specific components may be effectively adapted. It is proposed here that this is a highly prospective source of lessons, but one not as commonly

pursued as it should be, possibly due to the effort and level of policy knowledge required.
4. *Operational and technological options*, less dependent than the above on contextual variation, including 'hardware' such as communication devices or fire suppressant delivery systems, 'software' such as computer programs or training modules, or specific community education strategies. As already discussed, this is the main focus of lessons management in the sector: generally already catered for and effective if well done and properly resourced.

The above instructs us to exercise due care in choosing where to seek lessons from. The second caution is to recognize that the assumption that any lesson-drawing will, if undertaken and implemented, lead to improvement in policy—the assumption of direct, positive use of information. A significant literature in public policy and political science deals with the utilization of information in public policy: policy learning involves the generation of information, which will be used or ignored in various ways. Separating the following four forms of utilization allows a brief exploration of this issue (adapted and simplified from the typology of Hezri (2004), with the core concepts being generally consistent with other literature):

- **Instrumental utilization**: where scientific and other 'expert' information directly influences policy in a positive manner. This is rarely observed, as more than 'expert' knowledge or hard data typically informs political and policy choices, and very rarely does one line of information suffice to inform a policy decision in isolation form other information sources. Discussing the often called for practice of 'evidence-based policy', Head (2008) defined three forms or 'lenses' of evidence used in formulating policy: systematic ('scientific') research; program management experience ('practice') and political judgement. Any policy practitioner or political decision maker would recognize this, whether or not they agree with the resulting decisions.
- **Conceptual utilization**: where information and research 'seep' into policy thinking, slowly manifesting as change over time, combined with other information inputs, in the way problems are framed or in new policy decisions and directions. This is a much more

common form of utilization than instrumental, but the influence of a particular form of information or lesson is difficult to separate from others.
- **Tactical/symbolic utilization**: where new information or a lesson leads to further information being gathered to inform policy, rather than driving a near-term change. This may be justified if the new information or lesson learned is not sufficiently certain and requires further investigation, or it may be a delaying tactic to avoid policy change or the allocation of further resources.
- **Political utilization**: where information is used without reference to its rigour or validity, to support a previously held value, policy position or political goal. The information or lesson may be questionable or it may be rigorous and defensible, but the decision to deploy the information is based on its suitability as 'ammunition' in a political sense. Often, this involves carefully selective data or information or situations (including lessons from incidents), at times stripping information from any qualifications or context. This form of utilization is common in public and political debates, and may be deliberately manipulative or it may be unwitting (people are attracted to information or instances that support their existing beliefs).

As we progress through the above series of more detailed considerations of policy learning and lesson-drawing, things become more complicated and both positive and negative implications emerge, but at least our understanding of the possibilities for policy learning become more nuanced and thus, hopefully, more useful. A further complication is that DRR can be argued to be a particularly challenging sector for policy learning.

Disasters: A Difficult Learning Environment?

Many in the DRR sector sense that disasters present a prominent and difficult policy problem, that they are different in kind and degree to many others. The assumption should be tested: exceptionalism is common in policy and political debates, where one's own specialty or area of greatest concern is felt to be more important and/or more complex and difficult than others. The emphasis and urgency placed on disasters and their impacts on human and economic development and the environment in international policy noted above certainly justify the claim of importance, or difference in degree. As well, the rising costs of disasters in lives, livelihoods, assets and environmental quality suggest a significant scale (*difference in degree*) of policy problem. Whether significant effort is expended in addressing DRR becomes a question of social and political will, weighing the perceived importance of DRR against other societal priorities.

From a public policy perspective, however, the question is whether DRR represents a challenge *different in kind*. That is, does DRR displays problem attributes that make policy responses harder to design and implement? This can inform us more in terms of the different policy approaches: a problem may be big and difficult, but knowing *why* it is so is what can inform the policy response. It can be argued that sustainability policy problems exhibit a number of difficult problem attributes more often and more often in combination, making them particular challenges (Dovers, 1997), and further that DRR shares many of the same problem attributes (Handmer & Dovers, 2013). Disasters as policy problems exhibit deep uncertainty, variable and extended spatial and temporal scales, unclear policy and property rights and responsibilities, potentially severe impacts, high levels of connectivity between key variables and factors, systemic causes of problems (i.e. vulnerability), a mix of public and private interests, and insolubility without the coordinated engagement of multiple policy actors. These attributes certainly portray a difficult policy target, and serve to explain to some degree what many would judge to be slow progress notwithstanding the evolution of policy directions in line with the Sendai Framework. Recognizing the different policy problem attributes invites clearer focus on possible policy remedies (for example, see discussion of policy integration models below).

In terms of policy learning, a smaller number of factors play a role in challenging our ability to accrue lessons. Bluntly, disasters do not happen often enough, or in a similar enough fashion event-to-event, as every disaster event takes place in a specific context of place and time. Thus, while there are always lessons to be drawn from an event and our response, there are limited 'policy experiments' that equal replicable tests of policy options. As discussed above, there are limits to transfer of policy lessons across very varied social, physical, climatic, hazard and political contexts, although with care this can be done. That presents a difficulty, but careful management of information and lessons can accrue intelligence over time.

Other Policy Sectors

More difficult is the fact that the precursors of disasters—that is, people being vulnerable—arise not because of disaster policy but because of policy decisions and non-decisions in *other policy sectors*. Disaster policy and emergency management largely operate to address the negative effects of people being placed in the face of hazards through land use planning, poverty, socio-economic marginalization, displacement and other human-determined factors. Even the most frequent 'natural' disasters, caused by climatic variables, are now exacerbated by human-induced climate change. This means that many, if not most, of the policy levers for DRR aimed at reducing vulnerability either pre-, during or post-event are within the policy reach of various fields of social, economic and environmental policy, but not within reach of disaster policy or emergency management. While major policy platforms recognize this and call for 'whole-of-government' or 'whole-of-society' approaches (see above), disaster-oriented adjustments to social and economic policy at a systemic level are rare: why?

First, however, costly disaster impacts are, they may not be high on the agenda of non-disaster policy sectors and portfolios, except perhaps after disasters when impacts are felt and pleas for attention emerge. Importantly, this is the stage when assistance is often forthcoming, which can lessen the importance of DRR in sectors that are regularly supported post-impact: things turn out alright with government or NGO assistance and insurance, so why worry when other priorities remain? The focus on mitigation rather than mostly on response in international and national policy seeks to address this.

Second, whether disasters are, for other policy sectors, *different in degree* and thus deserving of greater attention may be validly argued against. Other priorities and factors than DRR matter for policy and decision makers across all relevant policy sector (planning, communications, emergency health services, poverty alleviation, infrastructure, etc.). For example, while it is apparent that land use planning decisions past and present have placed people in vulnerable situations from a DRR perspective, disaster mitigation is only one of many considerations that planners must take into account, including housing affordability, private property rights, economic efficiency and transport and commuting logistics (see March & Dovers, 2017). At the margin, trading off a little more safety *versus* better housing affordability and access to employment is a value judgement, albeit one hopefully informed by quality information. Similarly, a health agency or NGO asked to build contingency capacity for disaster relief faces balancing that against more certain near-term health services provision that are their standard mandate.

Third, it should be recognized that 'whole-of-government' policy initiatives are hard to do. Australia's national framework states this need as a guiding principle (Commonwealth of Australia, 2018, 8):

> Integrated action. Efforts to reduce disaster risk must be integrated across sectors, not progressed in silos.

While such policy integration would gain universal support, the structure of governments is by definition compartmentalized (i.e. in silos), with specialized agencies dealing with a particular policy sectors (government Minister/Secretary, with departments and authorities implementing decisions and programs), across numerous sectors such as finance, transport, health, education, communications, defence and more. Creating structures and processes to coordinate across these silos is difficult no matter what sectors or issues are involved, and 'cross-cutting' issues such as many aspects of DRR create particular challenges, as they are at once every department's potential concern and no one agency's sole responsibility. While many mechanisms are in place, such as national DRR committees and inter-agency collaborative procedures, practitioners, researchers and even official policy (e.g. Commonwealth of Australia, 2018) consider more could be done. However, in terms of policy learning, there is a considerable body of literature and evidence in the cognate policy field of environment and sustainability that describes policy integration strategies that could be explored for options potentially relevant to DRR (e.g. in Europe, Lenschow, 2002; in Australia, Ross & Dovers, 2008; Management Advisory Committee, 2004).

Mechanisms for Policy Learning

The above has been largely at the level of general concepts and frameworks, so we can now look briefly at the practicalities of policy learning. The first practicality is that policy and political agendas change, often in an uneven fashion over time, and that the opportunity to apply lessons and improve policy therefore are similarly uneven (Bennett & Howlett, 1992; Kingdon, 1984). There are, however, 'hooks and windows' that, if identified, may improve in using policy lessons that have been learned in a constructive fashion. Obviously, immediately post a disaster is a significant time of policy change, however that period of time may also feature rushed decisions. Disaster events are an 'unpredictable' policy window (Howlett, 1998), along with others such as swift shifts in public sentiment or the unexpected fall of a government or government minister/secretary. Other policy windows are more predictable, such as elections and the lead up to budgets or defined policy reviews.

Post-disasters, formal inquiries offer unpredictable but regular opportunities for policy learning and fulfil this role often in most jurisdictions. However, post-event inquiries are generally focussed on a particular event, and the variation between disaster events, especially across hazard types (flood, wild fire, cyclone, etc.) limits the possibilities for higher-level policy and institutional lesson-drawing. A recent Australian study that examined multiple inquires established that there were strong themes in the recommendations of inquiries across sub-national jurisdictions, inquiry types and hazards (Cole et al., 2018), suggesting that 'meta-learning' across multiple inquiries would be profitable. A searchable data base of post-event inquiry reports has consequently been constructed, to make easier the understanding and communication of lessons across hazard events and jurisdictions (https://tools.bnhcrc.com.au/ddr/home).

However, Cole et al. (2018) found that recommendations (and thus possible policy and operational changes) focussed very strongly on the activities of emergency management agencies themselves, much less on other policy sectors, and very little on the role of individuals, households, volunteers or private firms. That is not consistent with the strong focus in national and international DRR policy on shared responsibility and whole-of-society approaches. This, along with reservations about the adversarial style of some inquiries (Eburn & Dovers, 2015), suggests that the form and process of post-event inquiries could be revisited to maximize their policy learning potential.

In terms of other measures to encourage positive policy learning, these will be often specific to a jurisdiction, but seven can be advanced here to illustrate options. The first is to encourage more analysis of policy and institutional settings outside of the DRR sector, to identify reforms in those sectors that would enhance DRR. This may be difficult for those in the sector to undertake for political and skills reasons and is likely best done by independent applied policy researchers. The second is in research and indeed wherever possible to communicate and emphasize the principles and links across major international policies such as Sendai and the SDGs, to highlight the established logic of modern approaches to DRR and to remind non-DRR agencies of their endorsement by almost all governments of the world. The third is to seek to increase the 'policy literacy' of the DRR sector and professionals within it, not of their own policy settings (which they assumedly know well), but of general public policy, to aid the interaction and perhaps collaborations between DRR and other relevant sectors. This is not a criticism, but recognizing that public policy and adjacent disciplines of public administration, law and political science are not often incorporated in DRR training and education programs. The fourth is the converse of this: to seek to embed DRR materials in the training and education of highly relevant professions and disciplines such as land use planning, economics and infrastructure provision, where its coverage is generally lacking or patchy. Fifth, there is a need to communicate and publish the imperatives and policy options of DRR outside the disaster and emergency management community and the forums used by that community. Too much excellent and potentially useful information and policy possibilities are seen only by DRR researchers and practitioners: the likely already converted. Influential and potentially interested and supportive individuals in other policy sectors do not read disaster journals or emergency management bulletins.

The sixth is a difficult one: establishing a constructive and informed coverage of DRR issues by the popular media. Media coverage in the lead up to, during and immediately post-event is often crucial to communicating hazard information and avenues for assistance. However, media coverage in the aftermath of disasters can be too often unconstructive and divisive, for example, the following headlines—unfortunately all too typical—from major newspapers following recent Australian wildfires:

- State cops fire blame.
- Resign? Worthy idea, fat chance.
- Green ideas must take blame for deaths.
- After the fires, the buck has to stop somewhere.
- Fireys 'blunders' to blame for deaths.
- Oppositions wants Minister sacked over fire.
- Bureaucrats may be fanning the flames.
- Bureau chiefs contributed to fire havoc.
- Public scents blood in [event] report.

Such a public discourse is not conducive to a reasoned policy debate which is understandable to the broader public and thus likely to lead to well-understood and effective policy reform. It is notable that many such adversarial headlines emerge during the course of post-event inquiries, which themselves at times can become adversarial and generate social division and blame. Sustained and informed communication with the media is required, along with perhaps promulgation of balanced 'opinion pieces' and the like in the wider media by those familiar with DRR and the options for proactive policy change (see also the fifth suggestion above).

The final option is similarly difficult: to establish and maintain capacities to gather, analyze and communicate policy lessons across time, events, jurisdictions and the multiple policy sectors wherein the causes of and remedies to vulnerability lie. If policy learning is to be shared so that individual and organizational policy experience and expertise is enhanced and policy learning becomes institutionalized, such capacities are vital. Existing mechanisms and systems of communication exist largely within emergency management and disaster agencies, with some spread across jurisdictions, but far less so across the important other policy sectors identified above. A major area for further research and policy discussion needs to be about how, in a given political system, such mechanisms can be created.

Conclusion

The aim of this chapter has been to explore in some more detail than usual the easily agreed but always difficult prospect of policy learning in DRR, and across other relevant policy sectors. The concepts and frameworks presented above are not novel in DRR or especially elsewhere, but offer opportunities for a greater degree of focus and specificity in where we can seek policy lessons from, for what purpose, and how opportunities to learn can be identified and enhanced. It was emphasized above that policy lessons can arise unexpectedly, but we know that they will, and that windows of opportunity for policy change can arise predictably or unpredictably, but again we know that they will occur. That makes both a lot like disasters: we know they will happen but not when. Aligning those three dynamics may be difficult, but certainly worthwhile.

REFERENCES

Australian Institute for Disaster Resilience. (2013). *Lessons management*, Handbook no.8. AIDR.
Bennett, C. J., & Howlett, M. (1992). The lessons of learning: Reconciling theories of policy learning and policy change. *Policy Sciences, 25*, 275–294.
COAG (Council of Australian Governments). (2011). *National strategy for disaster resilience: Building the resilience of our nation to disasters*. Council of Australian Governments.
Cole, L., Dovers, S., Gough, M., & Eburn, M. (2018). Can major post-event inquiries and reviews contribute to lessons management? *Australian Journal of Emergency Management, 33*(2), 34–39.
Commonwealth of Australia. (2018). *National disaster risk reduction framework*. Commonwealth of Australia.
Connor, R., & Dovers, S. (2004). *Institutional change for sustainable development*. Edward Elgar.
Donahue, A. K., & Tuohy, R. (2006). Lessons we don't learn: A study of disasters, why we repeat them, and how we can learn them. *Homeland Security Affairs, 2*(2), 1–28.
Dovers, S. (1997). Sustainability: Demands on policy. *Journal of Public Policy, 16*, 303–318.
Eburn, M., & Dovers, S. (2015). Learning lessons from disasters: Alternatives to Royal Commissions and other quasi-judicial inquiries. *Australian Journal of Public Administration, 74*, 495–508.
Handmer, J., & Dovers, S. (2013). *Handbook of disaster policies and institutions: Improving emergency management and climate adaptation* (2nd ed.). Routledge.
Head, B. (2008). Three lenses of evidence-based policy. *Australian Journal of Public Administration, 67*, 1–11.
Hezri, A. A. (2004). Sustainability indicators system and policy processes in Malaysia: A framework for utilization and learning. *Journal of Environmental Management, 73*, 357–371.
Howlett, M. (1998). Predictable and unpredictable policy windows: Institutional and exogenous correlates of Canadian Federal agenda-setting. *Canadian Journal of Political Science, 31*, 495–524.
Kingdon, J. W. (1984). *Agendas, alternatives and public policy*. Little, Brown.
Kletz, T. A. (2001). *Learning from accidents* (3rd ed.). Oxford.
Lenschow, A. (Ed.). (2002). *Environmental policy integration: Greening sectoral policies in Europe*. Earthscan.
Management Advisory Committee. (2004). *Connecting government: Whole of government responses to Australia's priority challenges – Summary of findings*. Commonwealth of Australia.

March, A., & Dovers, S. (2017). Mainstreaming urban planning for disaster risk reduction. In K. Vella, & N. Sipe (Eds.), *Australian Handbook of Urban and Regional Planning*, 231–246. Taylor & Francis.

May, P. (1992). Policy learning and policy failure. *Journal of Public Policy, 12*, 331–354.

Milton, N. (2010). *The lessons learned handbook: Practical approaches to learning from experience*. Chandos Publishing.

Rose, R. (2005). *Learning from comparative public policy: A practical guide*. Routledge.

Ross, A., & Dovers, S. (2008). Making the harder yards: Environmental policy integration in Australia. *Australian Journal of Public Administration, 67*, 245–260.

Savoia, E., Agboola, F., & Biddinger, P. D. (2012). After Accident Reports (AARs) to promote organizational and systems learning in emergency preparedness. *International Journal of Environmental Research and Public Health, 9*(8), 2949–2963.

… CHAPTER 3

Na Ara Ahurea: Envisioning Collaborative Governance in Disaster Risk Reduction in Aotearoa

Christine M. Kenney

Introduction and Background

The indigenous peoples of Aotearoa New Zealand, Māori, are cultural guardians for communities, land and environments in their tribal regions and apply a communitarian approach to addressing these stewardship responsibilities (Kenney & Phibbs, 2014). Thus, Māori have a history of collective agency and instituting collaborative actions to ensure community well-being in the context of natural hazard events (Kenney & Phibbs, 2015). Contemporary exemplars of the effectiveness of Māori cooperative responses to disasters include the quick actions of Ngāi Tahu following the Canterbury and Kaikōura earthquakes (The New Zealand Herald, 2016) as well as the rapid mobilisation of the Ngāti Awa volunteer army in response to the Edgecumbe flood in April 2017 (Bay of Plenty Times,

C. M. Kenney (✉)
Massey University, Palmerston North, New Zealand
e-mail: C.Kenney@massey.ac.nz

© The Author(s), under exclusive license to Springer Nature Singapore Pte Ltd. 2022
H. James et al. (eds.), *Disaster Risk Reduction in Asia Pacific*, Disaster Risk, Resilience, Reconstruction and Recovery,
https://doi.org/10.1007/978-981-16-4811-3_3

2017; Scoop NZ, 2017). In both instances, the disaster management actions of local Māori stakeholders were further assisted by Iwi (tribes) residing in other parts of New Zealand who drew on assets to provide additional human support and material resources.

The collective Māori asset base, which is estimated to be worth NZ$40 + billion (Solomon, 2013), has and will again be mobilised in part or entirety, to secure community well-being in response to an increasing incidence of natural hazard events in New Zealand. This willingness on the part of Māori to mobilise significant human capital and material resources in response to natural hazard disasters has garnered considerable interest from central government and local authorities (Johnson et al., 2014). As an exemplar, the effectiveness of Māori approaches to disaster management is specifically acknowledged in the Technical Advisory Group's (TAG) *Ministerial Review Better Responses to Natural Hazard Disasters and Other Emergencies in New Zealand* (Department of Prime Minister and Cabinet, 2017).

Improving Emergency Management Responses to Natural Hazard and Other Disasters

The purpose of the technical advisory group's review was to generate information and recommendations to inform New Zealand's emergency response capabilities and ensure that the broader disaster management framework is well placed to meet future challenges. As part of this process, the review panel visited regions that had recent experiences of responding to disasters. It also evaluated best practice emergency management infrastructures evidenced in Australia, the United Kingdom, the United States and Canada. The findings from previous evaluations of emergency management systems were examined, and recommendations drawn from analyses of recent disaster management responses in New Zealand, including the Port Hills fires, and the Bay of Plenty weather events, were scrutinised.

The review identified a number of areas for strengthening New Zealand's emergency management infrastructure. Recommendations included enhancing emergency management legislation to incorporate professional standards and an expanded system of audit and assurance, establishing a national emergency management agency, and allocating primary authority for local states of emergency to local governance and group controllers (Technical Advisory Group Department of Prime

Minister and Cabinet, 2017, p. 2). More specifically, despite ample evidence as to capabilities, the review established that the resources, skillsets and social capital maintained and mobilised by Māori to assist in emergency responses, were not recognised in current legislation (Technical Advisory Group Department of Prime Minister and Cabinet, 2017, p. 18). Review findings also highlighted that national and regional emergency management stakeholders' engagement and relationships with Māori were not consistently well managed. In addition, consultation with Māori around emergency management planning often occurred late in the strategy development phase, which resulted in Māori communities' disaster management aspirations and needs not being adequately recognised in local Civil Defence and Emergency Management plans (Technical Advisory Group Department of Prime Minister and Cabinet, 2017, p. 3). Mobilising marae to act as welfare centres in the event of a disaster, for example, is a costly process and the review found that government processes for reimbursing costs incurred by marae and mobilising support resources, were considered by Māori to be 'complex, bureaucratic and lacking in clarity' (Technical Advisory Group Department of Prime Minister and Cabinet, 2017, p. 18).

The review's findings are consistent with previous research findings that have documented the tensions and marginalisation of Māori in relation to emergency management in New Zealand (Kenney & Phibbs, 2014). One exemplar is the lack of communication between Māori responders and the local emergency management infrastructure during the 2004 Manawatu-Rangitikei floods in the central North Island of New Zealand (Hudson & Hughes, 2007). History was repeated following the 2010–2011 Canterbury earthquakes when coordinating an integrated response between the Māori Recovery Network and the emergency management infrastructure was delayed because communication with Civil Defence took eight days to be established and required external mediators (Solomon, 2012). The Māori Recovery Network was well linked with communities in the Eastern suburbs of Christchurch, the areas of the city that were most severely impacted by the earthquakes, and had key information about local conditions as well as unmet needs in the broader community (Kenney & Solomon, 2014). The delay in integrating the Māori response with the formal disaster management response contributed to the absence and/or inadequate provision of essential services, including freshwater delivery and the provision of portable toilets (Paton et al., 2014).

Urban marae (Māori community centres) previously registered as civil defence hubs were not initially operationalised as welfare centres and when formally activated, tensions developed between marae leaders and formal responders in regards to situational governance (Lambert, 2014). Volunteering by Māori responders was also discouraged which created tensions for Māori around engaging with and assisting the mainstream response (Phibbs, Kenney & Solomon, 2015). The experience of an Auckland-based Māori construction and demolition company provides a case in point. Company representatives arrived in Christchurch the day after the February 22nd 2011 earthquake to provide excavation and demolition support. When an initial offer of help was refused by the national emergency management infrastructure, the company partnered with overseas search and rescue actors and provided exhumation assistance in the central city (Phibbs, Kenney & Solomon, 2015). A further exemplar is the marginalisation of the Māori wardens, whose efforts to conduct needs assessments in the Eastern suburbs of Christchurch, which were hard hit by the Canterbury earthquakes, met with resistance from the New Zealand Police. Although the wardens were formally deployed at the request of the Crown, the Police preferred that the wardens' activities were restricted to providing security services (Kenney & Phibbs, 2015).

The lack of recognition or understanding of Māori frontline responders' concerns, including the absence of Māori cultural values and practices within search and rescue protocols, also created tensions (Shepherd et al., 2017). As a consequence, Māori professional responders reported enacting cultural practices in secret in order to ensure their spiritual well-being, particularly when overseeing the care of the deceased (Phibbs, Kenney & Solomon, 2015). Subsequent to responders' experiences during the 2010–2011 Canterbury earthquakes, Māori Urban Search and Rescue (USAR) workers have requested the incorporation of Māori cultural values and practices in emergency management training planning and implementation as well as search and rescue protocols. Comprehensive consultation with key Māori cultural experts will be vital to facilitating this outcome.

The Technical Advisory Group's report (Department of Prime Minister and Cabinet, 2017) recognised the need for wider engagement and consultation with Iwi, other Māori institutions and agents, in order to develop a way forward for Iwi to take an expanded role in regional emergency management. To that end, TAG Report recommendations advocate for Iwi participation at every level of Civil Defence, including governance, stating:

> The current legislation intended that emergency management would be a consortium of territorial and regional effort (exercised through regional Groups)... We recommend retaining the joint committee governance with Iwi added. (Department of Prime Minister and Cabinet, 2017, p.19)

Legislation is proposed as one instrument for clarifying the role of Iwi in regional disaster governance, planning, coordination and response as well as developing contextually relevant processes for local governance engagement with Iwi. Key recommendations in this regard include formal recognition of Iwi capabilities that are relevant to emergency management and Iwi engagement in regional CDEM coordinating Executive Groups (CEG) and joint operational committees. The Resource Legislation Amendment Act (2017), has been proposed as a potential template for designing processes that will foster these outcomes and more broadly facilitate effective engagement between Iwi and regional emergency management authorities. The Act (2017), is a measure that was designed and introduced by the New Zealand Government to facilitate the second stage of reforming the Resources Management Act (1991).

RESOURCES MANAGEMENT, MANA WHAKAHONO-O-ROHE AND IWI MANAGEMENT PLANS

The New Zealand Resources Management context imposes statuary obligations on local authorities under the Local Government Act (2002) and the Resource Management Act (1991) to recognise, protect and provide for resident tribal values and interests.

However, acknowledgement of Iwi resource management concerns has been subject to regional variability. In order to ensure recognition of Iwi aspirations pertaining to regional development and sustainability the new Resource Legislation Amendment Act 2017 contains a mechanism for facilitating Iwi participation in local government decisions. The key inclusion in the Act is a new approach to strengthening Iwi participation in regional planning, the Mana Whakahono-a-Rohe amendment. First operationalised in the Bay of Plenty (Saunders, 2017), the amendment provides an avenue for Iwi to engage in collaborative governance specifically pertaining to environmental planning and resources management.

Within legislation and local authorities' statutory policies and practices, Mana Whakahono-o-Rohe is more generally considered a tool for developing Iwi Participation Arrangements (IPAS), structures that will foster Iwi engagement with regional authorities and potential involvement in broader areas of regional governance. These arrangements commonly take the form of written memoranda of understanding signed by representatives of local bodies and Iwi authorities. The memoranda contain stipulations regarding local authorities' obligations and processes for consultation with Iwi as well as the role of Iwi in the preparation and amendment of local policies and plans. Procedures for collaboratively monitoring and evaluating collective governance processes, decisions and the outcomes of decisions, are also usually outlined within the memoranda. However, in practice there is considerable inconsistency in regional understandings, particularly in regards to the nature of Iwi accountabilities and liabilities. Ongoing assessment of the ways in which Mana Whakahono-o-Rohe is variously operationalised at the regional level is key to identifying potential conflicts of interest between local authorities and Iwi as well as informing the creation of methods to resolve disputes. Further to refinement and proper implementation Mana Whakahono-o-Rohe may create a pathway for local bodies to meet their obligations to Iwi. Key areas of accountability include Iwi concerns about stewardship of tribal lands, mining, land development and the health of waterways, resident flora and fauna. As Iwi (tribal) Management Plans (IMPs) are regularly drawn on to assist urban and regional councils in meeting these responsibilities, IMPS are afforded statutory recognition under the Resource Management Act (1991).

Iwi Management Plans are in effect strategic development documents lodged with local authorities by Iwi or hapū (extended kinship structures), that address regional tribal aspirations and specific concerns in regards to resource management issues (Saunders, 2017). Plans may address single issues, but frequently encompass environmental, cultural, economic, and spiritual aspirations as well as Iwi values. Common concerns include stewardship issues pertaining to areas of Iwi significance including wahi tapu (heritage sites), and Iwi expectations regarding tribal involvement in the development and protection of resources and potentially natural hazards management. The Resource Management Act (1991) contains an explicit requirement that IMPs must be considered by local governments when preparing or changing regional policy statements and district plans. Therefore, IMPS are also a vehicle for Iwi to create partnerships with regional authorities that will advance Māori development aspirations and provide opportunities for Iwi to shape regional resilience. Operationalised through the context of a Mana Whakahono-o-Rohe framework, IMPS could equally constitute an effective mechanism for advancing Iwi involvement in regional disaster management planning, governance, and infrastructures.

From a Māori perspective, Mana Whakahono-o-Rohe may be understood as the process of establishing mutually respectful relationships between regional authorities, local councils, lifeline agencies and Iwi, and enacting those relationships through effective regional governance. Further to the recommendations tabled in the Technical Advisory Group's review (2017), the Mana Whakahono-a-Rohe framework has been considered a potential template for amending the Civil Defence and Emergency Management (CDEM) Act (2002) to facilitate Iwi engagement in formal emergency management structures. There are no restrictions to engagement under the current legislation, however, anecdotally, resistance to engagement has been evidenced by both the Crown and tangata whenua on occasion. Amending the CDEM Act (2016) could expedite the development of a collaborative disaster management governance framework that would be adapted for regional implementation throughout Aotearoa New Zealand. An initial conceptualisation of how the Mana Whakahono-o-Rohe process might be adapted to shape Iwi engagement with regional CDEM governance structures is presented in Fig. 3.1.

Although the engagement framework may constitute a first step towards envisioning collaborative disaster governance in regional Aotearoa New Zealand, the Mana Whakahono o Rohe process is not universally accepted, and formal Iwi engagement in disaster governance will require considerable deliberation. Potential Iwi governance responsibilities, accountabilities, liabilities, capabilities and reporting lines need to be clarified. Engagement, operational and governance tensions also need to be identified and addressed, while targeted research and consultation with Iwi, on the part of regional CDEM groups and local authorities, will be crucial to informing and negotiating agreements on such matters.

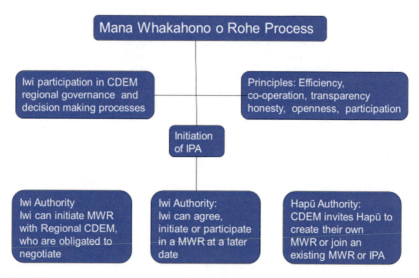

Fig. 3.1 Potential framework for Iwi engagement with CDEM regional disaster governance structures (*Source* Adapted from Resource Legislation Amendment Act, 2017)

Challenges to Implementation of Collaborative Disaster Management

There are also a number of challenges associated with establishing effective collaborative disaster management governance and operational structures when viewed from a Te Ao Māori perspective (Māori world view). A key concern is that initial government recommendations focus on embedding Māori involvement in disaster management governance solely at the regional level (Department of Prime Minister and Cabinet, pp. 3, 8). These recommendations align with key messages presented in the recently released National Disaster Resilience Strategy (2019), which highlights the strengths of Māori and asserts that 'partnering with Māori to build disaster resilience is essential (MCDEM Department of Prime Minister and Cabinet, p. 21)'. Yet, Iwi, hapū and whānau (Māori tribes, communities and families) respond to a significant natural hazard disaster or contexts where a state of emergency has been invoked in accordance with cultural dictates. Collectivised governance and communitarian approaches to providing support are rapidly operationalised on a nationalised basis, so resources are mobilised and distributed by multiple Iwi. Collaborative governance legislation that siloes Iwi engagement in operational governance at the regional level within pre-existing vertical command and control structures, may undermine integrated disaster risk reduction governance and responses to catastrophic disasters in local settings. Some Māori stakeholders have expressed concerns in regards to a perceived lack of recognition for Māori disaster governance aspirations at the national level (Phibbs et al., 2015). However, a broader concern is that limiting Māori engagement in this manner is contrary to the priorities and recommendations presented in the Sendai Framework for Disaster Risk Reduction (UNISDR, 2015).

A further consideration is that when a national state of emergency is declared in New Zealand, the government has statutory authority to operationalise a national emergency management response and local CDEM governance arrangements may become null and void (*Civil Defence and Emergency Management Act*, 2016). This was the case during the 2010–2011 earthquakes in Canterbury, although subsequent to the earthquakes Ngāi Tahu (the regional tribe) were legislated a limited statutory governance role in the redevelopment of Christchurch within the Canterbury Earthquake Recovery Authority Act (2011). Currently, there is no specific legislative mechanism for ensuring Iwi engagement in national disaster management governance. Anecdotal evidence suggests that the consistent lack of representation of Iwi in national governance structures has impacted relationships between Iwi and the Crown and strengthened Iwi concerns about the transparency and accountability of government-led actions in disasters. Concerns have also been expressed informally, that the lack of representation is a deliberate ploy to prevent Māori from playing a more active role in disaster governance. Such concerns have the potential to negatively impact the mobilisation of Iwi assets and resources to support urban and rural communities affected by natural hazard disasters and need to be explored.

An additional critique is that suggestions regarding Crown engagement in disaster governance with Māori, primarily focus on partnering with Iwi. This standardised approach to developing collaborative disaster management governance could facilitate situations where regional authorities engage with local Iwi who are inactive or have no interest or capabilities in disaster risk reduction. In contrast, urban Māori, displaced or relocated Iwi and Māori organisations that are active in disaster reduction may be excluded from governance arrangements. A further possibility is that local authorities' perceptions of Iwi economic, social and political capitals may inadvertently lead to privileging of some Iwi with additional disaster risk information and mitigation resources, while less affluent Iwi may experience inequitable access to resources and/or support. Potentially noteworthy in this regard is the first establishment of a corporate emergency operations centre (EOC) and tribal 'Emergency Response Framework' (Te Rūnanga o Ngāi Tahu, 2018) by affluent Iwi Te Rūnanga o Ngāi Tahu. While this is a significant and much needed development in terms of tribal emergency management capabilities, the iwi received considerable support from Canterbury CDEM Group agents.

Recent developments in the professionalisation of emergency management in New Zealand have also seen Te Rūnanga o Ngāi Tahu become the sole Iwi (tribe) invited to join the national consortium tasked by the Department of Prime Minister and Cabinet with developing and implementing national emergency management leadership training. The leadership programme is targeted at regional emergency controllers and recovery managers and has been expanded to include key stakeholders from various ministries, local authorities and other organisations active in the emergency management sector. However, the absence of broader Māori representation in this forum raises questions of transparency around inclusiveness and the constitution of the consortium.

In addition to NGOs and other key stakeholders not currently engaged with the consortium, a number of Iwi have demonstrated considerable resourcefulness and best practices disaster management in the aftermath of recent states of emergency. The Ngāti Awa response to the 2017 Edgecumbe Floods constitutes a case in point. Potential marginalisation and/or exclusion of Māori stakeholders from regional disaster management governance both nationally and in the regions draws attention to the hierarchical nature of the field of disaster management. Bourdieu (1996) defines a 'field' as: A structured social space that contains people who dominate and others who are dominated and he asserts that constant and permanent relationships of inequality operate inside such spaces. Drawing on Bourdieu's (1996) perspective, it may be inferred that the disaster management governance field constitutes a metaphysical and hierarchically ordered network of social relations. Structures, such as conditions in the disaster governance field, emergency management legislation and policies, the professional narratives and actions of CDEM actors produce a particular habitus (Bourdieu, 1977), which in turn shapes identity and agency. In doing so, habitus hierarchically positions Iwi, CDEM and local authority actors and influences power relations within the field of disaster management governance in New Zealand. The Ministry of Civil Defence and Emergency Management's (MCDEM) response to the Technical Advisory Groups recommendations, may constitute an exemplar.

The Ministry has agreed that recognition of Iwi emergency management capabilities is essential and seeks greater recognition and understanding of Iwi/Māori emergency management views, practices and the role of marae as support hubs in disasters (MCDEM, 2018, p. 25). Legislation is also deemed necessary to clarify the role of Iwi in planning for and responding to disasters, to enable Iwi representation on regional CDEM coordinating executive groups and to ensure regional CDEM Groups consult with Iwi/Māori when developing local emergency management plans (MCDEM, 2018, p. 26). However, the Ministry is resistive to drawing on the Mana Whakohono–a-Rohe framework as a model for potential changes to the Civil Defence and Emergency Management Act (2016) and does not support Iwi being accorded membership or voting rights in regards to CDEM Groups. Presently, CDEM groups select governance representation independent of ministerial approval; however, the proposed establishment of a national emergency management agency, professional standards and related legislative changes may reduce levels of autonomy within the regions. Future representation on regional disaster management and governance structures will likely be influenced as a result of the proposed restructure, including recognition of the diverse roles and responsibilities of Iwi in emergency management. It is therefore essential that Māori concerns regarding government acknowledgement of Iwi and other Māori agents' participation in disaster management governance, mobilisation of cultural assets and emergency management capability development are comprehensively addressed. The qualitative research project: 'Māori, Catastrophic Events, and Collective Development of Culture-based Disaster Management Theory and Practice' outlined in this chapter is an initial step towards that outcome.

Research Design

The principal aim of this research is to advance Māori disaster management theory, knowledge and practice through generating empirically rich understandings and conceptually innovative knowledge regarding the diverse roles of Māori attributes in managing catastrophic disasters to:

(i) create the first comprehensive Māori disaster management theory and implementation framework
(ii) innovate the ways Māori and the New Zealand emergency management infrastructure collaborate in response to disasters;
(iii) extend current knowledge and theory within the social science of disasters field.

Overview: The research project is envisaged as Community-Based (and led) Participatory Research (CBPR), an effective approach for facilitating trusting relationships with research partners, and promoting well-being in Indigenous communities. Te Whakamāramatanga (The enlightenment) the Māori narrative research methodology selected to frame this qualitative research, was developed to conduct research with Māori impacted by adversity and is thus highly suitable for shaping the research design and process. More broadly, the research is designed by and for Māori, addresses Māori concerns, and is implemented by Māori researchers in accordance with Māori values and research practices. Te Reo (Māori language), a key element of Māori identity and well-being will be embedded at every level of the research, and a Māori Advisory Group comprised of kaumātua (elders) will provide ethical, linguistic and cultural oversight of the research until completion.

The research design evidences respect for local ways of knowing, and promotes intergenerational dissemination of research practice knowledge and skillsets in Māori communities. Disrupting inherent power differentials between researchers and researched communities is also essential to decolonising research conducted with Māori communities. Therefore, the project is being developed in the context of a partnership between the Māori researchers and participants situated within community settings in Wellington, Canterbury, Hawke's Bay and the Bay of Plenty. These research sites were selected based on empirical evidence that these areas are considered high risk for significant natural hazard events as well as consultation with Māori stakeholders and local CDEM authorities in these regions.

Participant consultation and recruitment: Discussions with key Māori actors have facilitated marae access and community interest in the proposed research. Participant recruitment is purposive and will be achieved with support from Māori leaders, kaumātua, marae networks and through snowballing methods. Research participation is sought from Māori adults (n60 + individuals), aged between 20 and 65, who have relationships with their local marae or Māori communities, and will mobilise to support their communities in a disaster. Emergency managers (n10-15), employed in regional MCDEM and council offices will also be invited to share their professional views regarding New Zealand's disaster management infrastructure in semi-structured individual interviews.

Data Collection and Analysis: The oral tradition of passing down Māori knowledge, values and practices through conversation, stories and waiata (songs) is a valued aspect of Māori culture, and all mediums of information are acknowledged within the research. Kanohi ki te kanohi, the act of face-to-face communication, is embedded within the methodology, and actioned through hui a wānanga (workshops), dialogical, and semi-structured interviews to collect Māori participants' knowledge, experiences and views. Interviews may be held in English and/or Te Reo to enhance knowledge capture. Digitally recorded interview data will be transcribed verbatim. Member checking of interview transcripts is being used to verify the credibility, and reliability of transcribed data. 'Talk' is analysed in paragraph format using a narrative unit approach to reduce the risk of de-contextualised analysis. Investigator and theoretical triangulation is being applied to reduce data misinterpretation and emergent themes will be checked with participants to ensure accuracy of interpretation.

Analysis of Māori disaster management attributes, their contextual applicability in diverse settings and relationships between disaster management actors will be enhanced by using a bricolage of case study methods to compare participants' experiences, views, knowledges and practices. Māori methodological processes and concepts are core to data analysis. Yet multiple conceptual lenses will be applied to data analysis to ensure that participants' 'talk' is interpreted and Māori disaster management theory developed using a Māori 'gaze' that is contemporaneously nuanced by global socio-political externalities while considering the broader theoretical influences of disaster social science. Māori conceptualisations of disaster management and governance will be examined with reference to culturally situated socio-environmental approaches to disaster recovery. Sets of understanding about cultural attributes will be developed through characterising descriptions in terms of the meanings given by participants to values, practices, others' actions and social situations. Generating, and interweaving in-depth understandings of regional perspectives, practices and relationships within communities as well as between communities, CDEM and local authorities, will provide a comprehensive overview of Māori disaster management and governance. Finally, knowledge dissemination and co-authorship of publications will be negotiated during an initial Hui a wānanga. Māori knowledge shared during the research will constitute participants' intellectual property. New knowledge, theory, frameworks and practices developed by the research will be co-owned by Māori, the researchers, and host academic institutions.

Initial Phase of Research

The research proposal was peer-reviewed through the Massey University Human Ethics Committee (MUHEC) online approval system in September 2018. The proposal was deemed to be of low ethical risk and generated a MUHEC low-risk notification number: 4000019854. Community engagement in the research process commenced at a Hui a Wānanga (research development workshop), conducted at Te Kakano o Te Aroha Marae from 5 to 7th of October 2018. Provisional findings from the workshop and initial focus group interviews indicate that ensuring Māori self-determination of emergency management responses by and within Māori communities is a key concern. Participants' talk suggests that Māori identity is collectivised when enacted in emergency management contexts and generates a communitarian perspective on emergency management governance. Māori approaches to emergency management are therefore conceived as collaborative and reinforce community unity in times of adversity regardless of existing tensions and agendas at play within local social relations. Emergent findings suggest that shaped by collective identity Māori approaches to emergency management governance and practice are strongly characterised by collective responsibility, authority, agency, action and accountability. The ways in which these diverse elements are co-constitutive and Māori emergency governance may be positioned in relation to other emergency management actors and institutions, is presented in the following Fig. 3.2.

While this discussion is informed by provisional findings from current research, future analytical findings may challenge current data interpretations, Fig. 3.2 clearly showcases Māori approaches to emergency management governance and practices as cyclical, horizontal and relational. In contrast, emergency management governance embedded within formal response agencies and institutions relies on coordinated incident management systems (CIMS being operationalised in the aftermath of

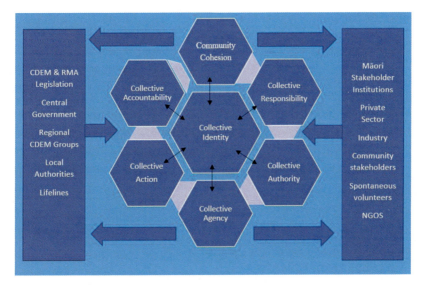

Fig. 3.2 Draft Māori emergency management governance model showing potential relationships with other stakeholders (© This figure is not to be used or reproduced without the permission of the author Dr C. Kenney)

disasters through a vertical hierarchy of command). Tensions in relation to establishing collaborative linkages between the two emergency management approaches are self- evident, therefore negotiating collaborative DRR strategies and practices will be essential to ensuring New Zealand's resilience to disasters.

Conclusion

The Framework developed during this research will require localised action and encourage the new National Emergency Management Agency, which has replaced the former Ministry of Civil Defence and Emergency Management MCDEM, to engage with Māori, and incorporate cultural diversity into a new collaborative governance approach to disaster management policies and practices. To date, such collaborations have been few, and rarely included the distinct Māori knowledge, values and practices that facilitate social well-being in differing disaster contexts. Bringing Māori cultural attributes into conversation with globally accepted risk reduction concepts and practices is crucial for developing both a comprehensive Māori disaster management theory and implementation framework as well as contributing to the reimagining and refinement of New Zealand's emergency management infrastructure policies and practices. More broadly, Māori disaster management approaches and practices have global relevance and resonate with international emergency management priorities and objectives, including the Sendai Framework for Disaster Risk Reduction (2015).

References

Bay of Plenty Times. (2017). *Edgecumbe clean up moves into 'recovery' phase.* Retrieved 23 April; viewed 19 June 2017. http://www.nzherald.co.nz/bay-of-plentytimes/news/article.cfm?c_id=1503343&objectid=11842863

Bourdieu, P. (1977). *Outline of a theory for practice* (R. Nice, Trans.). Cambridge University Press.

Bourdieu, P. (1996). *On television.* (P. Parkhurst, Trans.). The New Press.

Civil Defence and Emergency Management Act. (2016). (New Zealand) Retrieved 29 September 2018 from: http://www.legislation.govt.nz/act/public/2016/0088/latest/DLM6648809.html?src=qs

Hudson, J., & Hughes, E. (2007). The role of marae and Māori communities in post disaster recovery: A Case study, *GNS Science Report, 2007/15.* GNS Science.

Johnson, L., Kenney, C., Johnston, D., & Du Plessis, R. (2014). New Zealand case study. In M. Pelling (Ed.), Pathways for transformation: Disaster risk management to enhance development goals. A commissioned report to inform the Global Assessment of Disaster Risk Management (GAR) July 2015. Retrieved 8 September 2018 from: https://www.unisdr.org/we/inform/publications/49568

Kenney, C., & Phibbs, S. (2014). Shakes rattles and roll outs: The untold story of Māori engagement with community recovery, social reliance and urban sustainability in Christchurch, New Zealand. *Procedia Economics and Finance, 18*, 754–762.

Kenney, C., & Solomon, Sir M. W. (2014). Māori community-led disaster risk management: An effective response to the 2010–2011 Christchurch Earthquakes. *UNISDR Scientific and Technical Advisory Group Case Studies – 2014.* http://www.preventionweb.net/files/workspace/7935_kenneyandsolomon.pdf

Kenney, C., & Phibbs, S. (2015). A Māori Love Story: Community-led Disaster Management in response to the Ōtautahi (Christchurch) Earthquakes as a framework for action. *International Journal of Disaster Risk Reduction, 14*(1), 46–55. https://doi.org/10.1016/ijdrr.2014.12.010

Lambert, S. (2014). Indigenous peoples and urban disaster: Māori responses to the 2010–12 Christchurch earthquakes. *Australasian Journal of Disaster and Trauma Studies, 18*(1), 39–48.

Local Government Act. (2002). Retrieved 27 September 2018 from: http://www.legislation.govt.nz/act/public/2002/0084/latest/DLM170873.html

Ministry of Civil Defence and Emergency Management. (2019). *National disaster resilience strategy Rautaki ā-Motu Manawaroa Aituā.* Department of Prime Minister and Cabinet.

Ministry of Civil Defence and Emergency Management. (2018). *Delivering better responses to natural disasters and other emergencies - Government response to the Technical Advisory Group's recommendations.* Department of Prime Minister and Cabinet (published August 2018). Retrieved 22 September 2018 from: file:///F:/!%20A%20A%20ANU/govt-repsonse-tag-report-aug2018.pdf

Paton, D., Johnston, D., Mamula-Seadon, L., & Kenney, C. (2014). Recovery and development: Perspectives from New Zealand and Australia. In N. Kapucu & K. T. Liou (Eds.), *Disaster & development: Examining global issues and cases* (pp. 255–273). New York.

Phibbs, S., Kenney, C., & Solomon M. (2015). Ngā Mōwaho: An analysis of Māori responses to the Christchurch earthquakes. *Kotuitui: New Zealand Journal of Social Sciences Online, 10*(2), 72–82. https://doi.org/10.1080/1177083X.2015.1066401

Resources Management Act. (1991). Retrieved 19 September 2018 from: http://www.legislation.govt.nz/act/public/1991/0069/211.0/DLM230265.html

Resource Legislation Amendment Act. (2017). Retrieved 19 September 2018 from: http://www.legislation.govt.nz/act/public/2017/0015/27.0/DLM6669131.html

Saunders, W. (2017). Investigating the role of Iwi management plans in natural hazard management: A case study from the bay of plenty region. *GNS Science Report 2017/50* (published March 2018). GNS Science.

Scoop NZ. (2017). *Overwhelming support for Ngati Awa volunteer army.* Retrieved 19 June 2017 from: http://www.scoop.co.nz/stories/AK1704/S00582/overwhelming-support-for-ngati-awavolunteer-army.htm

Shepherd, D., McBride, D., & Lovelock, K. (2017). First responder well-being following the 2011 Canterbury earthquake. *Disaster Prevention & Management, 26*(3), 286–297. https://doi.org/10.1108/DPM-06-2016-0112

Solomon, Sir M. W. (2012). *Keynote address.* Recover reconnect rebuild. MASS (Māori Academy of Social Science) Conference. November, 28–30. Canterbury University.

Solomon, Sir M. W. (2013). The significance of the development of the Māori economy and the longer term perspective. *2013 Spring Overview.* New

Zealand Business & Parliament Trust. Retrieved April 2014 from: http://www.nzbpt.org.nz/assets/Uploads/Ta-Mark-Solomonsaddress.pdf

Technical Advisory Group - Department of Prime Minister and Cabinet (2017). Ministerial Review - Better Responses to Natural Disasters and Other Emergencies. Wellington: Department of Prime Minister and Cabinet (published 17 November 2017), Retrieved 20 September 2018 from: https://www.dpmc.govt.nz/our-business-units/ministry-civil-defence-emergency-management/ministerial-review-better-responses

Te Rūnanga o Ngāi Tahu. (2018). *Emergency response framework*. Te Rūnanga o Ngāi Tahu.

The New Zealand Herald. (2016). *Takahanga marae serves last dinner after Kaikoura quake as Red Cross sets up centre*. Retrieved 18 June 2017 from: http://www.nzherald.co.nz/nz/news/article.cfm?c_id=1&objectid=11751819

UNISDR. (2015). *Sendai framework for disaster risk reduction 2015–2030*. The United Nations Office for Disaster Risk Reduction. https://www.undrr.org/publication/sendai-framework-disaster-risk-reduction-2015-2030

CHAPTER 4

Improving Multi-Agency Governance Arrangements for Preparedness Planning and Response: Implementing the *Integrated Approach* in Australia

Alan Ryan

Introduction: The Need for an Integrated Approach

War is a humanitarian disaster and wars impose levels of operational complexity that fall most catastrophically on marginalised and vulnerable populations. So where we once considered humanitarian assistance and (natural) disaster response in isolation from the scourge of armed conflict, now we must consider disaster response as a complex problem requiring an integrated civil–military–police response. The lessons of

---

A. Ryan (✉)
Australian Civil-Military Centre, Queanbeyan, Australia

© The Author(s), under exclusive license to Springer Nature Singapore Pte Ltd. 2022
H. James et al. (eds.), *Disaster Risk Reduction in Asia Pacific*, Disaster Risk, Resilience, Reconstruction and Recovery,
https://doi.org/10.1007/978-981-16-4811-3_4

Australia's recent offshore deployments suggest that Australia's governments must create a flexible, adaptive and strongly coordinated 'All-Hazards' approach to policy planning and operational cooperation whenever we deploy military, police and civilian personnel to deal with a crisis or emergency. If Australia is to maximise its advantages in personnel, technology and resources, it needs to better coordinate the efforts of the many agencies involved in preparing, planning and executing operations. That imperative does not require significant organisational adjustments. It does mean that we need to develop an operational mindset that goes beyond interagency cooperation to achieve an integrated whole-of-government culture.

We live in an era of complex, protracted and interconnected security challenges rather than one characterised by discrete, stand-alone crises. Conflicts (or 'man-made crises') are often overlayed on humanitarian, ecological or developmental disasters. The past twenty years has seen Australia move from a relatively short-term model of offshore deployments to more extended and frequent overseas commitments. The ever-increasing array of government and non-government agencies committed to building preparedness, disaster prevention and crisis response both domestically and internationally means that this work is core business for a growing workforce. This chapter examines disaster risk reduction, resilience and recovery in its broadest context. It considers how the fundamental principles of multi-agency coordination apply across the full spectrum of crisis contingencies.

National policy-making must reflect the fact that we live in an era where protracted conflict and mass-casualty disasters together represent massive security and humanitarian challenges. National and international crisis response involves an ever-expanding array of actors. No single organisation or agency is capable of deploying more than a portion of the suite of capabilities required in crisis response. The 2004 Management Advisory Committee report *Connecting Government* argued that culturally whole-of-government was a relative strength for Australia and that institutional cultural reform was more important than machinery of government structural change. The report suggested that the whole-of-government approach was 'particularly suitable for complex and longstanding policy issues, sometimes referred to as 'wicked problems'. They defy jurisdictional boundaries and resist bureaucratic routines' (Management Advisory Committee, 2004, p. 10). In the time since then, the digital revolution and consequent public sector culture change has continued unabated. Accordingly, contemporary government requires systems that better support the interagency strategic analysis that supports joint action. We also need to be more deliberate in preparing the whole-of-government team that we will send overseas and into harm's way.

Thoughtful readers will ask how the proposed *Integrated Approach* departs from current practice. After all, we already have a mature and effective crisis management framework which is founded on a matrix of the Australian Government Crisis Committee; standing interdepartmental committees (IDCs); and ad hoc Interdepartmental Emergency Task Forces (IDETFs) (Prime Minister and Cabinet, 2016). This chapter endorses that framework but suggests that more needs to be done to ensure that integration occurs not only horizontally and vertically, but that it achieves greater conceptual and cultural cohesion. As Candel argues (2019, p. 5) 'even if an integrated approach might be effective and desired' it needs to be *feasible*. While for the usual work of government a fully integrated approach is usually unnecessary, it does become essential when effectiveness and efficiency are measured in lives saved. At present departments and agencies work together, they do not necessarily work as one.

Both individually, and collectively, states benefit from acting to address the root causes of human suffering. Addressing the political dimensions of disaster risk reduction and recovery is only a start. The 2017 World Bank report *Crisis Response and Resilience to Systemic Shocks* argued that to be resilient states need the capacity to prevent, mitigate, and/or respond effectively to shocks in the following three dimensions:

- Economic resilience: the capacity of the fiscal and financial systems to absorb shocks.
- Social resilience: the extent to which individuals are supported to recover from systemic shocks.
- Resilience to environmental shocks: enabling physical structures and the agricultural economy to withstand natural disasters and recover from them (World Bank, 2017, p. 11).

Increasingly the line between domestic and offshore crisis response is blurred. Australian crisis managers, whether civilian, military or police must often deploy over large distances and work alongside international, non-governmental and private sector partners. All too often military forces have taken on roles that are more appropriately civilian. Sometimes this is caused by a lack of civilian capability, but all too often it is caused by the fact that military planning capability can pre-empt or even swamp the development of civilian response options. The Australian government's evaluation and assessment of its whole-of-government mission in Afghanistan determined that:

> Whenever a whole-of-government mission is considered, all departments and agencies involved should participate in an interagency planning team . . . The whole-of-government planning approach should be tailored to accommodate all participating agencies. (ACMC, 2016, p. 20)

While the specific circumstances of each operation will differ, similar principles come into play in every contingency where lives are at stake. Instead of emphasizing what distinguishes crises from each other, there is value in investing more effort in determining the best way to coexist, coordinate and/or coordinate in disaster risk reduction and recovery in advance of deployments. Failure to do so invariably leads to unbalanced mission teams and ultimately to retrospective efforts to re-engineer the deployment.

The lessons learned from recent operations involving Australian and partner coalition states (most notably in protracted operations in Afghanistan) have demonstrated the importance of optimising culture, training and human behaviour. The lessons of international conflict response in Afghanistan (or Iraq, Timor or the Solomon Islands) are not a prescriptive model for the future. We do not know what strategic shocks await us. However, the experience of almost two decades of continuous complex operations conducted among vulnerable and marginalised populations provides us with lessons that are directly applicable to other developmental, humanitarian or ecological disasters. Whether disaster is the consequence of intentional acts or environmental factors, crisis responders need to work with colleagues across agencies, from the NGO sector, international organisations and other countries. An obvious lesson is that countries that possess the advantages of good intelligence; excellent information technology; resilient bureaucracies and highly educated human capital should be more resilient and capable of helping each other than they have in the recent past.

Learning and Applying the Lessons of Digital Age Strategic Leadership

Government departments and agencies everywhere are alert to the requirement for more agile, adaptive responses to contemporary security challenges. Levels of liaison and interconnectedness are generally higher than they have ever been. Government agencies enjoy instantaneous communications, access to unprecedented levels of information, and employ the most highly qualified professional staff in history. Yet planning and operational responses are still constrained by institutional siloes and are largely reactive to the crisis of the moment. We are reactive to events because we do not always adopt a means of assuring institutional memory that works across the entire government system. This chapter draws a link between the challenges that government faces in mobilising personnel to deal with conflict and the similar challenges of mounting disaster response and recovery operations. In many cases, the personnel involved in these operations are the same, so there is an advantage in building more coordinated civil–military–police relationships to maximise the impact of coordinated policy, planning and operational execution. Australia is not unique; we can benefit from innovations in public administration that are driving a global trend to more joined-up government.

Launching the United Kingdom's *Civil Service Workforce Plan* in 2016 the Honourable Matt Hancock MP, Minister for the Cabinet Office, stated that the digital revolution had transformed the way we work (Hancock, 2016). He observed '*any particular technology is only a tiny part of the solution – maybe ten per cent. Ninety percent is about culture, training and human behaviour*'.

Digitisation has had an enormous impact on our strategic and operational environments. But the human factor remains the key to effective leadership in all circumstances. Simply relying on collecting data, or even conducting lessons analysis is not enough. Because we operate human systems, we need to factor in how we learn and adapt as people. We cannot expect to rely on our databases to do that for us.

Organisations like the Australian Civil-Military Centre and the British Stabilisation Unit have derived lessons from operations that demonstrate that if we are to achieve an integrated approach, we need to radically reconceive how we think of public sector leadership and the way that we prepare officials, military and police for the challenges ahead. There is nothing 'heroic' in the model of leadership proposed. Whether it is supervisory, peer, or 'leading-upwards', strategic leadership is a core professional function. These days no one can say that providing leadership is not part of their job description.

An aspect of the professionalization of leadership is that we have become less reliant on models of charismatic 'top-down' leadership. That does not mean that we no longer value positive leadership traits such as good communication skills, empathy and providing guidance by example. It does mean that we are more aware of the mistaken tendency to assume that organisational successes and failures are all solely the result of the senior leader's performance. Leadership researchers call it 'the romance of leadership' (Meindl et al., 1985; Wong & Gerras, 2017). Any contemporary discussion of leadership lessons needs to consider the organisational culture and policy context at least as much as the personal attributes of successful leaders.

Concentrating on leadership in crisis is also potentially misleading. That is because focusing on crisis response, whether for disaster remediation or the prosecution of conflict distracts us from the real issue. If you work in government and are engaged in the business of employing national and international resources in other peoples' countries then you have a job for life. Crisis events are everyday business in foreign and national security affairs. The global proliferation of conflict; state failure; and increased challenges to human security suggest that we need to replace notions of crisis response as being exceptional with a professional, but routine approach to natural and man-made disasters—that includes conflict.

This shift in our perception of disaster management poses a dilemma. If 'crisis' is the new normal, do we reorganise government as one big crisis response agency? Or do we recognise that our strategic context has changed irrevocably and that government institutions need to adapt rather than maintain inadequate levels of capability in institutional siloes. Disasters are usually defined by poor preparedness and inadequate resources—there is nothing 'natural' about disaster (O'Keefe et al., 1976). We can ameliorate the effects of disasters, if we accept that complex operations are a whole-of-government responsibility.

For many government personnel, this requirement means that no longer can we regard deployments offshore as the exception in a domestically oriented career. Globalisation means that the national security workforce, just like the private sector, must be immediately capable of doing its work in contested, austere, insecure and often violent environments. This imperative requires a level of preparedness by civilian and police personnel that more closely approximates that traditionally maintained by the military. That means that we need to think more seriously about what sort of guidance about our expectations of leaders we provide to civilian, police and military personnel.

Leaders whose only experience is of policy work or providing transactional services in well-resourced capitals, with robust infrastructure, are unlikely to provide credible leadership in complex conflicts and disasters. Whereas in the past, like Lincoln and his generals, we had the luxury of time to allow the 'right' leaders to emerge, today we do not have that luxury. We need the right people in the right jobs in advance of strategic shocks.

The British *Civil Service Workforce Plan* recognises the fact that what worked in the past will not work now and what is required is a fundamentally transformational reconsideration of what is involved in public service. As Minister Hancock suggests:

> No longer should we take people with no experience of an area or job and throw them in at the deep end because they have a gap in their experience. Gone are the days of the gifted amateur. Today's world is too complex and demands are too high. (Hancock, 2016)

Good government requires professionals, properly educated, appropriately trained and ready to deploy if that is required. The requirements of preparedness are much higher for personnel than ever before as government call on small, expert teams rather than large bureaucracies or conscripted military labour forces. Government must organise itself, less in functional hierarchies and more as an adaptable learning organisation flexible enough to reconfigure to meet changing circumstances.

This imperative does not remove the requirement for government departments. Civilian agencies need to emulate the military 'Joint' approach, maintaining responsibility for raising, training and sustaining subject matter expertise, but being ready to contribute resources to integrated civil–military–police taskforces.

A digital workforce is networked—as opposed to a clerical workforce which is hierarchical. Senior leaders are still expected to assume responsibility and direct the application of resources to accomplish strategic objectives. But in an era of instantaneous communications and comprehensive connectivity, we need to see leadership as more organic than hierarchical. Schools of government and leadership training courses are promoting the practice of *Adaptive leadership* (Heifetz et al., 1997, 2009). The evidence from contemporary operations suggests that without adopting a networked and devolved adaptive leadership model of decision-making we are not maximising the benefit of our other advantages.

Contemplating the effect of instantaneous communications on the fight against Al Qaeda Iraq (AQI), General Stanley McChrystal observed that it *slowed* rather than accelerated decision-making. This was because:

> Repeatedly, we navigated approval processes that went all the way to the Pentagon or the White House for strikes against terrorist leaders we'd located, for the deployment of forces, or for the implementation of information campaigns. Communications should have been instantaneous but decisions never were. The aggregate effects were crippling.

There are two aspects to the impact of digitisation on strategic action. The first is **speed**. By this is meant our reaction time in the cycle of strategic and operational decision-making. Too slow and we surrender the advantage that force capability, intelligence, national and coalition resources confer on us. But if our strategic reactions are faster than our opponents' we are far more likely to prevail in conflict. The second issue is **cohesion**. By this, we mean whether we continue to act within existing institutional structures and only seek to coordinate our plans and actions. Or do we pursue a truly cooperative approach to the integration of ends, ways and means? Just settling for coordination between agencies, rather than higher-level integration, implies that the result of our efforts may equal the sum of its parts—maybe less. Integrating national efforts, together with closer cooperative relationships with international partners, opens the possibility that the strategic effect will be more than the sum of its parts.

In both areas of speed and cohesion, we are lagging badly in changing our culture, training and behaviour to match the possibilities of digitisation. We may have acquired the valuable tool of Big Data, but the way that we do things and the limitations we impose on our best and brightest reflects a commitment to rigid models of command and control. We fail to utilise the advantage of our extraordinary resource in human capital.

If we are to maximise the benefits of adaptive leadership we need to match our behaviours, organisational arrangements and mind-sets to the overwhelming advantage that our command of technology and information provides us. As John Lewis Gaddis lamented 'we're good at educating hedgehogs, who know one big thing and much less adept at training foxes, who know lots of little things and have the agility to cope with them' (Gaddis, 2009). Enabled by technology undreamt of only a decade ago, we must develop people who can identify connections, make decisions and react faster than ever before. If we can do that, and replicate it at the international coalition level, then we have a greater chance of controlling events rather than simply reacting to them. We might even conceive of operations and campaigns measured in years not decades. But to do this we must develop an Integrated Approach to national security based on the principle of 'joined-up' government (Ryan, 2016, 2017). Recent scholarship has identified different ways of articulating the integrated approach. Space does not permit a detailed analysis in this chapter, but as Candel suggests the 'four dimensions of policy integration distinguished are: (i) policy frame, (ii) subsystem involvement, (iii) goals, and (iv) instruments.' (Candel, 2019, p. 3). Crisis responders rarely have the leisure to deliberately conceptualise their response, instead, it needs to become part of their organisational DNA and that can only be achieved through education, training and realistic exercises in advance of crises.

The Integrated Approach: Building on the Lessons of Experience

The first principle of lessons learned is to avoid having to learn the lesson in the first place if others have already done it for you. Australia, the United States, the United Kingdom, Canada and New Zealand have long employed broadly similar approaches to developing assessment architectures that 'distil lessons that can build on previous experience and that will assist decision-makers, policy experts, planners and practitioners... in considering future whole-of-government responses to complex contingencies' (ACMC, 2016, p. 5). Of these five countries, the British have made the most progress in translating hard-won operational experience into policy and practice.

Within the British government, the Stabilisation Unit is a cross-government unit supporting UK government efforts to tackle instability overseas. It is the immediate counterpart of, and a model for, the Australian Civil-Military Centre. It is comprised of civil servant staff members from twelve government departments, as well as serving military and police officers. Established in 2007, the Stabilisation Unit:

- provides the link between civil, military and police efforts to build stability overseas;
- facilitates cross-government working and lesson-learning in planning for, and responding to, conflict; and
- captures and shares lessons and examples of best practice on stabilisation work (UK Stabilisation Unit, 2017).

Importantly, the Stabilisation Unit has placed lesson-learning at the core of its contribution to government capability. The core philosophy of the British approach is the adoption as policy of what is called the 'Integrated Approach'. Derived from the British experience of operations (Defence Committee, House of Commons, 2010) and reflecting bipartisan political support, British whole-of-government operational culture accepts that:

> Integration is primarily driven by the process of people from different institutions and different disciplines working side by side at several levels to ensure that their perspectives and activities reinforce each other. Integration requires low-level cooperation and mid-level coordination, supplemented by high-level alignment of overall strategic objectives. Integration should improve the flow of information, contribute to a shared understanding of stabilisation challenges and responses, reduce policy and delivery 'silos', and ensure greater effect on the ground.

This approach requires:

- high-level alignment at the strategic level;
- coordination at the operational level; and
- cooperation at the tactical level.

It recognises that leadership is exercised at every level and that systems founded on maintaining tight central control are anachronistic.

This principle is not just relevant to the alignment of national security efforts; it is applicable to every aspect of national policy-making where more than one department or agency is involved. In Australia in 2015 the former Secretary of the Department of Prime Minister and Cabinet,

Professor Peter Shergold, undertook a review of government processes in response to the disastrous failure of a number of major Australian Government policy programs. He observed that clustering expertise in one department worked best:

> for activities that are more transactional, where scale breeds efficiency and the connection to policy objectives, stakeholders and the broader environment is less critical. For complex major projects . . . a more bespoke, agile capability is required. The notion of establishing a 'tiger team' is one that should be adopted. It would assist the APS [Australian Public Service] to meet future challenges of government program delivery, particularly with new, large and complex initiatives. (Shergold, 2015, p. 50)

There are few government projects more complex than a decade-long, multi-agency commitment to an offshore coalition operation in a conflict-affected and impoverished country or region. This is an experience that has become all too common for Australian government departments and agencies. So adopting the integrated approach of forming bespoke, inter-agency ('tiger') teams is essential if we are to devolve authority and responsibility to those leadership teams in government that need it to be effective.

AN INTERAGENCY TOOL TO IDENTIFY AND MAINTAIN THE STRATEGIC POLICY AIM

Implementing the Integrated Approach requires both vertical and horizontal connectivity within government, and increasingly with international, non-government and private sector actors. For this to occur it must be informed by a cross-agency approach to problem solving.

The United Kingdom has adopted a well-thought-through national model for integrating strategic policy planning and management. Titled a *Joint Analysis of Conflict and Stability* (JACS) this model provides a 'tool to strengthen... [cross-government]... approaches to tackling overseas conflict and stability and identify the situation-specific interventions that will be most likely to succeed on helping to prevent conflict and build stability' (UK Stabilisation Unit, 2017, p. i). It is designed to build a 'shared understanding of the causes, actors and drivers of conflict and agreement on the key priorities for... intervention to promote stability, security and long term peace' (UK Stabilisation Unit, 2017, p. i). The document is publicly available on the Stabilisation Unit's website. The fact that it has been made public demonstrates that achieving interagency coordination is not rocket science, it is the result of deliberate coordination and promoting a joined-up culture across government.

The JACS underpins the implementation of the Integrated Approach and provides an off-the-shelf methodology for the 'Tiger Team' approach advocated by Professor Shergold. Whenever a strategic issue necessitates a national strategic response a cross-agency team or task force is formed and made responsible for identifying and maintaining clarity as to what are the government's strategic objectives. It is adaptable to the particular strategic context and can be led, or co-led from the most appropriate department/s.

The utility of the joint interagency analytical tool is not restricted to dealing with conflict, it is equally useful in building domestic and international capacity to deal with the full range of complex scenarios necessitating a multi-agency response. The JACS model is a tool to support governments by providing: an interagency appreciation of the strategic context; a rationale for engagement and decision-making; and risk management through identifying competing interests and the potential harmful consequences of various courses of action. The UK National Security Council requires that all government strategies for conflict and fragile states are accompanied by a common interagency conflict analysis. It is a requirement that our own national security and crisis response framework could well emulate.

Initially, and perhaps not surprisingly, there was a perception within some stakeholder departments in Her Majesty's Government that such a tool could be either time or resource consuming. There was a sense, common to most bureaucracies, that as people came to understand the strategic contexts of offshore operations, a new approach would not be needed. In most governments, we still have to break the expectation that with regard to their own portfolio policy responsibilities, government departments are sovereign. While such an approach made sense in clerical model bureaucracies the age of the omnipotent permanent departmental head is over. Departments and agencies routinely share information, resources and services. Good strategic policy requires more than simple consultation, it requires a common approach.

This is the situation within the United Kingdom. There is a rising demand for JACS to be conducted as Departmental Heads and senior officials realise that conducting policy analysis in siloes is inefficient. Ultimately, cross-agency coordination needs to occur if offshore operations are to be carried through to completion. Deferring this common effort only increases the cost of operations, extends their duration and risks greater loss of life. Of all the analytical tools that individual departments use, only the JACS methodology is both comprehensive in its approach to the issue, and also builds cross-departmental oversight and ownership.

The British model provides a precedent that could easily be adapted to the Australian context. If we are to build a strategic culture in Australia, we need to shift away from our traditional reliance on mounting a military operation and then retrospectively introducing civilian policy and operational elements. A national security strategy must be founded on networked conversations across national security portfolios, it can never work if it is the product of only one department or agency.

Conclusion

The requirement for an integrated national operational culture will persist as a requirement for effective disaster prevention, risk reduction and recovery. But workable solutions already exist, only requiring some changes in institutional approaches and political understandings of strategy. Contemporary understanding of the application of digital technology and networked systems approaches to public administration provides one way forward. The answer is not a single strategic document or more White Papers, but a change in the way we conceptualise our preparedness and long-term planning.

Assessment tools such as the JACS provide an opportunity to break down stove-piped contingency and crisis planning and develop shared interagency positions as issues develop, not years into a deployment. We require flexible approaches that utilise existing departmental and agency expertise, but which go beyond the interdepartmental committee approach. That approach ensures consultation; it does not meet the Digital Age imperative for joined-up government.

Our future security rests in the hands of the successive generations of highly intelligent, talented people now working their way through the community of operational responders, be they civilian, police or military. It is our responsibility to ensure that they understand the nature of strategic leadership that they must provide. They will only be able to do this if we provide the ongoing training, education and transparent interagency processes to set them up for success. It is time to move past departmental siloes and to conceive of strategy, and our strategic workforce, at the national level.

There is no perfect or perfectible model of integrated government. Mistakes will continue to be made and information flows will always be unsatisfactory. But the answer to those problems is not to double down and reinforce institutional stovepipes. Every country has to find its own path to promoting cohesion across its civilian, military and police agencies. But we can make great advances by emphasising that operational culture is not rooted in service or departmental ways of doing things. The challenge of leadership in the Digital Age is to ensure that everyone, from those deployed on the ground, to the Prime Minister, understands the nature of the missions facing them and their role in it. That imperative doesn't mean that everyone must know everything, it means that we need to continue to seek out simple, robust tools to promote strategic cohesion in spite of the fog and friction of events.

REFERENCES

Australian Civil-Military Centre. (2016). *Afghanistan: Lessons from Australia's whole-of-government mission.*

Candel, J. J. L. (2019). The expediency of policy integration. *Policy Studies.* https://doi.org/10.1080/01442872.2019.1634191. Retrieved 31 July 2019 from https://www.tandfonline.com/doi/full/10.1080/01442872.2019.1634191

Department of Prime Minister and Cabinet. (2016). *Annual report 2015–16,* crisis management. Retrieved 2 August 2017 from https://www.pmc.gov.au/sites/default/files/publications/annual_reports/2015-16-HTML/results/prime-minister-and-cabinet.html

Gaddis, J. L. (2009). 'What is grand strategy?' The Karl Von Der Heyden Distinguished lecture, Duke University, 26 February 2009, Retrieved 31 July 2019 from http://indianstrategicknowledgeonline.com/web/grandstrategypaper.pdf

Hancock, The Right Hon. M. (2016). 'Speech at the Launch of the Civil Service Workforce Plan 2016–2020', UK Cabinet Office, Retrieved 26 April 2017 from https://www.gov.uk/government/speeches/workforce-future-plan-matt-hancock-speech

Heifetz, R., Grashow, A., & Linsky, M. (2009). *The practice of adaptive leadership.* Harvard Business Press.

Heifetz, R. A., & Laurie, D. L. (1997, January–February). The work of leadership. *Harvard Business Review*, 124–134.

House of Commons, Defence Committee. (2010). *The comprehensive approach: The point of war is not just to win but to make a better peace*. Seventh Report of Session 2009–10. Retrieved 27th April 2017 from https://www.publicati ons.parliament.uk/pa/cm200910/cmselect/cmdfence/224/224.pdf

Independent Evaluation Group/The World Bank. (2017). *Crisis response and resilience to systemic shocks lessons from IEG evaluations*. Retrieved 15 October 2018 from http://ieg.worldbankgroup.org/sites/default/files/Data/Evalua tion/files/building-resilience.pdf

Management Advisory Committee. (2004). *Connecting government: Whole of government responses to Australia's priority challenges*. Commonwealth of Australia. Retrieved 31 July 2019 from https://www.apsc.gov.au/sites/def ault/files/connectinggovernment.pdf

Meindl, J., Ehrlich, S. B., & Dukerich, J. M. (1985). The romance of leadership. *Administrative Science Quarterly*, 30(1), 78–102. Retrieved 8 May 2018 from http://www.wiggo.com/mgmt8510/Readings/Readings11/mei ndl1985asq.pdf

O'Keefe, P., Westgate, K., & Wisner, B. (1976). Taking the naturalness out of natural disasters. *Nature*, 260(5552), 566–567.

Ryan, A. (2016). *Delivering 'joined-up' government: Achieving the integrated approach to offshore crisis management*. ASPI Strategic Insights Paper. Retrieved 26 April 2017 from https://www.aspi.org.au/publications/delive ring-joined-up-government-achieving-the-integrated-approach-to-offshore-cri sis-management/SI111_joined-up-government.pdf

Ryan, A. (2017). National-level operations—Achieving strategic results through 'joined-up' government. *Blamey Oration*. Royal United Services Institute, Tasmania. Retrieved 26 April 2017 from https://www.linkedin.com/pulse/ strategic-cohesion-fundamental-security-dilemmas-new-world-alan-ryan

Shergold, P. (2015). *Learning from failure: Why large government policy initiatives have gone so badly wrong in the past and how the chances of success in the future can be improved*. Australian Public Service Commission. Retrieved 4 May 2017 from http://www.apsc.gov.au/publications-and-media/current-publications/learning-from-failure

UK Stabilisation Unit. (2017). *Joint analysis of conflict and stability guidance note*. Retrieved 2 August 2017 from http://sclr.stabilisationunit.gov.uk/pub lications/programming-guidance/1232-jacsguidance/file

Wong, L., & Gerras, S. G. (2017). Beware the romance of leadership. *War on the Rocks*. Retrieved 8 May 2017 from https://warontherocks.com/2017/ 02/beware-the-romance-of-leadership/

CHAPTER 5

'Blackfella Way, Our Way of Managing Fires and Disasters Bin Ignored but "Im Still Here"': Australian Aboriginal Governance Structures for Emergency Management

Bevlyne Sithole, David Campbell, and Steve Sutton with contributions from O. Campion, C. Brown, G. Daniels, A. Daniels, C. Brian, J. Campion, D. Yibarbuk, E. Phillips, G. Daniels, K. Daniels, B. Hedley, M. Radford, A. Campion, H. Hunter-Xenie, I. Sutton, and S. Pickering

INTRODUCTION

Evidence of principles and strategies to include remote Australian Aboriginal communities in Emergency Management (EM) in Australia abound. For example, the existence of the definitive national strategy called Keeping our Mob Safe is evidence that the government acknowledges

---

B. Sithole (✉)
Research Institute for Environment and Livelihoods, Charles Darwin University, Darwin, Australia
e-mail: bevlyne.sithole@cdu.edu.au

© The Author(s), under exclusive license to Springer Nature Singapore Pte Ltd. 2022
H. James et al. (eds.), *Disaster Risk Reduction in Asia Pacific*, Disaster Risk, Resilience, Reconstruction and Recovery,
https://doi.org/10.1007/978-981-16-4811-3_5

and sees a need to engage more effectively with remote Australian Aboriginal communities. The strategy clearly identifies the desire and willingness of Australian Aboriginal communities to engage. Further, the strategy states that the development of effective partnerships between remote Australian Aboriginal communities and emergency management-related agencies is the key to developing resilience (e.g. DFES, 2016). Hossain (2013) explains that the changing direction of approaches to emergency management to a program designed by and for the people in certain disaster-prone areas requires reform of the current governance framework, which until now has failed to meet the needs of vulnerable populations and ignores local resources and capacities. Aboriginal public policy is currently formulated against a backdrop of public commentary of 'dysfunction' and social collapse (Sullivan, 2010, p. 16). The role of the state has expanded significantly while that of the communities has contracted across many policy areas. Buckle (1998) finds that communities see themselves as central to effective EM and expect to have input into local policies and programs. Consequently, the statement by an Aboriginal elder in 2016 that—'*Blackfella way, our way of managing fires and disasters bin ignored but 'im still here*' questions the effectiveness of current efforts and state commitments. Where communities feel left out of the process subsequent challenges to disaster management agencies is likely and frequent (Buckle, 1998). The expectation by Aboriginal communities that their knowledge and practices be fully integrated into current emergency management planning and programs is neither new nor surprising especially as the national strategy documents recognize the existence of traditional knowledge and experience. The Council of Australian Government's (COAG) National Strategy for Disaster Resilience (NSDR) notes that the context of disaster management has changed, and the balance

---

D. Campbell
University of South Australia, Adelaide, Australia

Steve Sutton with contributions from O. Campion, C. Brown, G. Daniels, A. Daniels, C. Brian, J. Campion, D. Yibarbuk, E. Phillips, G. Daniels, K. Daniels, B. Hedley, M. Radford, A. Campion, H. Hunter-Xenie, I. Sutton, and S. Pickering
Charles Darwin University, Darwin, Australia

Bushfire and Natural Hazards CRC, Melbourne, Australia

of responsibilities between governments and communities needs to be fundamentally re-organized (COAG, 2011, p. ii). What does it take for Aboriginal communities to participate meaningfully and for their participation to result in actual shifts in policy and practice?

Cornwall (2002) uses spatial metaphors to define and describe spaces where the state and communities interact to open up or extend opportunities for citizens to participate. Cornwall (2002) defines the space as arenas where voices and ideas jostle for attention. Consequently, communities can and often operate in different types of spaces. One of the types of spaces mentioned is created spaces. In the context of this chapter, created spaces are where the state mandates the form of interaction with the remote community. Communities act inside and outside these created spaces. Aboriginal people struggle with and try to engage with the disconnections that are apparent in the way the state operates on the Country, and the realities they encounter among their people. According to Yunupingu and Muller (2009, p. 158): "'Country' is an Aboriginal English term that recognizes the relationships, authority and responsibilities of particular groups of Traditional Owners to particular areas of land and sea'. Cornwall and Coelho (2004) note that these types of spaces are not something that should be opened up or assumed; rather they argue that these spaces should be shaped through the exercise of agency in which different knowledges and interests interact. They also observe that the available room to reshape existing spaces and negotiate boundaries indicates a growing interest to define and characterize the nature of interactive spaces between the state and other actors. Campbell et al. (2015) describe three ways of dealing with Aboriginal peoples as '*you can do to them, for them or with them*'. Further, they find that historically, the experience among Aboriginal peoples is '*the done to or done for experience. We need to be doing it with them*'. Paternalism is present and best demonstrated by the Northern Territory Intervention in 2007 which shows clearly the absolutist nature of control by the state over Aboriginal peoples, characterized by the state as a benevolent actor delivering for communities who are seen as passive recipients. Richard Trudgen's (2012) book, *When Warriors lie down and die*, underlines the fatigue and sense of 'irrelevancy' remote communities feel when facing the state. McIntyre (2007) finds that the constant perception that remote communities are spaces defined as 'a failed society' where basic standards of law and order and behaviour have broken down is used to justify government interest to continue with paternalism. Martin (2009) cites Murphree's principle on bureaucratic behaviour which indicates that the state often finds it hard to relinquish control to the extent that would make these local spaces conducive for communities to effectively act or be involved.

So resentment and challenges over state monopoly over spaces for emergency management are inevitable. Research in the Northern Territory shows that communities are still not active within the current EM framework (Campbell et al., 2015; Michaels, 2016; Sangha et al., 2017; Sithole et al., 2017, 2019). Morley et al. (2016) argue that while it appears that many procedures are in place across a range of spatial scales from local through to Territory-wide, the level of engagement is still very limited and non-consultative. But as Smith (2002) asks, is there an imperative for the government to do things differently? This chapter considers the spaces for Aboriginal communities to interact with the state over EM in west and central Arnhem Land, Northern Territory (NT) Australia; it considers the extent to which communities have been integrated into emergency management planning.

Consultations in West and Central Arnhem land, Northern Territory

This chapter focuses on remote communities in Arnhem Land in the NT. Within the analysis, the term, 'community,' is problematic and is used here very broadly to include growth towns and sometimes populations from outstations. We acknowledge the incredible diversity within these communities and with that the different relationships that groups within the broader community have with the state. Consequently, it is crucial to analyse and understand what 'state' means when they say they are working with the community. The 'state' is also a problematic term used variously to sometimes refer to the Northern Territory Government and other times the Federal government. Where general statements are being made, the term, 'state,' is inclusive of both, and, when necessary, distinctions will be made. The issues of representation, knowledge and legitimacy become important. The opinions considered here are those provided by Aboriginal people's residing in remote locations in Arnhem Land, NT. These were gathered by community-based Aboriginal research practitioners who used participatory tools including key interviews and focus group discussions. Short key interviews were also conducted with some of the Northern Territory Emergency Service (NTES) staff, the government coordinating officer and other organizations in the community. The territory government and the Federal government are considered as separate, but connected entities.

Discussions at three consultative workshops were conducted with communities. The first consultative workshop in March 2016 was held in Darwin and explored the traditional knowledge needed to manage bushfires and natural hazards in the landscape for the good of country and of people. The second workshop was conducted at Yellow Water and included end-users and community representatives. The third consultative workshop was conducted on the banks of the Blythe River to provide opportunities for more Aboriginal people to attend in July 2016. For the workshop in Darwin, communities identified key knowledge holders from west and central Arnhem Land and these were then invited to attend the focus group discussions. The group was comprised of traditional elders, ceremony leaders and firemen in the region. Invitations were extended to all leaders, individuals who were recognized knowledge holders (Djunkayi, Traditional Owners) or people who sit on the relevant emergency management-related key committees. Interest in the workshop was considerable and a number of senior lawmen who typically avoid government workers' consultative processes exercised their seniority and replaced more junior community members who had planned to attend. Wider participation was also constrained by budgetary limits. At the workshop, facilitation was led by one of the elders who has facilitation experience and every attempt was made to gain the trust among the participants so they felt they were able to speak and be listened to. A flexible approach was adopted to the languages spoken with an emphasis on dialogue. The pace was dictated by the participants who expressed such interest that discussions continued into break times and even after the meeting ended. The Indigenous facilitator sometimes documented discussion on butcher's paper to draw out the underlying governance framework and leadership principles.

The second and third workshops were held in country and were conducted over several days. Invitations were open and the location of the consultative workshop on the banks of the Blyth river at Nimiriwili on the country of the Rembarrnga people was significant as a meeting place for many clans in the cultural cosmology of the Aboriginal people of Arnhem Land. The camp aimed to engage a wider group and be inclusive of women and young people. There were more than 45 people in attendance, though it was fluid as people came and left as was convenient to them. Aboriginal people were drawn from west and central Arnhem Land and the Roper Gulf district. This mixed group included senior men and women as well as young people which allowed for a good discussion about the intergenerational transfer of knowledge, experience and responsibility. The third workshop at Yellow Water, near Ngukurr, included end-users and community members. Though many end-users were invited, few turned up for the workshop. At this workshop issues with emergency management, in general, were discussed and the nature of current relationships between communities and end-users. There were many 'break-out' conversations in the camp—taking place in several languages. More importantly, the workshops accommodated the cultural norms of Aboriginal society, including proscriptions against talking with certain specific classificatory 'kin'.

Emergency Management Arrangements in the Northern Territory

Every year, communities in remote areas of the NT face devastating losses caused by disasters. Bushfires, floods, storms and other hazards have significant impacts on communities, the economy, infrastructure and the environment. To build resilience nationally, the COAG agreed to adopt a resilience-based approach to disaster management on 7 December 2009, recognizing that a national, coordinated and cooperative effort is needed. A Working Group of the National Emergency Management Committee (NEMC) was tasked by COAG to coordinate the development of a National Strategy for Disaster Resilience (the Strategy). Crucially, the Strategy acknowledges that a resilience-based approach is a shared responsibility between governments, communities, businesses and individuals. The purpose of it is to provide high-level guidance on disaster management to all these sectors. However, the Legislation in place for BNH management in the NT does not refer to resilience or community engagement. The *Bushfire Management Act (NT)* 2016 provides a hierarchical structure for planning and managing bushfire. The Act establishes the NT Bushfires Council and Regional Bushfires Committees. While the Council has a number of ex-officio members, Regional Committees are broadly constituted with members being chosen from the regional community. For regions such as the Arnhem Bushfires Region, the Regional Committee is largely comprised of Aboriginal community members. The legislation provides an emphasis on planning and mitigation, rather than the exclusion of fire. The *Emergency Management Act (NT) 2013* provides structures and procedures for the management of natural hazards and other emergencies. This legislation also has a hierarchical structure with the establishment of a Territory, Regional and Local Controllers as well as Territory and Regional Emergency Management Committees. The Act calls for the creation of Territory and Regional Emergency Plans and provides for the creation of local Emergency Plans where the Council so directs the Territory Controller.

Authority for the finalization of the Emergency Plans rests with the Territory Controller, who must consult regional controllers. While not stated, it seems the Regional Controller will consult the Regional Emergency Committee in the establishment of the Plan. The Regional Emergency Committee comprises eleven ex-officio officers and one community representative nominated by the Regional Controller.

Clearly, the structures established in the two NT Acts result in quite different delivery of services on the ground. While Regional Committees provide the *Bushfires Management Act* linkages to the community, the *Emergency Management Act* is dominated by structures populated with representatives of the government. This creates a strongly hierarchical 'command and control' approach with little or no legislative emphasis on engaging with the community at a local level. Both Acts rely on a Western bureaucratic conception of leadership and authority. While the *Bushfire Management Act's* approach to the management of fire in the landscape is some approximation of Aboriginal approaches, it is not clear that either statute reflects Indigenous approaches to leadership and decision-making (Ganter, 2016; Haque, 1997; McRae-Williams & Gerritsen, 2010).

Despite omissions in legislation, BNH agencies and related government actors are demonstrating a willingness to engage more actively with NGOs and civil society/communities at various stages in the BNH management cycle. The 2016 submission by the Australasian Fire and Emergency Services Authorities Council (AFAC) to the Victorian parliamentary inquiry into bushfire preparedness states that '*collective action by people preparing for and responding to bushfires will invariably achieve better results than individuals acting alone*' (AFAC, 2016). The difficulty for bureaucracies appears to be that this is a complex undertaking. Responsibilities in BNH management can be overlapping, interdependent, ambiguous and often conflicting (McLennan & Handmer, 2014). Different views exist on what disaster management should achieve, how, and where the capacity lies, and what roles should be expected of various parties. McLennan and Handmer (2014) find that inclusive governance presents significant challenges to current governments. Inclusive governance frameworks should bring together government and communities in emergency management to get better outcomes. But Sithole et al. (2017) find that state agencies have little understanding of the existing local institutions and tend to bypass them rather than engage with them. Further, the diversity of communities, their interests and dynamics are not considered. Ranger groups have become proxies for Indigenous communities and in some places, the few representatives on the ranger committee become de facto community. Engagement with the community proper, not merely a subset however comprised, is required to develop programs leading to resilience. Through community, engagement agencies can build relationships which obviate the range of social/cognitive factors which impede the development of resilience (Paton, 2003, 2016; Paton et al., 2015). The key social/cognitive factor impeding community action has been shown to be trust (Paton, 2007; Paton & McClure, 2013). Agency engagement with communities provides the platform for developing trust. We argue in this chapter that real and effective engagement with communities needs to be re-thought in order to build that trust and we explore the kind of spaces needed to re-engage with traditional structures.

Aboriginal Arrangements for Emergency Management in Remote Communities

Aboriginal people have deep knowledge and tested practices for responding to hazards that revolve around the performance of ceremonies. There are clans who own and hold the knowledge and ceremony for different kinds of hazards. Within these clans, individuals are knowledge holders for a hazard. These clans have well-developed interdependent relationships with other clans. Ceremonial and cultural elders had deep knowledge of the cultural and spiritual dimensions of BNH. Engaging with these clan groups and individuals is crucial to harnessing local knowledge and practice for hazard management. Not all this knowledge is public. The cyclone story presented in the ARD film demonstrates the intricate relationships Aboriginal people have with natural hazards. They do not always see hazards negatively. It is important to note that keeping the songs and ceremony alive is seen as a key part of managing

BNH, sometimes deflecting and other times managing multi-clan level responses. Currently, not enough ceremonies are being performed and people are constrained by their obligations through Centrelink or job providers so attendance is low. Further, strict school attendance conditions mean that young people are growing up with limited or no experience of the ceremony and without the requisite knowledge for living with and managing natural hazards in the future. Aboriginal people are often conflicted about participating in ceremony and actions in country that address BNH as this may jeopardize their welfare benefits or job conditions.

Current BNH structures and decision-making pathways for hazard planning and responses at the community level are well developed but are not linked with the Indigenous structures. Most of the communities were not aware of who was a member of the local emergency management committees. These are not always the right people to be in those positions and represent a small number of people who should be involved. The state is not always aware or prepared to engage with the complexity and the numbers required for it to be a genuinely credible engagement process. Communities believe by their actions that the state operates as if they are unaware of the complex system of connections, responsibilities and knowledge on BNH that is available through the community (Sithole et al., 2017). For example, for bush fires the decision-making involves Traditional Owners (TO), Mingiringiri, Djungkayi [2], Clan Groups and Land Managers/Ranger groups (see Fig. 5.1). These are classificatory land management responsibilities. A Djungkayi is a 'manager' of land through his mother's descent group. No decision, no matter how pressing, should be made without at least the Mingiringiri and the Djungkayi, but there are many others involved as indicated in Fig. 5.1.

But these arrangements are not connected to the formal EM framework and operate in parallel and sometimes in conflict with the existing state framework. Participants felt that the existence and importance of these relationships are not known by EM agencies and poorly understood by the younger members of the community. It is also clear that the presence of the state EM framework has not always impacted positively on the traditional framework. The Aboriginal leadership framework includes different paths of responsibility, Firemen, Traditional Owners and Djungkayi among others. The state needs to be aware of these pathways and what they represent in terms of differing responsibilities to

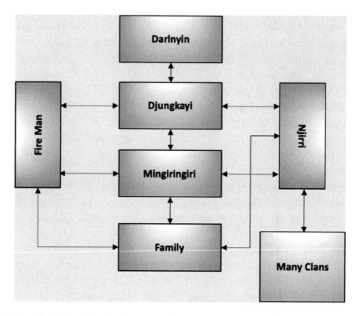

Fig. 5.1 Aboriginal leadership and decision-making structure

country and people. The nature of current membership to communities where the NTES staff depend on and are linked in with two rather than more individuals in a community with 13 clans all recognizing their own structures means that there is a large component of the community that is feeling left out of BNH. Those two individuals that are involved acknowledged that they feel overwhelmed and their participation is limited because they do not have the right to represent and they do not have the right information. Each hazard has its own structure. For example, for bushfires, the emphasis is on shared responsibility for decision-making with well laid out actions communicated via message sticks.

Importantly, the Aboriginal peoples see a role for themselves in BNH as part of their responsibility for looking after Country and have mapped out the spaces where they and the state can interact (Sithole et al., 2019). This is a crucial role that requires people to live on Country and meet their obligations. This includes conducting ceremony and transferring knowledge to the next generation of leaders in a process that enables them to 'hand over the key, clan and kinship'; to ensure young people are trained in 'the right way' to know-how leadership works in relation to country and BNH. Aboriginal peoples are clear on what constitutes good leadership and for BNH, their argument is that the 'right people/leaders should be involved'.

A more detailed schema of the discussions was prepared to indicate the desirable characteristics in leaders (Fig. 5.2).

Crucially, this would include knowing what constitutes the community and then moving forward to identify the leadership in each component identified within the larger community. The state continues to see communities as undifferentiated unit. This is problematic as it isolates leaders/individuals from their constituency. A leader within the Aboriginal context is only able to make certain decisions that they are authorized to make, and that power derives both from the clan and their connection to the Country. Some of the components for 'acting right' or

Fig. 5.2 Essential Aboriginal leadership skills

'talking right' for Country and BNH requires understanding the connections, presence on the country, and the observance of Aboriginal law. Emergency management represents an opportunity for collaboration with Aboriginal peoples and inclusion of Indigenous knowledge (ceremony, song and story) more prominently into BNH management practice.

Communication is fundamental to ensuring understanding. Aboriginal people stress the importance of combining existing traditional communications. Here the communication medium, as much as the content, and direction of information flow is an important part of the connection to the land and a reminder that people serve country. A series of safety principles emerged as critical learnings for future leaders (Fig. 5.3). It was also recognized that good planning was important and included consideration of all knowledge systems. This was expressed as needing to;

- Walk in the footsteps of elders/ walking in the community.

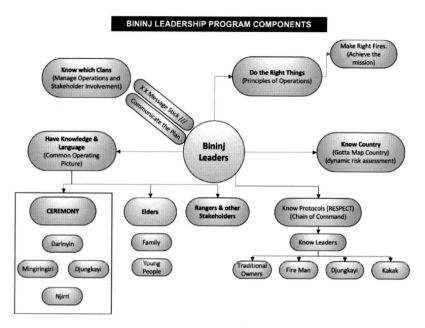

Fig. 5.3 Components identified as key knowledge areas for decision-making pathways

- Remember behaviours and actions have an impact on clans; and.
- Know how to read and explain signs on country.

These practices are not currently integrated into emergency management.

ATTITUDES TOWARDS COMMUNITY STATE ENGAGEMENT ON EM

Attitudes among Aboriginal communities indicate pessimism regarding the state's commitment to real engagement. Questions like *'where are my people, where is my power'* are common in focus group discussions with members of remote communities. Another response was *'here we just standing invisible, the government, they don't approach Aboriginal people, it's been there for many years but it is invisible'*. Even talking about engagement and collaboration elicited sceptical responses such as when one elder at a workshop at Blythe River stated—*'Your words don't work'*, and another at the Yellow Water workshop muttering *'the government is the biggest hazard we face'* underlining the current impatience with so-called consultations and dissatisfaction with the way the state is engaging with the communities on BNH. Communities indicated that they are pushing for involvement so that *'the government can work the right way with communities'* (Workshop on the Blythe). There was also no trust that the state genuinely wanted to engage. Some indicated that the state had no interest and pointed to the nature of current interactions where one respondent says *'the government holds the keys'* and *'when they do things they leave us in the dust'*. Another respondent pointed to the lack of accessibility of the process and documents to the community as evidence of reluctance to engage (Sithole et al., 2017). So, when communities ask *'what engagement'* it is difficult to see the shift that government says they are making towards more inclusive planning and response in BNH. One response says the state only works in their committees; they don't want to really work in the Aboriginal way. Thus according to one elder, they are *'pretending to have authority, and they don't go much further to real authority'*. Generally, communities feel that current arrangements do not engage with them adequately. State actors indicated that there are often difficulties in getting the right people, or getting consistent engagement in meetings, so there is a heavy reliance on a few Aboriginal people. The conclusion was that in most groups Aboriginal governance arrangements have been crushed.

Other comments were made related to the state community relationships during cyclone events where there is a reliance on external volunteers and limited involvement by the community. Stories were told about Tropical Cyclone Lam where voices were ignored in favour of state protocols that operate in tension with existing Aboriginal systems. Some of the tasks external volunteers were asked to perform could have been performed by Aboriginal people. One elder stated, '*we got boys in the ranger group and the community, they got paperwork, but still they don't get them*'. While some discussions indicate the presence of a '*tug of war*' between Aboriginal peoples and the state, indications suggest that the community does not feel that the contest is equal or that fair outcomes are possible. Statements indicate the strong desire for elders and leaders to become more active and influential in emergency management. However, the 'four big pillars' for Aboriginal emergency management are not being considered. These include incorporating existing knowledge of Country and how to look after it; supporting the strengthening of Aboriginal people's connection to Country and the importance of ceremony, law and living the right way on country. Finally, recognition of the value of having people living on Country in their homelands. This goes against the state's approach requiring people to be congregated in one place in order to deliver services. Having present knowledge holders on Country in continuity who are available to lead, transfer knowledge and communicate signs about emergency management is crucial. Without an appreciation of these pillars, community-level emergency management will continue to fail.

Concern over the disconnect between Aboriginal ways of doing things and the state way of doing things is highest among the elderly and the local leaders. Remote communities argue that emergency management arrangements that genuinely include them will produce the best outcome (Sithole et al., 2019). They caution against the state assuming that it is easy 'to accommodate', 'bring in', 'adopt' or 'integrate'. To illustrate the challenges of state community relationships, comments were made about the Aboriginal ranger groups that are working on Country under the Caring for Country Program. Ranger groups are now working on various forms of Indigenous-owned land including Indigenous Protected Areas. Generally, they have sought to bring together Aboriginal ways and scientific knowledge in a 'two tool-box' approach (Russell-Smith et al., 2009).

The reality is that some ranger groups are seen to be responding more to the imperatives of external funding agencies or the state than to the needs of the communities on whose land they are operating. Similarly, communities argue that the state ignores their rights and responsibilities in emergency management as they are more focused on external rather than local community imperatives (Sithole et al., 2019). Consequently, there is strong concern among communities about levels of 'capture' of community space by the state under the guise of the 'two toolbox' approach. One of the comments indicates the willingness to explore options that would make the programs respond to local concerns and expectations: *'They make programs Balanda way; how do we make programs that are suitable for us?'* Capture is used here to explain how the state can end up meeting external demands without really including local imperatives. At best, Aboriginal communities were concerned that their engagement is being 'squeezed out' and worst they are completely ignored. As one elder argued, on Aboriginal lands EM must necessarily engage in a meaningful and more nuanced way to include Aboriginal people.

Opportunity does exist to meet the demands, as one young person challenged, *'we need the elders to take control, why aren't Traditional Owners doing anything*? This indicates that the frustration the wider communities are starting to feel with the emergency management is not confined to the state but also towards the Aboriginal arrangements. State actors indicate that one of the big challenges for engagement is a lack of awareness of who to engage with and how. Discussions indicate the tendency of the state to follow a path of least resistance and work with one or two Aboriginal people. These people become the de facto community, a position that is problematic for the community they purport to represent. According to one elder, the practice by the state to privilege one or two individuals is detrimental to the relationships that those individuals have with their own clans and within the wider community. Their positions are questioned and therefore they only provide false comfort to the state that they are doing things in the right way.

It was clear from the discussion, that communities are diverse and have multiple overlaying structures and that for a large part these remain hidden from agency view. It was important to raise this question—*'What about all these clans, all mingling and the struggles between the tribes, can Balanda work with us mob?'* What is the best way to engage with these multiple jurisdictions? Participants described the complexity of the governance arrangements over the fire and other natural hazards and underscored the importance for the government to engage with the *'right people'*, the *'holders of knowledge'*, those with *'relationship to the hazard'* and those who hold the *'rights to the hazard'*. According to some participants, if the government wants to talk about fire they should talk bushfire to *'fire men, if they want to talk about cyclones they should talk 'cyclone people' and if whirly whirly, they gotta speak with the right people, hold that relationship, story, ceremony and song'*. Talking or involving just any individual is seen as not talking at all. While the participants were clear on the need to get involved, they argue that one of the important prerequisites is for EM to talk to the right people, because that *'is the right way to keep families safe'* and *'is the right way to heal our people'*. Appreciating the diversity over responsibilities and ownership of BHC underscore the need for EM to adapt to different situations in different communities and revisit their conception of community representation and engagement.

Prospects for Effective EM at the Community Level

In this chapter, we addressed the issue of engagement with remote Australian Aboriginal communities in EM. We asked the question, what does it take for Aboriginal communities to participate meaningfully and for their participation to result in actual shifts in policy and practice? Evidence indicates that while policies exist, real engagement at the ground level is absent. Intermittent, ongoing special measures by the state are proof that the normal processes of government are not working in Remote Australia (Walker, 2009). For example, current provisions for EM as provided by the NT policy and programmes do not obligate the state to engage with the levels that communities would find desirable. But Howitt et al. (2012) find that despite efforts to better match emergency service responses to the needs of Aboriginal communities (see for example Remote Indigenous Communities Advisory Committee, 2007), the capacity of Australian emergency services to work with Indigenous communities remains somewhat limited and problematic (see also Sithole et al., 2019). The report for EM in the NT does not mandate the requirement for community engagement. While national reviews and strategy emphasize the value of community in EM, communities feel their current engagement is dependent more on the good manners of individuals in the EM framework than on genuine commitments. Research shows that community resilience is dependent on the stock of human and social capital present in the community. The value of existing capacities has been highlighted in research and includes knowledge of the environment and local hazards, the ability to cope and ability to access help from outside, and the importance of local/traditional knowledge (in terms of understandings of risk, hazards, and coping strategies). Hunt (2013) finds that without genuine engagement with Indigenous people it will be difficult to meet the targets of the COAG. Howitt et al. (2012) argue that the characterization of Aboriginal communities as vulnerable presents them as victims in need of protection from the government and also assigns superiority to experts and agencies rather than the affected communities themselves. According to Royal Commission on Aboriginal Deaths in Custody (RCIADIC) (RCIADIC 1991:509), appropriate solutions will be found by considering what Aboriginal people and their organizations are actually doing and how they relate to the broader society. Sithole et al. (2017) observe that communities feel their capacity to strengthen their own resilience has been weakened by successive governments' Indigenous policies. Smith (2002) suggests we consider the concept of jurisdictional devolution to look at local governance and self-determination. Clearly, the devolution agenda needs to move past empowering lower structures of the state to act for communities and identify opportunities for conjuring spaces where more effective coupling between the parallel arrangements for EM can be achieved.

We have established that the available spaces for engagement over EM, even where they are present, are restrictive and inaccessible. In some places, the communities are not even aware spaces for engagement exist. The state dictates what size and form these spaces are, and it is generally dependent on the good manners of the individuals operating on the ground. State attempts to incorporate the Aboriginal way for EM are fraught with challenges. The level of complexity of the spaces proves challenging to state officials who often are ill-prepared to deal with communities. Walker (2012) suggests that it is imperative to reframe governance in a way that recognizes the essential interdependence between the formal apparatus of the state and its publics. Further, Walker (2012) argues for spaces which would ensure that there's more capacity for local decision-making, local involvement, as well as less government by remote control and fly-in fly-out forces, but the challenge would be to convince other layers of the state to relinquish control. When these attempts are not well thought out or haphazard, then the communities raise the issue of 'capture' where the state pretends engagement by doing the absolute minimum rather than what is required or what would be preferred by communities. Data presented show communities questioning state understanding of nuance, of the local situation and the culture. Absence of the right people in the space is equated as absence of space for EM, while ignorance of the Aboriginal way, the law and the practice and ceremony render the current EM efforts inappropriate and ill advised (Sithole et al., 2017).

The existence of parallel arrangements for EM challenges the relevance of centralized planning in a sector where there is a shift towards a people centred-planning process. The state should not have a monopoly over delivering safety to the community (Sithole et al., 2019). The continued ignorance of, and or discounting of, local structures is a weakness in current planning frameworks. Langton (2001) argues that if, as the common law now holds and native title survives, then the Aboriginal jurisdictions, or the juridical and social spaces in which such laws are practiced, must also survive. Thus, as Smith (2002) argues, by implication this means that jurisdictional devolution is about power-sharing, and the process of developing a system of inter-related jurisdictional parts. Communities believe that their community identity and collective values are a crucial part of their safety and resilience (cf. Veland et al., 2010). But, Betts (2007) questions the readiness of existing institutions to find a middle ground and to accept the validity of community history and culture. Smith (2002) states that in one form or another, Aboriginal people have been fighting for jurisdictional devolution for a very long time. These consultations suggest that this is indeed a legitimate question for EM personnel in Northern Australia. There are many clans, each with its own structures, knowledge holders and practices. There is a need to ensure the development of local disaster plans that work with those structures, identify the community priorities, recognize and include traditional knowledge about hazards, risk and the triggers for predicting their impact (see Morley, 2015). The question is when will the government accept the reality of an alternative world view and engage with it in a way that benefits the community and EM in general. Howitt et al. (2012) suggest that emergency service agencies need to frame their own responses and services in terms of Aboriginal cultural understandings. There is a deeper challenge for service agencies to engage with Aboriginal worldviews and negotiate what is appropriate as well as effective spaces for building local capacity for building resilience to support recovery in emergency settings. Thus as Veland et al. (2010) state a priority in developing approaches that limit conflict is ensuring that local, state and national authorities offer recognition and understanding of these local institutions, and develop strong relationships with them.

The presence of the formal EM framework has not always impacted positively on its informal counterpart. In fact, Howitt et al. (2012) found that the evacuation state intervention of the Kiwirrkurra community directly exacerbated the existing vulnerabilities of the community. Absence of engagement with, or exclusion from the local planning process 'shames' those who should be involved and as Campbell et al. (2015) find, it entrenches the view that Aboriginal governance is ill-equipped to deliver government programs effectively. The recognition of Indigenous law and structure determines participation in processes and issues. At present, the government is ignoring this. The state must show a genuine willingness to give up control over EM in order for communities to engage in a practical and meaningful way. Participants' views are consistent with Ellemor (2005), that BNH management governance structures need to include Indigenous community capability as part of the process rather than universally applying a command and control approach. Morley et al. (2016) suggest that disaster planning processes could strengthen the resilience of the community if they enabled greater community ownership of the planning, response and recovery process. These local structures and relationships are often ignored since they have been too difficult for bureaucracies to map (McRae-Williams & Gerritsen, 2010). In the EM realm, however, there is the potential to utilize these structures to build new leadership and decision-making arrangements that enhance the resilience of remote communities. Without this sort of engagement and adaptation, it is likely that there will be significant delays in achieving national goals for fulfilling their 'shared' responsibility.

CONCLUSION

Spaces for engagement where they exist should be conducive spaces that aim to satisfy the desire to engage 'the right way'. Arguments that the *'blackfella way, our way of managing fires and disasters bin ignored but 'I'm still there'* indicate a missed opportunity by the state. These systems exist and are robust, highly valued and but for the most part are ignored. Calls to reassess spaces for engagement in Aboriginal EM in the NT offer a real opportunity for an alternative way. This requires that governments revisit their understanding of the term 'community' and Aboriginal 'institution' as these have a crucial bearing on the nature of and process of engagement. The devolution agenda needs to move beyond decentralized structures of the state and be reflected in the way communities become part of, rather than spectators in, EM. If the state desires good outcomes on community safety, then expanding the space for an emergency should not be a matter of choice, but an urgent imperative.

The pressure to redefine these spaces to engage in is not all towards the state. There is also pressure from within communities who are starting to question 'their invisibility' and their elders' inaction. On the one hand, this has led to communities seeking to organize and more actively engage in articulating their demands and aspirations for an effective space. The state will not find a 'failed state,' but people starting to reassert themselves and wanting to be involved. However, wanting to be involved requires commitment and leadership and these are elements that the communities have spent time exploring and exposing. While heavy-handed statism is a fact of life for more Aboriginal people, there is optimism that the state will come to realize that real participation requires a nuanced and more culturally informed approach to EM. Safety is not something the state should feel they must deliver, especially when communities want to share the burden.

Acknowledgements We acknowledge the traditional owners of Gunbalanya, Maningrida, Ramingining and Ngukurr and all other actors in local organizations who were part of the BNHCRC Scoping resilience in Northern Australia Study (AITSIS ethics clearance); BNHCRC/HEPPP Training Project at the Charles Darwin University; and the BNHCRC funded project on Developing effective management partnerships in remote communities in Northern Australia (CDU ethics).

References

AFAC. (2016). *Bushfires submission 24; Inquiry into fire season preparedness*. Environment and planning standing committee, Victoria. Melbourne, Parliament of Victoria.

Betts, R. (2007). *Community engagement in emergency management—Uncertainty, risky, and challenging: Flood management conference Warnambool.*

Buckle, P. (1998). Re-defining community and vulnerability XE "vulnerability" in the context of emergency management. *The Australian Journal of Emergency Management, 13*(4), 21–26.

Campbell, A., Paton, D., & Buergelt, P. T. (2015). Learning to co-exist with environmental hazards: Community and societal perspectives and strategies. *Advances in Environmental Research, 43,* 1–25.

Cornwall, A. (2002). *Making spaces, changing places: Situating participation in development.* IDS Working Paper 170. Brighton, Sussex BN1 9RE, Institute of Development Studies.

Cornwall, A., & Coelho, V. S. P. (2004). *Spaces for change? The politics of citizen participation in new democratic arenas.* Zed.

COAG. (2011). *COAG review of natural disaster relief and mitigation arrangements: Improving emergency management outcomes for remote indigenous communities in Northern Australia.*

DFES. (2016). *Community engagement framework our approach to making interactions meaningful and creating community action.* Retrieved from http://www.dfes.wa.gov.au/aboutus/corporateinformation/plansandstrateg iespublications/dfes-ce-framework.pdf

Ellemor, H. (2005). Reconsidering emergency management and indigenous communities in Australia. *Environmental Hazards, 6*(1), 1–7.

Ganter, E. (2016). *Reluctant representatives.* Australian National University Press.

Haque, M. S. (1997). Incongruity between bureaucracy and society in developing nations: A critique. *Peace & Change, 22*(4), 432–462. https://doi.org/10.1111/0149-0508.00061

Hossain, M. A. (2013). Community participation in disaster management: Role of social work to enhance participation. *Antrocom Online Journal of Anthropology, 9*(1). Retrieved from https://pdfs.semanticscholar.org/26f5/ae5317 32723dee7ef1c5ca564b886ce73f53.pdf

Howitt, R., Havnen, O., & Veland, S. (2012). Natural and unnatural disasters: Responding with respect for indigenous rights and knowledges. *Geographical Research, 50*(1), 47–59.

Hunt, H. (2013). *Engaging with indigenous Australia—Exploring the conditions for effective relationships with Aboriginal and Torres Strait Islander communities.* Issues paper no. 5 produced for the Closing the Gap. Clearinghouse Janet Hunt Retrieved from https://www.aihw.gov.au/getmedia/7d54eac8-4c95-4de1-91bb-0d6b1cf348e2/ctgc-ip05.pdf.aspx?inline=true

Langton, M. (2001, October 5). *Ancient jurisdictions: Aboriginal polities and sovereignty.* A paper presented as a keynote address at the Australian History Association Conference—Challenging Histories Conference, State Library of Victoria. Melbourne.

Martin, R. B. (2009). Murphree's laws, principles, rules & definitions. In B. B. Mukamuri, J. M. Manjengwa, & S. Anstey (Eds.), *Beyond proprietorship: Murphrees's laws on community-based natural resources management in southern Africa*. Weaver Press.

McIntyre, G. (2007). An imbalance of constitutional power and human rights: The 2007 Federal intervention in the Northern Territory. *James Cook University Law Review, 14*, 86–114.

McLennan, B., & Handmer, J. W. (2014). *Sharing responsibility in Australian disaster management: Final report for the sharing responsibility project*.

McRae-Williams, E., & Gerritsen, R. (2010). Mutual incomprehension: The cross cultural domain of work in a remote Australian Aboriginal community. *International Indigenous Policy Journal, 1*(2).

Michaels, C., Tofa, M., & James, G. (2016). *Literature review on community resilience in remote north Australia*.

Morley, P., Russell-Smith, J., Sangha, K. K., Sutton, S., & Sithole, B. (2016). Evaluating resilience in two remote indigenous Australian communities. *Australian Journal of Emergency Management, 31*(4), 44–50.

Morley, S. (2015). *What works in effective Indigenous community-managed programs and organisations*. CFCA Paper (32). Retrieved from https://aifs.gov.au/cfca/publications/what-works-effective-indigenous-community-man aged-program/background

Paton, D. (2016). *Being afraid effectively: Cross-cultural perspectives on disaster risk reduction: Professorial lecture series*. Retrieved from http://www.cdu.edu.au/about/professorials

Paton, D., Buergelt, P., & Campbell, A. (2015). Learning to co-exist with environmental hazards: Community and societal perspectives and strategies. *Advances in Environmental Research, 43*(1), 1–23.

Paton, D., & McClure, J. (Eds.). (2013). *Preparing for disasters: Building household and community capacity*. Springfield.

Paton, D. (2007). Preparing for natural hazards: The role of community trust. *Disaster Prevention and Management: An International Journal, 16*(3), 370–379. https://doi.org/10.1108/09653560710758323

Paton, D. (2003). Disaster preparedness: A social-cognitive perspective. *Disaster Prevention and Management: An International Journal, 12*(3), 210–216. https://doi.org/10.1108/09653560310480686

Russell-Smith, J., Whitehead, P., & Cooke, P. (Eds.). (2009). *Culture, ecology and economy management in North Australian savannas: Rekindling the Wurrk tradition*. CSIRO Publishing. Royal Commission into Aboriginal Deaths in Custody (RCIADIC) (E Johnston, QC, Commissioner). National Report of the Royal Commission into Aboriginal Deaths in Custody.

Sangha, K. K., Sithole, B., Hunter-Xenie, H., Daniels, C., Yibarbuk, D., James, G., Chritsie, M., Gould, J., Edwards, A., & Russel Smith, J. (2017). Empowering indigenous communities in natural disaster prone Northern Australia. *International Journal of Mass Emergencies and Disasters*, 35(3), 137–153.

Sithole, B., Campion, O. B., & Hunter-Xenie, H. (2019). Hazard smart remote communities in Northern Australia—Community led response to disaster preparedness. *Australasian Journal of Environmental Management*, 31(4), 1324–1540.

Sithole, B., Hunter-Xenie, H., Yibarbuk, D., Daniels, C., Daniels, G., Campion, O. B., Namarnyilk, S., Narorroga, E., Dann, O., Dirdi, K., Nayilibibj, G., Phillips, E., Daniels, K., Daniels, A., Daniels, G., Turner, H., Daniels, C. A., Daniels, T., Thomas, P., ... Brown, C. (2017). Living with Widditjth—Protocols for building community resilience. In D. Paton, & D. Johnston (Eds.), *Disaster resilience: An integrated approach* (2nd ed.). Charles C. Thomas.

Smith, D. (2002). *Jurisdictional devolution : Towards an effective model for indigenous community self-determination*. CAEPR Discussion Paper, Issue 233.

Sullivan, P. (2010). *The Aboriginal community sector and the effective delivery of services: Acknowledging the role of indigenous sector organisations*. Desert Knowledge CRC. Alice Springs.

Trudgen, R. I. (2012). *Why warriors lie down and die*. Why Warriors Pty Ltd.

Veland, S., Howitt, R., & Dominey-Howes, D. (2010). Invisible institutions in emergencies: Evacuating the remote indigenous community of Warruwi, Northern Territory Australia, from Cyclone Monica. *Environmental Hazards*, 9(2), 197–214.

Walker, B. (2012). *The challenge, conversation, commissioned papers and regional studies of remote Australia*. RemoteFocus. Alice Springs. Retrieved from https://eprints.utas.edu.au/15067/3/remoteFOCUS_Compendium_August_2012%5B1%5D.pdf

Walker, W. R., & Skowronski, J. J. (2009). The fading affect bias: But what the hell is it for? *Applied Cognitive Psychology*, 23(8), 1122–1136.

Yunupingu, D., & Muller, S. (2009). Cross-cultural challenges for indigenous sea country management in Australia. *Australasian Journal of Environmental Management*, 16(3), 158–167.

PART II

Education and Capacity

CHAPTER 6

Facilitating Effective DRR Education and Human Survival: Intentionally Engaging the Transformative Education-Paradigm Shift Spiral

Petra Buergelt and Douglas Paton

INTRODUCTION

The period in which we are living is [...] a turning point in the very history of the earth itself. We are living a period of the earth's history that is incredible turbulent and in an epoch in which there are violent processes of change that challenge us at every level imaginable. The pathos

P. Buergelt (✉) · D. Paton
Faculty of Health, University of Canberra, Canberra, Australia
e-mail: Petra.Buergelt@canberra.edu.au

D. Paton
e-mail: Douglas.Paton@cdu.edu.au

College of Health and Human Sciences, Charles Darwin University, Darwin, Australia

© The Author(s), under exclusive license to Springer Nature Singapore Pte Ltd. 2022
H. James et al. (eds.), *Disaster Risk Reduction in Asia Pacific*, Disaster Risk, Resilience, Reconstruction and Recovery,
https://doi.org/10.1007/978-981-16-4811-3_6

of the human being today is that we are totally caught up in this incredible transformation, and we have significant responsibility for the direction it will take. What is terrifying is that we have it within our power to make life extinct on this planet. Because of the magnitude of this responsibility for the planet, all our educational ventures must be keep in mind the immense implications of our present moment. This is the challenge for all areas of education. For education, this realisation is the bottom line. When setting educational priorities, every educational endeavour must keep in mind this immense implication of our present moment. (O'Sullivan, 2002, p. 2)

Over the last few decades, research has repeatedly shown that the education strategies used to develop the disaster risk reduction (DRR) capabilities and relationships required to reduce the risk of extreme natural events and facilitate the development of adaptive capacities have been ineffective (Buergelt et al., 2017). While this state of affairs could be interpreted as education per se not working, a critical exploration and analysis of the worldview and beliefs underpinning current and alternative education approaches suggest that a different explanation warrants consideration. In this chapter, we firstly propose that the ineffectiveness of current DRR education efforts derives from being based on the totalitarian, mechanistic, positivistic, rational and capitalistic worldview prevailing in Western cultures to maintain its power. We secondly suggest that adopting the Indigenous metaphysical, nature-based, unified and egalitarian worldview can represent a more appropriate foundation for developing effective DRR education and the social-ecological relationships required to facilitate the development of sustainable DRR beliefs and practices based on the principle of people living in harmony/balance with nature, themselves and others (Griffith, 2014). These relationships, in turn, can represent a context for cultivating the individual and collective adaptive capabilities that contemporary DRR seeks to develop (Buergelt et al., 2017). Transformative pedagogies are required to create this paradigm shift.

To set the scene for this discussion, we first explore the nature and importance of philosophical worldviews. We then discuss how the fundamental beliefs of the Western worldview are the source of disharmonious relationships between humans and nature, disease and 'natural' disasters and how these beliefs create educational strategies that disempower people to maintain the status quo. Next, we examine how the prevailing Western worldview is challenged by a new worldview within the Western culture: social constructionism. This examination builds the bridge for being open to, and understanding, the Indigenous worldview. Following, we will explore how the Indigenous worldview comprises fundamental beliefs that aim at having people living in harmony with nature and thus creates a framework for embedding in every aspect of culture and society educational strategies and practices that foster the development of enduring harmonious socio-environmental relationships. Living in harmony with nature, self and others, in turn, supports the development and application of DRR outcomes as a result of its fundamental focus of empowering people. We conclude with a discussion of transformative educational pathways that could be adopted to facilitate the adoption of the empowering thinking and action that is implicitly evident in Indigenous beliefs and practices.

WORLDVIEWS, LEARNING PROCESSES AND EDUCATION

> Every transformation of [the human species]... has rested on new a metaphysical and ideological base; or rather, upon deeper stirrings and intuitions whose rationalised expression takes the form of a new picture of the cosmos and the nature of humanity. (Mumford, 1957, p. 179)

The philosophical worldviews people hold, the ways people are learning and the education strategies that flow from them, create in a dialectical dance the world we live in and influence DRR. The underlying worldviews comprise people's fundamental beliefs about the origin and development of the universe (cosmology), the nature of the world/reality (ontology) and what can be known, what constitutes valid knowledge epistemology and what constitutes the most valid and reliable way to establish knowledge (Babbie, 2010; Denzin & Lincoln, 2011). What people believe about the origin of the universe influences aspects of reality they can see and believe can be known, and what they believe constitutes valid knowledge. The interpretations derived from these worldviews drive people's actions.

The worldviews people come to hold derive from iterative processes of continuously learning from interpreting their experiences. How people interpret their experiences, in turn, is influenced by the culture prevailing where they live through socialisation processes. Cultures socialise their members into their particular ways of thinking. The meanings people attribute to their experiences are predominately learned through informal interactions with other people (e.g. education, television, magazines, music, internet) (Denzin, 2004; Williams, 2008). Over time, the worldviews we learned can become so entrenched that they become habitual, taken-for-granted and unconscious.

Whether the fundamental worldviews and the ensuing social systems and individual ways of thinking and behaving, are serving members of these culture are reflected in the health and well-being of its members and by the longevity of a culture (O'Sullivan, 2002). The culture and society created based on the Western worldview have become dysfunctional; they create suffering and environmental disasters rather than fulfilling its objectives of ensuring the health and well-being of citizens and other living creatures (O'Sullivan, 2002). This dysfunctionality extends to DRR, resulting not only in public education practices being ineffective and peoples' individual and collective capacity to respond to extreme natural events declining, but also contributing to the risk of extreme natural events and disasters increasing, (Buergelt et al., in press; Paton & McClure, 2013). Consequently, if we are honest with ourselves, we have to admit that the Western worldview is no longer serving us and thus inappropriate. Let us turn to critically illuminating how the current Western worldview created this crisis.

Dominant Western Worldview: Source of Disharmonious Relationships, Suffering and Disasters

Fundamentally, Western cultures commonly ascribe to a totalitarian cosmology and to mechanistic, positivistic and rational ontologies and epistemologies (Griffith, 2015; Reason, 1995). In the Western view of cosmology, the universe was created by a single male God through a single command. Because Christian theologies perceive respect for and protecting nature as challenging God's authority and will, nature is treated disrespectfully and destroyed (Griffith, 2014, 2015). The mechanistic, positivist and rational worldview believes that reality exists independent of thought and knowledge is based on a dualism between mind and reality. According to this perspective, there exists a:

real world made up of real things we can identify, operating according to natural causal laws which govern their behaviour laws which we can deduce by analysing the operation of the component parts. Mind and reality are separate: the rational human, drawing on analytical thought and experimental methods, can come to know the objective world. So the objective world spawns the objective mind, which becomes detached, analytical and thus in the end uncaring and cold. Human progress is dependent on the processes of science, the purpose of which is the pursuit of knowledge for its own sake. (Reason, 1995, p. 2)

Western ontology does not believe the existence of invisible aspects of reality and separates nature, land, law, medicine, song, story, dance, and painting (e.g. natural sciences, geography, legal studies, medicine, social sciences, philosophy, humanities, art) (Griffith, 2015). This separation extends into DRR; it is something that is seen and treated as being independent of nature, people's everyday lives and societal processes (e.g. community development). People socialised in the Western world, typically assumes that there exists only one absolute reality or truth which can be known. Because reality is believed to be an objective view of the world—a mirror of what we see, all that humans know they know from their sensory experiences of the outside world (Reber, 1995). Consequently, people in Western cultures typically only acknowledge aspects of reality that can be observed, operationalised, and measured (objective facts) as knowledge (Sexton, 1997). Nonphysical concepts, like consciousness, thoughts, spiritual beliefs, are not viewed as valid knowledge and thus, typically not included in scientific analyses. This aspect has led to DRR being dominated by approaches derived from the natural sciences and engineering, rather than from people's lived experience and their underlying cultural and societal influences.

From the perspective of this worldview, knowledge is *posteriori* and humans learn by building an internal representation of reality based on their experiences (Gergen, 1985). Experts are seen as possessing intelligence and knowing; people are seen as not knowing and passively receiving knowledge. The lived experience of people and their perspectives are not seen as valid knowledge. According to this worldview, reality, including human behaviour, is governed by mechanical system of laws and hence knowledge is stable, ahistorical and enduring, and can be accumulated (Gergen, 1985). This view underpins the belief that defining these laws will allow explaining, predicting and controlling human behaviour.

Because this worldview assumes that individuals' behaviour is the outcome of external forces determined by universal laws, people believe that individuals' behaviour exists independently of the world, including the natural environment (Diesing, 1991).

People also presume that nature (body) and mind are separate (Cartesian mind–body split) (Misra, 1993). Western philosophers like Socrates and Descartes championed the belief that only humans have intelligence, that nature could not teach anything, and that abstract scientific knowledge is more valid than people's own knowing (Reason, 1995). Scientific discoveries based on positivism, in tandem with capitalism and Christianity, fundamentally shifted how humans interact with nature (Clover, 2002; Griffith, 2014). The positivistic reductionistic scientific worldview disconnected humans from nature and many of the issues we experience from the living conditions created by capitalism (Rowe, 1990). As a result, members of Western cultures commonly grow up disconnected from nature; become alienated from, and dishonouring, nature, their bodies and their experiences; and lose their innate and concrete embodied knowing (Reason, 1995). They also commonly perceive their relationship with, and value of nature, largely in anthropocentric terms (Clover, 2002; Paton et al., 2015).

Being conditioned to perceive themselves as being separated from nature means that people believe they are independent of nature and can exist without nature. This resulting anthropocentric belief sees nature as a resource to be conquered, owned, controlled and managed (Buergelt et al., 2017; Paton, 2015). Nature is perceived as only having a value as an amenity that is useful to humans and a resource that can justifiably be exploited to benefit people. Therefore, people in Western cultures are capitalising on the resources and amenities sourced from nature and undervaluing both nature (in its own right) and the importance of maintaining harmonious relationships with nature for their survival (Buergelt et al., 2017). As a result of these views, DRR has focused on controlling, managing and combating nature rather than identifying and addressing human agency in the causation and prevention of disasters.

Despite the tangible indicators of climate change and the growing incidence of disasters, most Western people remain generally unaware of, and abrogate their responsibility for, their role in causing extreme natural events and disasters occurring (Buergelt et al., 2017). The Western worldview hinders people from experiencing, perceiving and understanding the intrinsic value of nature, that they are one with nature, interact with nature in dialectical ways and are dependent on nature for being themselves and for their health/well-being. Because they are largely unaware of their reciprocal relationships with nature, people miss seeing that the ensuing disharmonious relationships they created with nature increases the risk of extreme natural events occurring.

Taken together, the Western worldview led to increasingly disharmonious relationships between human beings living in Western cultures and the rest of nature resulting in humanity experiencing an emotional, psychological, political, and socioecolgocial crisis (Clover, 2002; Grande, 2000; Griffith, 2015; Reason, 1995). Importantly, increasingly disharmonious socio-environmental relationships are contributing to the occurrence of extreme natural events, and to their impacts being more serious and enduring (Buergelt et al., in press; Paton et al., 2015). However, it is challenging for Western people to become aware of this worldview. The fundamental beliefs are largely taken-for-granted and unconscious; the objective mind created by this worldview cannot see the lens it has created and how and why this lens itself is its own creation (Reason, 1995). Educational approaches and programs created by this worldview thus tend to disempower people as they are designed to socialise people into the Western cultures to maintain the status quo and to produce a capable workforce (Griffith, 2014).

Education in Western societies is given to people at designated times typically during childhood and young adulthood or for specific purposes during adulthood (e.g. preparing people for disasters). Education focuses primarily on the visible observable aspects of the world. Knowledge is passed on by experts who teach specialised and abstract theories created by discipline-specific quantitative research. Knowledge is taught in subjects that separate knowledge into distinct components including nature (natural sciences), land (geography), law (legal studies), medicine, story and song (social sciences and humanities), dance and painting (art). Knowledge is taught by passing on theoretical or conceptual information via books or online sources, and via teachers/experts standing in front of a room lecturing to a large number of students. It is easy, quick and cost-effective education.

However, as Freire (2017) argues, traditional Western pedagogy perpetuates Western cultures and, in the process, weakens and oppresses citizens by treating them as lacking knowledge and needing to be educated rather than acknowledging and drawing out their innate embodied knowledge. Western pedagogy reinforces the weakening and oppressing of citizens by modelling oppressive attitudes and practices. That is, citizen apathy, which commonly citizens are blamed for, is not the fault of citizens but results from the traditional Western pedagogies inherently disempowering people to keep them manageable and to maintain the power of the ruling few.

The renowned cultural historian and ecologist Thomas Berry (1993; cited in O'Sullivan, 2002) and acclaimed author Susan Griffith (1995, cited in O'Sullivan, 2002) suggests that the current Western worldview is dysfunctional for our present circumstances. They call for urgently reassessing the Western worldview and to transform towards a worldview that will heal and guide us. O'Sullivan (2002) emphasises that altering the course requires transforming the underlying worldview and the whole cultural system. The social constructionist worldview that has been emerging in the last decades is assisting us in reassessing the current totalitarian, mechanistic, positivistic and rational Western worldview and might be a valuable bridge towards appreciating the Indigenous worldview.

Social Constructionist Worldview: Challenging the Predominant Western Worldview

> Many writers and commentators are suggesting that the current worldview or paradigm of Western civilization is reaching the end of its useful life. It is suggested that there is a fundamental shift occurring in our understanding of the universe and our place in it, that new patterns of thought and belief are emerging that will transform our experience, our thinking and our action. ... we can see the costs of this progress in ecological devastation, human and social fragmentation, and spiritual impoverishment. So if we fail to make a transition to new ways of thinking ... our civilization will decline and decay. ... This emergent worldview is multifaceted: it has been particularly described as systemic, holistic, more feminine. (Reason, 1995, p. 42)

The totalitarian, mechanistic, positivistic and rational worldview is being challenged by the social constructionist worldview. This new worldview emerged at the end of the twentieth century in response to advances in relativity, quantum mechanics and the notion of the self-regulating universe. These advances show that nature and humans are one and deeply connected in a symbiotic relationship and that people are active autonomous beings that are self-regulated (Reason, 1995).

Social constructionism assumes that reality is multiple, relative, historical, transitory, and unknowable rather than singular, objective and knowable (Sexton, 1997). Knowledge is seen as constructed reality, invented, and ambiguous rather than representative of reality, discovered, objective, and certain (Reason, 1995; Wortham, 1996). To make sense of their environment, people construct knowledge in relation to the particular culture at a particular time through actively interpreting their perceptions. That is, perception is not directly representing the natural world but is mediated, organised, enriched and interpreted (Reber, 1995). Constructed meanings are neither final nor definite. Because each individual experiences a unique set of events within their life, each individual constructs a unique reality. Diversity is valued rather than a problem to overcome (Sexton & Griffin, 1997).

From the perspective of this worldview, knowledge is also relative; it changes across time and depends on varying historical and cultural arrangements (Gergen, 1985). The constructive nature of knowledge implies that knowledge is generated by individuals themselves rather than determined by universal laws as empiricists propose; knowledge is something people co-create through interacting with the environment rather than as something people have (Hayes & Oppenheim, 1997). The knowledge individuals can gain is only limited by their current genetic makeup (Plotkin, 1995), and the prevailing culture and society (Hayes & Oppenheim, 1997; Nightingale & Neilands, 1997). Consequently, people can change their reality through the way they act and interact within the limits set by their environment. Knowledge being contextual implies that humans can proactively adapt to their environment by constantly creating new knowledge and that everything humans do involves their body (Goncalves, 1997). Mind and body are inseparable. As a result, this worldview considers nonphysical concepts, like thoughts, opinions, or consciousness, as meaningful.

To shed light more on how individuals and cultures construct knowledge and learn, we utilise systems theory (Bronfenbrenner, 1977; Nelson & Prilleltensky, 2010) and symbolic interactionism (Blumer, 1969; Charmaz, 2014). Both social paradigms suggest our minds 'initially operate through preconceptions; these preconceptions not only shape our interpretations of the world but also impinge on the world itself' (O'Sullivan, 2002, p. 3). Our minds constantly create the world and society; the world and society and cultural systems create our minds (Smith, 2015).

This co-creative dance between people and society means, on the one hand, humans are autonomous beings that can through symbolic interactions construct, negotiate, modify, resist or reject the meanings they learn. People are active agents who are inherently capable of actively creating their own experiences/world and of thinking about their actions rather than responding mechanically to stimuli in their environment (Flick, 2019; Williams, 2008). Reality and knowledge are not independent of the humans mind—what people perceive is not merely what they observe. Instead, what they observe is created by properties of the observers' mind, by cognitive and affective operations (Reber, 1995) that function to integrate and synthesise new stimuli with previous experience/knowledge to construct new knowledge. This continuous learning process allows people to modify their knowledge during their lifetime in response to changes in their environment. Thus, it is not important whether knowledge is true but whether knowledge is viable, for only viable knowledge enables people to create outcomes that serve them. Hence, constructing meaning assists people to evolve and adapt.

On the other hand, human agency is constrained or expanded by the physical and social context in which action is contemplated and occurs. People constantly try to make sense of their environment and to create an equilibrium with their changing environment through adapting to changes. Because much of life is routine, people unconsciously interpret what others say, adapt their responses and respond with largely taken-for-granted habitual actions (Blumer, 1969; Charmaz, 2014). Habitual actions enable individuals to respond to situations with economy of thought and action (Dewey, 1922). Interpretations and actions are largely unconscious unless interrupted by change or challenge such as extreme natural events. If the routine of situations is disrupted by unusual experiences people are forced to change their interpretations and actions because they do not work anymore (Denzin, 1992). As a result, people redefine their selves. For this reason, epiphanic experiences often represent turning-point experiences in individual lives, which result in reconstructions of the self/identity.

The two-way reciprocal creative process happens through minds organising themselves and maintaining homeostasis to achieve equilibrium or balance/harmony between our internal cognitive presumptions/interpretations and perceptions/experiences by self-monitoring interactions with the environment and adjusting interpretations and actions based on this feedback (O'Sullivan, 2002). When we can make sense of the world and accomplish our goals there is no need for adjustment. However, when there is a persistent mismatch a cognitive crisis occurs old habitual modes of perceiving and interpreting become dysfunctional. When worldviews become dysfunctional, people and societies need to evolve and shift their cognitive systems or viewpoints in ways that enable them to deal with the new situation; people and society need to adapt by transforming themselves.

Because the social constructionist worldview argues that knowledge is co-created by people interacting and exchanging knowledge (Gergen, 1985), it follows that, to be effective, education must be conducted in collaboration with others; people need to be able to construct knowledge together. This worldview empowers citizens to build their individual and collective adaptive capacities to improve their situation.

By challenging the reality that the totalitarian, mechanistic, positivistic and rational Western worldview created, the social constructionist worldview assists in becoming aware of the operation and impacts of this worldview (Denzin & Lincoln, 2011). The constructivist paradigm validates the Indigenous worldview—a worldview that has proven its value as it has enabled Indigenous peoples to survive for millennia and to still be alive despite the brutal forces of colonialisation. Both paradigms hold similar tenants, but the Indigenous worldview is more comprehensive and sophisticated. It is to a discussion of the Indigenous worldview we turn now.

METAPHYSICAL, NATURE-BASED, UNIFIED AND EGALITARIAN WORLDVIEW: SOURCE OF HARMONIOUS RELATIONSHIPS, HEALTH/WELL-BEING AND DRR

This section provides insights into the sophisticated Indigenous worldview of Indigenous peoples living Australia, this worldview is comparable to those of other Indigenous peoples around the world (Griffith, 2015).

The Australian Aboriginal cosmology is laid down in the creation or dreamtime stories. According to these stories several female and male metaphysical beings or ancestor spirits created the land and all creatures by travelling across undifferentiated space and engaging in totemic acting out what they had dreamed (Broom, 1994; Griffith, 2015; Lawler, 1991). Importantly, throughout their travels they discovered through observation, experience, and learning both behaviours that created harmony and thus joy, health and well-being and those that interrupted harmony and thus created pain, chaos and disease (Lawler, 1991). These creation stories not only share of how the world was created but also act as a guide for humans how to interact with nature and each other in ways that maintain harmony. Thus, obedience to, and maintaining of, the dreamtime/nature laws is paramount for Indigenous peoples as this ensures the 'fertility, stability, and security of the entire society' (Lawler, 1991, p. 260).

Ontologically, Indigenous people distinguish between two different yet equally real realms of existence or realities (Lawler, 1991; Myers, 1986). One reality is the physical, visible objective world, which is the ordinary external world which humans can experience through their senses (land). The other reality is the metaphysical, invisible subjective world, which is transcendent to, and immanent in, nature (dreaming/spiritual). These two modes of reality are believed to be mutually exclusive yet inextricably and dialectically intertwined: the invisible world creates and influences the visible world and the visible world recreates and influences the invisible world. Australian Indigenous people live in and shift between both worlds. Experiencing the physical world gives access to the invisible world and thus to realising metaphysical creative powers (Lawler, 1991). Hence, Australian Aboriginal peoples value growing their awareness by honing their cabilities to distinguish aspects of the physical world. As a result, they are able to communicate with nature and each other more effectively.

Australian Indigenous peoples view all creatures as one and equal (Posey, 1999). They believe that there exists an essential creative life force or spirit (Broome, 1994; Griffith, 2015; Lawler, 1991). All creatures consist of the common universal consciousness of this primary creative force. That is, all creatures, including humans, share a common origin (i.e. all creatures are manifestations of the greater cosmos) and every aspect of the natural world contains the spirit of the metaphysical energy that created the world. Therefore, all creatures, including humans, are intimately connected—every creature within the universe influences human beings; human beings influence every creature within the universe.

While every creature is a manifestation of the greater cosmos, the life force expresses itself in many forms in the visible world. As a result, Indigenous people see all creatures as people like them and are aware of the interdependencies with all creatures. They see nature as allies - they look after the land; the land looks after them. Because humans and nature are seen as being related and interdependent, Indigenous people relate to nature based on the fundamental cultural values of reciprocity, respect, kindness, gentleness and restraint.

Australian Indigenous peoples recognise and value the wisdom of all creatures. For them all nature is 'knowledgescape' (Griffith, 2015). Nature is seen as sharing the same consciousness of the ancestors and thus containing all the knowledge of the original creation. Therefore, for Indigenous peoples, nature is an extension of mind and body and is their greatest teacher. Earth is seen as a library in which books are the different aspects of nature. They see and understand the knowledge of animals and plants. In their eyes, exploring any phenomena of nature, including humans, provides insights into the inner working of the universe. This unity and intimate relationship inspires and obligates Indigenous people to adore, respect and keep the earth in its original purity and potency as nature contains all the mystery and knowledge of the original creation. As a result, Indigenous peoples know nature intimately like family, care for nature and feel responsible for looking after land.

As a consequence of this intimate, reciprocal relationship, the self of Australian Aborigine is located in the land and they draw deeply from harmonious relationships with the land for their physical, psychological and spiritual health and well-being (Griffith, 2015; Lawler, 1991). If their self is separated from the land, both their sense of self and the land are diminished and suffer disease. Their awareness of this intimate unified relationship inspires and obligates Indigenous people to value, respect and keep nature in its original purity and potency. In fact, for Australian Aboriginal peoples, the recreating and passing on of the physical world or nature is the purpose of their life.

Nature has also highly influenced how Indigenous peoples organised culture and society. They practice democracy based on the model nature provides for democracy: 'ecocratic wisdom' (Griffith, 2015). The intimate connection between people and the land means that living in harmony with nature is essential for physical, psychological and spiritual survival and thriving. Hence, Australian Indigenous culture and society are designed to protect nature by ensuring that people live in harmony with nature (Griffith, 2015). Ecological truths are encoded in the stories that are repeatedly told through ceremonies/rituals, song, dance and painting intricately connecting Aboriginal people with nature and country to constantly recreate and nurture these intimate relationships.

Because of their worldview, Aboriginal people did live in harmony with nature and looked after nature. They developed over millennia individual, cultural and social capabilities of living together in harmony with nature and each other that enabled them to adapt to change, to survive and to thrive (Broome, 1994; Griffith, 2014, 2015; Lawler, 1991). The metaphysical, nature-based, unified and egalitarian beliefs lead to Indigenous peoples developing an education that aims at enabling people distinguishing ever finer subtleties of life to gain a deeper knowledge of nature to access the creative powers and live in harmony/balance with nature, themselves and others (Griffith, 2015).

METAPHYSICAL, NATURE-BASED, UNIFIED AND EGALITARIAN WORLDVIEW: CREATES EDUCATION THAT EMPOWERS PEOPLE

The knowledge and education strategies used in Aboriginal cultures are highly sophisticated (Buergelt et al., 2017; Buergelt & Paton, in press; Griffith, 2015; Lawler, 1991; Yunkaporta, 2019). Knowledge and education have been skillfully, diligently and systematically created over at least 60,000 years of observation, experience and insight, and passed on for as many years (Lawler, 1991). Indigenous education strategies are ecologically informed, emotionally charged and morally binding (Lawler, 1991). Living in nature, and learning from nature, is at the core of education (Griffith, 2015; Yunkaporta, 2019). The education methods are used implicitly and continuously in all interactions among and between people and nature throughout life and are oral, experiential, multimodal and collective (Buergelt et al., 2017).

In alignment with the cosmological, ontological and epistemological worldview Indigenous peoples hold, the purpose of education is to draw out from within people both physical and spiritual wisdom so they discover their true primordial nature and understand life intimately and holistically, reflecting the true meaning of the Latin source of education *educare* 'to draw out' and 'to lead' (Buergelt & Paton, in press; Buergelt et al., 2017). Accordingly, education focuses on both the visible and invisible aspects of the world (Griffith, 2014). All vital elements of life including nature, land, law, medicine, ceremony, story, song, dance, painting and living are seen as united rather than fragmented as in Western education and as needing to be in harmony for health and wellbeing to be present (Buergelt et al., 2017). Everybody teaches everybody constantly the local nature-related knowledges created over millennia. New and deeper knowledge is introduced in stages in accordance with the maturation of the mind; it is only given when elders passing on that knowledge determine through deep listening and observation that people are ready to understand that knowledge and to use the knowledge responsibly. In each initiation new language and experiences are given that enables the initiate to connect the visible physical and invisible metaphysical worlds to comprehend the invisible realms.

Engaging in the transformative quests especially via arts and nature is central to Indigenous education (Buergelt & Paton, in press; Buergelt et al., 2017). Directly experiencing our true nature and acquiring the wisdom of the ancestors required engaging in a quest that challenged physically, psychologically and spiritually. Nature and arts are the allies of this quest. Nature is seen as reflecting the true nature of humans for humans are intimately connected with nature; they are nature and nature is them. Accordingly, the more people interact with and know about nature, the more they get to know about ourselves and the spiritual, invisible world. Hence, nature is seen as a friend and teacher, which cradles and restores, imbues with diverse ways of knowing and provides challenges required for cultivating critical capabilities and maturing. Entomologically, arts is rooted in the Latin *artus* referring to 'joints and connecting the parts' and the German word for arts *Kunst* is linked to 'knowledge' and 'to know how, to be able', indicating that arts is capable of encoding, carrying over and connecting us with our inner wisdom, which is the true knowledge of the ancestors (Buergelt & Paton, in press). Thus, diverse forms of arts are deeply embedded in all parts of life.

Indigenous education strategies synergise many, if not all, the elements that Western science increasingly discovers as critical. They indicate that Indigenous peoples had, and in many cases continue to have, an excellent understanding of how people learn (Lawler, 1991). Because of the sophisticated holistic education, Indigenous people are 'landknowers' (Griffith, 2015). As a result, traditionally, Aboriginal peoples are highly sensitive to the knowledge embedded in the land. Dream time stories connect Aboriginal people with country and these stories contain highly complex knowledge systems of ecological understanding with the power of generating and determining social behaviour to maintain harmony. Thus, each group has specific ceremonies, stories, songs, dance and other cultural and spiritual ties that link them to the local knowledge embedded in the specific place where they live. Consequently, maintaining direct links with country are crucial for maintaining knowledge and obligations to maintain those connections form the core of individual and collective identity (Posey, 1999).

Children learn their relational positions and roles in the kinship system, the emotions and their sharing, and the dramatisation of emotions through experiencing intimate relationships (Lawler, 1991). Children are involved with their kin to create a 'sense of the world as an extension of the self' and to expand their concerns to the entire world (Lawler, 1991, p. 248). Emotions that foster that purpose are reinforced; emotions that detract from that purpose are discouraged and punished. Language and thought are being carefully connected to lived experience and perceptions in ways that encourage finer distinctions (Griffith, 2015). The language is always linked to the earth's topography so that the physical world is retained in and mirrors the psychic world and the psychic world is retained in and mirrors the physical world. This way nature and creatures including people create and reflect each other in a circle of reciprocity.

Aboriginal education seems to contain and synergise all the elements that Western science increasingly discovers as critical: continuous, focus on comprehending, action learning, experiential learning, transformative education, discovery education, using different modes that engage all senses, and scaffolding. In particular, the Indigenous pedagogy is consistent with Freire's (2017) pedagogy of the oppressed; a critical pedagogy approach that empowers educators to liberate people from oppression by consciously co-creating knowledge in a two-way education process that is characterised by authentic dialogues, critical thinking and constant interaction of theory and practice.

A growing body of empirical evidence generated by Western science from different disciplines demonstrates now what Indigenous peoples across the world have always know namely that nature spaces and living in harmony with nature is the source of mental and physical health, well-being and individual and collective adaptive capacities (Buergelt et al., 2017; Paton et al., 2015). In particular, growing up in nature, and with people who value nature, instils in people a desire and the ability to live in harmony with nature and to develop collaborative and cooperative relationships with other people and place (Griffith, 2014; Paton et al., 2015; Thompson et al., 2008). Harmonious relationships between people and nature also contribute to DRR by increasing people's sense of belonging to people and places (Paton et al., 2015).

Based on the above discussion we suggest that Indigenous worldviews, knowledges, sensitivities and practices hold rich potential for learning and elaborating how to develop cultures, societies and individual and collective adaptive capacities capable of addressing current challenges humanity is facing and (re)creating health/well-being of humans and nature. Consequently, (re)learning the capability of living in harmony with nature is a key to reducing the risk of extreme natural events and disasters (Buergelt et al., 2017). Accordingly, there is merit in listening to and learning from Aboriginal people and working together with them to integrate and transcend both knowledge systems. Indigenous and non-Indigenous peoples collaborating two-way might be the key transformative pathway required to shift beliefs and practices in ways humanity needs to survive and thrive.

To create individual, cultural and social shifts required to enhance DRR, a transformation of the fundamental beliefs Western cultures hold about cosmology, ontology and epistemology is required. Due to the Western worldview being so entrenched in all aspects of Western life, achieving such a shift is unlikely to arise easily (Berkes et al., 2003). Thus, transformation needs to be intentionally created and facilitated. Transformative learning and education, which we explore next, can accomplish this task.

Transformative Learning and Education

> Social change cannot happen without individual psychic change; physical health cannot be separated from planetary well-being; self-conceptions cannot be carved off from conceptions of the anima mundi. We make our world, and our world makes us, in some obvious and in some very subtle ways. This transformative potential is to be celebrated. (Morrell & O'Connor, 2002, p. xx)

The question is, however, how this transformative potential can be accomplished—how does education needs to look like to be effective in reducing the risk of extreme natural events occurring and building individual and collective adaptive capacity? From our exploration, we identified, in addition to (re)learning from Indigenous peoples, transformative learning and education as a key transformative pathway.

Transformative learning and education emerged to restore social justice, peace and nature by addressing inequalities and the destruction of the environment (Morrell & O'Connor, 2002). Transformative education challenges the view that emerged from the Western worldview that education needs to serve solely the global marketplace and suggests a more integral transformative vision (O'Sullivan, 2002). Drawing from various types of Indigenous knowledges to shape their pedagogical strategies transformative learning creates;

> experiencing a deep, structural shift in the basic premises of thought, feelings, actions. It is a shift of consciousness that dramatically and permanently alters our way of being in the world. Such a shift involves our understanding of ourselves and our self-locations; our relationships with other humans and with the natural world; our understanding of relations of power in interlocking structures of class, race, and gender; our body-awareness; our visions of alternative approaches to living; and our sense of possibilities for social justice and peace and personal joy. (O'Sullivan et al., 2002, p. xvii)

Transformational experiences can fundamentally alter people's ways of thinking and thus, how they are perceiving the world, feel and act (Erhard et al., 2013; Mezirow, 1997, 2012; Willis, 2012). Transformative learning creates shifts in being that enhance people's awareness, authenticity, responsibility, openness and formal and post-formal operational thinking skills such as perceiving the invisible world, thinking holistically and interdependently, seeing interactions between past-present-future, being receptive to new information and critically questioning information, critically reflecting on their experiences and interpretations, managing their thinking and taking other people's perspectives (Buergelt et al., in press). People become more capable of effectively engaging in discourse or dialogue to arrive at a best dependable, tentative working judgement regarding a belief; developing beliefs, feelings and actions that work better; taking actions based on their reflective insights and critically assessing the outcomes of their actions. Transformative learning empowers citizens' critical thinking and increases the likelihood of them becoming more socially responsible agents of their lives and the communities in which they live. Transformative learning lays the foundations for citizens to learn how to take effective social actions (Mezirow, 2003).

The transformative learning literature is increasingly expanding the view promoted by Mezirow (1991) that transformative learning occurs through rational ways of being and knowing by generating mounting evidence of extra-rational ways of being and knowing (Buergelt & Paton, in press). According to Mezirow (1991, 1997, 2003), transformative education aims at intentionally initiating and facilitating rational transformative learning processes that enable people to shift or reframe their frame of reference. Transformative education utilises discursive and critical dialectical processes that challenge people's taken-for-granted frames of reference to encourage them to critically reflect on and examine the assumptions they and others hold, and to see alternative points of view and redefine problems from a different perspective (Mezirow, 1997). The dialectical processes entail examining, questioning, challenging and revising perceptions (Mezirow, 1991).

To create a shift in worldviews, Sutton (1989) argues for a fundamental shift in attitudes towards ourselves and about our relationship with nature in ways that (re)develop an effective partnership with the rest of nature. Transformative education needs to critically question and challenge current education and how it has contributed to the current world, and be linked to individual and collective spirituality, subjectivity, ecology, interconnectedness, local places, diversity and communion (O'Sullivan, 2002). More specifically, O'Sullivan (2002) proposes that transformative learning must include education that stimulates the awareness that the current worldview and associated cultural practices are dysfunctional; develops the capacities to manage denial, despair and grief and to take responsibility for the world we created; critically examines the worldview and associated masculine hierarchical power structures that create the current world; and addresses the saturation of information that leads to an unconscious civilisation.

Clover (2002) emphasises that transformative education needs to address the ecological crisis. Ecological knowledge and knowing, a lived process of knowing that has been built and refined through cumulative process among generations over millennia though the interaction of age-old knowledge and daily lived experiences in a changing environment, gave cultures and societies the expertise to function and survive. However, ecological knowing is rapidly eroded and silenced through Western education and urbanisation to give more power to Western socialisation that maintains the status quo:

> The so-called age of Enlightenment…forced all other learning and knowledge into darkness… [rendering] invisible other ways of knowing such as native or traditional knowledge, people's spirituality, and especial all women's knowledge. (Shiva, cited in Clover, 2002, p. 161)

Clover (2002) suggests that this transformation can be accomplished by transformative education being reconceptualised within a holistic ecological framework that focuses on human–nature relationships and being based on peoples' cultural and ecological identities that reflect their relationships with the places in which they live. Education needs to weave environmental issues into cultural, political and economic discourses. It is about learning to live in harmony with nature and each other (Clover, 2002). It is about building upon people's knowledge and avoiding knowledge being in the hands of few irresponsible people, challenging cultural homogenisation, consumerism whilst promoting life-centred ecofeminist values. Therefore, education needs to create opportunities for people to imagine and work towards life-centred forms of development via education practices that are lodged in place using nature and communities as sites for learning, focusing on experiencing and studying the interrelationship between humans and the rest of nature.

To realise the benefits of this approach, educators need to be facilitators who create a supportive and trusting environment that makes it safe to explore, experiment, express and share, and learn from mistakes; provide the knowledge and support required for constructing coherent meaning; nudge transformation through questioning and model transformed attitudes and behaviours (Stewart, 2012). At the heart of this approach are actively creating genuine two-way interaction with people to dissolve barriers to gaining new knowledge and to co-construct knowledge.

However, over the last decade, extra-rational transformative pathways are gaining increasing recognition (Buergelt & Paton, in press; Nicolaides et al., in press; Taylor & Cranton, 2012). These extra-rational transformative learning pathways include most importantly nature (e.g. Lange, 2012; O'Sullivan, 2002, 2012); creative arts (e.g. Kasl & Yorks, 2012; Kokkos, 2021; Lawrence, 2012; Tyler & Swartz, 2012) and soul work and spirituality (e.g. Dirkx, 2012; O'Sullivan, 2002, 2012). These extra-rational transfromative pathways are consistent with the key characteristics of Indigenous education, pointing to Indigenous education being intrinsically transformative.

Conclusion

In conclusion, accomplishing DRR requires a shift from the Western worldview towards the Indigenous worldview. The increase in magnitude and frequency of extreme natural events and disasters, and the ineffectiveness of current DRR education strategies, is the result of the totalitarian, mechanistic, positivistic and rational worldview that dominates in Western cultures. The Western culture and society created based on the Western worldview have become dysfunctional; they create suffering as a result of emotional, psychological, political, and socioecolgocial crisis and the devastation of the very source of our existence (Buergelt et al., 2017; Clover, 2002; O'Sullivan, 2002; Reason, 1995).

This cultural and societal dysfunctionality renders DRR efforts ineffective. The Western worldview results in educational practices that disempower citizens and culture and society that disconnects people from nature and creates humans living in disharmonious relationships with nature (Buergelt et al., 2017; Freire, 2017). Disharmonious relationships increase the risk of extreme natural events and disasters, and that undermines the individual and in the collective capacity to respond to extreme natural events (O'Sullivan et al., 2002; Paton & McClure, 2013). Consequently, the Western worldview is inappropriate for our current circumstances and there is a pressing need to transform our ways of being and thinking towards a worldview that will heal us and guide us towards creating a culture and society that supports health/well-being and thriving (O'Sullivan, 2002).

Social constructionism challenges the Western worldview and validates the Indigenous worldview. While the social constructionist and Indigenous worldviews hold similar tenants, the Indigenous worldview is more comprehensive and sophisticated. The metaphysical, nature-based, unified and egalitarian beliefs Indigenous peoples across the world hold led to them creating cultures and societies that create harmonious relationships with nature and health/well-being (Broome, 1994; Griffith, 2014, 2015; Lawler, 1991). Thus, Indigenous worldviews hold a rich potential for developing cultures, societies and individual and collective adaptive capacities capable of accomplishing humans and nature being healthy.

To create the fundamental individual, cultural and societal shifts required to develop DRR, a transformation of the philosophical beliefs Western cultures hold is required. Due to the Western worldview being so entrenched in all aspects of Western life and enabling people in power to maintain their power, achieving such a shift is unlikely to arise on it is own (Berkes et al., 2003). Consequently, this transformation needs to be intentionally created and facilitated. Besides (re)learning from Indigenous peoples, transformative education pedagogies hold great transformative potential. Both education strategies provide a wealth of alternative and innovative ways that could be used by the DRR community to co-create with citizens pedagogies and knowledges that empower them to live in harmony with nature, themselves and others. That is, transformational education and transformation of worldviews are interdependent and happen in an iterative spiral-like process. To reduce the risk of extreme natural events and ensure human survival this transformative education—paradigm shift spiral needs to be intentionally engaged.

We have a critical choice to make. We can continue to cling to the worldview that creates suffering and the extinction of life including us or we can wake up, accept responsibility and intentionally engage in educational endeavours that transform our dysfunctional Western worldview towards Indigenous worldviews that have been successful in creating a world that enabled humans to adapt to change, to survive and to thrive. DRR scholars and practitioners around the world are in a unique position to play a vital role in leading this transformation. Will you accept this leadership and focus your energies on creating this transformation?

References

Babbie, E. R. (2010). *The practice of social research* (12th ed.). Wadsworth Cengage.
Berkes, F., Colding, J., & Folke, C. (2003). *Navigating social-ecological systems: Building resilience for complexity and change*. Cambridge University Press.
Blumer, H. (1969). *Symbolic interactionism: Perspective and method*. Prentice-Hall.
Broome, R. (1994). *Aboriginal Australians* (2nd ed.). Allen & Unwin.
Buergelt, P. T., & Paton, D. (in press). Restoring the transformative bridge: Remembering and regenerating our Western transformative ancient traditions to solve the riddle of our existential crisis. In A. Nicolaides, S. Eschenbacher, P. T. Buergelt, Y. Gilpin-Jackson, M. Mitsunori, & M. Welch (Eds.), *The Palgrave handbook on learning for transformation*. Palgrave Macmillan.

Buergelt, P. T., Paton, D., Campbell, C. A., James, H., & Cottrell, A. (in press). *Killing two birds with one stone: Utilizing natural hazard threats to develop adaptive and thriving communities, and reduce the risk of disasters.* In R. Wallace (Ed.), Northern research futures: Northern Research Futures. ANU Press.

Buergelt, P. T., Paton, D., Sithole, B., Sangha, K., Campion, O. B. & Campion, J. (2017). Living in harmony with our environment: A paradigm shift. In D. Paton & D. Johnston (Eds.), *Disaster resilience: An integrated approach* (2nd ed) (pp. 289–307). Charles C. Thomas.

Bronfenbrenner, U. (1977). Toward an experimental ecology of human development. *American Psychologist, 32,* 513–531.

Charmaz, K. (2014). *Constructing grounded theory: A practical guide through qualitative analysis.* Sage.

Clover, D. E. (2002). Toward transformational learning: Ecological perspectives for adult education. In E. O'Sullivan, A. Morrell, & A. O'Conner (Eds.), *Expanding the boundaries of transformative learning* (pp. 159–172). Palgrave.

Denzin, N. K. (1992). *Symbolic interactionism and cultural studies: The politics of interpretation.* Blackwell.

Denzin, N. K. (2004). Symbolic interactionism. In U. Flick, E. von Kardorff, & I. Steinke (Eds.), *A companion to qualitative research* (pp. 81–87). Sage.

Denzin, N., & Lincoln, Y. (2011). *The SAGE handbook of qualitative research* (4th ed.). Sage.

Dewey, J. (1922). *Human nature and conduct.* The Quinn and Baden Company.

Diesing, P. (1991). *How does social science work?: Reflections on practice.* University of Pittsburg Press.

Dirkx,. (2012). Nuturing soul work: A Jungian approach to transformative learning. In E. W. Taylor & P. Cranton (Eds.), *The handbook of transformative learning theory, research and practice* (pp. 116–130). Jossey-Bass.

Erhard, W., Jensen, M. C., & Granger, K. L. (2013) Creating Leaders an ontological/phenomenological model. In S. Snook, N. Nohria, & R. Khurana (Eds.), *The handbook for teaching leadership.* Sage.

Flick, U. (2019). *An introduction to qualitative research* (5th ed.). Sage.

Freire, P. (2017). *Pedagogy of the oppressed.* Penguin.

Garnett S. T., Sithole B., Whitehead P. J., Burgess C. P., Johnston F. H., & Lea T. (2008). Healthy country, healthy people: Policy implications of links between indigenous human health and environmental condition in tropical Australia. *The Australian Journal of Public Administration, 68,* 53–66.

Gergen, K. F. (1985). The social constructionist movement in modern psychology. *American Psychologist, 40,* 266–275.

Goncalves, O. F. (1997). Foreword. In T. L. Sexton & B. L. Griffin (Eds.), *Constructist thinking in counselling practice, research, and training* (pp. 157–173). Teachers College Press.

Grande, S. (2000). American Indian identity and intellectualism: The quest for a new red pedagogy. *International Journal of Qualitative Studies in Education*, *13*(4), 343–359.

Griffith, J. (2014). *A country called childhood: Children in the exuberant world*. Counterpoint Berkeley.

Griffith, J. (2015). *Savage grace: A journey in wildness*. Counterpoint Berkeley.

Hayes, R. L., & Oppenheim, R. (1997). Constructionism: Reality is what you make of it. In T. L. Sexton & B. L. Griffin (Eds.), *Constructist thinking in counseling practice, research, and training* (pp. 19–40). Teachers College Press.

Kasl, E., & Yorks, L. (2012). Learning to be what we know: The pivotal role of presentational knowing in transformative learning. In E. W. Taylor & Cranton, P. (Eds.), *The handbook of transformative learning: Theory, research, and practice* (pp. 503–519). Jossey-Bass.

Kokkos, A. (2021). *Exploring art for perspective transformation*. Brill.

Lange, E. A. (2012). Transforming transformative learning through sustainability and the new science. In E. W. Taylor & P. Cranton (Eds.), *The handbook of transformative learning: Theory, research, and practice* (pp. 195 – 211). Jossey-Bass.

Lawrence, R. L. (2012). Transformative learning through artistic expression: Getting out of our heads. In E. W. Taylor & P. Cranton (Eds.), *The handbook of transformative learning: Theory, research, and practice* (pp. 471–485). Jossey-Bass.

Lawler, R. (1991). *Voices of the first day: Awakening in the Aboriginal dreamtime*. Inner Traditions International.

Misra, G. (1993). Psychology from a constructionist perspective: An interview with Kenneth J. Gergen. *New Ideas in Psychology*, *11*, 399–414.

Mezirow, J. (1991). *Transformative dimensions of adult learning*. Jossey-Bass.

Mezirow, J. (1997). Transformative learning: Theory to practice. *New Directions for Adult and Continuing Education*, *1997*(74), 5–12.

Mezirow, J. (2003). Transformative learning as discourse. *Journa of Transformative Education*, *1*(1), 58–63.

Mezirow, J. (2012). Learning to think like an adult: Core concepts of transformation theory. In E. W. Taylor, & Cranton, P. (Eds.), *The handbook of transformative learning: Theory, research, and practice*. Jossey-Bass.

Morell, A., & O'Connor, M. A. (2002). Introduction. In E. O'Sullivan, A. Morrell, & A. O'Conner (Eds.), *Expanding the boundaries of transformative learning* (pp. xv–xx). Palgrave.

Mumford, L. (1957). *The transformations of man*. Allen & Unwin.

Myers, F. (1986). *Pintupi country, Pintupi self*. Smithsonian Institution Press.

Nelson, G., & Prilleltensky, I. (2010). *Community psychology: In pursuit of liberation and well-being*. New York: Palgrave.

Nightingale, D., & Neilands, T. (1997). Understanding and practicing critical psychology. In D. Fox & I. Prilleltensky (Eds.), *Critical psychology: An introduction* (pp. 68–84). Sage.

Nicolaides, A., Eschenbacher, S., Buergelt, P. T., Gilpin-Jackson, Y., Mitsunori, M., & Welch, M. (in press). *The Palgrave handbook on learning for transformation*. Palgrave Macmillan.

O'Sullivan, E. (2002). The project and vision of transformative education: Integral transformative learning. In E. O'Sullivan, A. Morrell, & A. O'Conner (Eds.), *Expanding the boundaries of transformative learning* (pp. 1–12). Palgrave.

O'Sullivan, E., Morrell A., & O'Conner, A. (Eds.) (2002). *Expanding the boundaries of transformative learning*. New York: Palgrave.

O'Sullivan, E. (2012). Deep transformation: Forging a planetary worldview. In E. W. Taylor & P. Cranton (Eds.), *The handbook of transformative learning theory, research and practice* (pp. 162–177). Jossey-Bass.

Paton, D., & McClure, J. (2013). *Preparing for disaster: Building household and community capacity*. Springfield, Ill: Charles C. Thomas.

Paton, D., Buergelt, P. T., & Campbell, A. (2015). Learning to co-exist with environmental hazards: Community and societal perspectives and strategies. In *Advances in environmental research, Volume 43*. Nova Publishers.

Plotkin, H. (1995). *Darwin machines and the nature of knowledge: Concerning adaptions, instincts and the evolution of intelligence*. Penguin Books.

Posey, D. (1999). *Cultural and spiritual values of biodiversity: United Environment Programme*. Intermediate Technology Publications.

Reber, A. S. (1995). *Dictionary of psychology* (2nd ed.). Penguin Books.

Rowe, S. (1990). *Home place*. New West.

Reason, P. (1995). A participatory world. *Resurgence, 186*, 42–44.

Sexton, T. L. (1997). Constructivist thinking within the history of ideas: The challenge of a new paradigm. In T. L. Sexton & B. L. Griffin (Eds.), *Constructist thinking in counseling practice, research, and training* (pp. 3–18). Teachers College Press.

Sexton, T. L., & Griffin, B. L. (1997). The social and political nature of psychological science: The challenges, potentials, and future of constructivist thinking. In T. L. Sexton & B. L. Griffin (Eds.), *Constructist thinking in counseling practice, research, and training* (pp. 249–262). Teachers College Press.

Smith, J. A. (Ed.) (2015). *Qualitative psychology: A practical guide to research methods*. London, UK: Sage.

Stewart, M. (2012). Understanding learning: theories and critique. In D. Chalmers, & L. Hunt (Eds.), *University teaching in focus: A learning-centred approach* (pp. 3–20). ACER.

Sutton, P. (1989). Enviromental education: What can we teach? *Convergence, 22*(4), 5–12.
Taylor, E. W., & Cranton, P. (2012). *The handbook of transformative learning theory, research, and practice.* Wiley.
Thompson, C. W., Aspinall, P., & Montazino, A. (2008). The childhood factor: Adult visits to green places and the significance of childhood experiences. *Environment and Behavior, 40,* 111–143.
Tyler, J. A., & Swartz, A. L. (2012). Storytelling and transformative learning. In E. W. Taylor & P. Cranton (Eds.), *The handbook of transformative learning theory, research and practice* (pp. 455–470—177). Jossey-Bass.
Willis, P. (2012). An existential approach to transformative learning. In E. W. Taylor & P. Cranton (Ed.), *The handbook of transformative learning: Theory, research, and practice.* Jossey-Bass.
Williams, J. P. (2008). Symbolic interactionism. In Lisa M. Given (Ed.), *The Sage encyclopaedia of qualitative research methods.* Thousand Oaks, CA: Sage.
Wortham, S. (1996). Constructionism, personal construct psychology and narrative psychology: Comment. *Theory & Psychology, 6*(1), 79–84.
Yunkaporta, T. (2019). *Sand talk: How indigenous thinking can safe the world.* Text Publishing.

CHAPTER 7

All Singing from the Same Song Sheet: DRR and the Visual and Performing Arts

Douglas Paton, Petra Buergelt, Etan Pavavalung, Kirby Clark, Li-Ju Jang, and Grace Kuo

INTRODUCTION

Growing recognition of a need to encompass the role social and cultural processes play in the development and implementation of community-based disaster risk reduction (DRR) processes (Kulatunga, 2010; UNISDR, 2015) calls for exploring how this goal might be realized. This chapter explores one possibility; the potential for the performing (song) and visual arts, prominent socio-cultural media for

---

D. Paton (✉)
College of Health and Human Sciences, Charles Darwin University, Darwin, Australia
e-mail: Douglas.Paton@cdu.edu.au

P. Buergelt
Faculty of Health, University of Canberra, Canberra, Australia
e-mail: Petra.Buergelt@canberra.edu.au

E. Pavavalung · G. Kuo
Linali Village, Pingtung, Taiwan

© The Author(s), under exclusive license to Springer Nature Singapore Pte Ltd. 2022
H. James et al. (eds.), *Disaster Risk Reduction in Asia Pacific*, Disaster Risk, Resilience, Reconstruction and Recovery,
https://doi.org/10.1007/978-981-16-4811-3_7

communication and engagement in all countries, to complement existing approaches to DRR. The chapter examines whether song and artworks can represent social-environmental contexts which could be used to facilitate the development of DRR beliefs and actions (e.g., understanding warnings, preparedness, etc.). Finding evidence of a relationship between arts and DRR outcome would afford opportunities to use arts as a medium to support or complement DRR strategies to foster people's understanding of their social–environmental–hazard relationships and facilitate their ability to make informed choices about preparing for and/or responding to environmental challenge and change (Blumer, 1969; Paton et al., 2006; Twigg, 2015).

The exploration of these issues opens with a summary of work that explores whether song lyrics can map onto constructs linked to DRR. Discussion then shifts to offering a perspective on how artworks are being used to facilitate disaster recovery and cultural regeneration.

Song Lyrics and People's Relationship with Environmental Hazards

Music, a common and ancient medium of cultural expression and communication in all countries and cultures (Boer & Fischer, 2012), derives this ubiquity from shared neurological foundations that reflect the evolutionary origins of music (Cross, 2001; Overy & Molnar-Szacks, 2009; Peretz, 2006). A decision to embark on an exploration of whether song could play a role in DRR processes was prompted by evidence that song lyrics represent rich sources of information on people's beliefs, interpretations, motives and actions across a range of areas (Hu et al., 2009). For example, evidence that songs have the potential to inform the development of shared understanding of environmental risk (Lorenzoni et al., 2007; McAlister, 2012; Quarantelli & Davis, 2011; Turner & Freedman, 2004) affords opportunities to use songs to support risk communication

---

K. Clark
University of Tasmania, Launceston, TAS, Australia

L.-J. Jang
National Pingtung University of Science and Technology, Pingtung, Taiwan

activities. Music and song have been implicated in other areas of DRR interest.

For example, evidence exists to support the ability of songs to facilitate people's ability to cope with challenging circumstances and the emotional correlates of such experiences (Juslin & Laukka, 2004; Laukka, 2007; Levitin, 2011; North et al., 2000; Saarikallio & Erkkilä, 2007; Sloboda et al., 2001). This has clear implications for disaster recovery processes. Furthermore, this influence may extend from the psychological to the social domains of recovery. Songs can enable social bonding, the emergence and maintenance of sense of community, place attachment and help people develop social identities linked to their sharing of common experiences (Hallam, 2010; Hudson, 2006; Mattern, 1998; Stokes, 2004; Tekman & Hortaçsu, 2002).

It was lines of evidence such as these that prompted suggesting that music could complement other approaches to developing DRR beliefs and behaviours (Alexander, 2012). The next section begins the processes of answering Alexander's call for more work in this area by summarizing preliminary work into whether song lyrics can act as a medium for progressing DRR goals. The process of assessing whether they might map onto issues of DRR interest commenced with a search for appropriate song lyrics.

Song Lyrics and DRR

Because it provides extensive coverage of the musical genres in which disaster music is most common (Alexander, 2012; Fisher, 2008), Mudcat Café (www.mudcat.org) was the primary source of song lyrics. Using search terms such as *natural disaster, natural hazard, hurricane, flood, tsunami, earthquake, volcanic eruption*, etc.; 656 songs were identified.

These lyrics were then classified by several raters into one of several categories: 1—lyrics which describe an actual disaster; 2—lyrics which depict a hazard or disaster experience, but not a specific event; 3—lyrics which include recurring themes or motifs of disaster, but do not depict any hazard or disaster event/experience; 4—lyrics which use disaster as a metaphor or descriptive device for non-disaster related events and/or experiences; and 5—lyrics which do not relate to any hazard or disaster event/experience. An assessment of inter-rater reliability using Fleiss' Kappa revealed a $K = 0.601$, indicated substantial inter-rater agreement (Landis & Koch, 1977). Based on this classification, only songs whose lyrics fell into categories 1 or 2 were analysed. This resulted in 110 songs being analysed. The next section summarizes the key issues identified.

Lyrical Insights into DRR and Disaster Recovery

This section outlines the kinds of DRR themes present in the song lyrics examined. These cover a broad range of relevant issues, including risk acceptance, warnings, event impact and consequences, response, recovery and resilience. Examples of each are described next and start with lyrical examples of risk acceptance.

Risk Acceptance

> there's gonna be an earthquake in this town, there will be houses falling down, the fire hydrants will blow up, the streets will crack, the pipes will pop.... (The Earthquake Song – The Little Girls)

Warning – Importance of Observing Natural Signs

> when it rains five days and the skies turn dark as night, then trouble's takin' place in the lowlands at night...Backwater blues done call me to pack my things and go. (Backwater Blues – Bessie Smith)

Warning and Importance of Being Prepared (to Respond Rather Than React)

> when the sirens blowing, we gotta get going, watch for the tsunami, everybody running cause the waves stay coming... get your bottled water, gasoline, 100 boxes lean cuisine, toilet paper, four tons of rice.... (Tsunami Song – Frank Delima)

Ignoring Formal Warnings

> the trumpets warned the people,' you'd better leave this place!', but no one thought about leaving town, till death was in their face...Wasn't that

a mighty day, when the storm winds swept the town. (Mighty Day – James Taylor)

Warnings, Being Unprepared, Having to React (Rather Than Being Able to Respond)

years and years of warning, no evacuation plan, it was just if the waters rose, just get out if you can! (New Orleans – David Rovics)

Warning and Fatalism

People all take warning, and don't forget to pray, for you too may meet your maker, before the break of day. (Storm that Struck Miami – Fiddlin' John Carson)
    ... There ain't nothing you can do to stop it, just hope for the best. (Get Down, River – The Bottle Rockers)

Warnings and Lack of Societal Empowerment

It was in the daily papers, in bold letters was the writ, what would happen, when the big one hit, but every year they cut the funding, just a little more...Preparations must be made, they said, now is the time...thousands and thousands of people, abandoned by the state, abandoned by their country, just left to meet their fate. (New Orleans – David Rovics)

Warnings and Emotional Impacts and Panic

twas the grey of early morning, when the dreadful cry of fire rang out upon the cold and piercing air, just that little word alone is all it would require, to spread dismay and panic ev'ry where. (The Milwaukee Fire or the Burning of the Newhall House – J.W. Kelley)

Impact

way out in Mississippi valley, just among those plains so grand, rose the flooded Mississippi river, destroying the words of man, with her waters at the highest that all man has ever known, she came sweeping through the valley and destroying land and homes.... (The Story of the Mighty Mississippi – Kelly Harrell)

Having to React to Challenging Events

We can make it to the road in a home-made boat, that's the only thing we've got left that'll float, it's already over all the wheat and the oats, two feet high and risin. (Five Feet High and Rising – Johnnie Cash)

Lack of Response Resources

... there were no buses, no one charted any trains, there was no plan to rescue, all of those who would remain, all the people with no money, all the people with no wheels. (New Orleans - David Rovics)

Response and Emotional Impacts

... now sparking eyes and laughing lips, oh see the sudden change, the lips grow pale, the eyes in terror stare, as o'er the crowd roars suddenly the flaming avalanche. (The Iroquis on Fire – Zella Evans)

Response and Physical and Emotional Impacts

Blew down my log cabin, there's no shelter for me, food is all exhausted, I'm as weary as can be...Hear the winds a-howling, hear the roaring thunder crash. (Florida Flood Blues – Burke)

Response and the Value of Helping

...when you stretch forth a helping hand, it's a duty nobly done...Give the needy food and gown. (The Burning of Frisco Town – Bob Adam & Theron Bennett)

Response and Fatalism/Anxiety

it fell across our city like a curtain of black rolled down, we thought it was our judgement, we thought it was our doom, the radio reported, we listened with alarm. (Dust Storm Disaster – Woody Gutherie)

Recovery—Search for Meaning

... Some people say, it's what we deserve, for sins against god, for crimes against the world... (On that Day – Leonard Cohen & Anjani Thomas).

Resilience and Positive Outcomes from Experiencing Adversity

Up from the ruins around us, soon we shall rise in our might! Just as the dawn of the morning, follows the darkness of night, so from despair and affliction, may forever we aspire! Onward and upward out motto! Tried, tried but not lost in the fire! (Lost in the Fire – George Cooper & Edwin Christie)

Resilience—Reinterpretation of Consequences

My mama always taught me that good things come from adversity...We couldn't see much good in the flood waters when they were causing us to leave home, but when the water went down, we found that it had washed a load of rich black bottom dirt across our land. The following year we had the best cotton crop we'd ever had. (Five Feet High and Rising – Johnny Cash)

Resilience (and Fatalism)

> California earthquake, you just don't know what you've done...Lord we'll build ourselves another town, you can tear it down again. (California Earthquake – Rodney Crowell)

It is evident that lyrics can capture elements of hazard experience and map onto areas of DRR interest: hazard and disaster experience; circumstances, meanings and implications; importance of warnings and preparedness; and how disasters create both positive and negative outcomes for those affected. This analysis was unable to consider how composers and performers influence how meaning is conveyed. That the latter is a line of inquiry worth pursuing comes from an Honours thesis supervised by two of the authors (Petra Buergelt and Douglas Paton).

Curtin's (2017) Honours thesis discussed how song lyrics can inform understanding of Indigenous Reconciliation in Australia. From Curtin's analysis of the lyrics of 11 songs and commentary from performers from the album *Murundak* by the *Black Arm Band*, a grounded theory model emerged which illustrated how lyrics offered transformative pathways for healing the past and instilling hope for the future through fostering relationships and evoking meaningful understandings of Indigenous histories and cultures. The thesis concluded by offering support for how composers and artists could play transformational leadership roles and support social learning in ways that may foster reconciliation by facilitating the realization of a more unified national identity in Australia (Curtin, 2017). This analysis suggests that it would be important to add exploring how composers and performers influence how song facilitates the development of meaning and action in future research. Before discussing the implications of these observations, this chapter first explores how another artistic medium, the visual arts, can offer insights into disaster recovery, cultural reintegration and environmental understanding.

Visual Arts, DRR and Disaster Recovery

The origins of work on the visual arts stemmed from a visit by one author (Douglas Paton) to the 921 (1999) Earthquake Museum in Taichung, Taiwan. The museum not only acts as a memorial to those who tragically lost their lives in one of the most devastating earthquakes to affect

Taiwan, it also seeks to educate people about earthquake DRR. Regarding the latter, one area of the museum was set aside for exhibiting artworks painted by students from areas affected by the earthquake. One painting captured traditional beliefs about Taiwan's seismic activity.

Traditional Taiwanese beliefs about earthquake causation describe their occurring when a buffalo sleeping below the surface of the earth wakes up and turns over (Fig. 7.1a). One picture depicted its artist praying for the buffalo to remain asleep (Fig. 7.1b), thus depicting the potential for traditional beliefs to influence people's DRR choices. The content draws attention to actions (mitigation based on praying for buffalo to remain asleep) that need not map onto effective DRR thinking (e.g., focusing on prayer to mitigate seismic risk may lessen interest in other DRR options). In this case, artworks can provide insights into ways of thinking that need to be accommodated in DRR in the pursuit of developing more effective mitigation and protective actions. The potential for art to be included as a medium to support DRR and recovery planning, however, was supported by the fact that the 921 Museum used the art exhibits in an attempt to stimulate people's interest in DRR.

Throughout the 921 earthquake exhibition, posters inviting people to "learn from the 921 Earthquake and move forward to rejoice in growing from adversity" sought to encourage people to reflect on the artworks and think about their DRR beliefs and actions. While no attempt was made to assess whether viewing the artworks influenced people's DRR thinking or action, the intent behind the exhibition reinforces the value of exploring the role of visual arts in DRR contexts in future research. That the latter may be a fruitful endeavour is evident from evaluation studies that offer additional insights into the benefits that can accrue from the arts playing central roles in recovery and DRR settings.

For example, following a series of disasters in 2010 and 2011 in Queensland (Australia), Arts Queensland and the Australia Council for the Arts launched the Creative Recovery Pilot Project in Queensland (Arts Queensland, 2012). The project involved a managed approach to working with local communities, artists and arts workers to develop high-quality arts and cultural activities designed to meaningfully integrate the arts into broader community recovery and renewal efforts. In addition to supporting recovery, the evaluation of this initiative also demonstrated how arts and cultural activities could contribute to community capacity building (Arts Queensland, 2012).

Fig. 7.1 A depiction of traditional Taiwanese beliefs regarding the cause of earthquakes (**a**) and a painting of depicting the relationship between traditional beliefs and an activity used to mitigate risk (**b**) (*Source* Douglas Paton)

The evaluation also highlighted both the importance of flexibility to ensure that activities were responsive to community needs and the value of engaging with local government to integrate creative processes more fully into formal disaster recovery planning and process. Arts Queensland argued that the observed benefits warranted the building of an evidence base to gain better understanding into how artists and cultural organizations could engage in disaster preparedness, recovery and rebuilding at local levels. This is not the only example available to support the potential of arts to support DRR and disaster recovery goals.

Following the 2009 Black Saturday bushfires in Victoria, Australia, work undertaken by Arts Victoria (Arts Victoria, 2011) reinforced the potential for the arts to inform disaster recovery processes. The report on this project discussed benefits ranging from using the arts to create memorials inspired by community members collaborating with artists to providing a novel medium for community members to share stories and assist them to impose meaning on lives disrupted by a disaster to enhancing people's psychological and emotional well-being.

Like their Queensland counterparts, Arts Victoria highlighted how arts-based projects could inform community capacity building. The report also called for governments to include arts and Arts bodies in DRR and long-term disaster recovery response planning (Arts Victoria, 2011). In doing so, they also stated that adopting a flexible, community-oriented approach will be essential.

Because no two disasters are alike, and because this is a new area of research and practice, Arts Victoria (2011) argued that it is impossible to develop a single set of "best practice" guidelines for arts-based DRR and recovery work. Rather, a tailored approach is required to map local community needs onto arts-based activities in ways designed to support rebuilding in each community (Arts Victoria, 2011). An example of a tailored community-specific approach is discussed next.

While the next example of applying artworks in community settings describes artworks by an Indigenous artist, the example is not focusing on Indigenous art per se. Rather, the chapter is using this as an example of how emergent artwork afford opportunities for systematically inquiring into how art can be situated in community-based DRR and recovery settings. The implications of the latter also serve to introduce the contributions that Indigenous artists and artworks can make to DRR and recovery research.

Artworks, Tribal Culture, Environment and Disaster Reconstruction

In August 2009, Typhoon Morakot dumped 2854 mm of rain across central and southern Taiwan. The combined impact of rainfall, flooding, landslide, debris flow and mudflow hazards resulted in 699 deaths, the destruction of 1766 houses and some 140,424 households being flooded (Paton et al., 2016). Major impacts occurred in mountain areas, particularly in areas inhabited by several of Taiwan's Indigenous peoples.

The level of damage and residual risk from landslides and earthquakes precluded rebuilding in situ in many villages and townships, at least for some time. This reality stimulated developing a program of resettlement for the inhabitants of many affected, and predominantly mountain, communities in newly constructed villages (in lowland areas rather than traditional highland locations). While providing access to high-quality housing for those displaced, the resettlement process paid no heed to the secondary social, cultural, family, personal and environmental losses that the process of resettling people from traditional homelands to new areas created (Paton et al., 2016). One person affected in this way is one of the authors of this chapter, Etan Pavavalung.

While visiting a community whose members had experienced relocation following Typhoon Morakot, a sudden monsoonal downpour occurred just as one of the authors (Douglas Paton) was passing Etan's art studio in Linali Township (in 2014). Consequently, Paton was invited to take shelter in the studio. It was serendipitous that a researcher interested in disaster recovery should be passing, at that moment, the studio of an artist who was developing an artistic style and artworks with the specific intent of capturing the social, cultural and environmental impact of the typhoon disaster and its implications for social and cultural resettlement.

Etan Pavavalung is a Paiwanese (one of 16 indigenous tribes in Taiwan) artist from the *Tjavaran* tribal village. Paiwanese people have traditionally drawn on the *Tjaivuvu Mountain and River* not only for physical sustenance, but also as sources of inspiration for art and civic life. The extensive damage Morakot caused in Etan's township resulted in its inhabitants being relocated to lowland areas.

Etan's experience of the Morakot disaster and the consequences it created for his family and tribe motivated him to develop an artistic style and artworks to support cultural regeneration. The new art style and artworks were developed to capture and depict *Tjavaran* life stories, legends and philosophy and reimagine them in ways that assist sustaining the socio-environmental beliefs and practices at risk of being lost following resettlement after Morakot.

A New Art Style and Artworks

Paiwanese tribal beliefs and legends encapsulate relationships between people, land, spirituality and the universe. Artistic creations that reflect the interdependence between art, spirituality and reverence for nature have guided activities ranging from environmental protection (e.g., sustainable foresting and hunting) to identifying spiritually significant locations for worship, hunting and farming rituals and ceremonies. In Etan's work, this rich history of the relationship between art and socio-environmental interdependencies inspired his creating a new artistic style and artworks to support tribal disaster recovery and regeneration.

Artworks and Tribal Recovery and Regeneration

The severe impacts Typhoon Morakot created throughout southern Taiwan necessitated many Indigenous tribes being evacuated from their mountain village homes to foothill areas. For Paiwanese peoples, disasters that disrupt the socio-environmental balance pose significant challenges to people and culture. In response, Etan developed a new artistic style, "trace-layer-carve-paint", which embodies his native language, "vecik", (which translates as "writing") and which captures Paiwanese people's relationship with Mother Nature. This art style was specifically developed to emulate several social, built and natural environmental elements important to Paiwanese people and to express them in a manner intended to support the re-establishment of Paiwanese cultural identity following resettlement into locations where these environmental elements were limited or absent.

In *vecik*, the "trace" component includes patterns, text and lines that represent those found in land, forests and all living things. The meaning in these elements is deepened by "carving" lines and patterns into the wooden (rather than canvas) base of the artworks. The "layer" element emulates the characteristic layering effect seen in traditional slate houses and terraces, and "paint" mirrors the different colours that appear in nature of the four seasons. Hence, the "trace-layer-carve-paint" techniques symbolizes key elements in the built and natural environments

Fig. 7.2 The wind on the slope is very fragrant (*Source* Etan Pavavalung, 2014)

from which Paiwanese peoples traditionally draw cultural strength and power. This style is thus intended to offer Paiwanese people a medium through which they can reflect on their socio-environmental heritage and its capacity to act as a source of the spiritual strength and resilience required to confront challenges arising from having to adapt to the loss of spiritual homeland and learning to live in an alien (lowland, industrial, polluted) environment in harmonious ways.

The artwork in Fig. 7.2, "The Wind on the Slope is very Fragrant", uses "trace" and "carving" (which create a 3D flowing effect not visible in photographs) to symbolize how the air and wind in the home village move through pristine mountain environments. This imagery is intended to help tribal members recall the mountain environments that play fundamental roles in their spiritual life and livelihood.

Another example of this style, "Labored Breathing in another Foothill" (Fig. 7.3) draws on symbols envisioned to capture Paiwanese characteristics of self-reliance, perseverance and responsibility. Providing opportunities for people to reflect on these works is intended to facilitate their thriving as they endeavour to reconstruct traditional social and cultural life in their new villages following relocation after Morakot.

An important Paiwanese symbol in this context is the Taiwan lily, a cultural totem with significant roles in both Indigenous arts and in people's daily life. In addition to it representing a significant source of spirituality for Paiwanese people, it also symbolizes men's courage and capacity. As a cultural totem, the use of the lily in these artworks (Figs. 7.2 and 7.3) is intended to assist people to find hope in challenging circumstances, symbolize the emergence of new life following disaster and to increase the likelihood that cultural and spiritual reconstruction complement physical rebuilding (e.g., building houses and roads) efforts. The use of this symbolism also seeks to encourage people to reflect on the importance of re-creating harmonious relationships between people and

7 ALL SINGING FROM THE SAME SONG SHEET: DRR ...   137

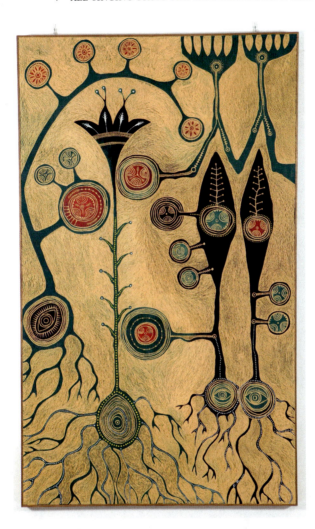

Fig. 7.3 Labored breathing at another foothill (*Source* Etan Pavavalung, 2013)

nature and building on this to develop their DRR processes. The relationship between artistic style and content in these works thus illustrates an example of the development of a local community-based approach to using art to facilitate adaptive responses to the consequences of a disaster.

The above discussion provided illustrations of how the visual arts have the potential to sustain or rekindle people's appreciation of traditional socio-environmental relationships and to remind them of the strengths and relationships they can call upon to support their resilience. It is the fact that the works were specifically developed with such goals in mind that illustrate how art can be linked to DRR and disaster recovery processes and outcomes. It is proposed that this affords communication and community engagement opportunities for developing and/or complementing existing approaches to community-based DRR and recovery and rebuilding planning and intervention. To realize any potential the *arts* have as a medium for community-based DRR, several issues need further consideration. These and their implications are discussed next.

Conclusions and Future Directions

The analysis of song lyrics provides insights into their capacity to encompass topics of DRR interest. Lyrics covered the negative (e.g., ignoring warnings, blame, panic, fear and fatalism) elements of people's beliefs, behaviours and experiences which DRR seeks to reduce. Lyrics also encompassed the positive processes and outcomes (preparedness, resilience and adaptation) which DRR strategies seek to engender. Composers and performers add another level of capability (Curtin, 2017), with their possibly playing roles in creating meaning around challenging events and experiences and playing transformative leadership roles in social change processes.

From a research perspective, these characteristics make song lyrics a potentially valuable source of information about people's experience of hazard events, their consequences and implications and the lessons they can learn from (others) experience. However, while constituting a source of research data, it cannot be assumed that song lyrics contribute to changing beliefs and behaviours, whether positively or negatively. There is much to be done before songs can be considered to represent a medium that can support the development and implementation of community-based DRR strategies. There are, however, several reasons for investing in this line of inquiry.

A significant reason for researching how song lyrics influence DRR derives from the fact that songs represent a medium towards which people gravitate and engage with naturally and frequently. This increases the potential for songs to reach diverse populations in voluntary and meaningful ways, increasing the potential for songs to influence people's thinking and to motivate actions encompassed in the lyrics (Glik, 2007; Marx et al., 2007). If, however, songs are to realize their DRR potential, several additional issues require consideration.

The songs analysed above represent several genres and covered different time periods. This kind of diversity raises questions regarding how and why people engage with "disaster" songs. While songs are listened to voluntarily, people differ regarding their genre and stylistic preferences, and no one genre will have universal appeal. The latter takes on additional significance when considering cross-cultural issues; musical styles, genre and melody vary considerably from country to country. Future work could explore how factors such as genre and artist influence popularity and whether and how this translates into changes in beliefs and actions (over both the short and longer term). Another issue concerns how to engage people if using song as part of a community engagement strategy.

Using song in DRR contexts could take advantage of the fact that song represents a medium that lends itself to active community engagement (Quarantelli & Davis, 2011). For example, social media could be used to direct people to links to, for instance, YouTube repositories of different songs that reinforce key elements of DRR messages (e.g., regarding warnings, preparedness, learning from events, etc.) depicted in song lyrics (see above). In this way, DRR strategies could be developed by referring people to a range of songs and in ways that allow people to select those they relate to most. This increases personal discretion regarding the songs accessed and assists the process of tailoring DRR to local and personal needs.

Another possibility is encouraging public and community involvement in composing and performing songs to support the attainment of DRR and recovery goals. Community singing has been linked to restoring spirits and encouraging perseverance (Walsh, 2007) and with developing informational, emotional and belongingness social support in recovery settings (Juslin & Laukka, 2004; Laukka, 2007; Levitin, 2011; North et al., 2000; Saarikallio & Erkkilä, 2007; Sloboda et al., 2001). Pursuing these ideas is supported by the potential for song to facilitate relational community engagement processes and places the arts in a position where they can function to complementing other community-based DRR activities.

The work covered in this chapter focused solely on lyrics. A comprehensive analysis would require attention being directed to examining other characteristics. Research thus needs to explore how characteristics such as genre, melody, tempo, mode and percussiveness contribute to meaningfulness and behaviour change (North et al., 2004).

Future research could include interviewing song writers to explore, for example, their motivation for writing lyrics and music (e.g., about the event, the people involved, the relationships, the outcomes and their perceived causes, intended audience and goals, etc.). Further research would need to explore the influence of individual and socio-cultural diversity (e.g., do all songs elicit the same response, the role the context and performer play in influencing attentiveness and outcomes, etc.) on the effectiveness of songs in DRR strategies.

It will be important to extend research into cross-cultural and cultural explorations of the relationship between music and visual arts in DRR outcomes. Regarding the role of song in this context, accommodating ethnomusicology viewpoints in future work (Harrison, 2012) would be a valuable addition to the research agenda. In addition to its coverage of lyrics, this chapter also explored links between DRR and visual artworks.

The visual arts present a more challenging research proposition than its performing arts (song) counterpart. The fact that songs can be broadcast to reach large numbers of people, are readily accessible to anybody from anywhere through several media, and include lyrics that clearly depict the kinds of event, object, action, relationship, etc., targets of interest in DRR work makes it an adaptable medium to use. In contrast, artworks do not generally enjoy comparable levels of accessibility. This does not, however, preclude their being included in future DRR and recovery research.

Anecdotal accounts of the inclusion of the art exhibition at the 921 Earthquake Museum in Taiwan and the work undertaken by Arts Queensland, Arts Victoria and by Etan Pavavalung in Taiwan illustrate how art is being used with the intent of supporting disaster recovery and cultural regeneration. The evaluation component of the Queensland and Victorian cases (see above) also furnished evidence for the role that both artist involvement and artwork creation could play in supporting not only disaster recovery and rebuilding, but also in facilitating future community capacity building. A need for such endeavours to be community specific was also emphasized (the origins and nature of Etan Pavavalung's artworks). Before discussing the implications of the latter, it is pertinent to consider how the above finding of positive outcomes from engaging in artistic activities does not automatically permit concluding that it was the artistic elements per se that were responsible for the observed outcomes. Other processes may be involved.

For example, the community-based nature of these endeavours meant that art-based activities brought people together to work on creative activities. This created a meaningful context in which social support from people who shared a challenging experience was available to participants. Engaging in artistic processes about challenging events can be emotionally cathartic. Furthermore, the development and application of new skills can develop self-efficacy (and collective efficacy if undertaken collectively).

Since emotional disclosure, social support, community participation, self- and collective efficacy have all been implicated in the development of DRR capabilities and recovery (e.g., Paton, 2013; Paton et al., 2014), it will be important to tease out the respective contributions of these competencies and those from art-related processes and works per se to the observed outcomes (or identify how they play interdependent roles in DRR and recovery). To pursue this approach, it is necessary to develop research questions that focus on articulating the specific influence of artworks on DRR and recovery outcomes. The fact that the Arts Queensland and Arts Victoria projects were event and community specific affords opportunities for exploring the relative contributions of artistic, social and competence elements to the outcomes observed. Another approach to exploring this can be gleaned from Etan Pavavalung's work.

The works of Etan Pavavalung discussed above were created in response to a specific event (Typhoon Morakot) and its consequences and with the goal of affording opportunities for community members displaced and relocated after Morakot to reflect on the artworks in ways intended to sustain social, cultural and environmental knowledges. Consequently, these artworks afford opportunities to test whether the imagery used in artworks can facilitate novel ways of socially constructing natural hazard risk and DRR processes.

For example, and hypothetically, it would be possible to explore whether Pavavalung's artworks did help "re-create harmonious relationships between people and nature" (the objective behind the development of vecik) in those displaces and whether and how people's engagement with artworks portraying the Taiwan Lily facilitated resilient responses and capacities to confront the novel and challenging circumstances created by the Typhoon and subsequent relocation. If, however, such hypotheses are to be tested, several issues require attention.

One concerns assessing how and to what extent traditional knowledges and beliefs were lost in order to provide a baseline to examine how artworks support cultural reconnection and knowledge acquisition and use. One approach that could be used here is to focus on youth and young adults. Anecdotal accounts from community members point to this population being most at risk of experiencing cultural disconnection.

Another issue involves assessing how people engage with artworks and how this facilitates cultural reconnection and knowledge acquisition. This could include, for example, dedicated exhibitions in the relocation villages, running narrated workshops around artworks and developing DRR thinking and actions in schools and community centres, and disseminating workbooks around art and DRR to school and community groups. While Pavavalung's work was introduced to illustrate how arts could be developed as a form of community-based disaster recovery and DRR activities, it is also necessary to consider the Indigenous origins of the imagery in the works prior to considering the wider applicability of the approach discussed above.

For example, although the stylistic and content development of Pavavalung's work derived from a specific event (Morakot), the imagery used was inspired by pre-existing cultural totems and imagery. This means that the ideas could be adapted in cultural settings where comparable cultural icons and totems exist, it may be less readily applicable and testable in populations where such culturally embedded imagery is absent. The latter is more likely in western populations. Consequently, more thought needs to be directed to how research questions could be developed and tested in non-Indigenous peoples (and particularly in western settings). Notwithstanding, the findings from the Queensland and Victorian studies suggest that investing in researching how and in what ways arts and art organizations can inform the development of comprehensive DRR and recovery strategies is worthwhile.

At the same time, the cultural specificity of Pavavalung's work opens opportunities for exploring the socio-environmental and DRR implications of Indigenous peoples visual and performance arts. Evidence for doing so is available elsewhere.

For example, King et al. (2007) discuss the rich environmental hazard imagery captured over centuries in Māori art in New Zealand. There thus exists evidence to suggest that developing roles for the arts in DRR and recovery/rebuilding settings will be a worthwhile endeavour. The cultural ubiquity of the arts increases the potential cross-cultural applicability of this approach. Work (being led by one author, Petra Buergelt) is currently being undertaken to explore links between art and capacity building in Indigenous peoples in Australia (Munipi) and Taiwan (Paiwanese (EP, GK) and Rukai). This project will provide further insights into how art informs DRR and cultural reintegration in Indigenous peoples and how the arts might be used to support DRR strategies. The next stage is to extend the thinking espoused in the Arts Queensland and Arts Victoria studies in Australia into researching arts and DRR relationships in western populations.

The systematic evaluation of the relationship between arts and DRR outcomes must be afforded a prominent place in future research. This will provide needed insights into how the effectiveness of arts-based activities compare to other risk communication strategies; whether it can be used effectively on its own, or if it should be used to complement other approaches.

References

Alexander, B. (2012). Hazards and disasters represented in music. In B. Wisner, J. Gaillard, & I. Kelman (Eds.), *The Routledge handbook of hazards and disaster risk reduction* (pp. 131–142). Routledge.

Arts Queensland. (2012). *Evaluation of creative recovery pilot project*. Department of Science, Technology, Innovation and the Arts.

Arts Victoria. (2011). *An evaluation of arts Victoria's and regional arts Victoria's bushfire initiatives*. Arts Victoria.

Boer, D., & Fischer, R. (2012). Towards a holistic model of functions of music listening across cultures: A culturally decentred qualitative approach. *Psychology of Music, 40*, 179–200.

Blumer, H. (1969). *Symbolic interactionism: Perspective and method*. Prentice-Hall.

Cross, I. (2001). Music, mind and evolution. *Psychology of Music, 29*, 95–102.

Curtin, N. (2017). *Singing for freedom: Australian Indigenous and non-indigenous artists and popular songs offering transformative pathways for healing the past and instilling hope for reconciliation in the future in Australia*. Unpublished Bachelor of Psychology Honours Thesis. Charles Darwin University.

Fisher, J. (2008). Sound recording reviews: People take warning! Murder ballads & disaster songs, 1913–1938. *Association for Recorded Sound Collections Journal, 39*, 149–151.

Glik, D. C. (2007). Risk communication for public health emergencies. *Annual Review of Public Health, 28*, 33–54.

Hallam, S. (2010). The power of music: Its impact on the intellectual, social and personal development of children and young people. *International Journal of Music Education, 28*, 269–289.

Harrison, K. (2012). Epistemologies of applied ethnomusicology. *Ethnomusicology, 56*, 505–529.

Hu, X., Downie, J., & Ehmann, A. (2009). Lyric text mining in music mood classification. Paper presented at the 10th International Society for Music Information Retrieval Conference. Retrieved from http://users.cis.fiu.edu/~lli003/Music/cla/34.pdf

Hudson, R. (2006). Regions and place: Music, identity and place. *Progress in Human Geography, 30*, 626–634.

Juslin, P. N., & Laukka, P. (2004). Expression, perception, and induction of musical emotions: A review and a questionnaire study of everyday listening. *Journal of New Music Research, 33*, 217–238.

King, D. N. T., Goff, J., & Skipper, A. (2007). Māori environmental knowledge and natural hazards in Aotearoa-New Zealand. *Journal of the Royal Society of New Zealand, 37*(2), 59–73. https://doi.org/10.1080/03014220709510536

Kulatunga, U. (2010). Impact of culture towards disaster risk reduction. *International Journal of Strategic Property Management, 14s*, 304–313.

Landis, J. R., & Koch, G. G. (1977). An application of hierarchical Kappa-type statistics in the assessment of majority agreement among multiple observers. *Biometrics, 33*(2), 363–374. https://doi.org/10.2307/2529786

Laukka, P. (2007). Uses of music and psychological well-being among the elderly. *Journal of Happiness Studies, 8*, 215–241.

Levitin, D. J. (2011). *This is your brain on music: Understanding a human obsession*. Atlantic books.

Lorenzoni, I., Nicholson-Cole, S., & Whitmarsh, L. (2007). Barriers perceived to engaging with climate change among the UK public and their policy implications. *Global Environmental Change, 17*, 445–459.

Marx, S. M., Weber, E. U., Orlove, B. S., Leiserowitz, A., Krantz, D. H., Roncoli, C., & Phillips, J. (2007). Communication and mental processes: Experiential and analytic processing of uncertain climate information. *Global Environmental Change, 17*, 47–58.

Mattern, M. (1998). *Acting in concert: Music, community and political action*. Rutgers University Press.

McAlister, E. (2012). Soundscapes of disaster and humanitarianism: Survival singing, relief telethons, and the Haiti earthquake. *Small Axe, 16*, 22–38.

North, A. C., Hargreaves, D. J., & Hargreaves, J. J. (2004). The uses of music in everyday life. *Music Perception, 22*, 41–77.

North, A. C., Hargreaves, D. J., & O'Neill, S. A. (2000). The importance of music to adolescents. *British Journal of Educational Psychology, 70*, 255–272.

Overy, K., & Molnar-Szakacs, I. (2009). Being together in time: Musical experience and the mirror neuron system. *Music Perception: An Interdisciplinary Journal, 26,* 489–504.

Paton, D. (2013). Disaster resilient communities: Developing and testing an all-hazards theory. *Journal of Integrated Disaster Risk Management, 3,* 1–17.

Paton, D., Jang, L.-J., & Liu, L.-W. (2016). Long term community recovery: Lessons from earthquake and typhoon experiences in Taiwan. In H. James & D. Paton (Eds.), *The consequences of Asian disasters: Demographic, planning and policy implications.* Charles C. Thomas.

Paton, D., Johnston, D., Mamula-Seadon, L. & Kenney, C. M. (2014). Recovery and development: Perspectives from New Zealand and Australia. In N. Kapucu & K. T. Liou (Eds.), *Disaster & development: Examining global issues and cases,* (pp. 255–272). New York, NY: Springer.

Paton, D., McClure, J., & Buergelt, P. T. (2006). Natural hazard resilience: The role of individual and household preparedness. In D. Paton & D. Johnston (Eds.), *Disaster resilience: An integrated approach.* Charles C. Thomas.

Peretz, I. (2006). The nature of music from a biological perspective. *Cognition, 100,* 1–32.

Quarantelli, E., & Davis, I. (2011). *An exploratory research agenda for studying the popular culture of disasters (PCD): Its characteristics, conditions, and consequences.* Disaster Research Center.

Saarikallio, S., & Erkkilä, J. (2007). The role of music in adolescents' mood regulation. *Psychology of Music, 35,* 88–109.

Sloboda, J. A., O'Neill, S. A., & Ivaldi, A. (2001). Functions of music in everyday life: An exploratory study using the experience sampling methodology. *Musicae Scientiae, 5,* 9–32.

Stokes, M. (2004). Music and the global order. *Annual Review of Anthropology, 33,* 47–72.

Tekman, H. G., & Hortaçsu, N. (2002). Music and social identity: Stylistic identification as a response to musical style. *International Journal of Psychology, 37,* 277–285.

Turner, K., & Freedman, B. (2004). Music and environmental studies. *The Journal of Environmental Education, 36,* 45–52.

Twigg, J. (2015). *Disaster risk reduction.* Overseas Development Institute.

UNISDR. (2015). Sendai framework for disaster risk reduction 2015–230. Retrieved from http://www.unisdr.org/files/43291_sendaiframeworkfordrren.pdf

Walsh, F. (2007). Traumatic loss and major disasters: Strengthening family and community resilience. *Family Process, 46,* 207–227.

CHAPTER 8

High Expectations, Low Recognition: The Role of Principals and Teachers in Disaster Response and Recovery in the Asia–Pacific

Carol Mutch

INTRODUCTION

In 2010/2011, the author was caught up in the devastating sequence of earthquakes in her hometown of Christchurch, Canterbury, New Zealand. The earthquakes themselves have been well-documented (see, for example, Aydan et al., 2012; Bannister & Gledhill, 2012; Canterbury, Earthquakes Royal Commission, 2012; Education Review Office, 2013; Potter et al., 2015; Thornley et al., 2013). Although the damage amounted to over 40 billion dollars, this disaster was only one of many to hit the Asia–Pacific region in the last decade (see, for example, Ferris & Petz, 2012; Ferris et al., 2013). What these disasters have in common, apart from their general location in the Asia–Pacific, is that

C. Mutch (✉)
Faculty of Education and Social Work, The University of Auckland, Auckland, New Zealand
e-mail: c.mutch@auckland.ac.nz

© The Author(s), under exclusive license to Springer Nature Singapore Pte Ltd. 2022
H. James et al. (eds.), *Disaster Risk Reduction in Asia Pacific*, Disaster Risk, Resilience, Reconstruction and Recovery,
https://doi.org/10.1007/978-981-16-4811-3_8

they hold some of the common misconceptions about disasters up to scrutiny. The 2010/2011 Canterbury earthquakes and the 2011 Japanese triple disaster were discussed in the report, *The year that shook the rich* (Ferris & Petz, 2012), highlighting that disasters do not just impact underdeveloped countries with limited economic and political stability but also wealthy, well-resourced nations with strong infrastructure. As the report states, "high-impact low-probability events can overwhelm the best prepared society" (Ferris & Petz, 2012, p. xi). Scientists and researchers predict that the effects of climate change will increase the frequency of unexpected and major events from extreme weather events, sea level rise and environmental degradation (Back et al., 2009; Dixon, 2017; Pittock, 2017; UNISDR, 2009, 2015). The 2012 Brookings Institute report (Ferris & Petz, 2012) concludes that we need to be prepared for a "new-normal" where a "once-in-a-century" disaster becomes a "once-in-a-generation" and new greater "once-in-a-century" disasters will overwhelm our current state of readiness and understanding (p. xii). It is no surprise, therefore, that the current focus for global disaster agencies is on improving disaster preparedness in order to lessen the catastrophic effects of these new mega-disasters (Ferris & Petz, 2012; Global Alliance for Disaster Risk Reduction and Resilience in the Education Sector [GADRRRES], 2017; Ranghieri & Ishiwatari, 2014; UNISDR, 2009, 2015). This chapter argues that, as part of disaster planning and preparedness, it is important to revisit aspects of prior disaster response and recovery efforts that worked effectively and to build these into future considerations (UNISDR, 2015). While this chapter cannot cover all the events of the last decade in the Asia–Pacific, it focuses on the author's research across five different countries and three different disaster types in order to highlight an under-researched and mostly unacknowledged force in positive disaster response and recovery—the local school.

After beginning a project in 2012 to document the stories of schools in post-earthquake Christchurch, I found myself invited to share the findings and conduct research into post-disaster stories in other schools in the region, namely, post-tsunami schools in Samoa, post-earthquake and tsunami schools in Japan, post-cyclone schools in Vanuatu and post-earthquake schools in Nepal. In this article, I share a qualitative comparative cross-case study of fifteen schools across the five settings—two developed countries and three developing countries—and then argue that the roles played by schools in disaster events are worthy of stronger consideration. First, I briefly synthesise some of the key literature relating to schools and disaster events. Next, I discuss the theoretical and methodological frameworks underpinning my research across the five settings. The findings are presented as three cross-country themes drawn from the analysis. In the discussion section, I argue that while there are high expectations for the roles that schools will, and do, play, schools are not well-supported to prepare for, or undertake, these roles. And, when their post-disaster roles are successfully concluded, the role of schools in disaster response and recovery is largely unacknowledged.

LITERATURE REVIEW

Disasters are described as the consequences of events triggered by natural hazards or human interventions that overwhelm the ability of local response services to manage or contain the impacts. Disasters are large-scale events, which seriously affect the physical, social and economic structure of the region. They are characterised by suddenness or lack of preparedness, unexpectedness of the size of the event and ensuing damage, and the inability of existing systems to cope. There is often large-scale death or dislocation, and a lack of immediate access to food, water, shelter and medical aid (Back et al., 2009; Ferris & Petz, 2012; Mutch, 2014a; Smawfield, 2013; Tatebe & Mutch, 2015; Winkworth, 2007).

Disaster agencies and scholars characterise the pre- and post-disaster phases as circular rather than linear. Thus, managing the eventuality and actuality of a disaster is ongoing and iterative. In this way, each phase impacts upon the one that follows, with the expectation that any learning that comes about from each phase will better prepare those facing the next iteration of a disaster event cycle. The regular occurrence of disasters over time has led to better understanding of risk and vulnerability and, therefore, the first phase relates to risk assessment, mitigation, prevention and preparedness. With warning of an imminent disaster event occurring (where the type of disaster allows for this possibility), early alert systems can set preparedness procedures, such as evacuations, in place, and response and recovery agencies can mobilise. Once the disaster has hit, response occurs at a variety of levels from individual and community to local, national and international organisations and agencies. The locality and severity of the disaster affect the response efforts and timelines, but response and recovery activities soon begin to overlap. The recovery phase is long and arduous and can be affected by subsequent events that hinder progress, such as further physical damage, social or political turbulence or outbreaks of disease. Eventually, reconstruction and rehabilitation begin and the people of the region adapt their new existence. The physical, emotional, psychological, social and economic implications linger for much longer (Dixon, 2017; Drabek, 1986; Gordon, 2004; Mooney et al., 2011; Smawfield, 2013; Tatebe & Mutch, 2015; UNISDR, 2007, 2015; Winkworth, 2007).

An examination of the relevant literature demonstrates that schools figure in all phases of the disaster process (Tatebe & Mutch, 2015). As schools are places of education, they include disaster-related content in their curricula and undertake evacuation drills (Mitchell et al., 2013; Tatebe & Mutch, 2015; UNISDR, 2007; Wisner, 2006). They play a part in community and family awareness of hazard awareness and disaster mitigation, such as community meetings, drills and mock evacuations (Mitchell et al., 2013; Tatebe & Mutch, 2015; UNISDR, 2007, 2009, 2015; Wisner, 2006). Schools also contribute to building community cohesion and connectedness which, in turn, enhances community resilience in times of disaster. Many schools bring communities together for social, cultural, sporting and educational activities and communities feel an affinity with the location and personnel (Callaghan & Colton, 2008; Direen, 2016; Duncan, 2016; Education Review Office, 2013; Mutch, 2014b, 2016, 2018a). Schools have both the physical facilities and, depending on the circumstances, the personnel to respond quickly to an emergency (Mutch, 2014a, 2014b, 2016; Smawfield, 2013; Winkworth, 2007). Should a disaster event ensue, schools are well placed to play a wide range of roles as immediate response and relief sites, communication centres, supply depots and support agency hubs (Direen, 2016; Mutch, 2014b, 2016, 2018a). As places of pastoral care, they have staff, or can access appropriate personnel, with the skills and knowledge to attend to the complex social, emotional and psychological needs of children, young people and their families in post-disaster contexts (Gibbs et al., 2013; Johnson & Ronan, 2014; Lazarus et al., 2003; Mutch & Gawith, 2014; O'Connor, 2013; O'Connor & Takahashi, 2014).

Table 8.1 is reproduced from an earlier publication (Mutch, 2014a) in which a comprehensive literature review analysed over 50 international sources relating to schools and disasters. It synthesises the role of schools in disaster preparedness, response and recovery at three levels: (a) supporting their wider community: (b) activities within the school itself; and (c) looking after the physical safety and social, emotional and psychological needs of the children and young people in their care.

Table 8.1 The role of schools in disaster preparedness, response and recovery

	Preparedness	Response	Recovery
Community	Schools as part of the disaster planning and preparedness process	Schools as relief centres and community response and communication hubs	Schools as community drop- in and rebonding centres
Schools	Schools as sites and facilitators of preparedness learning and activities	Schools as first responders or post-event response centres	Schools as pastoral care and agency hubs for staff, students and families
Children and young people	Schools as sites of integrated disaster learning inside and outside the curriculum	Schools as first responders and places of calm and security	Schools as screeners of severe responses and facilitators of appropriate recovery activities

Source Mutch (2014a, p. 19)

In conclusion, schools play a significant part, depending on the size and nature of the disaster, in response and recovery efforts. The role of schools as the "glue" that holds a community together through these phases is a strong feature of the literature (Direen, 2016; Duncan, 2016; Education Review Office, 2013; McDonald, 2014; Mutch, 2014a, 2014b; O'Connor & Takahashi, 2014; Shirlaw, 2014; Smawfield, 2013; Winkworth, 2007). In this chapter the focus is on the multiple roles played by principals and teachers immediately after the disaster, and over the short- and long-term recovery processes, such as housing, feeding or providing psychosocial support for their communities as they came to terms with the enormity of the event.

THEORY AND METHODS

The theoretical approach to this study was grounded in the notion that our experiences are viewed through social, historical and cultural lenses (Burr, 2015). Rather than seeking to establish the facts, this approach focuses on how the participants construct narratives of their lived experiences (Denzin & Lincoln, 2011) and how they make sense of the events in order to absorb them into their own personal histories (Gibbs et al., 2013). Storying disaster experiences has proved to be beneficial to the emotional and psychological recovery of disaster survivors (Appleton,

2001; Bonanno et al., 2010; Cahill et al., 2010; Gibbs et al., 2013; Mutch, 2013a; Peek et al., 2016; Salloum & Overstreet, 2012). To this end, the researcher used a range of qualitative and open-ended methods to allow participants to express their feelings and construct their narratives. With children, arts-based methods, storytelling and video-making were used (see, Mutch, 2013a). The focus in this chapter, however, is on the stories of the adults involved, primarily principals and teachers (for further information on how and why these participants were selected, see Mutch, 2018c). With adults, the main data gathering method used was semi-structured interviews. Because of the post-disaster context, it was important to build a relationship of trust before data gathering could begin. This meant prior visits to the locations to meet and share the purpose of the research and ensure all participants understood that participation was voluntary and that they could stop, take a break or withdraw if the interviews caused distress (see, for example, Mutch et al., 2015). It was also important to conduct the interviews in culturally appropriate ways, which might include beginning with a prayer, sharing food or exchanging gifts. The interviews were mostly conducted in English but, in Japan and Nepal, local interpreters helped as necessary. The interviews were transcribed and a constant comparative analysis method was used to code, categorise and collate themes from the data (Mutch, 2013b). Each interview was analysed independently for its own themes, before themes were analysed horizontally across participant type (e.g., principal, teacher or parent) within country and across country (Mutch, 2018b).

Overall, I conducted interviews with 40 adults and 90 children (see Table 8.2) from fifteen schools in the five countries, in some cases on more than one visit. Table 8.2 summarises the disaster settings and numbers and types of participants. This range of participants and settings provides an insight into similarities of principals' and teachers' responses despite their social, cultural, political or socio-economic differences.

FINDINGS

There are many common themes that arise from the analysis but those selected for this article elaborate on the roles of principals and teachers. The findings are presented in three sections: (a) immediate response and aftermath; (b) returning to school; and (c) longer term repercussions.

Table 8.2 Participants, settings and disaster types across the study

Setting	New Zealand (NZ)	Japan (J)	Samoa (S)	Vanuatu (V)	Nepal (N)
Disaster	2010/2011 Canterbury earthquakes	2011 Tohoku earthquake and tsunami	2009 earthquake and tsunami	2015 Cyclone Pam	2015 Gorkha earthquake
Participants	Five schools from five different locations; five principals, 12 teachers; ten parents and 72 children	Four schools from two different locations; one principal, four teachers; one parent	Two schools from two different locations; two principals; one teacher; one art educator	Two schools from two different locations; two principals; one deputy principal; one teacher	Two schools, two different locations; two principals; 18 children

Immediate Response and Aftermath

In New Zealand, Samoa and Japan, the disasters hit while school was in session. If students were in danger, principals' and teachers' thoughts were immediately on how to rescue or assist them. In Japan, the principal talked of schools telling children to run for their lives and not look back. In Samoa, one principal was on her way to school when she saw the tsunami:

> The earthquake hit just after 7 in the morning. I was walking to school. I was about halfway there when I felt it. I started to run so I could get to school before anything happened. At the gate I saw the wave. Many children were already in the classrooms with their teachers. They saw me and started running towards me. I tried to signal for them to go the other way. I turned away from the school and started running up the hill and they started to follow me. Some were screaming. Some were crying. The tsunami caught the latecomers. It was very sad. We sat under a shaded tree and said a prayer. (Principal, School S1)

One New Zealand teacher describes being at a water sports complex with 100 children:

My thoughts then were never, "We aren't going to get out" or that it would collapse, but my thoughts now when I look back is that the whole place could have fallen in. We were so jolted that we stood up, then we were jolted back down the force was so great. There was a group of children in the boat, and all we could see was the whole thing swamped with the big waves, and we couldn't even get to them. We tried to stand and go forward, but we were just knocked back…the lights went out, and the children were screaming. All I remember is the siren noise, and I went and grabbed a few of the Year 4 children out of the pool, and I just huddled with them. (Teacher, School NZ5)

Regardless of how frightened they were themselves, teachers and principals had to put on a brave face, *"I was guiding them back out, and I remember glass being on the carpet in the foyer, and we all had bare feet. I calmly told the children to watch out, and I walked them out"* (Teacher, School NZ5).

One Japanese teacher was taking his students for basketball when the earthquake hit, *"I was in the gym and I was worried about the lights falling down so I led the students to a safe place and was trying to calm them down"* (School, J3).

Another New Zealand principal describes how she felt when parents were coming to get their children:

I put on my principal's smile. Parents arrived and were standing outside. I realized then that I had an audience and my response needed to be calm and instantaneous. I had to look like I was in control. (Principal, School NZ1)

When the shaking stopped after the Japanese 2011 earthquake, teachers checked and tidied up the buildings:

The leader of the teachers said to check the school. Each teacher had to go to each floor and check if there were still any students inside. If we found students they had to go to the school grounds. (Teacher, School J2)

Principals and teachers were also worried about their own families: *"I was worried about the students but I couldn't stop thinking about my family"* (Teacher, School J2).

I was getting texts from my daughter who is a nurse and she was trapped in the hospital. My grandson was trapped at school and my schoolteacher husband couldn't leave either. I couldn't think of my family at the time and just had to assume they would be okay. (Principal, School NZ1)

In many cases the drills practised beforehand were put to good use:

The school was phenomenal. The children streamed out of the classrooms and down onto the field. The teachers were incredible. It was very prompt and very calm. (Parent, School NZ1)
During the training for earthquakes, students practiced to escape and the parents came to the school to take them home. The training for the tsunami was getting them to move to the shrine and if parents come, students can go with their parents. (Principal, School J1)

One principal commends the way her leadership team put their training into practice:

On the day, the leadership team kicked in and they were making sure the right thing happened. The training and up-skilling really worked for the school. They worked calmly and there was no personal heroism. (Principal, NZ1)

Principals and teachers often had to wait until all the children were collected. One Samoan principal said it was more than four hours before a friend or relative came to get all the children. In New Zealand, some parents were unable to collect their children, so the unclaimed children were taken to the local *marae* (cultural centre) to be cared for. A teacher describes her experience:

We had to wait until all the parents had picked up the children. I had one girl in my class whose mum didn't come for a very long time. As time went on, she got a little bit more worried, but I assured the kids that their parents were on their way and that there would be road blockages. When the mother arrived, she was in a real state... in tears and red-faced, and she was like, "The Cathedral's gone, there are people dead in the streets...." That was like the moment of reality. (Teacher, School NZ1)

When children were collected, teachers returned to their homes, if they could, to find out the extent of the damage:

In February our house broke in three places. We had water coming in with the rain, which was great with three young children. We had liquefaction to knee deep right through the backyard again, but luckily not through the house... It was horrendous. (Teacher, School NZ1)

In those settings where the disaster happened outside school hours, principals' and teachers' thoughts went to children and their families:

After the earthquake, I came to realise that most of the students in the affected area lost everything. Their houses were collapsed. They lost their books and their uniforms, some even lost their parents. I asked my Rotary friends in Australia to raise some funds to help the victimised families. (Principal, School N1)

Across the five settings, many teachers and principals were often also victims:

Our roof lifted off and there was water everywhere. The shutters below off and the glass in the windows broke. In the daylight, I could see how bad the damage was. Every neighbour had their roof blown off and water had come in. The bridge was down so no-one could get across. The telephone lines were all down. It was three days before there was any communication with the outside. (Deputy Principal, School V1)

Regarding my family – for almost two months my whole family, we stay outside because most people were frightened to go inside their houses even if they were only partially damaged. We stay in a tent and the whole neighbourhood stayed out with us. Fifteen families together. We shared everything and cooked together. (Principal, School N1)

Whether the event had happened inside or outside school hours, principals and teachers returned to school to inspect the damage so they could report to authorities and begin the clean-up. Even the teachers in Japan who were being moved to new schools in April returned to their former schools to help with the clean-up.

After the cyclone, I have to be a carpenter. I look at the classrooms and make a report. The Ministry came around to assess the damage. I ask parents to assist as I have no handyman. We still have things to be done. We have to spend school money on the roof. (Principal, School V1)

In some cases, the school was in use as a community shelter. In Japan, one principal had a conference with the local residents to explain what would happen with the local schools. His school had been used as a shelter for a month but the people still living there would be moved and three schools would use the buildings together. The children and teachers from two schools that were damaged would be bussed to their school. Two of the New Zealand schools were also community shelters:

> The school closed and the Army came in to clean up. They brought water tanks and set up community showers and washing facilities. It became a community hub. There was so much support here. Room 19 was set up as a coffee room. Children and parents felt safe here. (Parent, School NZ5)

While waiting for schools to reopen, principals and senior leaders worried about their staff:

> It was one big challenge for me because I've never been through this before. I wanted to meet with the teachers to tell them that the cyclone has passed but we have been affected. But I have to give time to my teachers because some of them have lost their own houses so I have to accept that they can't come to school if they are busy at home. (Principal, School V1)

While they were waiting for official permission to reopen their schools, principals and teachers made plans:

> Within that first week and a half, we were working out the safety of our school first. We were checking in with our staff to make sure that they were emotionally ready to support children, and also how our families were coping and what they [staff and students] might need when we got them back. (Principal, School NZ4)

Preparation for returning to school included ensuring that teachers would be able to cope with what they might face. In Vanuatu, one principal encouraged the teachers to tell their stories so that the children would know that they had suffered too. Principals described how they needed to look after their teachers, to allow them to express their emotions so they would be ready when the students returned:

We had a big debrief in the staff room. We had a chance to connect with the other staff to find out about all their different situations as some of the staff had lost homes and really suffered. The session was not just about commiserating, we were also celebrating that we were all still here. (Teacher, School NZ1)

Schools received information from their Ministries of Education on how to debrief the disaster when the students returned:

The MoE gave us two weeks to recover then we come back to school. They tell us to go slowly with the children so that they can forget about this. After a week when some start coming back, the teachers ask them about what happened to them – to tell their stories and we have lessons about safety precautions, what to do if there is another cyclone. (Principal, School V1)

We received support from the Ministry of Education—had a support team come in and meet with the staff about two days before we opened, and we talked about the kind of things we could do to support the children. To say: "It's okay to tell your story about what happened in that quake and the aftermath," and that it was good to tell the children that every story was important, and "the way you are feeling is a normal feeling...some people might feel differently [than] you about what happened, but however you are feeling is normal. (Principal, School NZ4)

Even before schools officially reopened, they found ways to support children and ease them back into routines. One New Zealand school set up informal classes in parents' or teachers' living rooms for the children in the area. In Samoa, they used four undamaged village houses. Bringing children together was helpful for them and enabled parents to have time to deal with the myriad of problems they now faced. In Nepal, one principal set up a mobile school:

We started a mobile school system. Because I saw that my students were frightened and sad. They had no food and nothing to do and their parents were busy with rescue work. I mobilise my teachers and we go to different places for one or two or three days. We let the children do drawing and painting and singing and dancing to make them happy. We feed them a small snack. We did more than 50 places. The parents appreciated what we started. (Principal, School N1)

Returning to School

Before school could start, there needed to be appropriate facilities for children to return to:

> When I got to my school, I found the roof of my classroom had gone. UNICEF provided tents but the school needed to decide who would use them. They decided on a younger class who wouldn't need desks and an experienced teacher – like me. (Teacher, School V1)

Schools let their communities know that their school was ready or that an alternative was available:

> Slowly, I started coming to school myself and visiting the parents. I invited them to inspect the school buildings. I made an awareness programme for them of what we would do if there was another disaster. Then I invited the children to come back and we did different things to remove the trauma – drama and singing and dancing. Slowly, we started to teach the classes. (Principal, School N1)

> We had a preparation day where kids could come in and see the school was still normal. The kids were amazing, we couldn't get over it, like it was security for them, it was really good. (Teacher, School NZ5)

Schools reported that it took time for their usual cohort of students to return:

> [When school resumed] we just made ourselves out there. We had a coffee morning straight away for the parents. We had lots of notices around the school saying, "Kia kaha [stand tall], we're strong, we can work through this together." And we kept referring to this as we welcomed the kids back. Half of them didn't come back, of course, because some of them had shifted away. Some of them were too scared to come back. Some parents were too scared to let their children come back, so there were a whole lot of different reasons why we didn't have our normal cohort. (Principal, School NZ2)

Often the basics were school's first priorities:

> Another challenge was supporting families. Their first priority was shelter, food and water. Many lost their homes and their jobs. To feed the children,

people donated local food and the school paid for meat. The teachers would take the food home and prepare it or show the children how to cook it. Then they ate together. (Principal, School V1)

Obviously, we kept on feeding kids, we've always done that to a certain extent but that became more evident. There were kids without lunches; there were kids without breakfasts. We just fed them as the need arose. Kids were really tired, so we would put cushions in the back of the room for them to sleep. (Principal, School NZ2)

Schools were grateful to the agencies, businesses and charities that helped out. They mentioned, for example, World Vision, Red Cross, Caritas, UNICEF, Presbyterian Support Services, the Salvation Army and Rotary International: "*In less than a month, UNICEF came and gave us some activities and sports equipment. That was good to keep the children coming to school*" (Principal, School V1).

Schools and volunteers from other areas, even other countries, offered their support:

Many principals from other schools came to help out. Many famous persons came to the school to visit students. Students participated in taiko (drumming), field trips and other activities. (Principal, School J1)

Through my Rotary friends we supported a thousand people. For 15 days we fed them – breakfast, lunch and dinner because they didn't have anything and they have to live outside. We built some temporary shelters out of bamboo and gave them some blankets. (Principal, School N1)

Different activities were provided for children to distract them from their sadness and encourage them to process their experiences. In Samoa, the five most badly affected schools benefitted from an ongoing art project where children wrote stories, painted pictures, made postcards and created puppets. The leader of the project commented that:

To begin with the art work had horrific and vivid images and the colours were muddy and dirty. As the project kept going, the children started to focus on lighter themes – trucks, bulldozers, Red Cross, the Army and gifts from donors. Later, they started drawing trees and plants growing back and birds and fish returning. (Personal communication, L. Latai, January, 2018)

Another important activity was to ensure that students were ready for any future disasters:

> After the February quake, the school organised a box full of beanies [warm hats] and safety blankets in the shed. It all felt a bit safer having the earthquake box in the shed under the school. My teacher made up a cellphone box. We put our cellphones in the box, so that if there was a really big aftershock, we could contact our parents. (Student, School NZ1)

In Vanuatu, Japan, New Zealand and Samoa, schools mentioned putting more emphasis on drills for all situations—earthquakes, fires, cyclones, tsunami and floods. One Japanese teacher said: *"The most important lesson is to take disaster education seriously so that people know what to do. Every day, they should be aware of evacuation routes and assembly areas"* (Teacher, School J3).

It was also important to get back to the normality of schooling as soon as was reasonable:

> As a school we wanted things to get back to normal. The teachers tried to create a place that was as normal as possible. The school was pretty undamaged, so that helped. When the children returned to school we reinforced the key message that the earthquake was a natural thing and it just happens. (Teacher 1, School NZ1)

Teachers kept going despite the difficulties in their own lives:

> We have to be strong. We have to have patience. We give what we can give to the best of our ability to help children so that they feel there is still someone there for them. We must be good role models – be strong instead of complaining. (Teacher, School V2)

Principals uniformly praised the response of their teachers:

> My teachers co-operated a lot. They understand that for six months we could not provide the proper salary. Some of my teachers had a lot of problems – their house collapsed and they lost everything. (Principal, School N1)

> Teachers, that's the interesting part, straight after February, teachers rallied round. Teachers are great. I can't say enough about how much strength,

how much integrity, how much they would go the extra mile to drop kids off, to look after kids in their classrooms after school, to buy them special treats, take them to McDonalds, all those sorts of things... to find clothes for them, to find a pram for a mother who didn't have a pram to wheel her baby to school. (Principal, School NZ2)

And in response, teachers praised their principals and senior leaders:

I've had a really supportive [senior leadership] team, and they have got in counsellors for staff and children and parents. They have provided opportunities for us to talk, just to chill out together. (Teacher, School NZ5)

The school looked out for the staff. There were constant e-mails and messages at morning teas and lunchtimes – that if staff were not coping to let management know as there was support and funding for relief teachers. Also, if we needed to go and sort things out with our houses, then we were encouraged to do so. (Teacher 2, School NZ1)

The efforts of schools did not go unnoticed by parents:

All these teachers are quiet heroes. I know there are teachers here that have lost their homes and some of them are living in the same situation as we are and they come to work and they get on with it. They do their job as best they can and they never ever show their frustration to the kids. (Parent, School NZ5)

Longer Term Repercussions

Many of the participants in the study mentioned how they had never experienced such a disaster and how under-prepared they were for the reality of it. Principals and teachers noted teaching about disasters or practising drills, but that neither they nor their students fully comprehended the enormity of a disaster until it happened to them. Another aspect they felt unprepared for was how long it would take for services to be up and running, for schools to be repaired and for their regions to get back to a semblance of normality. All this was to take a huge toll on their physical, emotional and psychological wellbeing.

8 HIGH EXPECTATIONS, LOW RECOGNITION: THE ROLE ... 163

That starts to wear down the staff, so we knew that we had to look after each other. We really had to look out for each other – be prepared, watch for the signs: "This teacher is not going to be at school tomorrow. I can just tell, she's looking shaky." (Principal, School NZ2)

We know from all the international literature that this will stay with people. I've got colleagues who've been diagnosed with cancer, with stress-related illnesses. They go to the doctor, get medical attention, but still there has been a gradual decline in teachers' well-being. Support staff here have been counsellors on the phone with crying parents. (Principal, School NZ5)

This was compounded by inadequate facilities, lack of resources and support being withdrawn too soon:

To begin with the children liked the tent. It was like playing house. But when it was hot, the tent was dry and dusty and when it rained the floor was full of puddles. After a few months the children wanted to go back to a regular classroom. (Teacher, School V2)

Yet schools tried to stay positive:

So almost two years later, we are still positive, we are still giving positive messages. We are still advocating for the school... but our reserves are running out. (Principal, School NZ1)

I'm so happy with my teachers because they adapt to the situation – even though they have never done teaching in a tent. They cope with that and with me doing the maintenance. Even though our records and stationery and our textbooks are wet, they find ways. (Principal, School V2)

Schools continued to look after their communities:

We also had the library open for parents to go in and have coffee in the morning and just to talk. There could only be four or five of them but they could all sit in there. If they wanted to cry, they could cry. You know, they could do whatever they wanted to, out of our sight. (Teacher, School NZ5)

Their support did not go unnoticed by their communities and had a positive effect:

They [the community] started caring more. They feel cared for; they start helping others. I've got a whole lot of people who would've actually come into the school offering to help other people in our community—people who they felt needed help. To me, that's the synergy of really strong relationships in a community. (Principal, School NZ2)

Yet with the ongoing nature of disaster recovery and the accumulation of secondary stressors, schools felt the strain:

We were affected for the whole year. More than 100 students could not come back. They were frightened and their parents did not want them to come to school. Last year the results of the examination were not so good. Students couldn't study. They are squeezed into a small tent with no lights – very difficult. (Principal, School, N1)

It's the cumulative things we are dealing with. People have got so many responsibilities, so much is going on and the big decisions are just not under our control. A teacher's performance has to be affected. It is not possible to carry on being the person of usual everyday circumstances. (Teacher, School NZ1)

In some cases, bureaucratic decisions, such as school relocations, closures and amalgamations, compounded the effects. In Japan, principals and teachers are relocated to new schools every few years. This meant that principals and teachers left behind the communities they had been through the disaster with and, in some cases, new principals and teachers arrived at traumatised schools with limited understanding of what the school community had been through. In Samoa and Japan, some damaged schools were demolished and rebuilt on new sites. While done with the best of intentions, students and staff had mixed feelings as they passed the old sites on their way to school each day. Also, in Japan, post-tsunami school mergers upset locals who felt that not rebuilding a school in their area would be another death knell for their communities. One New Zealand school described the permanent closure or amalgamation of nearly 40 schools in the disaster zone as "another aftershock". One teacher describes hearing the news about her school closure:

I was just sick in my stomach thinking, okay, what is it saying about jobs? What is it saying my child's school; other children's schools? . . . There wasn't enough information given out at the time, for you not to think about what does this mean for you, for your future. I mean, we're already living in houses waiting to be repaired, and we're going to lose my job now and my child's going to lose their school. (Teacher, School NZ5)

Although schools affected by closures and amalgamations in New Zealand protested, presented submissions, even took cases to court, most decisions remained unchanged. These decisions highlight how economic imperatives can override social concerns and community rebuilding in government recovery planning. One principal shares his frustration:

> How does that affect the staff? The emotional ties and the relationships are torn apart; families that have been associated with the school for decades have gone. That kind of link and historical connection and knowledge of the community and the school and its involvement goes as well. History goes; it travels with the people. [School NZ5] has been around for 141 years…it's not a place of recent history, we're looking at quite a significant place in the community. (Principal, School NZ5)

And through all this, principals and teachers had to hold everything together:

> They were so positive. I mean the teachers were going through more themselves about the whole merger and how it was going to work. They all had to apply for their jobs and all the rest of it. And yet they were so positive with the children. They did their best to make sure that when the merger occurred, that the children had a positive view of the whole thing. So, I take my hat off to the teachers because they were going through so much too… – the earthquake, the merger, the uncertainty themselves about how everything was going to happen. (Parent, School NZ5)

Discussion

Schools are significant places in society (Mutch, 2018c; Witten et al., 2003). They are charged with educating children and young people with the knowledge, skills, attitudes and dispositions that will prepare the next generation of citizens, workers and community members who will uphold the values on which that society is based. The evidence from the schools in this study highlights that principals and teachers see their role very much as service to their community and wider society. They are proud of their profession and go to extra lengths to support children and their families.

Schools play a significant role in building community connectedness and cohesiveness (Callaghan & Colton, 2008; Mutch, 2018c). When disaster hits, their commitment is taken to a new level (Education Review Office, 2013; Mutch, 2014b, 2018c).

If the disaster hits while schools are in session, principals and teachers become first responders, rescuing, evacuating, calming and caring for children, until there is somewhere for them to go (Mutch, 2014a; Tatebe & Mutch, 2015). In the case studies detailed here are specific examples of this "pedagogy of love and care" (O'Connor, 2013). In New Zealand and Samoa, teachers and principals waited many hours, until someone came to collect each child, making other arrangements, including taking students home, if they were not collected. They did this while hiding their anxieties about their own families. The Japanese principal in this study was trapped for five days with no food and only rationed water from a water tank, until the group he was with were rescued by helicopter. Without communication with the outside world, he had no idea if his own family had survived.

In each of the five disaster settings discussed in this chapter, principals and teachers lived in the area and were victims themselves. They had to deal with their own family deaths or injuries, personal losses of homes and possessions and the long, drawn-out rebuilding of their communities. Schools are often the first institutions re-opened, mostly in temporary make-shift conditions with only basic materials. Even before authorities had announced the formal reopening of schools, the principals in this study were finding ways to get back to a sense of regularity. One New Zealand principal borrowed a hard hat and boots and, with her caretaker, started assessing the damage and getting her school repaired. In Vanuatu, a principal called for the local community to come and help himself and his teachers tidy up the school grounds and repair the classrooms. In Nepal, another principal set up mobile schools going from shelter to shelter to give children activities to take their minds off the disaster. When school resumed, teaching took place in temporary shelters, tents, church halls and living rooms. In Christchurch, undamaged secondary schools ran two shifts of schooling—a morning shift and an afternoon shift—to get as many secondary school students back to school as soon as possible (Ham et al., 2012). In all cases, principals and teachers were simply expected to turn up to school and look after other people's children, providing them with a safe haven and a return to normality, despite whatever else they were dealing with themselves.

One of the problems teachers faced was that schools were often lacking the basics. While there were agencies, such as UNICEF or Red Cross, providing basic supplies, I also saw on my visits inappropriate donations provided by well-meaning donors. I watched as a group of parents in Vanuatu eagerly opened a box of educational supplies to find a full set of *Encyclopaedia Britannica*, when what they really needed was paper and pencils. When schools didn't have supplies, principals and teachers found creative ways to acquire them or, if they could, paid for them out of their own pockets.

Because of the place, both physical and social, that schools have in their communities (Callaghan & Colton, 2008; Mutch, 2018a; Witten et al., 2003), they are often used for a range of other post-disaster purposes besides education. In the case studies, they were places where families needing shelter or comfort, could come to sleep, eat or just talk. Again, principals and teachers took on these extra roles, distributing relief supplies, staying overnight at school, preparing food, offering support or whatever was required of them. And, this was on top of coping with their own trauma and family issues. While there was support from Ministries of Education and other agencies to begin with, it was often too little, was not always what was needed and was withdrawn too soon.

One of the areas where support was often lacking or withdrawn too soon was mental health support. While counsellors and support agencies might provide guidelines and some services, they were stretched thin and could only focus on the most severe cases. It was up to principals and teachers themselves to find ways to support each other, their students and their schools' families. This constant pressure led not only to a decline in principals' and teachers' emotional and psychological wellbeing but also in their physical health. In the New Zealand case, for example, Christchurch now has a mental health crisis (Hollis-Locke, 2017), with the government taking eight years before this was fully recognised. There were many stories of heart attacks, strokes, cancer, nervous breakdowns, suicides, alcohol abuse, family violence and other ways in which the post-disaster communities in these five case studies demonstrated that they were not coping—and again schools were bearing the brunt of these issues on top of their own.

To add to the stressors already mentioned (Gawith, 2013), many communities were then often impacted by bureaucratic decisions, such as the relocation, amalgamation or permanent closure of their schools.

Principals, teachers and communities were rarely consulted and the decisions went ahead without any consideration for the multiple ways in which schools might be affected (see, for example, Mutch, 2017).

Finally, when the post-disaster citations were read and the medals given out, principals and teachers were almost never included. They were simply considered to be "doing their job". While I don't wish to downplay the work of thousands of committed first responders, search and rescue, fire officers, army, police, ambulance services and so on—they are at least trained for these situations. Nor do I wish to downplay the many selfless volunteers who risked their lives to save or help others. In the case of principals and teachers, however, they did not have a choice about whether they could volunteer, they were simply expected to get on with what they had to do with little support or recognition.

Conclusion

This chapter shared findings from across five different disaster settings in the Asia–Pacific region, highlighting the role of principals and teachers in post-disaster contexts. Common themes arising across the five settings were that: (a) principals and teachers put their students first when they faced a disaster situation together; (b) principals and teachers returned to work despite often being victims themselves; (c) teachers focused on children's needs more than their own; (d) teachers tried to balance helping children to process their experiences safely with returning to normal school routines; (e) schools also needed to look after their school families and communities; (f) schools continued to provide the best education they could despite limited facilities, lack of resources and insufficient funds; (g) the stress of coping and trying to keep positive through a prolonged recovery period led to the decreased physical and mental wellbeing of teachers and principals; (h) bureaucratic decisions made by government agencies without consideration or consultation added to the stresses that schools were facing; and (i) little acknowledgement was given to principals and teachers of the heavy burden that they carry in post-disaster contexts.

To date, most accounts of the role of schools in disaster response and recovery are descriptive and related to a single event (see, for example, the chapters in Smawfield, 2013). What this study adds is a more detailed cross-case analysis that lifts these findings from anecdotal accounts to providing collective and comparative insights into post-disaster roles that are largely taken for granted and unacknowledged. While it cannot be claimed that *all* principals and teachers acted in these ways, it is significant that clear patterns of caring dispositions and supportive actions were displayed across these five different post-disaster settings.

The disaster risk reduction literature tends to focus on telling schools what they *should do* (see for example, UNISDR, 2007) although there is growing acceptance of the need to support the role of schools (GADRRRES, 2015; 2017; UNISDR, 2015). This study has focused on what schools, *did do* in these five post-disaster contexts. What is needed now is for these efforts to be better supported with appropriate training and funding so principals and teachers feel prepared when they are next called upon. And, when principals and teachers complete these roles beyond expectation, as those in this study have done, that they are recognised for their significant input into disaster response and recovery—we need them now and we are going to need them even more in the future.

References

Appleton, V. (2001). Avenues of hope: Art therapy and the resolution of trauma. *Art Therapy, Journal of the American Art Therapy Association, 18*(1), 6–13.

Aydan, O., Ulusay, E., Hamada, M., & Beetham, D. (2012). Geotechnical aspects of the 2010 Darfield and 2011 Christchurch earthquakes, New Zealand, and geotechnical damage to structures and lifelines. *Bulletin of Engineering Geology and the Environment, 71*, 63.

Back, E., Cameron, C., & Tanner, T. (2009). *Children and disaster risk reduction: Taking stock and moving forward*. Children in a Changing Climate Research. UNICEF.

Bannister, S., & Gledhill, K. (2012). Evolution of the 2010–2012 Canterbury earthquake sequence. *New Zealand Journal of Geology and Geophysics, 55*(3), 295–304.

Bonanno, G., Brewin, C., Kaniasty, K., & La Greca, A. (2010). Weighing the costs of disaster: Consequences, risks, and resilience in individuals, families and communities. *Psychological Science in the Public Interest, 11*(1), 1–49.

Burr, V. (2015). *Social constructionism* (3rd ed.). Routledge.

Cahill, H., Beadle, S., Mitch, J., Coffey, J., & Crofts, J. (2010). *Adolescents in emergencies*. Youth Research Centre, The University of Melbourne.

Callaghan, E., & Colton, J. (2008). Building sustainable & resilient communities: A balancing of community capital. *Environment, Development and Sustainability, 10*(6), 931–942.

Canterbury Earthquakes Royal Commission. (2012). *Final report* (Vols. 1–7). Canterbury Earthquakes Royal Commission.

Denzin, N. K., & Lincoln, Y. S. (2011). *The SAGE handbook of qualitative research*. Sage.

Direen, G. (2016). *My head is always full! Principals as leaders in a post disaster setting: Experiences in Greater Christchurch since 2010 and 2011 earthquakes* (Unpublished manuscript). Christchurch, New Zealand.

Dixon, T. (2017). *Curbing catastrophe: Natural hazards and risk reduction in the modern world*. Cambridge University Press.

Drabek, T. (1986). *Human system responses to disaster: An Inventory of sociological findings*. Springer-Verlag.

Duncan, J. (2016). *CPPA Inquiry into the Ministry of Education's post-earthquake response for education in Christchurch*. Canterbury Primary Principals, Christchurch, New Zealand.

Education Review Office. (2013). *Stories of resilience and innovation in schools and early childhood services. Canterbury earthquakes: 2010–2012*. Education Review Office.

Ferris, E., & Petz, D. (2012). *The year that shook the rich. A review of natural disasters in 2011*. London School of Economics, The Brookings Institution.

Ferris, E., Petz, D., & Stark, C. (2013). *The year of recurring disasters. A review of natural disasters in 2012*. The Brookings Institution, London School of Economics.

Gawith, E. (2013). The on-going psychological toll from the Canterbury earthquakes: Stories from one community. *Disaster Prevention and Management, 22*(5), 395–404.

Gibbs, L., Mutch, C., O'Connor, P., & MacDougall, C. (2013). Research with, by, for, and about children: Lessons from disaster contexts. *Global Studies of Childhood, 5*(3), 129–141.

Global Alliance for Disaster Risk Reduction and Resilience in the Education Sector. (2017). *Comprehensive school safety framework*. http://gadrrres.net/uploads/files/resources/CSS-Framework-2017.pdf

Gordon, R. (2004). *The social dimension of emergency recovery. Appendix C*. In Emergency Management Australia, Recovery, Australian Emergency Management Manuals Series No. 10 (pp. 111–143). Emergency Management Australia.

Ham, V., Cathro G., Winter, M., & Winter, J. (2012). *Evaluative study of co-located schools established following the Christchurch earthquake*. http://shapingeducation.govt.nz/wpcontent/uploads/2012/12/989-Co-located-schools-report-Final.pdf

Hollis-Locke, N. (2017, September 25). *Christchurch and the mental health crisis*. https://salient.org.nz/2017/09/christchurch-and-the-mental-health-crisis/

Johnson, V., & Ronan, K. (2014). Classroom responses of New Zealand school teachers following the 2011 Christchurch earthquake. *Natural Hazards, 72*, 1075–1092.

Lazarus, P., Jimerson, S., & Brock, S. (2003). *Helping children after a natural disaster: Information for parents and teachers* (Pamphlet). National Association of School Psychologists, Bethesda, MD.

McDonald, A. (2014). *Eastside story: The perceived impact of the Canterbury earthquakes on teacher performance* (Unpublished Master of Arts in Education thesis). University of Canterbury, Christchurch.

Mitchell, T., Jones, L., Lovell, E., & Comba, E. (2013). *Disaster risk management in post-2015 development goals: Potential targets and indicators*. Overseas Development Institute.

Mooney, M., Paton, D., de Terte, I., Jhal, S., Nuray Karanci, A., Gardner, D., Collins, S., Glavovic, B., Huggins, T. J., Johnston, L., Chambers, R., & Johnston, D. (2011). Psychosocial recovery from disasters: A framework informed by evidence. *New Zealand Journal of Psychology, 40*(4), 26–38.

Mutch, C. (2013a). Sailing through a river of emotions: Capturing children's earthquake stories. *Disaster Prevention and Management, 22*(5), 445–455.

Mutch, C. (2013b). *Doing educational research. A practitioner's guide to get started*. NZCER Press.

Mutch, C. (2014a). The role of schools in disaster preparedness, response and recovery: What can we learn from the literature? *Pastoral Care in Education: An International Journal of Personal, Social and Emotional Development, 32*(1), 5–22.

Mutch, C. (2014b). The role of schools in disaster settings: Learning from the 2010–2011 New Zealand earthquakes. *International Journal of Educational Development, 41*, 283–291.

Mutch, C. (2016). Schools as communities and for communities: Learning from the 2010–2011 New Zealand earthquakes. *School Community Journal, 26*(1), 99–122.

Mutch, C. (2017). Winners and losers: School closures in post-earthquake Canterbury. *Waikato Journal of Education, 22*(1), 73–95.

Mutch, C. (2018a). The role of schools in helping communities cope with earthquake disasters: The case of the 2010–2011 New Zealand earthquakes. *Environmental Hazards, 17*(4), 331–351. https://doi.org/10.1080/17477891.2018.1485547

Mutch, C. (2018b). *Analysing qualitative data using the latticework approach*. Te Whakatere au Pāpori Research Unit, University of Auckland.

Mutch, C. (2018c). The place of schools in building community cohesion and resilience: Lessons from a disaster context. In L. Shellavar & P. Westoby (Eds.), *The Routledge handbook of community development research* (pp. 239–252). Routledge.

Mutch, C., & Gawith, L. (2014). The role of schools in engaging children in emotional processing of disaster experiences. *Pastoral Care in Education, 32*(1), 54–67.

Mutch, C., Yates, S., & Hu, C. (2015). Gently, gently: Undertaking participatory research with schools post disaster. *Gateways: International Journal of Community Research and Engagement, 8*(1), 79–99.

O'Connor, P. (2013). Pedagogy of love and care: Shaken schools respond. *Disaster Prevention and Management, 22*(5), 425–433.

O'Connor, P., & Takahashi, N. (2014). From caring about to caring for: Case studies of New Zealand and Japanese schools post disaster. *Pastoral Care in Education: An International Journal of Personal, Social and Emotional Development, 32*(1), 42–53.

Peek, L., Tobin-Gurley, J., Cox, R. S., Scannell, L., Fletcher, S., & Heykeep, C. (2016). Engaging youth in post-disaster research: Lessons learned from a creative methods approach. *Gateways: International Journal of Community Research and Engagement, 9*(1), 89–112.

Pittock, B. (2017). *Climate change: Turning up the heat.* Routledge.

Potter, S., Becker, J., Johnston, D., & Rossiter, K. (2015). An overview of the impacts of the impacts of the 2010–2011 Canterbury earthquakes. *International Journal of Disaster Risk Reduction, 14*(1), 6–14.

Ranghieri, F., & Ishiwatari, M. (2014). *Learning from mega-disasters: Lessons from the Great East Japan earthquake.* World Bank Publications.

Salloum, A., & Overstreet, S. (2012). Grief and trauma intervention for children after disaster: Exploring coping skills versus trauma narration. *Behaviour Research and Therapy, 50*, 169–179.

Shirlaw, N. (2014). *Children and the Canterbury earthquakes.* Child Poverty Action Group.

Smawfield, D. (Ed.). (2013). *Education and natural disasters.* Bloomsbury.

Tatebe, J., & Mutch, C. (2015). Perspectives on education, children and young people in disaster education research. *International Journal of Disaster Risk Reduction, 14*(2), 108–114.

Thornley, L., Ball, J., Signal, L., Lawson-Te Aho, K., & Rawson, E. (2013). *Building community resilience: Learning from the Canterbury earthquakes.* Health Research Council.

UNISDR. (2007). *Towards a culture of prevention: Disaster risk reduction begins at school—Good practices and lessons learned.* United Nations International Strategy for Disaster Reduction Secretariat.

UNISDR. (2009). *Global assessment report on disaster risk reduction. Risk and poverty in a changing climate.* United Nations International Strategy for Disaster Reduction Secretariat.

UNISDR. (2015). *The Sendai framework for disaster risk reduction 2015–2030.* United Nations International Strategy for Disaster Reduction Secretariat.

Winkworth, G. (2007). *Disaster recovery: A review of the literature.* Institute of Child Protection Studies.

Wisner, B. (2006). *Let our children teach us. A review of the role of education and knowledge in disaster risk reduction.* UNISDR System Thematic Cluster/Platform on Knowledge and Education Geneva.

Witten, K., Kearns, R., Lewis, N., Coster, H., & McCreanor, T. (2003). Educational restructuring from a community viewpoint: A case study of school closure from Invercargill. *New Zealand Environment and Planning C: Government and Policy, 21,* 203–223.

CHAPTER 9

Planning and Capability Requirements for Catastrophic and Cascading Events

Andrew Gissing, Michael Eburn, and John McAneney

INTRODUCTION

Natural disasters are a significant risk globally (World Economic Forum, 2018). The extreme end of possible disasters, so-called catastrophic disaster risks, however, attract limited attention compared with either more frequent smaller and thus manageable events, or previous historical events. This is certainly the case in the context of the Australian

---

J. McAneney
Risk Frontiers, St Leonards, NSW, Australia

M. Eburn
Australian National University, Canberra, ACT, Australia

A. Gissing (✉)
Macquarie University, North Ryde, NSW, Australia
e-mail: andrew.gissing@riskfrontiers.com

A. Gissing · M. Eburn
Bushfire and Natural Hazards Research Centre, East Melbourne, Victoria, Australia

emergency management sector, which remains strongly response-focused. Previous reviews into the preparedness of the Australian emergency management sector have recognized this limitation (Australian Government, 2016; Catastrophic Disasters Emergency Management Capability Working Group, 2005; COAG, 2002; Crosweller, 2015; Government of Western Australia, 2017) and the same is true for many other Western nations (9/11 Commission, 2004; Davis, 2006; State of Oregon, 2018; US Government Accountability Office, 1993).

In what follows we review literature, policies and plans in order to identify key attributes of catastrophic events. We define crucial key elements to better inform planning and preparedness efforts to minimize the occurrence of catastrophic events. Implications for practitioners are discussed.

Defining Catastrophic Disaster Characteristics

The term catastrophe is widely used, and numerous definitions exist, though in many regards the true scale of a catastrophe is largely contextual. Common listed attributes allude to their extraordinary impacts that overwhelm the normal functioning of societies and require different approaches to their management (Quarantelli et al., 2006). In this sense they are different from more routine events which do not interfere with the normal functioning of the community.

For the Australian Emergency Management Committee, a catastrophe has to be: *beyond our current arrangements, thinking, experience and imagination* (Australian Government, 2018, p. 5).

In other words, a catastrophe is an event so big that it overwhelms our social systems and resources, and degrades or disables governance structures and strategic and operational decision-making (Australian Government, 2018).

The hallmarks of catastrophes are death and destruction, large-scale disruption, displacement of populations and public anxiety. Often these occur with little to no warning (such as large earthquakes), although they may also onset slowly, growing in size and duration, as in the case of droughts, disease and food shortages. After events that overwhelm the capacity of institutions and the community to cope, we may see emergency systems, communications and plans all failing and leaving leaders out of touch with what is happening on the ground. Local emergency response personnel may be directly impacted themselves, and thus unable to perform their professional roles. Resources from neighbouring regions may also be impacted or unavailable. Emergency leaders are confronted with overwhelming issues, of a scale, complexity and uncertainty that they have never experienced nor imagined. Information about impacts and needs of affected communities may be limited for days after an event, meaning that decisions will often have to be made in the absence of complete information. The event becomes subject to significant national and international media scrutiny, and inevitably, political involvement.

Some catastrophic events may be cascading in nature, escalating in their impacts as interconnected systems fail successively yielding yet further impacts and making recovery more complex and prolonged. Essential infrastructure—water, gas, sewage, power, healthcare, banking, transport, emergency response and communication—becomes severely disrupted. Restoration may take months and disease and fires may wreak further havoc. In some events, disruptions may reach global proportions.

Catastrophic events will typically impact large areas (Barnshaw et al., 2008) and may not respect borders or boundaries resulting in unclear accountabilities amongst responding agencies, and conflicting public messaging. Such disruption and confusion can reach global scales.

The recovery of communities may take many years, with the impacted population displaced, some choosing to relocate to other areas permanently. Many of those affected may suffer long-lasting psychological trauma. Economic losses can be severe as industry and agriculture are disrupted, businesses close down or make yet further demands on Government for recovery support.

Recent examples of catastrophic disaster include: September 11 Terrorist attacks in New York and Washington, USA (2001), Indian Ocean Boxing Day tsunami that struck multiple coastal states (2004), Hurricane Katrina, New Orleans, USA (2006), Cyclone Nargis, Myanmar (2008), Russian heatwave (2010), Haiti earthquake (2010), Christchurch, New Zealand earthquake sequence (2011) and Japanese earthquake and tsunami (2011). For Australia, the Spanish flu pandemic (1918–1919) stands out as one example of an event that overwhelmed Australia's management systems at the time and which resulted in extraordinary impacts (12,000 deaths). Tropical Cyclone Tracey in 1974 serves as an example of an event that completely overwhelmed an Australian city. The cyclone struck Darwin, the capital city of Australia's Northern Territory, leaving only 6% of the city's housing stock habitable (Stretton, 1975).

Crosweller (2015) believes a catastrophe in Australia is inevitable with many scenarios such as extraordinary floods, bushfires, tsunami, cyclones, pandemics, infrastructure failures and heatwaves all having annual probabilities of less than 1-in-500 years on average. Solar storms, large earthquakes and global volcanic mega-eruptions also pose a risk, but at even less frequent or uncertain probabilities. Our nation may also be susceptible to a series of smaller damaging events whose impacts compound into a much larger catastrophe. In some instances the interactions between complex systems (Boin & t Hart, 2010; Cavallo & Ireland, 2014; Masys, 2012; t Hart, 2013) or knowledge gaps due to poor information sharing (Alexander, 2010; Government Office for Science, 2012) may yield unimagined and unpredictable consequences. Almost no current Australian emergency manager will have experienced a nationally significant catastrophe event.

While many catastrophic disaster risks are either known or can be imagined, they are largely unappreciated as was illustrated in the cases of Hurricane Katrina (Comfort, 2005) and the Fukushima nuclear disaster (Funabashi & Kitazawa, 2012).

Management of Catastrophe

Although a catastrophic event by definition is difficult to manage emergency managers can act to reduce loss of life and property and help sustain the continuity of affected communities (Harrald, 2006). Response strategies that work for smaller, more frequent events will be quickly overwhelmed and prove ineffective. By necessity, community members become first responders (Tierney, 1993; Whittaker et al., 2015). Often the success of the response is reliant upon the capacities already present in communities. Social research has shown that rather than panic or be shocked and dazed, communities impacted by catastrophe typically act proactively and work to assist others forming groups often based on pre-disaster ties (Tierney, 1993). Emergent groups typically arise when the demands of the community are not being met by government or officials; when existing traditional structures are inadequate; or when the community feels it is necessary to become involved (Drabek & McEntire, 2003). Emergent groups often have the advantage of real-time situational awareness, knowledge of specific community vulnerabilities and can configure their responses to best meet local needs (Whittaker et al., 2015).

No one organization alone is capable of responding to all aspects of a catastrophe (Benini, 1999; Fugate, 2017). In the case of Hurricane Katrina some 535 organizations, ranging from non-government, commercial, infrastructure, emergent, interest and faith-based organizations, were involved (Comfort & Haase, 2006). There is a need to integrate and coordinate operations of a large number of disparate organizations (Boin & Bynander, 2015). This approach is embodied in the whole-of-community approach philosophy adopted by FEMA in the United States.

Traditional command and control methods of incident management that do not attempt to collaborate with communities are unlikely to be effective (Boin & t Hart, 2010; Drabek & McEntire, 2003; Nohrstedt et al., 2018; Quarantelli, 1988; Tierney, 1993). For example, Ellis and MacCarter (2016) concluded that the Incident Command System did not integrate well with groups that emerged following the Christchurch earthquakes in 2010 and 2011. A review of Australian emergency management plans revealed that rarely do these plans detail methods for the integration of community responses in the immediate aftermath of an event. One exception is the Victorian State Flood Plan, which outlines a strategy for the deployment of community liaison officers to support community groups with logistics and risk management.

Recognizing the capacity of the community itself to respond, it is essential to adopt a more flexible and collaborative approach to inspire, integrate, support and coordinate community efforts and allow for improvisation. Bureaucratic structures and processes such as disaster declarations and mandatory registration of spontaneous volunteers will only hinder community-led efforts (Kapucu & Van Wart, 2006). For example following September 11 there was little time or desire to develop a controlling structure over the flotilla of craft that spontaneously assisted the evacuation of some 300,000–500,000 people from lower Manhattan; attempting to do so may have only slowed and undermined the response (Wachtendorf & Quarantelli, 2003).

It must be recognized that the capacities of communities are not infinite and that there will still be a need for external supporting resources from across government, defence, humanitarian, infrastructure, non-government, community, faith-based and private sector organizations. For example following Hurricane Sandy (2012) some 70,000 utility workers were mobilized to restore infrastructure through mutual aid agreements and logistical support from the defence force (Kaufman et al., 2015).

An enhanced management model for response and recovery would be enabled by decentralized locally based decision-making. It would need to acknowledge emergent community groups, local innovations and existing networks (Boin & McConnell, 2007; Dynes, 1990; Kapucu & Van Wart, 2006) and be supported by higher-level coordination efforts (Carayannopoulos, 2017). At times to inform wider resource mobilization or overcome dysfunctional local relationships it may be necessary to supplement this approach with the forward deployment of a senior emergency management controller. This happened after the Christchurch earthquake (2011) and Cyclone Tracy (1974).

Success requires proactive responses to ensure that significant support can be provided to assist and mobilize the community when it is at its most vulnerable, often within the first 72 hours after a catastrophe when the scale of the consequences of an event may still be influenced. The early movement of significant resources, however, is complex, and there may be inevitable delays leaving impacted communities on their own. Decision-making to commit significant outside resources will take place under great uncertainty and in anticipation of catastrophic consequences (Fugate, 2011). In some instances, Australia is further challenged in mobilizing support to remote areas. For this reason, it is vital that planning to support communities be integrated with logistical components often managed by different organizations.

Understanding supply chains for key commodities will be time well spent. In many cases the private sector can be more efficient. During the response to Hurricane Sandy, for example, the private sector was able to move eight times the amount of food into affected areas compared with the combined responses of government and other non-government organizations (Kaufman et al., 2015).

Assessing and Developing Capability

Numerous Australian capability planning models are typically derivatives of the FEMA National Preparedness Goal which outlines a list of core capabilities from which capability targets are established based upon realistic disaster scenarios (US Department of Homeland Security, 2013). The application of capability models has not been consistent across Australia, with jurisdictions and individual agencies developing their own methods. Approaches have also focused on the emergency management sector and ignore wider community capacities. Recently, a set of national core capabilities have been defined as part of the Australian Disaster Preparedness Framework.

Response efforts to catastrophes must be guided by a specific set of operational priorities. For example the Hawaii Catastrophic Hurricane Plan sets out priorities to save lives and minimize suffering; stabilize and repair critical infrastructure; and maintain critical transportation and distribution networks (FEMA, 2015).

Catastrophic disaster plans must then be based on the achievement of defined priorities, but many assume the simple scaling up of existing arrangements (Crosweller, 2015) and provide equal significance to the provision of all defined capabilities. No guidance is provided as to what are the most important capabilities. If a response agency were to simply extend existing arrangements and capabilities designed to deal with frequent, small (routine) events to manage a catastrophic event this would spread resources too thinly and achieve little, even if their efforts were directed to the worst affected areas. Efforts to plan for all capabilities to be delivered to reasonable levels of effectiveness are simply unrealistic, and ignore the nature and scale of a catastrophic event.

Emergency management organizations must define what capabilities they are best able to provide in support of wider community efforts to best achieve operational priorities. This means altering of typical service delivery standards and mechanisms (Hanfling et al., 2012). Gissing (2016) proposes that priority capabilities should comprise: leading communities; facilitating coordination and supporting the efforts of communities and infrastructure providers; ensuring infrastructure is viable to allow the arrival of supporting resources; collecting and providing situational awareness to help influence community efforts; providing subject matter expertise to guide community capabilities; providing public information to activate and inform community responses; and to provide critical specialist resources, such as medical expertise and hazardous materials response. Capability planning by emergency management organizations should hence focus on the delivery of these functions as a priority over those for which a lower standard of delivery maybe acceptable. For other capabilities, planners should look to identify community capacity and to build community networks that may be quickly mobilized to assist in the first instance. As greater external support becomes available to support local community efforts service standards can be revised.

It is unrealistic to resource and fully prepare for all magnitudes of events (Heide, 1989; Quarantelli, 1986; Queensland Floods Commission of Inquiry, 2012), though without specific knowledge of society's risk appetite for emergency resourcing it is difficult for planners to define capability targets. Such definitions of risk appetite exist in other contexts for example prudential regulations for insurers; and land-use planning and building codes. The definition of societal risk appetite would assist to define scenarios in which emergency management organizations should plan to have sufficient capabilities and capacity to respond to and recover from assuming that such investment is cost-effective. However, this does not mean that planners should ignore catastrophic events; rather there needs to be a realization that emergency management will be unable to cope with the worst-case scenarios on their own. Moreover, consideration of their capabilities in the face of such scenarios will more clearly define the limits of what might be expected and the point at which their reliance on local capacity and external help comes into play. It is essential to understand the extent of capacity gaps that might arise and strategies required once traditional emergency management capabilities are overwhelmed (Fugate, 2017).

Discussion and Conclusions

Though the importance of integrating emergency response with community capacity emerges as a clear theme through the research literature, this is challenged by the reality that many communities tend to be disinterested in preparing even for frequently occurring risks such as floods, bushfires and heatwaves, let alone risks that may occur much more rarely (FEMA, 2017). Such disinterest operates within the wider background of increasing community expectations placed upon emergency services. This is evidenced by the blame game of public inquiries held after each significant natural hazard event.

There needs to be a shift in emergency management culture from rhetoric to honest dialogue with communities. There is a real limit to what emergency managers can achieve in the face of catastrophes. As the first responders, citizens need to be encouraged to develop a greater degree of self-reliance. In New Zealand citizens are told to expect that for the first 72 hours they may be on their own after a significant event. Similar messaging needs to be got across to the Australian public.

There is a need to identify measures that incentivize community participants to get involved. In the United States, the sharing of situational awareness information has been shown to incentivize large businesses to become involved and to utilize such information to better direct their own efforts to service impacted areas (Gissing, 2017).

The management of a catastrophe in Australia will ultimately require a nationally coordinated approach to ensure the capability and capacity of the nation will be available to respond. However, at present Australia lacks true national coordination frameworks that would enable such an approach (Eburn et al., 2019).

Overall, preparing for catastrophes must accept the inevitability of catastrophic events and move towards an inclusive emergency management model that embraces the whole of community. Such thinking must be championed by leaders to inspire cultures that are both focused on collaboration and preparedness in the context of catastrophic events. And lastly, instead of the traditional all-hazards all-agencies approach, Australian leaders should consider an all-hazards, nationwide whole-of-community approach to emergency management.

Acknowledgements This research was funded through the Bushfire and Natural Hazards Cooperative Research Centre and Macquarie University.

References

9/11 Commission. (2004). *Final report of the national commission on terrorist attacks upon the United States*. US Government.
Alexander, D. E. (2010). The L'Aquila earthquake of 6 April 2009 and Italian Government policy on disaster response. *Journal of Natural Resources Policy Research, 2*, 325–342.
Australian Government. (2016). *A capability roadmap: Enhancing emergency management in Australia 2016*. Attorney-General's Department.
Australian Government. (2018). *Australian disaster preparedness framework*. Department of Home Affairs.
Barnshaw, J., Quarantelli, E., & Letukas, L. (2008). *The characteristics of catastrophes and their social evolution: An exploratory analysis of implications for crisis policies and emergency management procedures* (Working Paper #90). University of Delaware Disaster Research Center.

Benini, A. A. (1999). Network without centre? A case study of an organizational network responding to an earthquake. *Journal of Contingencies and Crisis Management, 7*, 38–47.
Boin, A., & Bynander, F. (2015). Explaining success and failure in crisis coordination. *Geografiska Annaler: Series A, Physical Geography, 97*, 123–135.
Boin, A., & McConnell, A. (2007). Preparing for critical infrastructure breakdowns: The limits of crisis management and the need for resilience. *Journal of Contingencies and Crisis Management, 15*, 50–59.
Boin, A., & t Hart, P. (2010). Organising for effective emergency management: Lessons from Research. *Australian Journal of Public Administration, 69*, 357–371.
Carayannopoulos, G. (2017). Whole of government: The solution to managing crises? *Australian Journal of Public Administration, 76*, 251–265.
Catastrophic Disasters Emergency Management Capability Working Group. (2005). *Review of Australia's ability to respond to and recover from catastrophic disasters*. Australian Emergency Management Committee.
Cavallo, A., & Ireland, V. (2014). Preparing for complex interdependent risks: A system of systems approach to building disaster resilience. *International Journal of Disaster Risk Reduction, 9*, 181–193.
COAG. (2002). *Natural disasters in Australia*. Canberra, ACT.
Comfort, L. K. (2005). Fragility in disaster response: Hurricane Katrina, 29 August 2005. *The Forum*.
Comfort, L. K., & Haase, T. W. (2006). Communication, coherence, and collective action: The impact of Hurricane Katrina on communications infrastructure. *Public Works Management & Policy, 10*, 328–343.
Crosweller, M. (2015). Improving our capability to better plan for, respond to, and recover from severe-to-catastrophic level disasters. *Australian Journal of Emergency Management, 30*, 41.
Davis, T. (2006). *Select Bipartisan Committee to investigate the preparation for and response to Hurricane Katrina* (Final Report). US House of Representatives, February, 15.
Drabek, T. E., & Mcentire, D. A. (2003). Emergent phenomena and the sociology of disaster: Lessons, trends and opportunities from the research literature. *Disaster Prevention and Management: An International Journal, 12*, 97–112.
Dynes, R. R. (1990). Community emergency planning: False assumptions and inappropriate analogies. *International Journal of Mass Emergencies and Disasters*.
Eburn, M., Moore, C., & Gissing, A. (2019). *The potential role of the Commonwealth in responding to catastrophic disasters*. Bushfire and Natural Hazards Cooperative Research Centre.

Ellis, S., & MacCarter, K. (2016). *Incident management in Australasia*. CSIRO Publishing.
FEMA. (2015). *2015 Hawaii catastrophic hurricane plan*. FEMA, hawaii.
FEMA. (2017). *2017 National preparedness report*. https://www.fema.gov/media-library/assets/documents/134253
Fugate, C. (2011). *Remarks on Disasters*. Retrieved from https://www.c-span.org/video/?c1331898/user-clip-clip-craig-fugate-remarks-disasters
Fugate, C. (2017). *Building an emergency management baseline: Four non-negotiables*. IAEM Bulletin. Retrieved 25 February 2018 from: http://www.cadmusgroup.com/wp-content/uploads/2017/09/IAEM-Bulletin-Craig-Fugate-August-2017.pdf?hsCtaTracking=99c3908a-bb09-48dc-a079-6a88e8 8f0712%7C40836b9a-a8f0-4225-9aa5-3d38e1030e7c
Funabashi, Y., & Kitazawa, K. (2012). Fukushima in review: A complex disaster, a disastrous response. *Bulletin of the Atomic Scientists, 68*, 9–21.
Gissing, A. (2016, April). Planning for catastrophic disaster in Australia. *Asia Pacific Fire Magazine*.
Gissing, A. (2017). Disaster risk management: Insights from the US. *The Australian Journal of Emergency Management, 32*, 5.
Government Office for Science. (2012). *High impact low probability risks: Blackett review*. UK Government. https://assets.publishing.service.gov.uk/government/uploads/system/uploads/attachment_data/file/278526/12-519-blackett-review-high-impact-low-probability-risks.pdf
Government of Western Australia. (2017). *Emergency preparedness report*. https://www.oem.wa.gov.au/Documents/Publications/PreparednessReports/2017SEMCEmergencyPreparednessReport.pdf
Hanfling, D., Altevogt, B. M., & Gostin, L. O. (2012). A framework for catastrophic disaster response. *Journal of the American Medical Association, 308*, 675–676.
Harrald, J. R. (2006). Agility and discipline: Critical success factors for disaster response. *The Annals of the American Academy of Political and Social Science, 604*, 256–272.
Heide, E. A. (1989). *Disaster response: Principles of preparation and coordination*. C.V Mosby Company.
Kapucu, N., & Van Wart, M. (2006). The evolving role of the public sector in managing catastrophic disasters: Lessons learned. *Administration & Society, 38*, 279–308.
Kaufman, D., Bach, R., & Riquelme, J. (2015). Engaging the whole community in the United States. Strategies for supporting community resilience. *CRISMART, 41*, 151–186.
Masys, A. (2012). Black swans to grey swans: Revealing the uncertainty. *Disaster Prevention and Management: An International Journal, 21*, 320–335.

Nohrstedt, D., Bynander, F., Parker, C., & t Hart, P. (2018). Managing crises collaboratively: Prospects and problems—A systematic literature review. *Perspectives on Public Management and Governance*, *1*(4), 257–271.

Quarantelli, E. L. (1986). *Planning and management for the prevention and mitigation of natural disasters, especially in a metropolitan context: Initial questions and issues which need to be addressed* (Preliminary Paper #114). University of Delaware Disaster Research Center.

Quarantelli, E. L. (1988). Disaster crisis management: A summary of research findings. *Journal of Management Studies*, *25*, 373–385.

Quarantelli, E. L., Lagadec, P., & Boian, A. (2006). *Handbook of disaster research*. Springer.

Queensland Floods Commission of Inquiry. (2012). *Queensland Floods Commission of Inquiry: Final report*. Brisbane, QLD.

State of Oregon. (2018). *The state must do more to prepare Oregon for a catastrophic disaster* (Report 2018-03). https://sos.oregon.gov/audits/documents/2018-03.pdf

Stretton, A. (1975). *Darwin disaster: Cyclone Tracey*. Natural Disasters Organisation.

t Hart, P. (2013). After Fukushima: Reflections on risk and institutional learning in an era of mega-crises. *Public Administration*, *91*, 101–113.

Tierney, K. J. (1993). *Disaster preparedness and response: Research findings and guidance from the social science literature* (Preliminary Papers, 193). Disaster Research Center, University of Delaware.

US Department of Homeland Security. (2013). *Threat and hazard identification and risk assessment guide*. US Department of Homeland Security.

US Government Accountability Office. (1993). *Disaster management: Improving the nation's response to catastrophic disasters*. Report to Congressional Requesters, GAO/RCED-93-186.

Wachtendorf, K., & Quarantelli, E. L. (2003). The evacuation of Lower Manhattan by water transport on September 11: An unplanned 'success'. *Joint Commission Journal on Quality and Patient Safety*, *29*, 316–318.

Whittaker, J., McLennan, B., & Handmer, J. (2015). A review of informal volunteerism in emergencies and disasters: Definition, opportunities and challenges. *International Journal of Disaster Risk Reduction*, *13*, 358–368.

World Economic Forum. (2018). *The global risk report 2018* (13th ed.). http://www3.weforum.org/docs/WEF_GRR18_Report.pdf

CHAPTER 10

Development and Implementation of Disaster Risk Management Specialization Program: Philippine School of Business Administration-Manila and Quezon City Government Collaboration Towards Sustainable Development Solutions

Tabassam Raza, Jose F. Peralta, Thess Khaz S. Raza, and Carmelita R. E. U. Liwag

INTRODUCTION AND BACKGROUND

Philippines is an archipelago state, consisting of some 7,100 islands and islets, and covering a land area of approximately 300,000 km^2. She is exposed to high incidents of hazards such as typhoons, floods, storm surges, floods, tsunamis, earthquakes, volcanic eruptions, landslides

T. Raza (✉) · J. F. Peralta
Graduate School of Business, Philippine School of Business Administration (PSBA), Manila, Philippines
e-mail: tabassamr@psba.edu

© The Author(s), under exclusive license to Springer Nature Singapore Pte Ltd. 2022
H. James et al. (eds.), *Disaster Risk Reduction in Asia Pacific*, Disaster Risk, Resilience, Reconstruction and Recovery,
https://doi.org/10.1007/978-981-16-4811-3_10

and droughts. This, combined with poverty, leaves various communities throughout the Philippines in highly vulnerable situations. Of these, hydro-meteorological events including typhoons and floods, accounted for over 80% of the natural disasters in the country during the last half-century (Jha et al., 2018). In terms of disaster risk, Philippines ranked third among all of the countries with the highest risks worldwide according to the World Risk Report 2018, with index value of 25.14% (World Economic Forum, 2018). At least 60% of the country's total land area is exposed to multiple hazards, and 74% of the population is susceptible to their impact (GFDRR, 2017). The frequency and intensity of disasters, both natural and man-made, are on the rise. Their impact on our own well-being, livelihood and economy, including industries, is ever-increasing. The increasing impact of disasters on the numbers affected and on economic and material loss is logically explained by the increasing levels of vulnerability of people.

Essentially, the destruction caused by natural and climate related disasters has been associated with lack of personnel and institutions coping and adaptive capacities. In line with existing National and International laws, guidelines and agreements, we need to reinforce our Institutional and Personnel Coping and Adaptive Capacities (IPCACs) for DRR and CCA and build up the resilience of our communities, including the financial, industrial, and environmental sectors. In recent times where factors contributing towards vulnerability are widespread, the challenges posed to humankind by disasters, whether natural or man-made, are greater than ever. It basically indicates that the Higher Education Institutions (HEIs) have neglected disaster management as part of their study courses in the Philippines. The main objective of this research is to assess the IPCACs of a pilot Local Government Unit (LGU) in the Philippines (Raza & Peralta, 2019). The selection of Quezon City as pilot area was empirically done by collecting data from all candidate cities using the Key Informative Interviews (KIIs). The specialized Logical Decision for Windows (LDWs) software with built-in statistical tool was used to process the data collected through KIIs and select the top-ranked city as a pilot LGU. The 142 barangays of QCG were assessed through participatory process

---

T. Raza · T. K. S. Raza · C. R. E. U. Liwag
School of Urban and Regional Planning, University of the Philippines (UP-SURP), Quezon City, Philippines

by conducting three symposia and getting response to the survey questionnaire. It is done by determining if the personnel of the authorized institution have undergone DRR and CCA related training programs or have attained diplomas or specializations from any HEIs.

The IPCACs of the QCG and its barangays were found to be "Very Poor" to "Poor", based on the analysis of research data. This led to the estimating of the demand and eventually recommended the development of a formal education model for specialists on formulating solutions to effects of disasters on businesses, livelihood, and on the overall economy of the nation. Considering the above recommendation and the previous rigorous researches conducted for the provisions of solutions to the business continuity problems related to disaster impact in changing climate by PSBA-Manila since 2002, authors developed a curriculum for a formal DRM specialization under the existing MBA program (PSBA, 2017). It was done based on business continuity principles regarding the increasing intensity and frequency of natural and manmade disasters with negative impact on the national economy. Indeed, Graduate School of Business (GSB), Philippine School of Business Administration (PSBA), Manila, took the lead in introducing Disaster Risk Management (DRM) as a specialization/track in its existing Master of Business Administration (MBA) program (thesis program) (PreventionWeb, 2018). The School's MBA in DRM is a distinctive program in the Philippines and its main objective is to combine the strengths of general MBA core competencies in the areas of economics, finance, project research and development, marketing, production and operations, strategic management, and accounting, along with the intensive exploration of risk management fields, altogether making up an effective DRM towards sustainable development solutions.

The PSBA is the pioneer of DRM specialization and started developing MBA in DRM in 2014. Its request for acquiring Government authority to offer MBA in DRM program was initiated in September 2015 with Commission on Higher Education (CHED), the regulatory body of the Philippines in the field of Higher Education. The program was evaluated by the CHED assigned Technical Committee for Business Administration, Entrepreneurship and Office Administration. After more than 2 years of continuous consultation and communication with CHED on its approval, the PSBA became the first Higher Education Institution (HEI) in the Philippines to be granted Government Authority to offer MBA in DRM program in May 2017 (CHED, 2017). This program provides a unique opportunity to develop the skills required to be a professional in the field of DRM and business continuity for improving the quality of life of the people.

DRM is a dynamic and complex field demanding a wide scope of knowledge and expertise in multiple areas. This program takes a comprehensive approach covering a wide range of topics including financial mechanism for disaster risk reduction, planning, management, humanitarian logistics and supply chain, response, relief, recovery and the economics of disasters. These subject delivery mechanism includes blended learning mode, i.e. both face to face and online medium. The MBA in DRM Program is a 16-month full time study program requiring successful completion of 45 credits spanning four consecutive semesters. To learn from our global partners, there is an off-site study which consists of a 2–10 days excursion for qualified students. In this regard, PSBA-Manila has signed substantial numbers of Memorandum of Understanding (MOU) with local and international partners on knowledge and expertise exchange programs. After a keen evaluation and acquiring proper authorization, the MBA in DRM program was launched in the first semester of Academic Year 2017–2018. Initially, a total of 32 students, 24 Scholars from the QCG and eight (8) regular students were enrolled in the first and second semesters of the Academic Year 2017–2018. The School's MBA-DRM program provided students the enviable opportunity to work alongside leaders in the disaster risk field to develop national to local level DRM and Climate Change Adaptation (CCA) action plans. Twelve students graduated from MBA in DRM Program in Second Semester of Academic School Year 2018–2019. The thrusts of their theses were aligned with the achieving of the Sendai Framework priority areas, Paris agreement objectives and sustainable development goals. This outcome can be replicated as a good practice through the adoption and customization of the curriculum by other institutions to fill the demand of producing Planners and Decision Makers who can mainstream DRR and CCA in national and local sustainable development planning.

Statement of the Problem

The destruction caused by natural and climate-related disasters during twentieth century in the Philippines has been associated with the IPCACs, indicating that the HEIs have neglected disaster management as part of their study courses in the Philippines. This study seeks to answer the following questions:

1. What is the level of assessment in terms of QCG Barangays' existing Institutional and Personnel Coping and Adaptive Capacities (IPCACs)?
2. What kind of formal education program should be developed and implemented to enhance the Coping and Adaptive Capacities of the personnel who are directly or indirectly involved in developing and mainstreaming LDRRMP and LCCAP in the QC Comprehensive Land Use Plan (CLUP) and Comprehensive Development Plan (CDP)?

SCOPE OF THE LITERATURE REVIEW

Coping and Adaptive Capacities' Concepts

There exists an important difference between coping and adaptive capacities. Coping is typically used to refer to ex-post actions, while adaptation is normally associated with ex ante actions. This implies that coping capacity also refers to the ability to react and reduce the adverse effects of experienced hazards, whereas adaptive capacity refers to the ability to anticipate and transform structures, functions, or organizations to better survive any hazards (Saldaña-Zorrilla, 2007). In other words, the capacity to cope does not infer the capacity to adapt (Birkmann, 2011). This research used coping capacity for DRR to decrease or minimize vulnerability towards four thematic areas (i.e. Disaster Preparedness, Disaster Response, Prevention and Mitigation and Rehabilitation and Recovery) recognized under the National Disaster Risk Reduction Management Plan (NDRRMP) 2011–2028 (DND, 2011). Furthermore, the adaptive capacity is used in the context of CCA to improve adaptive capacity against vulnerability towards the seven strategy areas (i.e., Food Security, Water Sufficiency, Ecological Environmental Stability, Human Security, Climate Smart Industries and Services, Sustainable Energy and Knowledge and Capacity Development) as prioritized under the National Climate Change Action Plan (NCCAP) 2011–2028 (CCC, 2011).

Institutional and Personnel Adaptive and Coping Capacities Assessment

Local institutions and personnel's coping and adaptive capacities form the basis for assessment of disaster resilience. Local institutions play a critical role in supporting adaptation. Thus, expanding the institutional and personnel's coping and adaptive capacities are the integral parts in creating resilient societies (Grothmann et al., 2013). The Adaptive Capacity Wheel (ACW) by Gupta et al. (2010) was also considered in identifying institutional assessment parameters (Gupta et al., 2010).

Legal Foundation for Formal Education Program in Disaster Risk Management

The Republic Act No. 10121 known as *Philippine Disaster Risk Reduction and Management Act of 2010* emphasizes under its Section 2; Declaration of Policy to,

> a) Uphold the people's constitutional right to life and the property by addressing the root cause of vulnerability to disasters, strengthening the country's institutional capacity for disaster reduction and management building the resilience of local communities to disaster including climate change impact. (RP, 2010)

Further, the Republic Act No. 9729, or the *Climate Change Act of 2009* of the Philippines also provides legal basis for formulating policies, plans and programs to deal with business management resiliency in changing climate. Internationally, to deal with Disaster Risk Reduction (DRR) (RP-CoP, 2009), the United Nations (UN) and member countries showed their concern by formulating the Hyogo Framework for Action (HFA) in 2005 which set goals to reduce disaster losses by 2015. The HFA states that,

> At times of disasters, impacts and losses can be substantially reduced if authorities, individuals and communities in hazard-prone areas are well prepared and ready to act and are equipped with the knowledge and capacities for effective disaster management. (UNISDR, 2005)

Following the end of the HFA, the Sendai Framework was developed with seven targets through four priorities for action by the year

2030 focusing on DRR (UNISDR, 2015). Further, in December 2015, a conference among 195 countries was held in Paris, France which set goals for Climate Change that came to be known as "The Paris Agreement". Moreover, in September 2015 at the UN Sustainable Development Summit, a final document for the Sustainable Development Goals (SDGs) was developed, which lists 169 targets over 17 goals, each with its own indicators to measure compliance. The 13th SDG in particular focuses on Climate Action (UNDESA, 2018; UNDP, n.a.). It has to be noted that to create resilient urban environment and achieve sustainable development goals for present and future generations, the Institutional and Personnel's (e.g. planners and decision makers) Coping and Adaptive Capacities (IPCACs) building needs to be established and pursued towards Disaster Risk Reduction (DRR) and Climate Change Adaptation (CCA) (FIG, 2006).

OBJECTIVE OF THE STUDY

The main objective of this research is to assess the present Institutional and Personnel Coping and Adaptive Capacities (IPCACs) of Quezon City Government (QCG) and its barangays. It has to be done by determining whether or not its officials have undergone Disaster Risk Reduction (DRR) and Climate Change Adaptation (CCA)-related training programs or have attained diplomas or specializations from any Higher Education Institutions (HEIs).

RESEARCH METHODOLOGY

Intensive internal, external and online desk researches were used as a primary methodology to collect secondary data. Further, a participatory process was also applied by conducting strategic planning workshops and symposia involving Quezon City Local Government (QCLG) and Barangays representatives (Raza, 2018).

Furthermore, a descriptive research design using a combination of quantitative, qualitative and collaborative approaches is applied to analyze the existing QCG Barangays' Institutional Coping and Adaptive Capacities.

Research Location

Nine (9) candidate cities were considered including Mandaluyong, San Juan, Pasay, Makati City, Pasig City, Manila City, Markina, Taguig and Quezon City. The factors considered in ranking the cities with the most potential for being a pilot LGU include future commercial activity, need for technical assistance in planning, readily available data, major infrastructures, availability of funds for the research area of the city, exposure to hazards and political will (Raza, 2018). A Key Informative Interviews (KIIs) form consisting of the above selection criteria was developed. The specialized Logical Decision for Windows (LDWs) software with built-in statistical tool was used to rank and select the top-ranked city as a pilot LGU.

Level of Expertise Assessment

Level of Expertise Assessment/Gap Analysis serves as the summary of the quality and the extent of the coping and adaptive capacity assessment. In the context of this research, it is the numerical representation of the level of IPCACs to deal with DRR and CCA sensitivity to exposed sector, people and other elements at risk against an identified hazard (such as Earthquake, Landslides, Flood, Extreme Weather Event, Change in Precipitation Pattern and/or Rising Mean Temperature). To determine Institutional Coping and Adaptive Capacities (IPCACs) gaps, firstly, this study assessed the capacity parameters of DRR and CCA using 5 point Likert Scale (See Table 10.1 for modified verbal interpretation in the context of this study) (McLeod, 2019). These parameters include the level of basic information; institutional setup; organizational linkages; training, formal education, economic wealth, infrastructure,

Table 10.1 Verbal interpretation of level of expertise

Level of capacity/expertise	Verbal interpretation
5	Excellent
4	Good
3	Fair
2	Poor
1	Very Poor

Source McLeod (2019)

technology, and formal education. These were modified after National Economic Development Authority (NEDA) in 2008 and Local Government Academy (LGA) Local Climate Change Adaptation Planning, Guide Book 1 (DILG, 2014). Secondly, the Personnel Coping Capacity in terms of expertise level was assessed using the same Likert Scale towards four DRR priority areas comprising of disaster prevention and mitigation, disaster preparedness, disaster response and rehabilitation and recovery (RP-DILG, 2011). Finally, Personnel Adaptive Capacity was also assessed using Likert Scale (Table 10.1) but this time to determine the expertise level towards CCA thematic areas, i.e. Food Security, Water Sufficiency, Ecological and Environmental Stability, Human Security, Climate-friendly Industries and Services (Infrastructure), Sustainable Energy and Knowledge and Capacity Development.

ANALYSIS AND INTERPRETATION

Selection of the Pilot Area

The selection of City as the pilot urban area was empirically done by using the specialized software Logical Decisions for Windows (LDW) to process the pertinent collected data from all candidate cities. The LDW evaluated choices provided to select the pilot City by considering many variables/goals at once, separating facts from value judgments and explaining choice to others (swMATH, 2020). The explanation regarding the use of software LDW is provided in the previous sub-section.

Figure 10.1 shows the contribution of eight (8) selected variables' utility values in term of total utility value of each City.

The ranking of the candidate cities with corresponding utility values are shown in descending order (higher to lower utility values). It has to be noted that the variables/goals i.e. Future commercial activities, Availability of funds, Political will, Need technical assistance and Readily available data were the main determinants in placing Quezon City at Rank 1 and Mandaluyong City at Rank 8 with total utility score of 0.932 and 0.212, respectively as shown in Fig. 10.1 (Raza, 2015).

The location map of the Quezon City is shown in Fig. 10.2 (Raza et al., 2016).

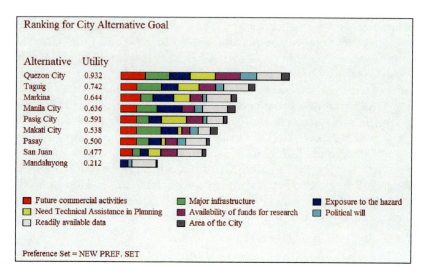

Fig. 10.1 Ranking results of the candidate cities (*Source* Raza, 2015)

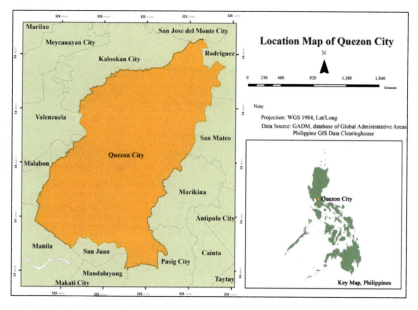

Fig. 10.2 Location of the Quezon City selected as pilot urban area (*Source* Raza, 2015)

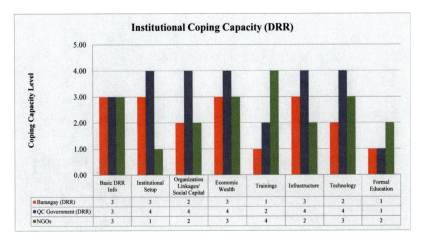

Fig. 10.3 Institutional Coping Capacity of QCG Barangays, QCG and NGOs

Institutional Coping Capacity Level of QCG Barangays, QCG and NGOs

The overall Institutional Coping Capacity (ICC) of QCG Barangays is rated 2.5 "Poor". Further, Fig. 10.3 portrays "Very Poor" ICC in terms of formal education and training; "Poor" in organizational linkages/social capital and technology and "Fair" for ICC in terms of basic DRR information, institutional setup, economic wealth and infrastructure. The overall ICC of QCG responsible offices/departments is "Good". However, it is "Very Poor" in terms of formal education and "Poor" in terms of training (Fig. 10.3). The Non-Government Organizations recognized by the QCG were also assessed. Figure 10.3 shows that the overall ICC of NGOs is "Poor". See Fig. 10.3 for other parameters' details.

Institutional Adaptive Capacity Level of QCG Barangays, QCG and NGOs

The overall Institutional Adaptive Capacity (IAC) of QCG Barangays is rated 2.0 "Poor". Further, the institutional setup, social capital, economic wealth, training and formal education are assessed as "Very Poor" (1) to "Poor" (2) for both QCG (responsible offices and department) and its

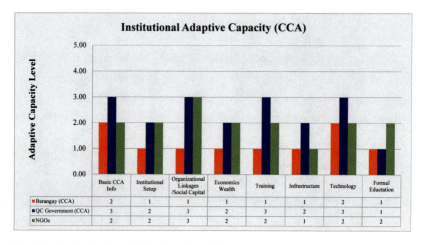

Fig. 10.4 Institutional Adaptive Capacity

Barangay Fig. 10.4). In the case of NGOs the overall IAC is "Poor". See Fig. 10.4 for more details.

Personnel Coping Capacity Level of QCG Barangays, QCG and NGOs

The overall Planners/Decision makers Personnel Coping Capacity (PCC) of QCG Barangays is rated 2.0 "Poor". Further, the disaster prevention and mitigation; preparedness, response; rehabilitation is "Fair". Furthermore, the PCC of the QCG responsible offices and departments overall expertise in all the DRR priority areas is also "Fair". However, PCC in terms of rehabilitation and recovery is "Poor". See Fig. 10.5 for more details.

Personnel Adaptive Capacity Level of QCG Barangays, QCG and NGOs

The overall Planners/Decision makers Personnel Adaptive Capacity (PAC) of QCG Barangays' is rated 1.0 "Very Poor" (Fig. 10.6). Further, the PAC in terms of food security is "Very Poor". Furthermore, the PAC of other CCA thematic areas is "Poor". The PAC of the NGOs is "Very

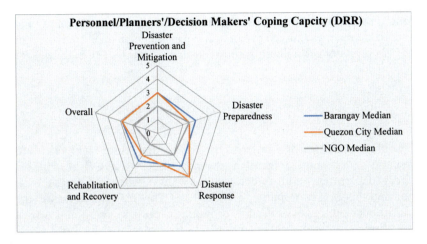

Fig. 10.5 Personnel Coping Capacity Level of QCG Barangays, QCG and NGOs

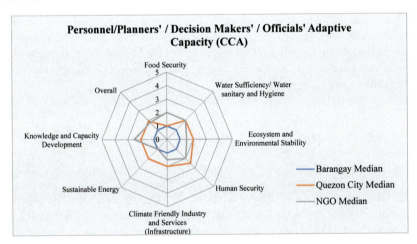

Fig. 10.6 Personnel Adaptive Capacity Level of QCG Barangays, QCG and NGOs

Poor" in terms of food security, climate friendly industry and ecology and sustainable energy, and ecosystem and environmental stability. However, PCC in terms of rehabilitation and recovery is "Poor". See Fig. 10.6 for more details.

INTERPRETATION OF THE ANALYSIS

The analysis of the collected data from 142 barangays of QCG done through a participatory process by conducting three symposia and a survey questionnaire revealed that the ICC of QCG responsible offices/departments and its Barangays is "Very Poor" in formal education and "Poor" in training (Table 10.1). The IAC, in terms of the institutional setup, social capital, economic wealth, training and formal education is assessed as "Very Poor" (1) to "Poor" (2) for both QCG (responsible offices and department) and its Barangays. Further, the overall PCC and PAC of QCG and its Barangays is rated 2.0 "Poor". In addition, the destruction caused in the country in the last decade by natural and climate-related disasters has been associated with the lack of IPCACs. This led to estimating the demand and development of a curriculum for a formal DRM education at HEIs level. The framework for developing formal education degree program specializing in DRM is provided in the next section.

FRAMEWORK FOR DEVELOPING FORMAL EDUCATION PROGRAM IN DRM

Due to the quest for a formal education to fill the country's demand for Disaster Management as based on the analysis of the data collected, the Graduate School of Business (GSB), Philippine School of Business Administration (PSBA), Manila took the lead in introducing Disaster Risk Management (DRM) as a specialization/track in its existing Master of Business Administration (MBA) program (thesis program). The School's Master of Business Administration (MBA) Specialization in Disaster Risk Management (DRM), the so called MBA in DRM is a distinctive program in the Philippines. Combining the study of general MBA core competencies in economics, finance, project research and development, marketing, production and operations, strategic management and accounting with intensive exploration of risk management fields is the main trigger for effective DRM. In fact, the DRM is a dynamic and complex field demanding a wide scope of knowledge and expertise in multiple areas. This program takes a comprehensive approach covering a wide range of topics including financial mechanism for disaster risk reduction, planning, management, humanitarian logistics and supply chain, response, relief, recovery and the economics of disasters. Figure 10.7 shows the Framework used to develop the said program. The following subsections provide a brief description of the activities that were performed to achieve the output of this study:

DEMAND ESTIMATION

The demand estimation basically builds the success of the process and analysis of Institutional and Personnel Coping and Adaptive Capacities (IPCACs) Assessment of the QCG as pilot urban area. Further, the demand estimation is also derived from a total of 43,768.00 Disaster Risk Reduction Management Councils (DRRMCs) in the country needing immediate assistance to implement RA 10121. These DRRMCs include 17 Regions, 81 Provinces, 145 Cities, 1,489 Municipalities and 42,036 Barangays. In addition, the recent bill regarding the creation of Department of Disaster Resilience (DDR), filed by at least 10 senators, is high on the list of priority bills in the Senate and the House of Representatives. The devastating typhoons, earthquakes and the Taal eruption struck the country successively; the lawmakers will do their best to pass vital legislation on the creation of the Department of Disaster Resilience Act of 2019 (Tamayo, 2020). Taking off from the interpretation of analysis, this further increased the demand for formally educated Disaster Risk Management Managers.

Therefore, the attainment of DRM specialization of MBA degree program in the context of this study will open new doors for Managers, Planners, Decision Makers, Economists, Engineers, Scientists, Social Scientists and Armed Forces Personnel, in the highly competitive field of DRM. Indeed, the DRM specialization of MBA will contribute in upholding the people's constitutional right to life and property and gear the nation towards achieving the objectives of Sendai Framework and Sustainable Development Goals by 2030.

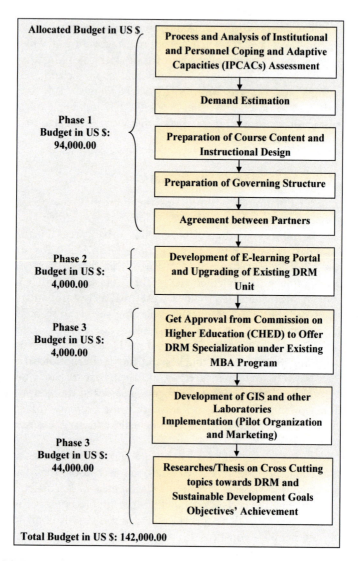

Fig. 10.7 Framework for Developing Formal Education Program (*Source* PSBA, 2017)

Preparation of the Courses and Instructional Design

A team of 6 experts was hired to review the existing courses and instructional design of the currently offered certificates or degree programs in the country or abroad. Recommendations drawn from the review were used to prepare the course description of the DRM related courses. Further, it was also applied in defining the entry points in restructuring available MBA courses and selection of new courses to build the Curriculum of MBA in DRM. Indeed, it allowed the estimation of the gaps in the existing course content, and recognized the efforts necessary to produce a sound set of courses. Further, it also allowed PSBA authorities to file an application to CHED to acquire Government Authority to launch the MBA-DRM program.

Preparation of Governing Structure

An ad hoc committee consisting of potential partners and other institution experts in the field of DRM were consulted through strategic planning workshop. The output of the workshop was used in preparing MBA-DRM program management arrangement, the administrative protocols, resource acquisition strategic plan, admission requirements, administration of entrance examination, thesis writing guidelines, foreign trip guideline, disaster risk management unit upgrading, research fellowship program organizational structure and resources, consent of the experts from the industry to teach courses in the curriculum and tuition fee schedule among others. A student handbook comprising of MBA-DRM governing structure is developed and it is readily available for download at PSBA official website.

Agreement Between Partners

Initial consultations with local and international schools, universities, institutions, departments and offices from public and private sectors were done. The output of the consultations led to an arrangement through Memorandum of Agreement, Memorandum of Understanding, Letter of Intention and Memberships. At present, PSBA has substantial number of partners and linkages with local and international organizations, institutions, departments, etc. These include the Office of Civil Defence,

Philippines, Quezon City Government, Philippines, Asian Institute of Technology, Thailand, Imperial Dunes LLC, Dubai, UAE, Sustainable Development Solution, USA, Global Alliance of Disaster Research Institute, Kyoto University, Japan, GS Fame Institute of Business, Jakarta and Lahore College for Women University, Pakistan, just to name a few.

Development of E-learning Portal and Upgrading of DRM Unit

Following the blended mode of instruction, the MBA in DRM modules are taught using both face to face and online teaching techniques. PSBA-Manila has developed in-house Moodle platform in the form of PSBA E-learning System.

To support the research element of the program, PSBA-Manila has upgraded Disaster Risk Management (DRM) Unit developed under the Graduate School of Business Research Center (GSBRC) since 2003. The unit has produced a substantial number of DRM related researches and published and presented them in local and international conferences, seminars and workshops. The unit also created a Research Fellowship Program. These research fellows are given an opportunity to take part in the Programs, Projects and Activities (PPAs) in the field of DRM and Business Management conducted by the DRM Unit. Further, all the research staffs of the school including research fellows are required to attend and participate in the periodic International events every year through the generous support by the Research Center and DRM Unit.

Government Authority to Offer MBA-DRM Program

The Commission on Higher Education (CHED)/Government authority is required in order to offer any formal education in the Philippines. The Philippine School of Business Administration (PSBA) is the pioneer of DRM specialization in its MBA program. The PSBA Manila started to develop MBA in DRM in 2014. Its request for acquiring Government authority to offer MBA in DRM program was initiated in September 2015 with Commission on Higher Education (CHED), the regulatory body of the Philippines in the field of Higher Education. The program was evaluated by the CHED assigned Technical Committee for Business Administration, Entrepreneurship and Office Administration. After 2 years of continuous communication with CHED on its approval, the PSBA became the first Higher Education Institution (HEl) in the Philippines to be granted with Government Authority to offer MBA in DRM program in May 2017.

Development of Geographic Information System (GIS) Laboratory and MBA-DRM Implementation

The MBA in DRM Program is a 16-month study requiring successful completion of 45 credits spanning four consecutive semesters. To learn from our global partners, there is an off-site study which consists of a 7- to 10-day excursion for the qualified students. Further, to comply with the wide range of topics covered by the program including the Geographic Information System (GIS), Risk Sensitive Land Use Planning, Risk Sensitive Development Planning, Community Based Disaster Risk Management, etc., a GIS laboratory was necessary. Thus, in this regard the School acquired hardware (20 computers and 1 Server), software and corresponding training to understand and implement integrated digital system. The GIS laboratory was also completed by acquiring GIS licenses.

Furthermore, 4 laboratory staff and a professor were sent for GIS training as part of the total cost of acquisition of the GIS licenses. After having the required facilities, course curriculum in hand, keen evaluation, and acquiring proper authorization, the MBA-DRM program was launched in the first semester of Academic Year 2017–2018. Presently, 24 Scholars from the QCG and eight (8) regular students are enrolled in the program. The School program provided students the opportunity to work alongside leaders in the disaster risk field to develop DRM and CCAM and Mitigation (CCAM) for national and locals covering programs, projects and activities with agencies and organizations. This is accomplished as a group project where the professor acts as the project manager and the students are given assignments to complete in a professional manner.

Thesis on Cross Cutting Topics Towards DRM and SDGs

The first pilot batch consisting of 12 Scholars from the QCG graduated with degree of MBA-DRM Program in the Summer Semester 2019 (May, 2019). Their theses/researches were done specializing in Disaster Management cross cutting the SDGs.

Conclusion

The analysis revealed that the IPCACs of the QCG and its barangays were "Very Poor to Poor" in the context of acquisition of formal DRM education and training. Further, the destruction caused by natural and climate-related disasters has been associated with the lack of IPCACs. To respond to the above challenge, MBA-DRM program was introduced. It is the key to expanding Institutional Coping and Adaptive Capacities of the personnel directly or indirectly involved in the development and implementation of the local to national risk sensitive agendas/plans. The DRM specialization has combined the strengths of general MBA core competencies towards business continuity and risk sensitive solutions. Certainly, altogether it makes up an effective DRM towards sustainable development solutions. The piloting of this specialization translated into identification of QCG functional problems and unique solutions by the first batch of QCG scholars. The MBA in DRM program is developed considering business continuity principles and increasing intensity and frequency of natural and man-made disasters and its negative impact on the national economy. Even though the development of this program was very challenging, its implementation opened new doors for its Graduates to become future managers, planners, decision makers and economists in the highly competitive field of DRM.

The DRM specialization program is taught with blended learning mode of instruction that includes face to face and online learning. It is of international coverage with periodic international conferences, research colloquia and symposia. Participatory and practice oriented thrust is one of the asset of this program. Indeed, this DRM specialization program will enhance the capacities of decision-makers and personnel involved in developing and implementing plans, programs, projects and activities in upholding the people's constitutional right to life and property.

Recommendations

- The existing MBA-DRM curriculum should be enhanced to develop it into a Master of Science in Disaster Risk Management (MS DRM) in the near future.
- The curriculum can be adopted and customized tailor-fitted by other institutions to fill the demand for producing Planners and Decision Makers who can mainstream DRR and CCA in national and local planning.
- Initiate application to include MBA-DRM in seeking the Environmental Planner's Licensure Examination under the Professional Regulatory Commission (PRC) of the Philippines.
- An online or spilt based Executive MBA-DRM Program should be developed from the existing MBA-DRM Program with the collaboration of partner Institution/s.
- Under the PSBA continuous learning policy, the GSB-PSBA should offer certificate courses consisting of one unit (18 hours) that will be selected from its existing General MBA and MBA in DRM curriculum. The Modules of these courses should be well-designed and ready for implementation using blended medium, i.e. both online and face to face teaching techniques.
- Proper training should be given to the Decision Makers, Planners and other personnel directly or indirectly involved in developing and implementing and implementation of LDRRMP, LCCAP, CLUP, CDP and other related plans.
- The courses obtained through the certificate program should be formulated to be accredited for any master's degree program offered by the GSB, PSBA-Manila and its partners.
- With CHED endorsement, the GSB PSBA-Manila should reach out to the public and private institutions to continue its traditional off-Campus classes to promote MBA in DRM in support of objectives of RA 10121.

Acknowledgements We would like to extend our gratitude to the former Hon Quezon City Mayor Herbert M Bautista and Chief of the Staff, Cdr. Aldrin C. Cuña for approving the Quezon City as pilot City for developing and implementing this so called MBA-DRM Program. I would also like to extend my gratitude to the current Quezon City Mayor Hon. Joy Belmonte for her continued support to the MBA-DRM Program.

Further, we are very grateful to Ms. Alicia C. Padua, Ms. Rose Laude from QC-CPDO, Ms. Frederika C. Rentoy and Andrea Valentine A. from QC-EPWMD, Dr Noel and Karl Michael E. Marasigan QC-DRRMO for sparing their precious time in providing their technical assistance during the study.

Last but not the least, we would also like to thank the Executive Board Members of PSBA Manila and Quezon City Government for providing overall moral, financial and technical support to achieve the objectives of this study.

References

Birkmann, J. (2011). First and second-order adaptation to natural hazards and extreme events in the context of climate change. *Natural Hazards, 58*(2), 811–840. https://doi.org/10.1007/s11069-011-9806-8

Climate Change Act (2009), Republic of the Philippines. Retrieved February 6, 2020 from http://www.gov.ph/2009/10/23/republic-act-no-9729/.

Climate Change Commission (CCC). (2011). *National climate change action plan 2011–2028*. Philippines: Climate Change Commission (2011) 1–128, Retrieved December 6, 2019 from https://policy.asiapacificenergy.org/sites/default/files/NCCAP_TechDoc.pdf

Commission on Higher Education (CHED), National Capital Region. (2017). 2nd Endorsement of Ms. Eleanor BA Fernandez OIC, Office of the Director IV, Office of the Programs, Standards Development, Granting Government Authority to the Philippine School of Business Administration-Manila to offer DRM as Specialization, Letter Dated, May 16, NCR Philippines.

DILG. (2014). *LGU guidebook on the formulation of Local Climate Change Action Plan (LCCAP)*. Department of Interior and Local Government.

DND, Republic of the Philippines. (2011). *PRIMER, the National Disaster Risk Reduction and Management Plan (NDRRMP) 2011–2028*. Department of National Defense, 1–10 Philippines. Retrieved June 20, 2020 from http://www.dilg.gov.ph/PDF_File/resources/DILG-Resources-2012116-ab6ce90b0d.pdf

FIG. (2006). *The contribution of the surveying profession to disaster risk management*. Fig Working Group 8.4, International Federation of Surveyors. frederiksberg, Denmark. Retrieved February 6, 2020 from http://extwprlegs1.fao.org/docs/pdf/phi152934.pdf

GFDRR. (2017). *Global facility for disaster reduction and recovery, Philippines*. Retrieved September 17, 2020 from https://www.gfdrr.org/en/philippines

Grothmann, T., Grecksch, K., Winges, M., & Siebenhüner, B. (2013). Assessing institutional capacities to adapt to climate change: Integrating psychological dimensions in the Adaptive Capacity Wheel. *Natural Hazards and Earth System Sciences, 13,* 3369–3384. https://doi.org/10.5194/nhess-13-3369-2013

Gupta, J., Termeer, K., Klostermann, J., Meijerink, S., van den Brink, M., Jong, P., Nooteboom, S., & Bergsmaa, E. (2010). The Adaptive Capacity Wheel: A method to assess the inherent characteristics of institutions to enable the adaptive capacity of society. *Environmental Science and Policy, 13,* 459–471.

Jha, S., Quising, P. F., Ardaniel, Z., Martinez, A. Jr., & Wang, L. (2018). *Natural disasters, public spending, and creative destruction: A case study of the Philippines* (ADBI Working Paper: 817). Tokyo.

Logical Decisions. (2020). *swMath.* Retrieved September 16, 2020 from http://swmath.org/software/16195

May, P. (1992). Policy learning and policy failure. *Journal of Public Policy, 12,* 331–354.

McLeod, S. A. (2019, August 3). *Likert scale, simply psychology.* Retrieved July 17, 2020 from https://www.simplypsychology.org/likert-scale.html

Philippine Disaster Risk Reduction and Management Act. (2010). Republic of the Philippines. Retrieved March 23, 2020 from http://www.gov.ph/2010/05/27/republic-act-no-10121/

PSBA. (2017). *Curriculum for the Degree of Master in Business Administration (MBA) Specialization in Disaster Risk Management (DRM).* Philippine School of Business Administration. Retrieved February 6, 2020 from http://psba.edu/curriculum/master-in-business-administration-mba-specialization-in-disaster-risk-management-drm/

PreventionWeb. (2018). *The knowledge platform for disaster risk reduction, academic programme, Master of Business Administration, Specialization in Disaster Risk Management (MBA-DRM).* Retrieved February 6, 2020 from https://www.preventionweb.net/academic/view/58436

Raza, T. (2015). *Risk sensitive land use and development planning model: Mainstreaming DRR and CCA into planner's and decision agenda, Quezon City, Philippines* (PhD Dissertation). School of Urban and Regional Planning, Quezon City, Philippines, University of the Philippines.

Raza, T. (2018). Localizing disaster risk reduction and climate change adaptation in planners' and decision makers' agenda: Technical comprehensive model, Quezon City, Philippines. *Procedia Engineering, 212,* 1311–1318. https://doi.org/10.1016/j.proeng.2018.01.169

Raza, T., Fan-Sheng, K., & Peralta, J. F. (2016). *Originating urban climate change adaptation planning guidepost: Urban Landscape Sustainability Framework (ULSF), Quezon City, Philippines.* Proceedings of the 11th international Symposium on Architectural Interchanges in Asia (ISAIA). September 20–23. Japan: Miyagi, 2016.

Raza, T., & Peralta, J. F. (2019). *Education capacity development and disaster resilience, disaster resilience and sustainable development*. Panel Discussion with the collaboration of Asian Institute of Technology (AIT), United Nations University, and ProSPER.Net, March 7–8, AIT, Thailand.

Republic of the Philippines, Department of Interior and Local Government (RP-DILG). (2011 June, 16). *National Disaster Risk Reduction and Management Framework (NDRRMF)*, 2/f, NDRRMC Building, Camp, General Emilio Aguinaldo, Quezon City, Philippines. Retrieved November 2, 2021 from https://www.adrc.asia/documents/dm_information/Philippines_NDRRM_Framework.pdf

Saldaña-Zorrilla, S.R. (2007). *Socioeconomic vulnerability to natural disasters in Mexico: Rural poor, trade and public response* (CEPAL Report 92). UN-ECLAC, Disaster Evaluation Unit, Mexico, ISBN 978-92-1-121661-5.

Tamayo B. (2020, January 20). *Disaster resilience Dept. is top Congress priority*. Manilatime.net. Retrieved February 6, 2020 from https://www.manilatimes.net/2020/01/20/news/top-stories/disaster-resilience-dept-is-top-congress-priority/675901/

UNDESA. (United Nation Department of Economics and Social Affairs). (2018). *Climate change: Sustainable development knowledge platform*. Retrieved July 25, 2020 from https://sustainabledevelopment.un.org/topics/climatechange

UNDP. (United Nation Development Programme). (n.a.). *Sustainable development goals, Goal 13: Climate action*. Retrieved February 6, 2020 from https://www.undp.org/content/undp/en/home/sustainable-development-goals/goal-13-climateaction.html#:~:text=The%20goal%20aims%20to%20mobilize,also%20to%20the%20other%20SDGs.

UNISDR. (2005). *Hyogo framework for action 2005–2015: Building the resilience of nations and communities to disasters*. Retrieved February 6, 2020 from www.unisdr.org/eng/hfa/docs/Hyogo-framework-for-actionenglish.pdf

UNISDR. (2015). *Sendai framework for disaster risk reduction 2015–2030*. Geneva, The United Nations Office for Disaster Risk Reduction. Retrieved February 6, 2020 from https://www.undrr.org/publication/sendai-framework-disaster-risk-reduction-2015-2030.

World Economic Forum (WEF). (2018). *The global risks report 2018* (3rd ed.). World Economic Forum.

PART III

Science Technology, Risk Assessment, Communities

CHAPTER 11

Vulnerability and Resilience Science: Concepts, Tools, and Practice

Susan L. Cutter

INTRODUCTION

Understanding that hazards are social constructions and do not exist independently of human activity goes back to the early work of Gilbert F. White, who according to many is the grandfather of hazards research. Beginning with his own dissertation where he proclaimed that "*floods are acts of god, but flood losses are acts of [hu]man*" (White, 1953), White was steadfast in his belief that hazards arise from the interactions of social, biological, and physical systems, and that disasters were as much a product of humans as the physical event itself (White, 1978, p. 230). The traditional view of hazards was as discrete events affecting the built environment on the one hand, and social systems on the other. The interaction between the event's impact on the built environment and the social systems created the disaster.

S. L. Cutter (✉)
Hazards and Vulnerability Research Institute and Department of Geography, University of South Carolina, Columbia, SC, USA
e-mail: SCUTTER@mailbox.sc.edu

Over time, a more nuanced and sophisticated understanding of the social construction of hazards and disasters evolved. Instead of a one-way flow from event to impact, we now understand the interactive nature of hazards and disasters whereby the natural systems influence and are influenced by changes in the built environment and social systems (Tierney, 2019). The reflexive nature of these interactions (natural systems, built environment, social systems) produces new risks (Beck, 1999). Simultaneously, such interactions occur within the broader contexts whereby social, economic, political, institutional, and historical processes that have altered these systems. In other words, events beyond our control do not create disasters rather they are a product of the existing social order created by past and ongoing processes (Tierney, 2014). There are two major constructs in natural hazards science that have evolved in the past half century that give rise to our present understanding of hazards and disasters and their impacts on people and the places where they live and work. These two constructs—social vulnerability and community resilience—also govern disaster risk reduction policies and practices from local to global scales.

This chapter explores the concepts of social vulnerability and community resilience, their measurement, and the practical application of social vulnerability and community resilience metrics in emergency preparedness and response with specific reference to the U.S. experience. The chapter poses five propositions: (1) vulnerability and resilience are linked but they are not the opposite of one another; (2) community resilience is multi-faceted and multi-hazard; (3) measurement is important in establishing the value proposition for community resilience; (4) vulnerability and resilience science must be translated into practice and resilience practice must inform science; and (5) acknowledgement of the limitations of science and practice is critical in disaster risk reduction. After initially exploring social vulnerability and community resilience concepts, the chapter moves to a detailed discussion of approaches to measurement as a foundational element in providing the evidentiary basis for disaster risk reduction policies and practices.

Vulnerability and Resilience Science

Vulnerability and resilience are complementary, yet represent two different approaches to understanding hazards and disasters and impacts (Cutter, 2018; Miller et al., 2010; Turner II, 2010). They are also driven by very different fundamental questions: (1) what circumstances create the social burdens of risk and how do these affect the distribution of risks and losses (e.g. vulnerability); and (2) what enhances or reduces the ability of communities to prepare for, respond to, recover from, successfully adapt to, or anticipate hazard threats (e.g. resilience), and how does this vary geographically?

Vulnerability

In its broadest sense, vulnerability is the potential for loss or some adverse impact or the capacity to suffer harm. In the disasters context, the UNISDR defines vulnerability as:

> The conditions determined by physical, social, economic, and environmental factors or processes which increase the susceptibility of an individual, a community, assets or systems to the impacts of hazards. (UNISDR, 2017a)

Vulnerability can characterize individuals (e.g. people, buildings), broader social groups such as the elderly, renters, female-headed households, or systems (either spatial-defined such as ecosystems, or a-spatial systems such as infrastructure, which could have a spatial element). Vulnerability crosses the divide between physical and/or environmental conditions to include not only social conditions and built environment/infrastructure as well.

Depending on orientation and training there are some discrepancies in the usage of vulnerability between scholars engaged in hazards and disasters research and those involved in topical areas of global environmental change research. This is primarily reflective of the different origins, paths, and questions asked by the research community of scholars (Adger, 2006; Fuchs & Thaler, 2018; Turner II, 2003). The place-based nature of vulnerability posits that the vulnerability of a place is a combination of the interaction between the inherent risk and mitigation efforts that influence the hazard potential (or exposure), which is then filtered through the geographic context (location, distance, elevation) which produces the biophysical vulnerability. At the same time, the hazard potential also leads to interactions with the socioeconomic characteristics and social conditions to produce the social vulnerability of places. The overall vulnerability of a place—such as city or neighbourhood—is the combination of social and biophysical vulnerability attributed to that place (Cutter, 1996, 2006). Vulnerability is a function of exposure (what or who is at risk of the hazard potential) and sensitivity (the degree to which people or places can be harmed) (Cutter, 1996).

Resilience

Resilience is the ability of a system to respond and recover from a disturbance, in this instance a hazard event or disaster. It includes the inherent conditions within the system to absorb the impacts, cope with the event, and in the longer term enhance the system's capacity to adapt or change in response to the event (Cutter et al., 2008). In ecological systems, the premise is bouncing back after a disturbance to a pre-impact state and maintaining functions. In socio-ecological systems, resilience is defined as bouncing forward after a disturbance, not merely bouncing back (Manyena et al., 2011), in other words, improvements in the conditions. The ubiquitous nature of the term resilience fosters widespread usage, ranging from the engineering systems who define resilience in terms of the structure to return to its original shape or form after being compressed, bent, or shaped (Linkov et al., 2014) to the health sciences who use resilience to describe the ability of individuals to adapt in the face of adversity, trauma, or stress (Ungar, 2018).

In the hazards context, resilience is defined thusly.

> The ability of a system, community or society exposed to hazards to resist, absorb, accommodate, adapt to, transform and recover from the effects of a hazard in a timely and efficient manner, including through the preservation and restoration of its essential basic structures and functions through risk management. (UNISDR, 2017a)

In reframing the resilience concept, this chapter uses the definition of resilience put forth by the U.S. National Academies because of its simplicity, expansiveness, and widespread acceptance. Accordingly, disaster resilience is the "*...ability to prepare and plan for, absorb, recover from or more successfully adapt to actual or potential adverse events*" (The National Academies, 2012, p. 2).

Like its counterpart vulnerability, resilience can be applied to multiple scales and units of analysis ranging from individuals (people, structures, businesses), groups (social groups, economic sectors), or systems (infrastructure, environmental), again in spatial or non-spatial terms. A further defining characteristic of resilience is that it can be an outcome (resilience to what), a process (resilience for whom) or both. There can be inherent or pre-existing resilience with systems or places, but given the post-event impacts there can also be adaptive resilience where social learning and improvisation take place to facilitate recovery after disaster. The disaster resilience of place model (DROP) describes these elements and highlights that the pre-existing or antecedent conditions within places include the inherent vulnerability and the inherent resilience as by-products of the intersection of social systems, natural systems, and the built environment (Cutter et al., 2008). In this model, vulnerability and resilience are not the same conceptually, nor are the opposite of one another, although linked. In simplified language, just because you are vulnerable, does not mean you lack resilience, a concept that also applies to places.

THE INTEGRATED NATURE OF COMMUNITY RESILIENCE

Communities come in all shapes and sizes and it is generally understood that communities are a collection of people and the systems that support them occupying a geographically delimited area usually at a sub-national, sub-province, or sub-state level of jurisdiction. Community resilience then becomes those capabilities that enhance or detract from its ability to prepare and plan for, absorb, recover from, or adapt to adverse events. Community resilience is more than a single sector, single capability, or single hazard construct; it encompasses all the assets and resources available in the community. Think of community resilience as a system of interdependent systems each of them having their own individual and collective resilience. This multidimensional nature is akin to a system of systems characterization of community resilience, or what many term the capitals approach (Berkes & Ross, 2013) and highlights the basic forms of capital within communities that enable them to develop, prosper, and recover when the disaster hits.

While the capitals pie can be split in many ways, in the disaster literature the capitals are divided into six main groupings (NASEM, 2019). Human or cultural capital includes the demographic characteristics and physical attributes of the community such as age, educational levels, special needs populations as well as the values and shared beliefs. Financial or economic capital is the totality of economic assets and livelihoods embodied in employment, personal wealth, type of economic activity in the community, and so forth. Built environment capital (or infrastructure) are the material assets in communities including buildings of all types—residential, commercial, industrial, institutional, schools—and infrastructure such as roads, water supply, power, communications, that are necessary to provide the critical services to residents. Political capital as referred to as institutional/governance capital is the access to resources and the power to influence the distribution of those resources for the betterment of the community, and to engage the community in those decisions. The provision of shared government, and key community resources—public safety, emergency response, jurisdictional coordination—is also included in this capital. Social capital is one of the most well-known but least operational element of community resilience. Social capital refers to the social networks and connectivity among individuals and groups that enhances trust, attachment to place, political engagement, collaborative decision making, and the social quality of life within the community. Lastly, natural or environmental capital is the natural resource base and environmental conditions that provide the basic building blocks for the community's livelihoods. These capitals produce the inherent resilience within communities and either advance or retard the capacity of communities to respond to hazard events before and after they occur.

Measurement Approaches

Measurement tools are helpful in identifying disaster risk and taking steps towards reducing it. They are also helpful in assessing and prioritizing needs and goals, understanding costs (investments) and benefits (results) of actions, and importantly evaluating the effects of different policies and/or approaches. In order for communities to make investments in resilience activities they need to document their current capacities. It is difficult to measure progress towards an established goal or recognize success if you do not have a starting point or baseline. Measurement tools cannot create a resilient community, but they can help guide it towards becoming safer, stronger, and more vibrant in the face of unanticipated events. One of the major benefits for measuring community resilience is to raise awareness and get stakeholder buy-in on what resilience means for that community and the need for and significance of becoming resilient.

Vulnerability Assessments

There are many approaches for assessing vulnerability some that address vulnerability to specific hazards (earthquakes, floods, hurricanes), particular locations such as coastal, mountains, small island nations, or specific spatial units (counties, cities, countries) (Hames, et al., 2017; Rufat, et al., 2015; Solangaarachchi et al., 2012; Titus et al., 2009). Most include quantitative data in the form of indices, which provide a descriptive analysis of vulnerability, mainly expressed solely as exposure or sensitivity. Social vulnerability indices focus primarily on the identification of those population characteristics influencing the social burdens of risk and empirically measure the social disparities in disaster impacts, preparedness, response, and recovery. When paired with exposure assessments or disaster loss data, social vulnerability indices provide a powerful tool for illustrating in an apolitical manner, the intersection of those places with the highest social vulnerability and the greatest damage and loss (Burton et al., 2018; Emrich, 2017; Emrich & Cutter, 2011; Oxfam America, 2017).

One of the most well-known social vulnerability indices is the Social Vulnerability Index (SoVI®) (Cutter et al., 2003). Starting with the conceptualization that social vulnerability is a multi-dimensional construct where age, socioeconomic status, race/ethnicity, gender, family structure, special needs populations, and housing tenure interact to produce the social vulnerability of places. SoVI® represents U.S. county (and sub-county) socioeconomic profiles based on decennial census input data. Using a principal components analysis to reduce the 29 input variables into multi-dimensional drivers, the SoVI® procedure identifies anywhere from 6–8 factors or components that roughly explain between 72 and 78 percent of the variance in the input data (Cutter & Morath, 2013; Rufat et al., 2019). The factors are summed (assuming equal weights) to produce an overall score which is then mapped by standard deviation for each enumeration unit into a 3-class or 5-class categorization representing high (top 20%), medium, and low (bottom 20%) vulnerability, or high (5%), medium high, medium, medium low, or low (bottom 5%) vulnerability. The mapping provides the comparison of the relative level of vulnerability across the desired study area, as illustrated for the entire United States by county (Fig. 11.1).

Originally developed at the county scale to coincide with U.S. emergency management functions, SoVI® is scalable to any enumeration unit

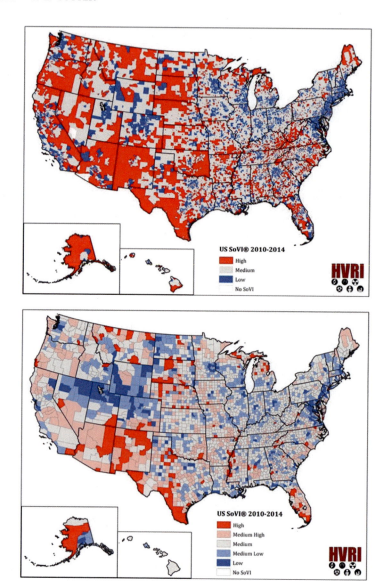

Fig. 11.1 SoVI® for the U.S. using 2010–2014 data by census tract (top) using a three-class categorization, and by county (bottom) using a five-class categorization

such as a census tract, metropolitan area, state, as long as the requisite input data are available. In the U.S. for spatial units smaller than a census tract, the quality and error estimates in the data are insufficient to produce a truly localized SoVI® metric using Census Data.

There are many replications of SoVI® outside of the U.S. for metropolitan areas such as Lisbon (Guillard-Gonçalves et al., 2015)and Bucharest (Armas & Gavris, 2013), and for selected regions such as the Yangtze River Delta in China (Chen et al., 2013), a flood-prone region of Zimbabwe (Maharani et al., 2016), and villages surrounding the Merapi volcano (Mavhura et al., 2017). On a national level, SoVI® was replicated for Norway (Holand & Lujala, 2013), Brazil (de Loyola Hummell et al., 2016), and Indonesia (Siagian et al., 2014). While the replications customize the input variables for the local context and meaning and use the enumeration unit most applicable to the study area based on national census data, the index construction methods remain the same. In each example, the output data are presented as a map showing the uneven distribution of social vulnerability across the study region.

Community Resilience Assessments

The development of community resilience metrics is not as mature as vulnerability indices. There are dozens of resilience measurement efforts, but there is no consistency among them in terms of purpose, target categories, input variables, scale, type of measurement, or practical application as a number of reviews highlight (Beccari, 2016; Cutter, 2016; Ostadtaghizadeh et al., 2015; Sharifi, 2016).

The single most important issue with empirically based community resilience metrics is that they are unusable by communities. Initially designed for theoretical or conceptual purposes not practice, they are too difficult to implement or use; input data are not available at the appropriate spatial scale, or they fail to engage with the totality of community assets, capacities, or programmatic needs (NASEM, 2019). It is also debatable as to whether the existing measurement efforts truly measure resilience and/or the resilience as defined by the community itself.

A second critical issue with the existing measurement efforts is the lack of external or internal validation and the inability to monitor change in resilience over time. It is unclear, for example, whether or not the computed indices are in fact measuring resilience as relatively few follow standard scientific principles of indexing, nor have they been correlated with some desired outcome measure (such as loss reduction). Further, most appear descriptive of pre-existing conditions at a single point in time and not repeated in the same place to track changes in resilience over time.

One example of a community resilience tool that has attempted to address the two criticisms above is the Baseline Resilience Index for Communities (BRIC) (NASEM, 2019). The original prototype for BRIC focused on five capitals for only the Southeast U.S. Improvements in our conceptual understanding and data availability led to a more expansive and comprehensive BRIC developed for the U.S. at the county level. Based on the theoretical Disaster Resilience of Place (DROP) model, described earlier in this chapter and the experience of the computationally intensive SoVI® metric, DROP employed a different indexing approach in its construction, and was computed using an excel spreadsheet.

Utilizing the capitals framework, input variables were selected based on the conceptual understanding of their contribution to resilience and then empirically tested to reduce high collinearity or lack of congruence within the capitals. The variables were normalized using linear min–max scaling (values ranging from 0 to 1), where 1 indicated increased resilience and 0 meant decreased resilience. There were an uneven number of input variables within each capital, requiring taking the simple mean for each. The mean score per capital (or sub-index) was summed to produce the overall resilience score which ranged from 0 to 6. As was the case with the SoVI®, equal weighting was used as there is no theoretical or conceptual basis for determining which capital is more important than the others. The geographic patterns of county resilience were mapped using a 5-category classification based on standard deviation and displayed as a map showing either the geographic variability in total BRIC score, or the geographic distribution of resilience based on the individual capitals.

In addition to the mapping display of information, the BRIC scores can be easily retrieved from the spreadsheet. In this manner, the user can quickly identify what capital is driving the resilience in that county (higher score closer to 1), and which capital or capitals are lagging (scores closer to 0). It is the latter where investments in resilience may produce improvements in overall scores (Table 11.1). Using census data based on sampling rather than actual counts, permitted the development of BRIC on five-year intervals (e.g. the Census American Community Survey product samples 20% per year, so a 5-year period is needed to get the 100% values). In comparing 2010 BRIC for example, with a 2015 BRIC

Table 11.1 Selected BRIC Scores by Capital and Change from 2010 to 2015

	St. Charles, Louisiana		Shelby, Iowa		Richland, South Carolina		Imperial, California		Presidio, Texas	
	2010	2015	2010	2015	2010	2015	2010	2015	2010	2015
Social	0.81	0.74	0.81	0.7	0.65	0.69	0.31	0.61	0.1	0.5
Economic	0.7	0.5	0.71	0.51	0.45	0.47	0.4	0.41	0.24	0.41
Housing & Infrastructure	0.47	0.27	0.63	0.33	0.29	0.31	0.42	0.27	0.27	0.14
Community	0.61	0.41	0.69	0.42	0.34	0.39	0.32	0.24	0.36	0.21
Institutional	1	0.64	0.94	0.51	0.39	0.4	0.23	0.36	0.17	0.32
Environmental	0.8	0.66	0.48	0.58	0.6	0.58	0	0.39	0.53	0.58
Overall Score	4.389	3.233	4.267	3.047	2.725	2.853	1.67	2.271	1.674	2.162

Source Author

illustrates changes in resilience over time and across space (Cutter & Derakhshan, 2018).

TRANSLATION INTO PRACTICE

Given the diversity of communities, a one-size-fits-all approach to disaster resilience practice is not possible given different levels of community engagement, investment levels, and needs. While the theoretical and conceptual approaches to social vulnerability and community resilience are important in advancing the science, they were constructed from the top-down with little, if any engagement with the community. If the goal is to translate such efforts into usable and useful information for communities, such information needs to not only be customized for the local experience, but it must provide multiple benefits (e.g. embedded in day-to-day practices such as planning) and such investments justified and the expected outcomes from such expenditures given the fiscal constraints in many communities.

MITIGATION AND RECOVERY AIDED BY SoVI®

There are a number of examples of the translation of social vulnerability into practice worth noting. In the U.S., all states are required to produce a hazard mitigation plan in order to maintain their eligibility for disaster relief resources including public assistance and mitigation. All plans require FEMA approval with updates every five years. The state plans summarize the county mitigation plans submitted to the state. All mitigation planning efforts follow the same guidelines and procedures put forth by FEMA (FEMA, 2016). Each plan (county and state) must include a hazard and vulnerability assessment outlining the range of hazards affecting the area, location, extent, frequency, probability of future occurrence, changing future conditions, and vulnerability of jurisdictions based on population characteristics and assets. FEMA encourages the use of mapping to illustrate the extent of hazards and the vulnerability. This risk assessment is the evidentiary basis for identifying and prioritizing mitigation actions at county to state jurisdictional levels. SoVI® was first used in South Carolina's state hazard mitigation plan in 2006 and became an example of best practice. Since then SoVI® appears in over a dozen state hazard mitigation plans and countless county, city, and regional mitigation planning efforts (see sovius.org for a listing).

After the 2015 extreme flood event in South Carolina, the Governor's goal was to prioritize recovery based on highlighting those most in need in terms of loss and capacity to recover. The intent was to avoid distributing scarce resources to those with less need and to avoid the risk crippling recovery for many citizens and communities by ignoring their capacity. These requirements required an apolitical mechanism for targeting areas with the greatest social vulnerability which also sustained large flood losses. SoVI® became the operational tool to achieve these goals by illustrating the intersection of FEMA verified loss counts with social vulnerability (Fig. 11.2). The inclusion of SoVI® became part of the South Carolina's long term recovery plan and the model used in other states for determining post-disaster recovery support. Since 2015, South Carolina, West Virginia, Louisiana, and Puerto Rico have used SoVI® to determine the unmet needs for recovery resources from the federal government (Govierno de Puerto Rico, 2018; SC Disaster Recovery Office, 2017; West Virginia Development Office, 2017).

Deployment of Community Resilience Tools

In the case of resilience, there are many more examples of the implementation of resilience measurement as they were developed for this purpose. In most instances, such tools were developed to establish baselines measurement ostensibly for priority investments such as the UNISDR's

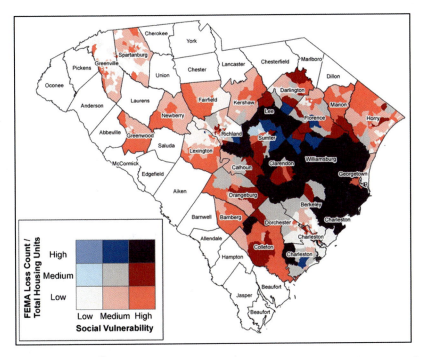

Fig. 11.2 SoVI® coupled with FEMA verified loss counts tells the story of where resources are needed to support flood recovery in the aftermath of the 2015 flooding in South Carolina (*Source* South Carolina Disaster Recovery Office [SCDRO], South Carolina Action Plan for Disaster Recovery [Columbia: South Carolina Department of Commerce, 2016, p. 18], https://www.sccommerce.com/sites/default/files/hud_submittal_action_plan_160719.pdf)

Disaster Resilient Scorecard for Cities (UNISDR, 2017b), or as guides for the self-assessment of resilience such as the Coastal Resilience Index (Sempier et al., 2010) or the City Resilience Framework used in the 100 Resilient Cities effort supported by the Rockefeller Foundation (ARUP, 2014, 2018). Those resilience frameworks deployed in multiple places include the NIST Community Resilience Planning Guide (NIST, 2016) and Zurich Flood Resilience Measurement Framework (Zurich Insurance Group 2019a, 2019b). Both incorporate a hybrid approach of top-down information with locally generated data collection and engagement in guiding resilience investments (NASEM, 2019).

The Baseline Resilience Indicators for Communities (BRIC) while temporally and spatially replicated had not moved beyond the research and development phase until very recently. In 2016, FEMA began a project to develop a strategy and tool for eliminating inconsistent risk assessments in planning and to provide a national baseline for risk assessment. Utilizing hazard (probability of event or observed historic frequency), consequence (exposure of the built environment plus social vulnerability), and resilience, the National Risk Index for Natural Hazards (NRI) provides web-based geospatial product for use by state and local entities for planning. The NRI includes SoVI® as the social vulnerability component and BRIC as the resilience element (https://hazards.fema.gov/nri/).

Conclusions and Limitations

Throughout the chapter, an effort was made to identify both the limitations of the science of vulnerability and resilience and its application. Clearly there is room for improvement in both. For example, more focus needs to be placed on resilience enhancement and vulnerability reduction but these must be done in concert with very clear emphases on who, what, where, and for whom the enhancement or reduction is targeted. There is a need for moving beyond the examination of the existing characteristics of the vulnerability or resilience of places (a static view), to more dynamic approach that examines the underlying drivers and their influence at multiple spatial and temporal scales. At the same time, the temporal and spatial patterns of vulnerability and resilience need more investigation in order to empirically demonstrate the relationship between the two concepts. Finally, there is a critical need for outcome measures. How do we know for sure whether we are measuring social vulnerability or resilience and how do we know it?

This chapter began with five simple propositions. First, vulnerability and resilience are indeed separate and distinct concepts, focusing on sensitivity to hazard impacts (vulnerability), and capacity to cope with such impacts. They are not the oppositional anchors of a pathway from vulnerability to resilience. Just because you are vulnerable does not mean you lack resilience and the corollary. Second, vulnerability and resilience are multi-dimensional and must be seen in their totality as antecedent or pre-existing conditions within communities. Also, community resilience is a part of the fabric of communities and thus can apply to wide range of hazards and stressors. Third, assessing baseline conditions is a prerequisite for establishing the value of resilience in terms of costs and benefits, and progress towards disaster risk reduction. Fourth, the translation of vulnerability and resilience science into practice is emerging, but there remains a valley between top-down and bottom-up approaches in the co-production of the new knowledge to advance resilience theory and practice. Finally, knowing more does not result in better practice or even risk reduction. Science and practice each have their limits in terms of perceived value, efficiency, and acceptance. It is only when communities exercise the leadership, commitment, and engagement with knowledge experts and knowledge experts learn from communities that the transdisciplinary ideal of community resilience can be achieved as we progress forward on the path to disaster risk reduction and a sustainable future.

References

Adger, N. W. (2006). Vulnerability. *Global Environmental Change, 16,* 268–281.
Armas, L., & Gavris, A. (2013). Social vulnerability assessment using spatial multi-criteria analysis (SEVI model) and the Social Vulnerability Index (SoVI model)-a case study for Bucharest, Romania. *Natural Hazards and Earth System Sciences, 13,* 1481–1499.
ARUP. (2014). *City resilience index: Understanding and measuring city resilience.* https://www.arup.com/perspectives/publications/research/section/city-resilience-index
ARUP. (2018). *City resilience index.* https://www.cityresilienceindex.org/#/
Beccari, B. (2016). A comparative analysis of disaster risk, vulnerability and resilience composite indicators. *PLoS Currents, 1*(14). https://doi.org/10.1371/currents.dis.453df025e34b682e9737f95070f9b970
Beck, U. (1999). *World risk society.* Polity Press.
Berkes, F., & Ross, H. (2013). Community resilience: Toward an integrated approach. *Society & Natural Resources, 26*(1), 5–20.
Burton, C., Rufat, S., & Tate, E. (2018). Social vulnerability. In S. Fuchs & T. Thaler (Eds.), *Vulnerability and resilience to natural hazards* (pp. 53–81). Cambridge University Press.
Chen, W., Cutter, S. L., Emrich, C. T., & Shi, P. (2013). Measuring social vulnerability to natural hazards in the Yangtze River Delta Region, China. *International Journal of Disaster Risk Science, 4*(4), 169–181.
Cutter, S. L. (1996). Vulnerability to environmental hazards. *Progress in Human Geography, 20,* 529–539.
Cutter, S. L. (2016). The landscape of disaster resilience indicators in the USA. *Natural Hazards, 80,* 741–758.

Cutter, S. L. (2018). Linkages between vulnerability and resilience. In S. Fuchs & T. Thaler (Eds.), *Vulnerability and resilience to natural hazards* (pp. 257–270). Cambridge University Press.

Cutter, S. L. (2006). *Hazards, vulnerability and environmental justice*. Earthscan, Sterling.

Cutter, S. L., Ash, K. D., & Emrich, C. T. (2014). The geographies of community disaster resilience. *Global Environmental Change, 29*, 65–77.

Cutter, S. L., Barnes, L., Berry, M., Burton, C., Evans, E., Tate, E., & Webb, J. (2008). A place-based model for understanding community resilience to natural disasters. *Global Environmental Change, 18*, 598–606.

Cutter, S. L., Boruff, B. J., & Shirley, W. L. (2003). Social vulnerability to environmental hazards. *Social Science Quarterly, 84*(2), 242–261.

Cutter, S. L., & Derakhshan, S. (2018). Temporal and spatial change in disaster resilience in US counties, 2010–2015. *Environmental Hazards, 9*(1), 10–29. https://doi.org/10.1080/17477891.2018.1511405

Cutter, S. L., & Morath, D. P. (2013). The evolution of the social vulnerability index (SoVI). In J. Birkmann (Ed.), *Measuring vulnerability to natural hazards* (2nd ed., pp. 304–321). United Nations University Press.

de Loyola Hummell, B. M., Cutter, S. L., & Emrich, C. T. (2016). Social vulnerability to natural hazards in Brazil. *International Journal of Disaster Risk Science, 7*, 111–122.

Emrich, C. T., & Cutter, S. L. (2011). Social vulnerability to climate-sensitive hazards in the Southern United States. *Weather Climate and Society, 3*(3), 193–208.

Emrich, C.T. (2017). *Social vulnerability and hazard analysis for Hurricane Harvey, background and methods*. Oxfam America. https://www.oxfamamerica.org/static/media/files/hurricane-harvey-background.pdf

FEMA. (2016). *State mitigation plan review guide*. FEMA FP 302-094-2. https://www.fema.gov/media-library-data/1425915308555-aba3a873bc5f1140f7320d1ebebd18c6/State_Mitigation_Plan_Review_Guide_2015.pdf

Fuchs, S., & Thaler, T. (Eds.). (2018). *Vulnerability and resilience to natural hazards*. Cambridge University Press.

Govierno de Puerto Rico. (2018). *Puerto Rico disaster recovery action plan*. Government of Puerto Rico, Puerto Rico, San Juan. https://www.cdbg-dr.pr.gov/wp-content/uploads/2018/08/2018-08-27-Action-Plan-with-Approval-EN.pdf

Guillard-Gonçalves, C., Cutter, S. L., Emrich, C. T., & Zêzere, J. L. (2015). Application of social vulnerability index (SoVI) and delineation of natural risk zones in Greater Lisbon, Portugal. *Journal of Risk Research, 18*(5), 651–674.

Hames, E., Stoler, J., Emrich, C. T., Tewary, S., & Pandya, N. (2017). A GIS approach to identifying socially and medically vulnerable older adult populations in South Florida. *The Gerontologist, 57*(6), 1133–1141.

Holand, I. S., & Lujala, P. (2013). Replicating and adapting an index of social vulnerability to a new context: A comparison study for Norway. *Professional Geographer, 65*(2), 312–328.

Linkov, I., Bridges, T., Creutzig, F., Decker, J., Fox-Lent, C., Kröger, W., Lambert, J. H., Levermann, A., Montreuil, B., Nathwani, J., Nyer, R., Renn, O., Scharte, B., Scheffler, A., Schreurs, M., & Thiel-Clemen, T. (2014). Changing the resilience paradigm. *Nature Climate Change, 4*(6), 407–409.

Maharani, Y., Lee, S., & Jin Ki, S. (2016). Social vulnerability at a local level around the Merapi volcano. *International Journal of Disaster Risk Reduction, 20*, 63–77.

Manyena, S. B., O'Brien, G., O'Keefe, P., & Rose, J. (2011). Disaster resilience: A bounce back or bounce forward ability? *Local Environment, 16*(5), 417–424.

Mavhura, E., Manyena, B., & Collins, A. E. (2017). An approach for measuring social vulnerability in context: The case of flood hazards in Mazarabani district, Zimbabwe. *Geoforum, 86*, 103–117.

Miller, F., Osbahr, H., Boyd, E., Thomalla, F., Bharwani, S., Ziervogel, G., Walker, B., Birkmann, J., van der Leeuw, S., Rockström, J., Hinkel, J., Downing, T., Folke, C., & Nelson, D. (2010). Resilience and vulnerability: Complementary or conflicting concepts? *Ecology & Society, 15*(3), 11. http://www.ecologyandsociety.org/vol15/iss3/art11

National Academies of Sciences, Engineering, and Medicine (NASEM). (2019). *Building and measuring community resilience*. National Academies Press.

National Institute of Standards and Technology (NIST). (2016). *Community resilience planning guide for buildings and infrastructure systems* (Vol. I and II). NIST. https://doi.org/10.6028/NIST.SP.1190v1 and https://doi.org/10.6028/NIST.SP.1190v2

Ostadtaghizadeh, A., Ardalan, A., Paton, D., Jabbari, H., & Khankeh, H.R. (2015). Community disaster resilience: A systematic review on assessment models and tools. *PLoS Currents Disasters, 1*(8). https://doi.org/10.1371/currents.dis.f224ef8efbdfcf1d508dd0de4d8210ed

Oxfam America. (2017). *Hurricane Harvey and equitable recovery: Mapping social vulnerability and intensity of wind and flooding from Hurricane Harvey in Texas.* Oxfam America. https://www.oxfamamerica.org/static/media/files/Hurricane-Harvey-Equitable-Recovery-Oxfam.pdf

Rufat, S., Tate, E., Burton, C. G., & Maroof, S. A. (2015). Social vulnerability to floods: Review of case studies and implications for measurement. *International Journal of Disaster Risk Reduction, 14*(4), 470–486.

Rufat, S., Tate, E., Emrich, C. T., & Antolini, F. (2019). How valid are social vulnerability models. *Annals of the American Association of Geographers, 109*(4), 1131–1153.

SC Disaster Recovery Office. (2017). *South Carolina Hurricane Matthew action plan*. SC Department of Commerce, Columbia. https://scstormrecovery.com/wp-content/uploads/2017/07/SC-Hurricane-Matthew-Action-Plan-Revised-HUD-Submittal-5-31-17-1-1.pdf

Sempier, T. T. Swann, D. L., Emmer, R., Sempier, S. H., & Schneider, M. (2010). *Coastal community resilience index: A community self-assessment, ocean springs: Mississippi-Alabama Sea Grant Program*. NOAA, MASGP-08-014. http://www.gulfofmexicoalliance.org/files/projects/files/83Community_Resilience_Index.pdf

Sharifi, A. (2016). A critical review of selected tools for assessing community resilience. *Ecological Indicators, 69,* 629–647.

Solangaarachchi, D., Griffin, A. L., & Doherty, M. D. (2012). Social vulnerability in the context of bushfire risk at the urban-bush interface in Sydney: A case study of the Blue Mountains and Ku-ring-gai local council areas. *Natural Hazards, 64,* 1873–1898.

The National Academies. (2012). *Disaster Resilience: A National Imperative* (p. 2). The National Academies Press.

Tierney, K. (2014). *The social roots of risk: Producing disasters*. Stanford University Press.

Tierney, K. (2019). *Disasters: A sociological approach*. Polity Press.

Siagian, T. H., Purhadi, P., Suhartono, P., & Ritonga, H. (2014). Social vulnerability to natural hazards in Indonesia: Driving factors and policy implications. *Natural Hazards, 70*(2), 1603–1617.

Titus J. G., Hudgens, D. E., Trescott, D. L., Craghan, M., Nuckols, W. H., Hershner, C. H., Kassakian, J. M., Linn, C. J., Merritt, P. G., & McCue, T. M. (2009). State and local governments plan for development of most land vulnerable to rising sea level along the US Atlantic coast. *Environmental Research Letters, 4*(7). https://doi.org/10.1088/1748-9326/4/4/044008

Turner, B. L., II. (2003). Framework for vulnerability analysis in sustainability science, Proceedings. *National Academy of Sciences of the U.S.A. (PNAS), 100*(14), 8074–8079.

Turner, B. L., II. (2010). Vulnerability and resilience: Coalescing or paralleling approaches for sustainability science? *Global Environmental Change, 20*(4), 570–576.

Ungar, M. (2018). Systemic resilience: Principles and processes for a science of change in contexts of adversity. *Ecology and Society, 23*(4), 34. https://doi.org/10.5751/ES-10385-230434

UNISDR. (2017a). *Terminology*. Retrieved February 2, 2017 from https://www.unisdr.org/we/inform/terminology#letter-v

UNISDR. (2017b). *Disaster resilience scorecard for cities*. UNISDR, Version 2.2. http://www.unisdr.org/2014/campaign-cities/ResilienceScorecardV1.5.pdf

West Virginia Development Office. (2017). *West Virginia Disaster recovery action plan.* https://wvfloodrecovery.com/wp-content/uploads/resources/WV-Action-Plan-hyperlinked_final_submission-to-HUD-042117.pdf

White, G. F. (1978). Natural Hazards and the third world-A reply. *Human Ecology, 6*(2), 229–231.

White, G. F. (1953). *Human adjustment to floods* (Research Paper No. 29). University of Chicago Press.

Zurich Insurance Group. (2019a). *Flood resilience measurement for communities (FRMC).* Retrieved August 15, 2019 from https://www.zurich.com/en/sustainability/flood-resilience/measuring-flood-resilience

Zurich Insurance Group. (2019b). *Flood resilience alliance.* http://repo.floodalliance.net/jspui/bitstream/44111/2981/1/941-PA-ZFRP-AdHoc-V7c-WEB.pdf

CHAPTER 12

Flood Hazards and Disciplinary Silos

Robert J. Wasson and Daryl Lam

INTRODUCTION

The sociologist of risk, Ulrich Beck (1992), reached the following profoundly important conclusion (as translated by Power, 1997):

> ...a paradigm shift in the understanding of risk is needed: a shift from the problem of knowing risk to the problem of the risks inherent in ways of knowing.

The risks inherent in ways of knowing are manifest in the different approaches and results of different relevant academic disciplines. Each attempt to know risk, or at least the hazard component of risk, notes that

R. J. Wasson (✉)
College of Science and Engineering, James Cook University, Cairns, QLD, Australia

Fenner School of Environment and Society, Australian National University, Canberra, ACT, Australia

D. Lam
Water Technology Pty Ltd, South Brisbane, QLD, Australia

© The Author(s), under exclusive license to Springer Nature Singapore Pte Ltd. 2022
H. James et al. (eds.), *Disaster Risk Reduction in Asia Pacific*, Disaster Risk, Resilience, Reconstruction and Recovery,
https://doi.org/10.1007/978-981-16-4811-3_12

risk also involves the exposure and vulnerability of human populations and their constructions. But each group of like-minded people attempting to know risks is often blind to the limitations of their views so that they don't understand the risks inherent in their ways of knowing. This problem can lead to serious underestimates and overestimates of risk.

Our focus will be on the hazards of extreme floods where the academic disciplines involved are engineering, hydrology, earth science, human history (particularly environmental history), statistics, and specialists in complexity. People trained in these disciplines are in universities, government agencies, NGOs, and insurance companies, and many are involved in risk governance.

The disciplinary "silo effect" comes about when isolation from colleagues in other disciplines, or even in one's own discipline, produces minimal contact, limited cross-fertilization of ideas and few challenges to norms. Within universities the effect results from prior training, funding opportunities that are often tightly focused, the pressures of teaching and committee work, the pressures of writing and publishing to maintain their positions and achieve promotion, speaking engagements, time consuming in-fighting to maintain power, strong advice to young academics from their supervisors to maintain a narrow focus, and community service. In government agencies there is often little or no incentive to seek new methods and ideas from, for example, university academics, and consultants will mostly use methods that have professional certification, for reasons of legal protection, and are therefore usually not at the forefront of thinking. But perhaps more difficult to overcome is suspicion by some of the rigour of other disciplines such as between engineers, natural scientists and historians.

To be clear, we are not suggesting that silos are unimportant: we need deep disciplinary knowledge to tackle really difficult disciplinary problems. But we also need people in silos to look beyond the boundaries imposed by themselves and their institutions to see what others are doing, learn from that experience and reflect on the weaknesses of their approaches in an effort to improve assessments of risk.

ESTIMATING EXTREME FLOODS

The Standard Approach

The standard approach used by engineers and hydrologists to the calculation of extreme flood magnitudes at a particular location is to fit a statistical function to discharge values measured at a gauging station. These statistical distributions include Gaussian, the Log-Pearson Type III (LP3), Generalized Extreme Value, and Gumbel (Viessman & Lewis, 2003). The best distribution is determined from a statistical goodness of fit test (Millington et al., 2011), although in some countries a particular distribution is mandated (e.g. the Log-Pearson Type III in the USA) without a sound physical basis). This data-driven approach dictates that only instrumentally recorded events are included in the development of flood estimates.

Limitations of the Standard Approach

The limitations of the standard approach to flood frequency analysis fall into five categories. First, the parameters of statistical distributions for flood frequency analysis do not have a relationship with flood-generating processes (Hubert et al., 2007; Wasson, 2016), such as rainfall, snowmelt, landslide lake and glacier lake outburst floods, spatial variability of runoff generation including large differences in infiltration rates. Also different probability functions fit to the same gauged data provide differing estimates of extremes (McMillan et al., 2010; Vasileski & Radevski, 2011). Further, commonly used Gumbel and Log-Pearson Type 3 (LP3) distributions also do not fit peak flow discharge times series with very fat tails associated with the occurrence of extreme floods (Sachs et al., 2012). Alternatively, Malamud and Turcotte (2006) have shown that flood peak data approximate a power law relationship, owing to the presence of fat tails, a topic to be returned to below.

Second, gauged record lengths are too short to be reliably used for accurate fits of probability distributions for calculation of extreme events, because floods are typically erratic and sometimes clustered in time, with short-term characteristics not necessarily representative of long-term behaviour. Analyses of gauged records show that the accuracy of estimates of extremes decreases with increasing return periods and skewness (McCuen & Galloway, 2010). Most alarming is the finding of Eychaner (2015) that a 500-year record from the Danube River is not long enough to constrain an estimate of floods with return periods greater than 100 years.

Third it is now commonplace to claim that gauged records are non-stationary (Milly et al., 2002); that is, the past is no longer representative of the future and future flood assessments must rely on deterministic hydrologic models that, for sound reasons, are unlikely to be possible (Montanari & Koutsoyiannis, 2012) and may not be verifiable or of predictive value (Oreskes et al., 1994). These authors therefore propose the use of stochastic process-based models informed where possible by historical data which is discussed below; they also suggest that non-stationarity is not as serious a problem as some have suggested. But the recognition of non-stationarity as a problem has produced some extraordinary solutions such as the inclusion of cyclic covariance structures in analyses (Jagtap et al., 2019) and even the deliberate truncation of record lengths (DeGaetano & Castellano, 2018).

Fourth, standard flood frequency analysis is based on "clearwater flows"; that is, flows with low sediment concentrations. In mountain streams sediment loads can be very large (such as in the Himalaya, Timor-Leste, Indonesia and The Philippines) creating debris floods and debris flows in channels with total volumes much larger than those that are produced by clearwater floods for the same rainfall amounts (Jacob et al., 2016). The estimation of the probability of such extreme floods (or hydro-geomorphic events: Sidle and Onda [2004]; and see Bodoque et al. [2015] and Naylor et al. [2017] for additional insights) cannot therefore be a simple extrapolation from a probability distribution based on the assumption that the floods are clearwater. In most mountains however there are few or no gauged records of floods of any type and regional flood frequency analyses (based on meagre gauged data) are sometimes used to estimate the probability of such events. They are likely to be underestimates because of high sediment loads. For hazard assessments in steep channels Jacob et al. (2016) recommend the combined use of methods from the earth sciences (hydrology, geomorphology, geology, including palaeoflood analysis and dendrohydrology), engineering geology, numerical modelling (for the range of ratios of water to sediment) for the estimation of design floods. An example of such a study in Canada is provided by Jacob (2005) and, while it is more limited than this Canadian study, the palaeoflood analysis by Wasson et al. (2013) in the central Himalaya takes account of the absence of a gauged record and also the non-clearwater characteristics of floods in this region.

Fifth, Baker (1988, 2007) has argued that advances in quantitative modelling in flood hydrology is distancing understanding between scientists and decision makers and the general public who rely more on perceptions that are more readily underpinned by examples of real extreme floods rather than statistical abstractions that appeal to scientists. He argues that flood sediments and other physical (i.e. real) manifestations of floods should be given greater attention in their own right for risk assessments rather than just being additions to the standard statistical approach. To this we can add historical accounts of extreme floods.

A Complexity Approach

For those who rely solely on gauged records fit by a probability function from which extrapolations are made to estimate unrecorded extremes, it is becoming increasingly clear that the best function for a wide range of phenomena, for both social and natural systems, is the power law (Sornette, 2009) including for flood peaks (Malamud & Turcotte, 2006). The theoretical basis of this function has been established by Thurner et al. (2018) as an expression of a driven critical phenomenon (not a self-organized critical phenomenon for which the input is constant but the outputs are power law distributed; Turcotte, 1999) with statistical behaviour as if it were at a phase transition or critical point (Thurner et al., 2018). Power laws indicate that extremes are not exceptional events because of their fat-tailed properties; that is, power laws, unlike thin-tailed distributions, provide estimates of extremes that are larger than those of other distributions and have an equal number of events in each size category, because they are scale-free, with significant implications for risk assessments. The existence of power laws also suggests that extremes and smaller events are produced by the same processes (Sornette, 2009), implying that large events are a result of amplification of the causes of smaller events.

The catastrophic nature of extremes is often seen as a surprise, even though they may be produced by the same processes as smaller and more usual events that are the objects of most attention. Such surprises are called Black Swans by Taleb (2007). Sornette (2009) goes further to introduce the idea of the "Dragon King", events that are even more extreme than those lying in the tail of a power law and that may be considered outliers and therefore, and unwisely, disregarded as errors of some kind. Dragon Kings point to mechanisms of generation that differ from those in a power law and can coexist with power laws. The conclusions to be reached from this co-existence is that there are several generative mechanisms for extremes, and they are not only a result of amplification of the causes of smaller events; extremes are underestimated by other distributions, and extremes are with us all the time. While these conclusions apply to earthquakes, wildfires and possibly landslides, there does not appear to be evidence of Dragon-King floods (Sachs et al., 2012) although they may be found in future analyses.

The approach adopted by Sornette and many others falls into the category of complexity studies. Complex systems consist of many interacting parts that can interact in different ways to produce different states through time. The interactions are also often non-linear, producing emergent properties that surprise, such as the extremes in the tails of power law distributions or as Dragon Kings. The approach is different from the analytical (or reductionist) method whereby a system is decomposed into its parts, the understanding of which is thought to lead to an understanding of the whole. Here lies another source of tension between the deep disciplinary knowledge mentioned above and a need to understand whole systems in their full dynamic complexity. Bottom-up modelling of hydrologic systems is an example of deep knowledge fed into a mathematical model for predictive purposes, but it is not a mature approach (England et al., 2014, and references therein). It seems more likely that further success will be achieved by starting with a "crude look at the whole" (Miller, 2015), represented by power laws, that is further analyzed by using deep disciplinary knowledge.

Other Approaches

As already mentioned, Baker (1988, 2007) sees a profound disconnect between the mathematical/statistical version of hydrology and the naturalist/historical science approach that is based on realized events rather than abstractions derived from extrapolations from gauged records. Whatever view is taken about the relevance of the past for the future, given the likely impact on hydrology of climate change and the idea that the past is no longer a guide to the future (Furlani & Ninfo, 2015), history will nonetheless continue to provide the only reliable information about the extremes that nature is capable of, providing estimates of extremes not available in gauged records, and also tests of hydrologic models for projections, analogous to the use of paleoclimatic reconstructions to test global climate models (see: https://pmip.lsce.ipsl.fr). Baker's view should be seen as a complement to other alternative methods, which will now be introduced.

Because most river flow gauging stations have been operational for decades rather than the centuries needed to identify real extremes and understand the long-term frequency of extreme events (Wilhelm et al., 2018), they can produce inaccurate results. It has been shown that in the absence of sufficient flow measurements, long-term flood characteristics can potentially be derived from palaeohydrological indicators (an idea mooted as early as 1917 by Fuller) such as flood sediments (most commonly slackwater deposits), fluorescent bands in corals, cave deposits (speleothems), erosional features, flood debris (including boulder deposits), tree rings and tree damage and the absence of vegetation within flood zones (Baker, 1987; Denniston et al., 2015; England et al., 2014; Isdale et al., 1998; Wilhelm et al., 2018). Also valuable are historical documents and records, paintings, photographs, oral histories, memorials and marks on buildings (e.g. Brázdil et al., 2006; Prieto & García Herrera, 2009; Prieto & Rojas, 2015). Incorporation of historical records in flood assessments began in the 1970s, although it began earlier in Germany and The Netherlands (K.M. Cohen, pers. comm., 2019), but only recently have methods been developed for their inclusion in quantitative analyses (Salinas et al., 2016); and in Europe historical records of extremes are increasingly being adopted in risk analysis (Kjeldsen et al., 2014). Moreover, historical data can help to bridge gaps between gauged records and palaeohydrological results.

There are several ways of using alternative information about extreme floods. The simplest is the comparison of peak discharges calculated from palaeostage indicators with gauged peak flows without formal flood frequency analysis. For the Llobregat River in Spain, Thorndycraft et al. (2005) showed, from slackwater deposits, that there have been larger floods than those found in the gauged record by a factor of about two. A similar result was found for the Gardon River in France where the maximum palaeoflood was 1.3 times the maximum gauged flood (Scheffer et al., 2003). Kale (2008) showed, by comparing the palaeostages of extreme floods in Peninsular India, that those since the 1950s have been larger than any in the last few centuries.

To a probability distribution created by the standard method can be added peak flows calculated from the modelling of peak discharges derived from palaeostages. Francés (2004) provides an account of this method in which he describes gauged data as systematic and palaeoflood and historical information as non-systematic, the latter always being censored. That is, a minimum threshold value is assigned where the palaeoflood and historical information are always greater. Systematic data are considered to be uncensored. Stedinger and Cohn (1986) examined censored and binomial data in a flood frequency analysis that employed a two parameter lognormal distribution, finding that the inclusion of historical and palaeoflood estimates improved flood estimates considerably. By combining gauged and palaeoflood data and using Bayesian inference Lam et al. (2017a) reduced the uncertainty in the magnitude of the 100-year return period flood by over 50%.

Using a flood frequency analysis in various parts of the USA Fenske (2003) showed that no palaeofloods known at the time of this publication came close to the magnitude of the Probable Maximum Flood (PMF), a theoretical construct calculated from the Probable Maximum Precipitation that is in turn estimated by, among other methods, transposing to a catchment of interest the maximum precipitation measured in a comparable area; a procedure that has many problems (Wasson, 2016). This is an important conclusion as large infrastructure, such as dam spillways, are designed for the PMF.

Historical hydrology is now an established field of enquiry. A number of studies of historical records have explored flood frequency and magnitude (Kjeldsen et al., 2014; Macdonald, 2013; Rohr, 2013; St. George & Mudelsee, 2018; Williams & Archer, 2002; Zong & Tooley, 2003) with development of robust statistical methods when historical data are included in flood frequency analyses (Gaál et al., 2010; Salinas et al., 2016). While many studies have demonstrated that the addition to gauged records of historical data increases estimates of the magnitude of floods of a particular return period (see Gaume & Borga, 2008), Mei et al. (2015) used historical events in the USA recorded before gauging had begun to show that in over 70% of the studied catchments the 100-year flood magnitude was reduced. The effect on estimates of magnitude is dependent upon the length of the historical records and the censoring threshold. For example, Francés et al. (1994) compared palaeoflood data with gauged data to show that the value of palaeoflood data varies depending upon the relative values of the number of floods in the gauged record, the length of the palaeoflood record, the return period of the flood of interest and the return period of the maximum magnitude of the flood that must be exceeded before a palaeoflood is recorded.

One of the values of historical palaeoflood data therefore lies in reducing the uncertainties in flood frequency curves by extending the gauged record with additional data by which to test the suitability of statistical distributions fit to flood flows. Also, palaeoflood analyses have demonstrated the existence of clusters of very large floods in time, revealing that the assumption of stationarity might be invalid for the derivation of the flood frequency curves (Wasson et al., 2013).

Historical hydrology can therefore provide a variety of evidence useful for flood risk assessment. Quantitative estimates of extremes can be integrated with gauged records to improve flood frequency analysis. But this is not all, and Baker's (1987, 1988, 2007) warning about the "unreality" of extreme discharge estimates from limited data, even if supplemented with historical data, should be heeded so that historical hydrology is not only used in flood frequency analysis. Frequency without magnitude can be of value, if there is evidence that the events were extreme, as can the classification of floods into categories of severity, although this approach may confuse hazards with vulnerability to hazards. And documentation of single extremes, if included in flood frequency analysis, can help constrain low return period estimates (St. George & Mudelsee, 2018), and also provide information about what nature can produce, even if the information cannot be included in flood frequency analysis. Or as expressed by Wilhelm et al. (2018),

> ... the common-sense recognition that what has actually occurred in the past could happen again has much more potential to provoke engaged and wise public response than the abstract prognostications provided by conventional practice, thereby facilitating greater community engagement, improved public understanding of risk, and better decision making',

a sentiment expressed earlier by Baker.

LIMITATIONS OF THE ALTERNATIVE APPROACHES

These approaches have many uncertainties and limitations. Many palaeostage indicators are not widespread, especially in low gradient large rivers, although this is also a limit on gauged data in many countries. Caves near rivers are required for the use of speleothem records, trees with rings are needed near rivers for dendrohydrology, appropriate corals have only been found in the tropics, and large blocks of rock to produce boulders that record the highest velocities are needed. Speleothems, lakes and tree-based records may only apply to small catchments, although in the case of tree scars Ballaesteros Canovas et al. (2017) have developed a method for regionalization to larger catchment areas. Tree ring thickness differences and scars can be produced by processes other than floods; mud in speleothems can come from the surface in drip water rather than in floods; and flood deposits in alluvial settings can be removed by extreme flows. Flood layers in lakes and reservoir sediments need to be distinguished from deposits produced by other mechanisms such as inter-flood particle settling, and flood layers may not be distinguishable if the available particle size range is narrow. Lacustrine records can be biased by land use changes that increase the delivery of sediment and thereby change the relationship between sediment characteristics and discharge, assuming that at least the youngest part of the record can be calibrated against a gauged record.

The interpretation of alluvial sediments requires an understanding of the vertical and lateral development of river channels and floodplains. Slackwater deposits, like tree scars, marks on buildings, and boulder deposits do not record the highest water level, but provide the stage below the maximum stage of a flood (although see Jarrett & England, 2002 for a more complete and somewhat different account); and the difference in estimated discharge can be as high as 20% (Lam et al., 2017b).

Dating of all these records is essential, which is likely to be most accurate in the case of tree rings and marks on buildings. Radiometric dating of sediments, however well done, has relative errors that make it impossible to determine the year or season of a flood. Radiocarbon dates refer to the time of death of an organism and not the time when the dated organic material was incorporated in sediment, a residence time problem that can only be dealt with by employing another tool such as optical dating. There are other chronologic problems that Wilhelm et al. (2018) introduce, but a new method not considered by these authors is based on viscous remanent magnetization of boulders rotated in Earth's magnetic field from which their time of deposition can be estimated (Berndt & Muxworthy, 2017).

Finally, it is important to note that there are few palaeoflood studies from large rivers where, of course, there are more people and infrastructure than on small rivers (K.M. Cohen, pers. comm. 2019). This lack of attention to spatial scale is largely a result of the priority given to analyses in bedrock gorges where the conditions for calculating flood magnitudes from flood deposits are most easily met. But there is a slowly increasing number of studies of large rivers, based on floodplain and river terrace sediments (e.g. Toonen et al., 2015; Wasson et al., in press).

DISCUSSION AND CONCLUSIONS

The literature on alternatives to the standard approach cited above is a fraction of the available material and almost all of it has been produced by earth scientists and environmental historians. Hydrologists, engineers and modellers in the main are not exposed to this material and continue to use methods for risk assessment that ignore a much wider range of information that has been shown to be of value for risk assessments. However, in Europe the EU Floods Directive (2007/60/EC) requires the inclusion of historical information in risk assessment, a requirement not yet adopted in many EU countries (Kjeldsen et al., 2014), and Australian Rainfall and Runoff (http://arr.ga.gov.au), produced by Engineers Australia and Geoscience Australia for the estimation of design floods, recommends the use of historical and palaeoflood records in conjunction with gauged records. There is also considerable expertise in the application of palaeoflood and historical hydrology in the USA, principally through the US Geological Survey (e.g. Jarrett, 1991). Surprisingly, despite high quality palaeoflood records in The Netherlands, there is no uptake among risk practitioners (Toonen and Cohn, pers. comm. 2019). In Russia the standard approach is used to estimate maximum extreme discharges based on gauged records, and palaeodata are not used (Sidorchuk, pers. comm. 2019).

So, some change is happening that integrates the standard and alternative approaches, but more is needed. However, there may be fundamental barriers to overcome. Our emphasis has been on the risks in ways of knowing, but there is also risk in not knowing. Agnotology is, at its simplest, the study of culturally created ignorance or doubt (Proctor & Schiebinger, 2008, two historians of science). Ignorance, or less pejoratively non-knowledge, can be in Beck's (1996) view something that one does not want or need to know or something that cannot be known. Ignorance can be useful as a political instrument (Croissant, 2014) to, for example, maintain hegemony in a field. Can the motivation of the purveyors of the standard approach to flood hydrology, ignoring either deliberately or by simply not knowing the alternatives, be expressed in the following way: I knew nothing of the alternatives to the standard approach, or I don't want to know about them, because they may challenge my hegemony. Of course, Beck's second category haunts us all. How to know the unknowable even though we suspect that it may be truly catastrophic?

For those who practice the standard approach there is another member of the menagerie of catastrophic animals involved in risk analysis: the Black Elephant which Ho (2018) describes as a cross between a Black Swan and "the elephant in the room". This is a problem that is visible but ignored, until it happens and then "we all feign surprise and shock, behaving as if it were a black swan" (p. 14). Is this a description of the behaviour of those who practice the standard approach and know that alternative methods can provide other and even better estimates of flood extremes but choose to ignore them? Gross (2007) argues that "ignorance and surprise belong together", and it is worth recalling Beck's (1992) fundamental point that the management of ignorance and its resulting surprises is a major feature of knowledge-based societies. Therefore, the reduction of ignorance, in all of its forms, is a critical issue in an increasingly connected and risky world that is becoming more vulnerable to climate change. However, Beck did not take account of the paradox that ignorance grows as knowledge grows, a phenomenon that Firestein (2012) argues benefits science, because it is at its most creative when uncertain as ignorance grows.

Returning to a key theme here, perhaps the most strident attack on disciplinary silos is from Ravetz (1993):

> When scientists restrict their discourse with others of the same or related specialties, their ignorance-squared can persist indefinitely. Traditionally, they have lived securely in their "ivory tower", supported by society in their narrowly focused pursuit of specialized knowledge. (p. 2)

Ignorance-squared refers to ignorance of ignorance, and in the title of the paper Ravetz refers to this as *The Sin of Science* and can be construed as a manifestation of the worst form of disciplinary silos. He also suggests an antidote, namely humility and,

> ... an attitude of openness to honest differences of opinion and perspective, and the possibility of error in oneself (enabling) a critical and constructive

dialogue without which there can be no progress, in science as in human affairs (p. 164),

a view reflected by Faber et al. (1993) for all environmental studies. All of the methods summarized here for the estimation of flood extremes and their probabilities are uncertain, therefore none can be considered superior, but each has its strengths and weaknesses and not all have been applied to the same scale of river. And all of those involved are trying their best to produce results of the highest quality to save lives and reduce impacts on infrastructure and ecosystems. Now there is a way forward in the many studies that have shown that together the standard and alternative approaches produce better results. We conclude by suggesting that each group struggling to know the hazard component of flood risk should honestly identify the risks inherent in their ways of knowing. And reflect on what they do not know rather than what they think they know. This suggestion is likely to be best operationalized by small groups that are grappling with well constrained problems; that is, too large a group may have many objectives that will make solutions using a mixed-method approach difficult to implement. In addition, workshops sponsored by professional organizations, particularly of engineers, to provide guidelines for improved flood forecasting that take account of alternative approaches are likely to have greater credibility than workshops organized by researchers.

Acknowledgements Helen James invited this chapter, Kim Cohen and Willem Toonen provided very helpful comments on a draft, Alexsey Sidorchuk provided information about Russia, and an anonymous referee provided helpful comments.

References

Baker, V. R. (1987). Paleoflood hydrology and extraordinary flood events. *Journal of Hydrology, 96,* 79–99.
Ballaesteros Canovas, J. A., Trappmann, D., Shekhar, M., Bhattacharayya, A., Stoffel, M. (2017). Regional floodfrequencey reconstruction for kullu district, Western Indian Himalayas. *Journal fo Hydrology, 546,* 140–149.
Baker, V. R. (1988). Cataclysmic processes in geomorphological systems. *Zietschrift für Geomorphologie, Supplement Issues., 64,* 25–32.
Baker, V. R. (2007). Hydrological understanding and societal action. *Journal of the American Water Resources Association, 34*(4), 819–825.

Beck, U. (1992). *Risk Society*. Sage.
Beck, U. (1996). Wissen oder Nicht-Wissen? Zwei Perspektiven reflexiver Modernisieurung. In U. Beck, A. Giddens, & S. Lash (Eds.), *Reflexive Modernisierung* (pp. 289–315). Suhrkamp.
Berndt, T., & Muxworthy, A. R. (2017). Dating Icelandic glacial floods using a new remanent magnetization protocol. *Geology*, *45*(4), 339–342.
Bodoque, J. M., Díez-Herrero, A., Eguibar, M. A., Benito, G., & Ruiz-Villanueva, V. (2015). Challenges in paleoflood hydrology applied to risk analysis in mountainous watersheds—A review. *Journal of Hydrology*, *529*(2), 449–467.
Brázdil, R., Kundzewicz, Z. W., & Benito, G. (2006). Historical hydrology for studying flood risk in Europe. *Hydrological Sciences Journal*, *51*, 739–764.
Croissant, J. L. (2014). Agnotology: Ignorance and absence or towards a sociology of things that aren't there. *Social Epistemology*, *28*(1), 4–25.
DeGaetano, A. T., & Castellano, C. (2018). Selecting time series length to moderate the impact of nonstationarity in extreme rainfall analyses. *Journal of Applied Meteorology and Climatology*, *57*, 2285–2296.
Denniston, R. F., Villarini, G., Gonzales, A. N., Wyrwoll, K.-H., Polyak, V. J., Ummenhofer, C. C., Lachniet, M. S., Wanamaker, A. D., Jr., Humphreys, W. F., Woods, D., & Cugley, J. (2015). Extreme rainfall activity in the Australkian tropics reflects changes in the El Niño/Southern Oscillation over the last two millennia. *Proceedings of the National Academy of Sciences*, *112*(15), 4576–4581.
England, J. E., Julien, P. Y., & Velleux, M. L. (2014). Physically-based extreme flood frequency with stochastic storm transposition and paleoflood data on large watersheds. *Journal of Hydrology*, *510*, 228–245.
Eychaner, J. H. (2015). *Lessons from a 500-year record of flood elevations*. Association of State Floodplain Managers, Madison Wisconsin,Technical Report 7, 25.
Faber, M., Manstetten, R., & Proops, J. L. R. (1993). Humankind and the environment: An anatomy of surprise and ignorance. *Environmental Values*, *1*(3), 217–241.
Fenske, J. (2003). Application of paleohydrology to corps flood frequency analysis. *US Army Corps of Engineers, Hydrologic Engineering Center*, RD-47: 28.
Firestein, R. (2012). *Ignorance. How it drives science*. OUP.
Francés, F. (2004). Flood frequency analysis using systematic and non-systematic information. In G. Benito & V. R. Thorndycraft (Eds.), *Systematic, palaoeflood and historical data for the improvement of flood risk estimation. Methodolocial guidelines* (pp. 55–71). CSIC-Centro de Ciencas Medioambientales.

Francés, F., Salas, J. D., & Boes, D. C. (1994). Flood frequency analysis with systematic and historical or paleoflood data based on the two-parameter general extreme value models. *Water Resources Research, 30*(6), 1653–1664.

Fuller, M. L. (1917). Discussion. Final Report of the Special Committee on Floods and Flood Prevention. *Transactions of the American Society of Civil Engineers, 81*(1400), 1269–1278.

Furlani, S., & Ninfo, A. (2015). Is the present the key to the future? *Earth-Science Reviews, 142*, 38–46.

Gaál, L., Szolgay, J., Kohnová, S., & Hlavcova, K. (2010). Inclusion of historical information in flood frequency analysis using a Bayesian MCMC technique: A case study for the power dam Orlík, Czech Republic. *Contributions to Geophysics and Geodesy, 40*(2), 121–147.

Gaume, E., & Borga, M. (2008). Post-flood field investigations in upland catchments after major flash floods: Proposal of a methodology and illustrations. *Journal of Flood Risk Management, 1*(4), 175–189.

Gross, M. (2007). The unknown in process. Dynamic connections of ignorance, non-knowledge and related concepts. *Current Sociology, 55*(5), 742–759.

Ho, P. (2018). Hunting Black Swans and taming Black Elephants. In J. W. Vasbinder (Ed.), *Disrupted balance. Society at risk. World scientific* (pp. 13–20).

Hubert, P., Tchiguirinskaia, I., Schertzer, D., Bendjoudi, H., & Lovejoy, S. (2007). Predermination of floods. In O. F. Vasiliev, P. H. A. J. M. Van Gelder, E. J. Plate, & M. V. Bolgov (Eds.), *Extreme hydrological events: New concepts for security*. NATO Science Series, IV. *Earth and Envoronmental Sciences, 78*, 185–198.

Isdale, P. J., Stewart, B. J., Tickle, K. S., & Lough, J. M. (1998). Palaeohdrological variation in a tropical river catchment: A reconstruction using fluorescent bands in corals of the Great Barrier Reef, Australia. *The Holocene, 8*(1), 1–8.

Jacob, M. (2005). Debris flow hazard assessments. In M. Jacob & O. Hungr (Eds.), *Debris Flow hazards and related phenomena* (pp. 411–443). Springer.

Jacob, M., Clague, J. J., & Church, M. (2016). Rare and dangerous: Recognizing extra-ordinary events in stream channels. *Canadian Water Resources Journal, 41*(1–2), 161–173.

Jagtap, R. S., Gedam, V. K., & Kale, M. M. (2019). Generalised extreme value model with cyclic covariate structure for analysis of non-stationary hydrometeorological extremes. *Journal of Earth System Science, 128*(14), 16.

Jarrett, R. D. (1991). Paleohydrology and its value in estimating floods and droughts. In R. W. Paulson, E. B. Chase, R. S. Roberts, & D. W. Moody (Compilers), *National water summary 1988–89-hydrologic events and floods and droughts*. U.S. Geological Survey Water-Supply Paper 2375 (pp. 105–116).

Jarrett, R. D., & England, J. F., Jr. (2002). Reliability of paleostage indicators for paleoflood studies. In P. K. House, R. H. Webb, V. R. Baker & D. R. Levish (Eds.), *Principles and applications of paleoflood hydrology*. Water Science and Application (Vol. 5, pp. 91–109). American Geophysical Union.

Kale, V. S. (2008). Palaeoflood hydrology in the Indian context. *Journal of the Geological Society of India, 71*, 56–66.

Kjeldsen, T. R., Macdonald, N., Lang, M., Mediero, L., Albuquerque, T., Bogdanowicz, E., Brázdil, R., Castellarin, A., David, V., Fleig, A., Gül, G. O., Kriauciuniene, J., Kohnová, S., Merz, B., Nicholson, O., Roald, L. A., Salinas, J. L., Sarauskiene, D., Šraj, M., ... Wilson, D. (2014). Documentary evidence of past floods in Europe and their utility in flood frequency estimation. *Journal of Hydrology, 517*, 963–973.

Lam, D., Thompson, C., Croke, J., Sharma, A., & Macklin, M. (2017a). Reducing uncertainty with flood frequency analysis: The contribution of paleoflood and historical flood information. *Water Resources Research, 53*(3), 2312–2327.

Lam, D., Croke, J., Thompson, C., & Sharma, A. (2017b). Beyond the gorge: Palaeoflood reconstruction from slackwater deposits in a range of physiographic settings in subtropical Australia. *Geomorphology, 292*, 164–177.

Macdonald, N. (2013). Reassessing flood frequency for the River Trent through the inclusion of historical flood information since ad 1320. *Hydrology Research, 44*, 215–233.

Malamud, B. D., & Turcotte, D. L. (2006). The applicability of power-law frequency statistics to floods. *Journal of Hydrology, 322*, 168–180.

McCuen, R. H., & Galloway, K. E. (2010). Record length requirements for annual maximum flood series. *Journal of Hydrologic Engineering, 15*(9), 704–707.

McMillan, H., Jackson, B., & Poyck, S. (2010). *Flood risk under climate change*. National Institute of Water and Atmospheric Research Ltd., New Zealand. NIWA Client Report CHC2010-033:55.

Mei, X., Dai, Z., Tang, Z., & Van Gelder, P. H. A. J. M. (2015). Impacts of historical records on extreme flood variations over the conterminous United States. *Journal of Flood Risk Management*. https://doi.org/10.1111/jfr3.12223:10

Millington, N., Das, S., & Simonovic, S. P. (2011). *The comparison of GEV, Log-Pearson Type 3 and Gumbel distributions in the Upper Thames River watershed under global climate models*. Department of Civil and Environmental Engineering, The University of Western Ontario.

Miller, J. H. (2015). *A crude look at the whole* (p. 245). Basic Books.

Milly, P. C. D., Wetherald, R. T., Dunne, K. A., & Delworth, T. L. (2002). Increasing risk of great floods in a changing climate. *Nature, 415*, 514–517.

Montanari, A., & Koutsoyiannis, D. (2012). A blueprint for process-based modeling of uncertain hydrologic systems. *Water Resources Research, 48*, W09555. https://doi.org/10.1029/2011WR011412

Naylor, L. A., Spencer, T., Lane, S. N., Darby, S. E., Magilligan, F. J., Macklin, M. G., & Möller, I. (2017). Stormy geomorphology: Geomorphic contributions in an age of climate extremes. *Earth Surface Processes and Landforms, 42*, 166–190.

Oreskes, N., Shrader-Frechete, K., Belitz, K. (1994). Verification, validation, and confirmation of numerical models in the earth sciences. *Science, 263*(5147), 641–646.

Power, M. (1997). From risk society to audit society. *Soziale Systeme, 3*, H.1, 3–21, https://www.soziale-systeme.ch/leseproben/power.htm

Prieto, M. R., & García Herrera, R. (2009). Documentary sources from South America: Potential for climate reconstruction. *Palaeogeography, Palaeoclimatology, Palaeoecology, 281*, 196–209.

Prieto, M. R., & Rojas, F. (2015). Determination of droughts and high floods of the Bermejo River (Argentina) based on documentary evidence (17th to 20th century). *Journal of Hydrology, 529*(2), 676–683.

Proctor, R. N., & Schiebinger, L. (Eds.). (2008). *Agnotology*. Stanford University Press.

Ravetz, J. (1993). The sin of science. Ignorance of ignorance. *Science communications, 15*(2), 157–165.

Rohr, C. (2013). Floods of the Upper Danube River and its tributaries and their impact on urban economies (c. 1350–1600): The examples of the Towns of Krems/Stein and Wels (Austria). *Environment and History, 19*, 133–148.

Sachs, M. K., Yoder, M. R., Turcotte, D. L., Rundle, J. B., & Malamud, B. D. (2012). Black swans, power laws, and dragon-kings: Earthquakes, volcanic eruptions, landslides, wildfires, floods, and SOC models. *European Physical Journal Special Topics, 205*, 167–182.

Salinas, J. L., Kiss, A., Viglione, A., Viertl, R., & Blöschl, G. (2016). A fuzzy Bayesian approach to flood frequency estimation with imprecise historical information. *Water Resources Research, 52*, 6730–6750.

Scheffer, N. A., Enzel, Y., Grodek, T., Waldmann, N., & Benito, G. (2003). Claim of largest flood on record proves false. *EOS, Transactions of American Geophysical Union, 84*, 109.

Sidle, R. C., & Onda, Y. (2004). Hydrogeomorphology: An overview of an emerging science. *Hydrological Processes, 18*, 597–602.

Sornette, D. (2009). Dragon-Kings, Black Swans and the prediction of crises. *International Journal of Terraspace and Engineering*, https://arxiv.org/pdf/0907.4290.pdf

St. George, S., & Mudelsee, M. (2018). The weight of the flood-of-record in flood frequency analysis. *Journal of Flood Risk Management*. https://doi.org/10.1111/jfr3.12512

Stedinger, J. R., & Cohn, T. A. (1986). Flood frequency analysis with historical and paleoflood information. *Water Resources Research, 22*(5), 785–793.

Taleb, N. N. (2007). *The Black Swan: The impact of the highly improbable*. Random House.

Thorndycraft, V. R., Benito, G., Rico, M., Sopeña, A., Sánchez-Moya, Y., & Casas, A. (2005). A long-term flood discharge record derived from slackwater flood deposits of the Llobregat River, NE Spain. *Journal of Hydrology, 313*, 16–31.

Thurner, S., Hanel, R., & Klimek, P. (2018). *Introduction to the theory of complex systems* (p. 431). OUP.

Toonen, W. H. J., Winkels, T. G., Cohen, K. M., Prins, M. A., & Middelkoop, H. (2015). Lower Rhine historical flood magnitudes of the last 450 years reproduced from grain-size measurements of flood deposits using end member modelling. *CATENA, 130*, 69–81.

Turcotte, D. L. (1999). Self-organized criticality. *Reports of Progress in Physics, 62*, 1377–1428.

Vasileski, D., & Radevski, I. (2011). Implementation of Gauss function in determining probability of floods at the gauge station "Dolenci" on the Crna Reka in Republic of Macedonia. *Geographica Pannonica, 15*(4), 113–118.

Viessman, W. J., & Lewis, G. L. (2003). *Introduction to hydrology*. Prentice Hall.

Williams, A., & Archer, D. (2002). The use of historical flood information in the English Midlands to improve risk assessment. *Hydrological Sciences Journal, 47*, 57–76.

Wasson, R. J. (2016). Uncertainty, ambiguity and adaptive flood forecasting. *Policy and Society, 35*, 125–136.

Wasson, R. J., Sundriyal, Y. P., Chaudhary, S., Jaiswal, M. K., Morthekai, P., Sati, S. P., & Juyal, N. (2013). A 1000-year history of large floods in the Upper Ganga catchment, central Himalaya, India. *Quaternary Science Reviews, 77*, 156–166.

Wasson, R. J., Ziegler A. D., Lim, H. S., Teo, E., Lam, D. Chuah, C. J., Higgitt, D., Rittenour, T., Singhvi, A. K., & Khairun, N. (2021). Episodically volatile high energy non-cohesive river-floodplain systems: Global review and new information from the Ping River, Thailand. *Geomorphology.382. 107658.*

Wilhelm, B., Cánovas, J. A. B., Aznar, J. P. C., Kämpf, L., Swierczynski, T., Stoffel, M., Stren, E., & Toonen, W. (2018). Recent advances in paleoflood hydrology: From new archives to data compliation and analysis. *Water Security, 3*, 1–8.

Zong, Y., & Tooley, M. J. (2003). A historical record of coastal floods in Britain: Frequencies and associated storm tracks. *Natural Hazards, 29*, 13–36.

CHAPTER 13

Theorizing Disaster Communitas

Steve Matthewman and Shinya Uekusa

INTRODUCTION

Sociologists have observed the emergence of communitas following disasters for as long as there has been a sociology of the subject. Communitas refers to such phenomena as mutual help, resource sharing, community action, community spiritedness, volunteerism and humanitarianism. While there are some affinities with social capital, there are also clear differences. We discuss their divergences in the section titled, "Communitas: What is it, why does it emerge and why should we theorize it?" Despite the longstanding recognition of communitas, little has been written about how it might be conceptualized, and much less still on what might limit it. This chapter examines both in order to identify ways of enhancing it; as such theorizing has practical import for disaster risk reduction (DRR) policy (Richardson et al., 2014, p. 212).

S. Matthewman (✉)
University of Auckland, Auckland, New Zealand
e-mail: s.matthewman@auckland.ac.nz

S. Uekusa
School of Culture and Society, Aarhus University, Aarhus, Denmark

© The Author(s), under exclusive license to Springer Nature Singapore Pte Ltd. 2022
H. James et al. (eds.), *Disaster Risk Reduction in Asia Pacific*, Disaster Risk, Resilience, Reconstruction and Recovery,
https://doi.org/10.1007/978-981-16-4811-3_13

We begin by considering the three factors responsible for communitas' emergence: the public nature of disaster, the limitations of authorities and the social nature of human beings. We then outline our motivations for writing this chapter, which are: to respond constructively to the critique that disaster studies suffers from a paucity of theory, to critique "disaster mythology" in public discourse, to offset the focus on top-down disaster recovery, to demonstrate a way in which communities might be a party to their own recovery and to reiterate the importance of social infrastructure (as discussions of recovery typically prioritize physical infrastructure).

Communitas is so commonly observed because it goes to the core of our humanity. Human being is being for others. We offer examples of successful mutual aid post-disaster, including at significant scale and in the unlikeliest of places. That said, communitas is not guaranteed to emerge. We discuss factors that limit communitas, focussing in particular on the degradation of social infrastructure that accompanies economic decline and civic withdrawal, and the "corrosive communities" which result from toxic chemical spills where protracted lawsuits, scapegoating and consequent community division all feature.

Disasters can destroy lives, environments and properties, but they do not usually destroy social institutions. This means that systems of privilege and prejudice remain in place. Here we draw upon the literature on social capital to think about differential outcomes following disasters. This leads into our concluding thoughts on how communitas might be enhanced for all.

Communitas: What Is It, Why Does It Emerge and Why Should We Theorize It?

As noted, communitas refers to improvisational social connections that render mutual aid when disaster strikes. It is one of the most consistently observed phenomena within the disaster literature. Indeed, it has been noted by sociologists of disaster for as long as there has been such study. Samuel Henry Prince (1920), the sub-discipline's progenitor, examined community reactions to the explosion of the French munitions ship Mont Blanc, in Halifax, Nova Scotia, on 6 December 1917. His analysis of that event revealed

> the role of catastrophe in stimulating community service, in presenting models of altruistic conduct, in translating energy into action, in defending

law and order, and in bringing into play the great social virtues of generosity, sympathy and mutual aid. (Prince, 1920, p. 58)

Communitas is but one word for this generally identified practice. Since Prince published his book in 1920, communitas has gone by many names within the disaster literature. A partial list includes: "altruistic community" (Barton, 1969), "brotherhood of pain" (Oliver-Smith, 1999), "disaster citizenship" (Remes, 2016), "emergency togetherness" (Drury et al., 2009), "extraordinary community" (Solnit, 2009), "post-disaster solidarity" (Oliver-Smith, 1999), "post-disaster utopia" (Wolfensburg, 1957), "pro-social behavior" (Rodríguez et al., 2006), "social utopia" (Fritz, 1961) and "therapeutic community" (Barton, 1969). Following Victor Turner (1969, 1986, pp. 101–102), our preference is to use communitas, a Latin term that captures the pure spirit of community, denoting more than togetherness; it also speaks to bonding, collective action and a society of equals. Despite tying notions of communitas to visions of the catastrophic, Victor Turner (1969, p. 154) never explicitly connected his concept to disasters. His wife, Edith Turner (2012, pp. 73–78, 83) did, recounting Linda Jencson's work on the Dakota floods of 1997, and Carl Lindhaus' work on Hurricane Katrina. She saw clear advantages from communitas for disaster response and recovery, and unlike her husband did not believe that communitas was necessarily only ever temporary.

While there are certain affinities between communitas and social capital, there are some notable points of difference. Communitas occurs in conditions of what Victor Turner calls "anti-structure", which is to say moments of social breakdown, or in exceptional circumstances, beyond quotidian experience. Social capital speaks more to a structured state. And unlike communitas, it has a long-recognized dark side. While disaster researchers are wont to see social capital as an unqualified good; early sociological writers on the subject noted that the networks through which social capital accrues are often based on exclusions. This perpetuates hierarchies and secures ongoing structural advantage (Bourdieu, 1986). The strategic and self-interested investment/return motivations that define social capital (Colclough & Bhavani Sitaraman, 2005, p. 479) are lacking in communitas. So, too, are the norms of reciprocity and mutual obligation (Coleman, 1988). Communitas is more of a public good. Social capital can work against the public good in that it restricts some from access to resources (because only connected members are eligible).

Indeed, social capital can even produce social bads, as in organized crime. There are additional points of difference. Communitas speaks to a society of equals sharing a common experience. Social capital does not. Communitas is place-based while social capital networks may be geographically dispersed. Communitas is the spontaneous formation of new bonds rather than the strengthening of pre-existing ones. Under conditions of communitas social bonds are strong, to the point of being intoxicating, whereas in cases of social capital they may be weak (Granovetter, 1973). Finally, as all of its progenitors use the concept, social capital inheres in individuals (Portes & Landolt, 1996), while communitas is a shared product of the collective.

There are three reasons for the emergence of communitas. First, it arises because disasters are essentially *social phenomena*. Threats and damage are public and shared. This bonds survivors, providing the basis for physical and emotional support. Collective adversity, then, creates social solidarity. Under such conditions, possessive individualism and political passivism are frequently among the first casualties (Preston & Firth, 2020; Solnit, 2009, 2020). *We are all in this together.* Second, collective action is further encouraged as current power structures are nowhere near as robust as is commonly thought. Indeed, the *prevailing power structures often dissipate*. Realization that official assistance is seldom in the right place at the right time in sufficient numbers gives civil society a boost. Although here it is only fair to note the concerted efforts by Disaster Risk Reduction (DRR) specialists across the last three decades to include communities/civil society in preparedness, mitigation and response activities, and those working in the area of community based disaster management (CBDM) who seek to do likewise.

Mutual aid from within this "society of equals" may be the only resource available. It is usually first responders, fellow citizens, who do the heavy lifting when disaster strikes (Tierney, 2003). Third, we are essentially *social beings*. We cannot exist alone. We are products of culture and collective labour. We share norms and relations, and are, to a degree unknown among any other species, remarkably altruistic (on this see also Peek, 2020). The word "altruism" is a sociological neologism, coined by Auguste Comte. Comte was moved to counter assertions that human nature is essentially selfish. He believed that people routinely suppress egoistical desires in service of the collective, to a degree unseen in any other species. He also felt that the work we do is largely undertaken for others. He coined the term "altruism" to describe this. It is derived from the Italian "altrui", which means "of others", "to others". For Comte, altruism was composed of three core instincts: attachment, benevolence and veneration. In a fit of modesty, he placed his revelation alongside Copernicus' work on the Earth's motion, declaring it "the chief discovery of modern science" (Quoted in Dixon, 2008).

Disasters throw this aspect of our species into sharp relief. Thomas E. Drabek and Enrico L. Quarantelli (1967, p. 12) concluded, disasters *"often bring out the best in individuals. Ability to endure suffering, desire to help others, and acts of courage and generosity come forth in times of crisis."* Similarly, Rebecca Solnit (2009, pp. 305–306) said that disasters reveal us to be resilient and generous, committed to the possibility of doing things differently, desiring of human connection and purpose. In disasters, then, a peculiar social energy emerges. Rendering assistance of all types gives new definition to life—a reason for being—which is being for others.

There are five motivations for theorizing communitas. First, disaster studies' own scholars regularly criticize their collective efforts for being "theory-lite" (Alexander, 2013; Tierney, 2010, p. 660). Second, it is important to challenge the enduring prevalence and power of "disaster mythology" within public discourse (Fischer, 2002), which is to say the idea that society breaks down during disasters. The sociology of disasters provisions us with a century's worth of empirical evidence showing that disaster situations do not conform to media stereotypes, or the fears of the powerful. Anomic states are rare, anarchic ones are rarer still. Third, while people and communities do not typically exhibit high-level alarm the same cannot be said of the media and other authorities, as detailed by the literature on "elite panic" (Clarke & Chess, 2008). Moreover, in disaster situations authorities frequently align in the service of elite interests at the expense of public and environmental wellbeing (Molotch, 1970), leading some to argue that the greatest harms wrought to the social fabric are the predatory actions of the most powerful rather than those at the bottom of the social order (Mutter, 2015). Rebecca Solnit (2020) is interesting in this regard. She writes: "There are nearly always selfish and destructive people, and they are often in power, because we have created systems that reward that kind of personality and those principles".

Examples of "recreancy", the failure of institutional players to perform their roles responsibly and to the expected standards of proficiency, also abound (Freudenburg, 1997, p. 33). In the absence of official assistance, communitas—assistance from proximate others—may be the *only* available resource (Wood et al., 2013, p. 143). Fourth, since interests diverge, this makes the efficacy of solely relying upon formal top-down "command and control" models of disaster recovery questionable in the extreme (Tierney, 2014, p. 203). In line with best-practice recovery (Aldrich, 2011), we also see a role for community empowerment. Enhancing the conditions that create communitas is one way to achieve it. As Edith Turner (2012, p. 3) has noted: "The benefits of communitas are quick understanding, easy mutual help, and long-term ties with others". Fifth, scholarship and policy on disaster recovery overwhelmingly focuses upon physical "lifeline" infrastructures, those hard technological systems that sustain life, like communication, energy and transportation systems, rather than social infrastructure. Yet research suggests that it is social rather than physical infrastructure that is the driver of resilience (Aldrich & Meyer, 2015; Klinenberg, 2018), and as such its development is increasingly being recognized as a vitally important tool for disaster management and risk reduction (UN Chronicle, 2016).

CATASTROPHES AND SOCIAL ENERGY: "JOY" IN DISASTERS

We have already alluded to the social energy that emerges post-disaster. Indeed, disaster scholars have long-seen what must be one of the most counter-intuitive occurrences in the social world: joy in disasters (Solnit, 2005, pp. 7, 306). This is also reflected in media reports. Public responses to a pandemic described as "beautiful" (Graff, 2020). Community responses to earthquakes described as "positive" (Sinani quoted in Povoledo, 2016) and "wonderful" (Quoted in Westgate, 2014). Responses to a train crash described as "beautiful" (Blaine quoted in Daley, 2016). A city-wide blackout giving citizens a "magical" time that was a "privilege" to experience (Mirsky, 2016). A flood described as a "positive experience" providing the community, with its "finest hour" (Turner, 2012, p. 74).

Solnit provides one explanation for this joy in disasters. She argues that disasters bring out the best in us. They reveal who we are. She concludes that we are resilient and generous, committed to the possibility of doing things differently, desiring of human connection and purpose (Solnit, 2009, pp. 305–306). Disasters also bind. Those in peril are rescued, the hungry are fed, the homeless are sheltered and the lonely are cared for. There is a kindness to strangers.

Grass roots organization can certainly be an awesome force. Garrett M. Graff (2020) wrote that "*[t]he public's response to the coronavirus will stand as a remarkable moment of national [US] mobilization*". In March 2020, in response to the COVID-19 pandemic, the British government called for a quarter of a million volunteers to come forward to assist senior citizens, those in isolation, and frontline medical staff who required supplies delivered. Over three times that amount offered to assist (Solnit, 2020). We are witnessing similar acts the world over, from the young volunteers in Hyderabad who are supplying the city's precarious workers with food packages, to the helpers in Wuhan who are ferrying essential medical workers between hospital and home, to the programmers in Latvia who organized a hackathon to create optimal face shield components for 3D printers. "The shift is even more interesting than it first appears", George Monbiot (2020) states,

> Power has migrated not just from private money to the state, but from both market and state to another place altogether: the commons. All over the world, communities have mobilised where governments have failed.

At the risk of reiterating the obvious, this is no isolated example. Following Hurricane Katrina the "Cajun Army" of volunteers was credited with saving thousands of lives (Tierney, 2014, p. 203), more than 200,000 citizens offered shelter to strangers and tens of thousands helped out with the Gulf Coast clean-up (Solnit, 2009, p. 2). Similarly, people facilitated the evacuation of Manhattan following the September 11 attacks on the World Trade Center. Those with access to boats enacted "*the largest water evacuation in our history*" (Perrow, 2007, p. 297). These collective acts can even transcend seemingly intractable political differences. For example, as in the Indian Ocean tsunami of 2004 in Sri Lanka, where in the days immediately following the disaster the impossible happened: the army and community groups, the Liberation Tigers of Tamil Eelam (LTTE) and the government all worked together for the common good (Frerks, 2009, p. 8). Then there is the Bosnian and Serbian flooding of April 2014. A rapid deluge, the heaviest recorded, displaced a million people and caused thousands of landslides. The predicted economic damage was profound. Neighbouring countries like Croatia, Slovenia and Macedonia were quick to offer relief irrespective of ethnic background, but in Bosnia and Herzegovina the government was seen to be neglecting much of the population. Locals rallied to render assistance to each other in the absence of state protection. In northern towns like Samac, Muslims helped Serbs. Supporters of the football team

Red Star Belgrade, long-regarded as a hot bed of Serbian nationalism, took to social media to help emergency relief efforts in Bosnia and Croatia. In Banja Luka, Serbs came to the assistance of Muslims. During the war, Serb forces destroyed all of Bosnia's second city's mosques. "*Amid this tragedy, I am so delighted to see this solidarity between people who generously helped each other*", a local mufti said (Camdzic quoted in Geoghegan, 2014).

THE LIMITS OF COMMUNITAS: DEGRADED SOCIAL INFRASTRUCTURE AND A NEW SPECIES OF TROUBLE

While the above discussion is *typically* true of disasters, there is no iron law guaranteeing the emergence of communitas in disasters. Communitas can encounter limits. Identifying them has important implications for effective disaster risk reduction (DRR) strategy.

Severe deprivation can mean that some communities cannot self-organize as, to all intents and purposes, there is no community to be organized. In such circumstances, people live under conditions of co-presence rather than enmeshed in supportive social relations. Eric Klinenberg's (2002) study of the 1995 Chicago heat wave is instructional in this regard. It brings social ecology into consideration by comparing two climatically, demographically and socioeconomically similar communities, North and South Lawndale. Despite their likenesses, residents in these two locations experienced markedly different outcomes. North Lawndale had ten times the rate of fatalities of its neighbour. To explain this disparity we need to examine social infrastructure.

North Lawndale began losing its industrial base in the 1950s. Other commercial activities and public amenities soon followed. The underground economy replaced the formal one. Large swathes of the population left the area. As they dispersed, support networks stretched, sometimes to breaking point. More transient (and reclusive) people populated the hitherto stable neighbourhoods. City authorities also withdrew. When the heatwave came, poverty stopped people from cooling off inside. They either did not have, or could not afford to use, air-conditioning. Civic neglect and fear of crime compounded the problem. There was nothing to go out to, and open spaces were viewed as threatening.

The neighbourhood to the immediate south is an entirely different world. South Lawndale escaped the ghettoization that took place in North Lawndale, the vicious cycle of neglect, civic withdrawal, decline, vandalism and violence that leads to atomization. Moreover, it was boosted by constant Mexican and Central American in-migration. During the period in which North Lawndale's population halved, South Lawndale's grew by 30 per cent. The high population density gave the place a vibrant street life and plentiful commercial activity. A bustling place, it fosters sociability and mutual care. In South Lawndale, it is far harder to fall through the cracks. People feel safe in public. When the heatwave came, the elderly comfortably ventured outside. In so doing, others kept a neighbourly eye on them (Klinenberg, 2002, pp. 79–128).

Depletion of social infrastructure corrodes community spirit, so too do the "new species of trouble" that comes from modern toxins. Kai T. Erikson (1994, p. 141) argues that poisons create their own peculiar fears. He outlines three reasons for this. First, there is the nebulous nature of their harm. They present new challenges regarding detectability and duration. Toxins do obvious physical damage and they have profound psychological impacts. Fear is intensified as these threats typically evade bodily protection mechanisms, which is to say, our senses. We do not know when we are at risk. It can be years before there is decisive confirmation of contamination. Moreover, they seem to be disasters without conclusion. Toxic disasters have undefined lifecycles. They do not simply begin, exist and then end (Erikson, 1994, p. 147). Second, toxic events can create "corrosive communities" in which social bonds are weakened by prolonged litigation, victim blaming and community division, all of which undermines the prospects for recovery. Third, these disasters display widespread levels of recreancy. Just as health fails, so too do institutions (Freudenberg 1997). Numerous officials, agencies and institutions can let people down, compounding social stress (Picou et al., 2004). Ill-defined, imperceptible and therefore difficult to counter, communities tend to display profound feelings of inadequacy in the face of toxic events, at being out of control and being abandoned by authorities.

COMMUNITAS AND CAPITALS: MIGHT ONE BUILD THE OTHER?

Disasters do not permanently eradicate the obdurate features of social structure. The systems that disburse prejudice and privilege are resilient (Tierney, 2014, p. 237). Victimology records this: the isolated, weak, minorities and the less wealthy consistently fare worse in disaster situations (Matthewman, 2015, pp. 20–21). While communitas speaks to notions of people power and equality, it is clear that some people might be more powerful—and hence more "equal"—than others. Since communitas is fundamentally about human connection, the literature on social capital is drawn upon here to help elucidate such differences in fate. This serves as another way of framing our social infrastructure discussion and, as such, it will help to identify further barriers to the development of communitas.

Disaster and resilience researchers are not strangers to social capital theory. Social capital's role in bringing people together to facilitate effective disaster response and meaningful recovery is frequently highlighted (Tierney, 2014). Daniel P. Aldrich's (2012, pp. 31–34) scholarship is exemplary in this regard. Following Michael Woolcock (2002), he conceptualizes social capital in three different forms: bonding (within networks or homogeneous communities, i.e. people who are close), bridging (between networks or more loosely connected communities) and linking (across vertical gradients, i.e. connecting the people with authority figures). Social capital has many benefits, including the ability to access resources and work collectively towards recovery.

Limited literature is available on the conditions that increase and decrease inter-community and macro-level bridging or linking capacities, although there is work suggesting that socioeconomic status (SES) and race are significant predictors of social capital and the distribution of resources in recovery. For instance, Robert L. Hawkins and Katherine Maurer's (2010, p. 1785) study of Hurricane Katrina argues that SES and race remained significant barriers to bridging and linking social capacities.

In general, the more socially advantaged have broader connections (better bridging and linking capacities as more localized bonding social capital is often less important), while the more socially vulnerable have stronger localized social connections and better bonding social capital capacity (see Rivera & Nickels, 2014, p. 185). This can mean that wealthier citizens have more opportunity post-disaster to construct a world that favours them. As a senior authority in the Canterbury rebuild following the earthquakes of 2010 and 2011 said to us in an interview:

> I'd cynically say that consultation can also mean; that the rich will organize, just get what they want. So, for example, one of the biggest Christchurch City Council projects that has been done so far, was starting the Art Gallery, because the Art Gallery had this incredibly well organized group, the stakeholders, who said: "Unless we have the Art Gallery really super strong, base-isolated, the Rembrandts and Picasso's will never come back".

[P]eople who have got their shit together, they'll get what they want. While all that was happening; well, there wasn't anywhere for the poor people of the Eastern suburbs to go and play rugby league, they didn't have a field operating for a long time in those Eastern suburbs, while all those sorts of discussions were going on.

Don't forget ... the poor people that represented those poor and destitute people; they were so busy just helping [them] to survive. They don't want to submit about what happens to the Art Gallery, or whether swimming pools get built necessarily, they're just flat out.

So, that's the thing about these environments, the leaders get busy, but the well-resourced leaders can continue to operate and lobby, and kind of get what they want. (Sutton, 2018)

At this point, the discussion will profit by drawing on the work of Pierre Bourdieu (1986) as his scholarship unpicks the nexus of interests and the network effects that accrue from combined forms of capitals that result in social advantage. Bourdieu (1986) uses capital theory to refer to almost any resource: capital might be *economic* (e.g. cash and financial assets), *cultural* (e.g. attitudes, education, knowledge, language, past experience, skills), *social* (e.g. networks and group memberships) or *symbolic* (e.g. visibility, stereotypes, social status). These capitals can intersect with each other and convert into/from the other(s) (Bourdieu, 1993). For Bourdieu, capital possession determines social position, particularly within the related domains of labour market and education. It is equally applicable to disaster zones. The total amount, quality and interplay of capitals combines to determine resource-level and social standing. This impacts upon individuals and communities' disaster experiences. Those with more capital possession will likely experience higher resilience and vice versa (Obrist et al., 2010; Wilson, 2012). Importantly, for Bourdieu (1993), the value of capital is determined through the interplay between field and habitus. Fields are the specific social spaces where individuals compete for the distribution of capital. Habitus refers to the internalized, taken-for-granted elements of social structure. These structural factors are typically disregarded in accounts of social capital.

Individuals are seen as strategic and rational social agents who acquire particular types of capital that are valuable in, and applicable to, particular social situations (fields). In a field certain capitals are valuable, but, in different fields (or rapidly changing fields as is the case during disasters), the same capital may be worthless. In other words, agents do not simply act in the world. They are also constrained by habitus and by context (field) (Uekusa, 2017).

Our own research has shown numerous cases where foreigners, following Bourdieu's analysis, could be said to have not developed field-specific habitus to possess the minimum capital (e.g. language competency, correct religious persuasion) to become "proper" and therefore fully accepted members of the social field. This has, for example, seen them placed at risk as they were unable to understand tsunami evacuation warnings, and seen them placed at a disadvantage when negotiating with their insurance companies over earthquake damage to their homes. "Satoshi", a Japanese man involved in social services in Tohoku, explained to us that foreign students at an evacuation shelter following the Great East Japan Earthquake were forced to remain separate from the rest of the group by the evacuation shelter managers because of perceived language barriers. Other issues soon emerged:

> The members of the neighbourhood association, who were running one of the emergency evacuation shelters, said straight out, "I don't like foreign students" or "I'm anti-foreigners". When I asked them about the reason, they said that, since a major university is near-by that place, it was stormed by the foreigners. And it was we, the elderly, who were running the soup kitchen and giving food to the young, whether it is office workers or foreigners. Somehow it doesn't feel right, does it? I understand that a shelter is the place where anyone can come. The point is that the people from the community were operating the shelter to help each other, but there were people who didn't belong to the neighborhood. And it's like we are working so hard, but what? These people came to the shelter and just stayed there without helping others. And even if you understand there is language barrier or whatever, emotionally you just can't accept it. ("Satoshi" 2014)

In addition to alerting us to the resilient system of social structure, Bourdieu's theory offers another important element: the role of symbolic capital, which refers to standing, value, recognition, prestige. External support may focus on those most visible or deemed most deserving. Stereotypes, often invented, manipulated and/or perpetuated via the media, may become a strong predictor for who will accrue capital by finding favourable external support (Lee et al., 2015). Some communities with better symbolic capital such as the Vietnamese Catholic community in Eastern New Orleans after Hurricane Katrina (Leong et al., 2007) and the Filipina community in Tohoku after the Great East Japan Earthquake (Lee, 2012) might have garnered more, and more positive, public attention, resulting in additional external support and extended social and political networks. This contrasts markedly with communities that have negative or limited symbolic capital such as African-American communities and Tohoku marriage migrant women in the same respective disasters. In both cases, these groups were negatively stigmatized and stereotyped, and they suffered accordingly (see South End Press Collective, 2007; Uekusa, 2018).

CONCLUDING THOUGHTS: HOW MIGHT COMMUNITAS BE ENHANCED?

In this chapter we have seen how "human beings reset themselves to something altruistic, communitarian, resourceful, and imaginative after a disaster" (Solnit, 2009, p. 18). Individuals band together for the collective good, new forms of social capital are generated and people risk their lives to save anonymous others. We have known as much for a century, ever since Prince's (1920) pioneering work. Numerous subsequent studies, including, as Scott Knowles (2011, p. 213) notes, landmark texts like *The Effects of Strategic Bombing on German Morale* (1947) and *Human Reactions in Disaster Situations* (1954), have come to the same conclusion: "*disasters bring out prosocial and innovative behaviors in communities*".

That said, while commonplace, we know that communitas does not always flourish. This is particularly the case where social infrastructure has degraded because of ongoing economic disaster, and where communities have "corroded" in the face of toxic disasters. Moreover, we also know that communitas varies between disasters. Brian K. Richardson et al., and and's (2014, p. 211) study of a small Texan community struck by Hurricane Ike, for example, draws our attention to "community characteristics, such as leadership, demographics, length of community residence, community size, and sense of community or closeness during everyday circumstances" as determining characteristics for "*foster[ing] communitas during disasters*".

Given its significance for disaster recovery, it behoves us to learn more about communitas. How might we enhance it? We are still a long way from being able to create communitas at any time, in any place, or at any scale. Moreover, this situation only ever appears to be temporary (Hearn, 1980, p. 316); although it is certainly the case that many people volunteer their time, labour and skills in support of activities that support the social good during non-disaster times as well. Yet Tomohide Atsumi's (2014, p. 152) study shows "*that the state of post-disaster 'paradise' can be maintained, at least intermittently*" by donating funds and volunteering labour to help those struck by other disasters. This creates social bonds between groups even when the direct experience of a particular disaster is not shared. Similarly, it has been observed that positive media exposure can do much the same (O'Brien & Mileti, 1992). This leads to our first suggestions: fundraising, volunteering and responsible media representations of disasters are all helpful. Even potentially corrosive communities have demonstrated that they can collectively cope with toxic events, but they do need to be motivated, skilled and organized (Kaniasty & Norris, 2004, p. 218). This takes us to our second tranche of suggestions: clearly institutional systems that support community organization are to be welcomed and those that encourage robust regulatory oversight, with strong "polluter pays" policies and swift resolution of legal claims would be beneficial too.

By developing social infrastructure and social capital, we build resilience and we create a potent force for disaster risk reduction as well as disaster recovery (Nakagawa & Shaw, 2004). Daniel Aldrich and Michelle Meyer (2015, pp. 262–263) provide us with three practical suggestions here. The first is time banking and community currency. These incentivize volunteering (for example, for every hour of labour for the community that is undertaken, a person is rewarded with an hour of help in kind or community money that can be spent at a local retailer). The second suggestion is to run focus groups and social occasions. These strengthen social connections and build trust. Ideas here include block parties and school information evenings. Third, they recommend civic planning that encourages social mixing, and the possibility of even fleeting encounters with other people. This harks back to older ideas like the creation of "neighbourhood commons" built by and for local residents—barbecue pits, picnic tables, community gardens—which facilitate socializing and allow groups to make their own marks upon their environment (Linn cited in Hirsch, 2015, p. 113). Sally Carlton and Suzanne Vallance (2018) have shown that in post-disaster Christchurch, for example, where most of the central city was destroyed or damaged beyond repair by earthquakes, transitional urbanism projects undertaken by the community became important sites for social capital generation.

Finally, we can revisit Bourdieu's framing to bring in additional suggestions, which gives us the opportunity to go beyond individual and group capacities to consider more *structural* remedies:

- *Cultural capital:* Creating community centres, community empowerment and mobilization programmes; policies promoting educational equality (including equality of access and opportunity), skills provision, language education, minority language promotion (multilingualism); challenging traditional gender roles, deconstructing racial stereotypes.
- *Economic capital:* progressive taxation; provision of: financial assistance and social welfare, affordable housing and public housing; funding for community incentives, employer incentives, employment/work experience schemes.
- *Social capital:* Enhancing networking capacities; encouraging community events and group memberships; social media promotion (as a community binding agent); helping communities develop social infrastructure and the general conditions for people to flourish (e.g. shops, recreational facilities, community centres, good public transportation, public healthcare); greater outreach to include those seen as hard-to-reach, inclusion as consultants in recovery.
- *Symbolic capital:* Anti-discrimination legislation; affirmative action programs; policies aimed at promoting inclusivity; strong media watchdogs to prevent negative stereotyping and misreporting.

While there is merit in all of the abovementioned suggestions, the only real way to ensure an enduring society of equals is through the redistribution of resources (and see: Portes & Landes, 1996).

References

Aldrich, D. P. (2011). The power of people: Social capital's role in recovery from the 1995 Kobe earthquake. *Natural Hazards, 56*(3), 595–611.
Aldrich, D. P. (2012). *Building resilience.* The University of Chicago Press.
Aldrich, D. P., & Meyer, M. (2015). Social Capital and Community Resilience. *American Behavioral Scientist, 59*(2), 254–269.

Alexander, D. (2013). Talk no.1: There is nothing more practical than a theoretical approach to disasters. *Disaster Planning and Emergency Management*. Retrieved from http://emergency-planning.blogspot.co.nz/2013/05/talkno-1-there-is-nothing-more.html

Atsumi, T. (2014). Relaying support in disaster-affected areas: The social implications of a 'pay-it-forward' network. *Disasters, 38*(S2), S144–S146.

Barton, A. H. (1969). *Communities in disaster: A sociological analysis of collective stress situations*. Doubleday.

Bourdieu, P. (1986). The forms of capital. In J. G. Richardson (Ed.), *Handbook of theory for the sociology of education* (pp. 241–258). Greenwood Press.

Bourdieu, P. (1993). *Sociology in question*. Sage.

Carlton, S., & Vallance, S. (2018). The commons of the tragedy: Temporary use and social capital in Christchurch's earthquake-damaged central city. *Social Forces, 96*(2), 831–850.

Clarke, L., & Chess, C. (2008). Elite and panic: More to fear than fear itself. *Social Forces, 87*(2), 993–1014.

Colclough, G., & Sitaraman, B. (2005). Community and social capital: What is the difference? *Sociological Inquiry, 75*(4), 474–496.

Coleman, J. (1988). Social capital in the creation of human capital. *American Journal of Sociology, 94*, S95-120.

Daley, M. (2016). After Hoboken train crash, heroes act before politicians talk. *The Daily Beast*. Retrieved 29 September 2016 from https://www.thedailybeast.com/after-hoboken-train-crash-heroes-actbefore-politicians-talk

Dixon, T. (2008). Encounters with positivism: Making moral meanings in Victorian Britain. *British Academy Scholarship Online*. https://doi.org/10.5871/bacad/9780197264263.003.0003

Drabek, T. E., & Quarantelli, E. L. (1967). Scapegoats, villains, and disasters. *Trans-action, 4*, 12–17.

Drury, J., Cocking, C., & Reicher, S. (2009). The nature of collective resilience: Survivor reactions to the 2005 London bombings. *International Journal of Mass Emergencies and Disasters, 27*(1), 66–95.

Erikson, K. (1994). *A new species of trouble: Explorations in disasters, trauma, and community*. Norton.

Fischer, H. W. (2002). Terrorism and 11 September 2001: Does the 'behavioural response to disaster' model fit? *Disaster Prevention and Management, 11*, 123–127.

Frerks, G. (2009). *Macro dynamics of a mega-disaster: rethinking the Sri Lanka tsunami experience, national safety & security and crisis management: Megacrises in the twenty-first century* (pp. 7–9). Ministry of the Interior and Kingdom Relations.

Freudenburg, W. R. (1997). Contamination, corrosion and the social order: An overview. *Current Sociology, 45*(3), 19–39.

Fritz, C. E. (1961). Disasters. In R. K. Merton & R. A. Nisbet (Eds.), *Contemporary social problems* (pp. 651–694). Harcourt.
Geoghegan, P. (2014). Bosnia under water. *London Review of Books Blog*. Retrieved 28 May 2014 from https://www.lrb.co.uk/blog/2014/may/bosnia-under-water
Graff, G. M. (2020). What Americans are doing now is beautiful: The public's response to the coronavirus will stand as a remarkable moment of national mobilization. *The Atlantic*. Retrieved 19 March from https://www.theatlantic.com/ideas/archive/2020/03/inspiring-galvanizing-beautiful-spirit-2020/608308/
Granovetter, M. (1973). The strength of weak ties. *American Journal of Sociology*, 78(6), 1360–1380.
Hawkins, R. L., & Maurer, K. (2010). Bonding, Bridging and linking: How social capital operated in new Orleans following Hurricane Katrina. *British Journal of Social Work*, 40, 1777–1793.
Hearn, F. (1980). Communitas and reflexive social theory. *Qualitative Sociology*, 3(4), 299–322.
Hirsch, A. B. (2015). Urban barnraising: Collective rituals to promote communitas. *Landscape Journal*, 34(2), 113–126.
Kaniasty, K., & Norris, F. H. (2004). Social support in the aftermath of disasters, catastrophes, and acts of terrorism: Altruistic, overwhelmed, uncertain, antagonistic, and patriotic communities. In R. J. Ursano, A. E. Norwood, & C. S. Fullerton (Eds.), *Bioterrorism: Psychological and public health interventions* (pp. 200–229). Cambridge University Press.
Klinenberg, E. (2002). *Heat wave: A social autopsy of disaster in Chicago*. University of Chicago Press.
Klinenberg, E. (2018). *Palaces for the people: How social infrastructure can help fight inequality, polarization, and the decline of civic life*. Crown.
Knowles, S. G. (2011). *The disaster experts: Mastering risk in Modern America*. University of Pennsylvania Press.
Lee, F., Yamori, K., & Miyamoto, T. (2015). The relationship between local residents and media during recovery: Lessons from "star disaster-affected areas" in Taiwan. *Journal of Natural Disaster Science*, 36(1), 1–11.
Lee, S. (2012). The earthquake experiences and new challenges of 'multicultural families': How to understand the transnationality of marriage-migrant women (translation ours). In H. Komai & E. Suzuki (Eds.), *Foreign immigrants and the great East Japan earthquake* (pp.65–74). Akashi Shoten.
Leong, K. J., Airriess, C. A., Li, W., Chia-Chen, A., Ying, W., Keith, V., & Adams, K. (2007). From invisibility to hypervisibility: The complexity of race, survival and resiliency for the Vietnamese-American community in Eastern New Orleans. In K. A. Bates & R. S. Swan (Eds.), *Through the eye of Katrina: Social justice in the United States* (pp. 171–188). Carolina Academic Press.

Matthewman, S. (2015). *Disasters, risks and revelation: Making Sense of our times*. Palgrave Macmillan.

Mirsky, S. (2016, April 1). What happens when the power goes off. Or, how to enjoy a blackout. *Aeon*. Retrieved from available: https://aeon.co/videos/what-happens-when-the-power-goes-off-or-how-to-enjoy-a-blackout

Molotch, H. (1970). Oil in Santa Barbara and power in America. *Sociological Inquiry, 40*(1), 131–144.

Monbiot, G. (2020, March 31). The horror films got it wrong. This virus has turned us into caring neighbours. *The Guardian*. Retrieved from: https://www.theguardian.com/commentisfree/2020/mar/31/virus-neighbours-covid-19

Mutter, J. C. (2015). *The disaster profiteers: How natural disasters make the rich richer and the poor even poorer*. St. Martin's Press.

Nakagawa, Y., & Shaw, R. (2004). Social capital: A missing link to disaster recovery. *Journal of Mass Emergencies and Disasters, 22*(1), 5–34.

O'Brien, P., & Mileti, D. S. (1992). Citizen participation in emergency response following the Loma Prieta earthquake. *International Journal of Mass Emergencies and Disasters, 10*(1), 71–89.

Obrist, B., Pfeiffer, C., & Henley, R. (2010). Multi-layered social resilience: A new approach in mitigation research. *Progress in Development Studies, 10*, 283–293.

Oliver-Smith, A. (1999). The brotherhood of pain. Theoretical and applied perspectives on post-disaster solidarity. In A. Oliver-Smith & S.M. Hoffman (Eds.), *The angry earth. Disasters in anthropological perspective* (pp.156–172). Routledge.

Peek, L. (2020). *The ties that bind*. The Natural Hazards Center, Boulder, Colorado. Retrieved 20 March from https://hazards.colorado.edu/news/director/the-ties-that-bind

Perrow, C. (2007). *The next catastrophe*. Princeton University Press.

Picou, S. J., Marshall, B. K., & Gill, D. A. (2004). Disaster litigation, and the corrosive community. *Social Forces, 82*(4), 1493–1522.

Portes, A., & Landolt, P. (1996, May–June 26). The downside of social capital. *The American Prospect*, p.18+. Gale Academic OneFile. Retrieved 5 September 2020 from https://link-gale-com.ezproxy.auckland.ac.nz/apps/doc/A21093810/AONE?u=learn&sid=AONE&xid=ba8d68ba

Preston, J., & Firth, R. (2020). *Preparing for the 2020 Coronavirus pandemic in the United Kingdom: From the neo-liberal state to radical mutual aid*. Palgrave Pivot, UK.

Prince, S. H. (1920). *Catastrophe and social change*. Columbia University.

Povoledo, E. (2016). After earthquake in Italy, 'half the town no longer exists'. *The New York Times*. Retrieved 24 August from https://www.nytimes.com/2016/08/25/world/europe/amatrice-italyearthquake.html

Remes, J. A. C. (2016). *Disaster citizenship: Survivors, solidarity and power in the progressive era*. University of Illinois Press.
Richardson, B. K., Siebeneck, L. K., Shaunfield, S., & Kaszynski, E. (2014). From 'no man's land' to a 'strong community': Communitas as a theoretical framework for successful disaster recovery. *International Journal of Mass Emergencies and Disasters, 32*(1), 194–219.
Rivera, J. D., & Nickels, A. E. (2014). Social capital, community resilience, and Faith-based organizations in disaster recovery: A case study of Mary Queen of Vietnam Catholic Church. *Risk, Hazards & Crises in Public Policy, 5*(2), 178–211.
Rodriguez, H., Trainer, J., & Quarantelli, E. L. (2006). Rising to the challenges of a catastrophe: The emergent and prosocial behavior following Hurricane Katrina. *The Annals of the American Academy of Political and Social Science, 604*(1), 82–104.
"Satoshi". (2014, October 13). Interview: Social services worker. *Tohuku*.
Solnit, R. (2005, October). The uses of disaster: Notes on bad weather and good government. *Harper's Magazine*, pp. 31–37.
Solnit, R. (2009). *A paradise built in hell: The extraordinary communities that arise in disasters*. Viking.
Solnit, R. (2020). The way we get through this is together: The rise of mutual aid under Coronavirus. *The Guardian*. Retrieved 14 May from https://www.theguardian.com/world/2020/may/14/mutual-aid-coronavirus-pandemic-rebecca-solnit
South End Press Collective. (2007). *What lies beneath: Katrina, race, and the state of the nation*. South End Press.
Sutton, R. (2018, April 30). *Interview: CEO of the Canterbury Earthquake Recovery Authority*. Christchurch.
Tierney, K. (2003). Disaster beliefs and institutional interests: Recycling disaster myths in the aftermath of 9–11. In L. Clarke (Ed.), *Terrorism and disaster: New threats* (pp. 33–51). New Ideas, Elsevier.
Tierney, K. (2010). Growth machine politics and the social production of risk. *Contemporary Sociology: A Journal of Reviews, 39*(6), 660–663.
Tierney, K. (2014). *The social roots of risk: Producing disasters*. Stanford University Press, Stanford.
Turner, V. (1969). *The ritual process: Structure and anti-structure*. Aldine Publishing.
Turner, V. (1986). *The anthropology of performance*. PAJ Publications.
Turner, E. (2012). *Communitas: The anthropology of collective joy*. Palgrave Macmillan.
Uekusa, S. (2018). *Social vulnerability, resilience and capital in disasters: Immigrants, refugees and linguistic minorities in the 2010–2011 Canterbury and Tohoku disasters* (PhD Thesis). University of Auckland, New Zealand.

Uekusa, S. (2017). Rethinking resilience: Bourdieu's contribution to disaster research. *Resilience: International Policies, Practices and Discourses*, 1–15. https://doi.org/10.1080/21693293.2017.1308635

UN Chronicle. (2016). The relevance of soft infrastructure in disaster management and risk reduction. *UN Chronicle, LIII*(3). Retrieved from https://unchronicle.un.org/article/relevance-softinfrastructure-disaster-management-and-risk-reduction

Westgate, J. (2014). Fieldnotes from Christchurch: 'A wonderful disaster'. *Australian Centre for Culture, Environment, Society and Space*, Retrieved 7 December from https://www.uowblogs.com/ausccer/2014/12/07/fieldnotes-from-christchurch-a-wonderful-disaster/

Wilson, G. (2012). *Community resilience and environmental transitions.* Taylor & Francis.

Wolfensburg, M. (1957). *Disaster: A psychological essay.* Free Press.

Wood, L. J., Boruff, B. J., & Smith, H. M. (2013). When disaster strikes... How communities cope and adapt: A social capital perspective. In D. C. Johnson (Ed.), *Social capital: Theory, measurement and outcomes* (pp. 143–169). Nova Science Publishers Inc.

Woolcock, M. (2002). Social capital in theory and practice: Where do we Stand? In J. Isham, T. Kelly, & S. Ramaswamy (Eds.), *Social capital and economic development: Well-being in developing countries* (pp. 18–39). Edward Elgar.

CHAPTER 14

Use of Scientific Knowledge and Public Participation in Disaster Risk Reduction and Response in the State of Sikkim, India

Vinod Sharma

Sikkim—From Response to Preparedness

Sikkim is the second smallest state of India and is located between 27°5′N to 28°9′N and 87°59′E to 88°56′E. It has an area of 7096 km² and is bound by Nepal in the west and large stretches of the Tibetan plateau in the north. Bhutan and Chumbi Valley of Tibet lie in the east and Darjeeling district in the south. The State of Sikkim is stretched over 112 km from north to south and 64 km from east to west. Sikkim has 47.80% of forest cover. It is a part of eastern Himalayan global biodiversity hotspot with the large amount of forest cover (FSI, SFR 2015). The largest portion of Sikkim is in its North-Western region where, a large number of mountains are present with the altitude of about nine thousand metres which includes the famous Kanchenjunga (8598 metres), the third highest peak in the world (Fig. 14.1).

V. Sharma (✉)
Indian Institute of Public Administration, New Delhi, India

Fig. 14.1 Map of Sikkim

Sikkim lies in a highly seismic zone of IV and V of the Indian seismic zone. Steep slope terrain makes it vulnerable to the various geophysical and hydro-meteorological disasters. The state characterized by weak geology, comprising sedimentary and low-grade metamorphic rocks which are prone to landslides.

Managing disaster risks and reducing the risks to a great extent is based on scientific knowledge and evidence-based technique. The losses caused due to the disasters can be greatly reduced by the use of technology-based disaster risk reduction techniques. There are many different conceptual frameworks for risk reduction.

In the last decade, India has moved from reactive emergency responses to being proactive and implementing disaster preparedness and risk reduction (Sandeep Tambe, 2018). The Disaster Management Act of 2005, provides a hierarchical institutional structure, with the National Disaster Management Authority (NDMA), State Disaster Management Authorities (SDMAs), and District Disaster Management Authorities (DDMAs) responsible for disaster management at the national, state, and district levels, respectively. The guidelines formulated by NDMA have proactive procedures for dealing with specific natural disasters. The National Disaster Response Force (NDRF) was formed under the Act by upgrading battalions of central paramilitary forces consisting of specialized teams trained in various types of natural and technological disasters (NDMA, 2011).

REVIEW OF POST-EARTHQUAKE RESPONSE STRATEGIES

In developing countries, the post-earthquake reconstruction consists of reconstruction of public amenities such as roads, bridges, schools, hospitals, and offices, and reconstruction of damaged houses. Rural houses reconstruction largely happens in situ. In such cases, housing insurance is uncommon, and victims often depend on the government for support (Hidayat, 2010). Consequently, 30–50% of post-disaster financial allocations are assigned to housing reconstruction (Freeman, 2004).

Indian responses to post-disaster reconstruction and the outcomes achieved have been diverse (Barenstein, 2010). Housing reconstruction in India began with CDA, which was adopted during the Latur earthquake of 1993 and Indian Ocean tsunami in 2004. Most of the planning, technology options, and implementation was top-down, resulting in low beneficiary satisfaction levels (Barenstein, 2010).

Difficult terrain, remote locations, and communication gaps with the local community were the main challenges faced by the Uttarakhand project (Mallik, 2014). Reconstruction projects funded by central government have been location-specific, such as prefabricated houses constructed for Leh flash flood victims in 2010 to provide shelter quickly as winter was fast approaching (Sandeep Tambe, 2018).

Sikkim was hit by a 6.9 magnitude earthquake of intensity VII on 18 September 2011, which triggered numerous landslides, causing damage to half of the 92,000 rural houses. Subsequently there was a massive collateral damage due to a combination of weak terrain, geology, fragile ecology, and heavy rainfall which amplified the impact of the earthquake, creating a multiplier effect resulting in hundreds of natural calamities in the form of landslides, boulder falls, and flash floods (Sharma, 2018).

The National Disaster Management Authority (NDMA) issued guidelines for the management of earthquakes in April 2007. These guidelines, however, do not specify any parameters or tools/mechanisms to assess the performance of states/union territories in a disaster. The guidelines identify six pillars on which earthquake management in India should be based on

1. earthquake-resistant construction of new structures;
2. selective seismic strengthening and retrofitting of existing priority structures and life line structures;
3. regulations and enforcement;
4. awareness and preparedness about earthquakes;
5. capacity development to include education, training, research & development, capacity building; and
6. Documentation and strengthening emergency response.

Post-Earthquake Initiatives

The present chapter deals with some of state policy, plans, and strategies for use of Science, Technology, and people's participation in resilient reconstruction disaster risk reduction in the state. Sikkim state reconstruction on principal of "Build Back Better" is a success story of resilient construction as given in Sendai Framework 2015–2030.

Following the 2011 earthquake, a post-earthquake assessment of the strengths and weaknesses of the various structures present in rural areas was carried out. It was found that stone masonry walls with mud mortar which are widely used as residential structures in the rural areas were the most affected structures and suffered maximum damage. However, it was also found that these structures had some earthquake-resistant characteristics as the deaths caused by these were very few.

The traditional house typically has a two-stories with a light ekra (bamboo reinforced wall) or wooden walling and plastered with mud or cement plaster on thick stone masonry walls. The rapid growth and development in the state have resulted in a transition in the construction choice from traditional houses to RC frame houses.

In a study conducted post-earthquake, it was discovered that 54,000 of the total 92,000 rural houses suffered various degrees of damage, but there were very few casualties. The findings of the study indicated that the superstructure of wooden framed houses with ekra walling and light iron-sheet roof was mostly intact. The stone masonry load-bearing walls laid on mud mortar and not having any reinforcement suffered maximum damage to the shear forces. Private houses with RC frame structure with brick masonry infill and iron-sheet roof performed well, showing only non-structural damage. This study was also published in the Current Science journal published by the Indian Academy of Sciences in May 2012 (Sharma, 2018) (Fig. 14.2).

Following the Sikkim earthquake, the Reconstruction of Earthquake Damaged Rural Houses (REDRH) project was conceived by the Rural Management and Development Department (RMDD). This project was launched in March 2012 and, both in terms of the number of houses to be rebuilt and the budget, is the single largest project ever implemented in

Fig. 14.2 Ruins of a house in 2011 earthquake

the state (Sandeep Tambe, 2018). The detailed project report and operational guidelines of the reconstruction project were prepared by RMDD, building on the experiences in the ongoing CMRHM programme, which was showing good results (Sandeep Tambe, 2018).

There are different approaches to post-disaster reconstruction of residential structures for example contractor-driven approach (CDA), the owner-driven approach (ODA), instant prefabricated housing (IPH), the departmental construction approach (DCA), and joint approach of department and owner, which is similar to and the cash transfer approach (CTA). The three most important factors during the rebuilding of the houses are the approach to be taken, technical support provided to the locals and the timely delivery of the construction materials (Fig. 14.3).

The state government had recently launched CMRHM, with INR 4.2–4.8 lakh provided to beneficiaries in instalments using ODA. Immediately after the earthquake, the Land Revenue and Disaster Management Department, Government of Sikkim (LRDMD) along with the gram panchayats (elected representatives at the village level) assessed the nature and quantum of the damage to rural housing. Based on this assessment, payments were released to the owners to undertake immediate temporary house repairs.

During the reconstruction phase the locals were not keen to rebuild them, traditional house design of ekra houses using locally available construction materials, particularly bamboo as they deemed it to be

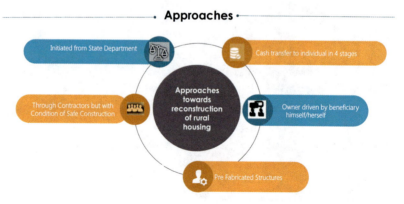

Fig. 14.3 Options for the post-disaster reconstruction in Sikkim of residential housing

vulnerable to disasters. As a result, the ongoing rural housing programme (CMRHM) promoted RCC (reinforced cement concrete) houses and had gained wide acceptance.

Accordingly, the state political leadership approved a four-roomed RCC frame house, in which the CMRHM house design was further reinforced with earthquake-resistant features and had the following core specifications:

a. Size: total floor area 56.20 m^2 (605 sq. feet)
b. RCC frame structure: with nine columns, plinth beam, roof beam, and sill band. Columns and beams with a cross-section of 0.3 m × 0.3 m, and sill band of 0.15 m × 0.15 m. Rings of 8 mm diameter with the ends bent at 135 degrees and spaced at 8 cm near the joints
c. Walls: brick walling over RCC frame or traditional ekra panels
d. Flooring: cement concrete
e. Roofing: RCC slab 0.1 m thick or CGI sheet sloping roof
f. Sanitation: toilet along with septic tank (Fig. 14.4).

This house design, incorporating earthquake-resistant features, was communicated to homeowners, masons, and field engineers using a mason training handbook with comic-book style illustrations in English, Hindi, and Nepali

The homeowner designed the house type appropriate to their lifestyle, family size, and budget. Flexible design options were permitted such as:

1. Toilet and kitchen were permitted outside the house, provided the size and design of the main house having a plinth of 56 m^2 conforms to the prescribed design. This is as per the prevalent traditional practice as many households use firewood extensively and toilets are not perceived as hygienic inside the house.
2. Plinth area option in two storeys: few cases came to light where the households own less than 56 m^2 of land. In these cases, the plinth area was compensated by building rooms on the second floor. The design of this two-storied house with new design was checked to ensure whether it was earthquake resistant, and prior administrative approval of the District Level Committee was also taken in this case.
3. Internal partition of ekra material: the transportation and head load costs of bricks especially for houses located at a distance from the

Fig. 14.4 Layout of a typical house

road head is quite substantial and is not adequately accounted for in the standard unit cost estimate. Hence, the internal partition of the house was permitted of ekra (wood reinforced bamboo) material instead of brick.

4. CGI roof option in select remote areas: option of CGI roof was permitted for beneficiaries in select remote areas in all districts to save on transportation costs with prior approval of District Level Committee.
5. Advisory to the beneficiary: advisory was provided to the beneficiary that the foundation of the house has been designed for maximum of two storeys with the roof of the second story having CGI sheet

roof. Any modification of design involving slab roof on the second story or subsequent storeys will need corresponding modification in the foundation and supporting reinforcement.
6. Parapet wall of brick masonry on the roof can be replaced with durable material with adequate strength.

The reconstruction of the houses was based on the guiding principle of the philosophy of Build Back Better. The earthquake-resistant houses were built in partnership with the homeowners. The core house design, building standards, construction material technical supervision, and co-financing capital were provided by the project.

The homeowner was free to choose between two approaches of department-driven implementation or homeowner-driven model. In homeowner-driven option, the homeowner took the lead in construction and the funds and construction material was provided to him after completing predefined milestones. While in the department-driven model, the department took the lead in the construction of the house. Needless to say, the homeowner-driven option was the most popular. Homeowners were empowered to make their own choice, which resulted in a greater satisfaction and buy-in and an increased willingness to invest more in earthquake safety and a reduction in dependency (Sharma, 2018).

Construction materials of high quality were made available to the homeowners by the project itself. The project procured the materials directly from the manufactures at lower rates outside the state and brought it to the area to be made available for the homeowners. This resulted in significant savings in the cost and ensured easy access to quality construction material for the homeowners. For each house, stock material in the form of 300 bags of cement and 26 quintals of TMT bars was provided (Sharma, 2018).

Therefore about 1.5 million cement bags and 13,000 MT of TMT bars were to be supplied for the construction process to run smoothly. This was a major logistics challenge to the project. The financing was provided in four instalments. Each instalment was disbursed to the homeowner after checking of the quality of the construction at every phase. In other words, the provision of grant was made contingent upon meeting minimum standards for good construction quality (Fig. 14.5).

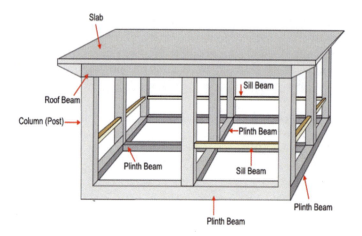

Fig. 14.5 Earthquake-resistant features

EARTHQUAKE-RESISTANT FEATURES

The new constructed houses were ensured to be earthquake resistant. Some guidelines for the construction were issued for the homeowners benefit and ensure a strong structure.

- RC frame structure with nine columns, plinth beam, roof beam, and sill beam.
- Columns and beams have cross-section of 0.3 m × 0.3 m, with the sill beam of 0.15 m × 0.15 m.
- Rings are of 8 mm dia with the ends bent at 135 degrees and a spacing of 8 cm near the joints.
- Use of quality building material: Cement and 500D TMT EQR bars of reputed brands were only used.
- Good workmanship: Simplifying the technical aspects by preparing easy to use IEC materials with adequate supervision by technical staff.
- Concurrent monitoring: Regular and concurrent monitoring of the houses under construction.

Guidelines and Capacity Building

- **Training of technical staff**: The local masons were trained in the technical aspects of house construction and management of block level stores in various training workshops. Also, the "Mason Training Handbook" was prepared in both English and Nepali to simplify the technical aspects of house construction. The book has been prepared in easy to understand illustrated format in comic-book style and translated into the local language. Knowledge upgradation programme for the masons was also organized in partnership with IIT Delhi under the Rural Housing Knowledge Network (RHKN) initiative of MoRD.
- **Training of accounts staff** to maintain accounts and management of block level stores by the storekeepers has also been conducted.
- **Record keeping**: Record keeping at District, Block, and Block Level Stores has been simplified by providing pre-printed registers and training has also been conducted.
- **Establishing a web-based MIS in an IT challenged environment**: While other parts of the country have been reaping the benefits of the IT revolution, the northeast region is largely digitally marginalized. In this challenging environment, the successful demonstration of this functional web-based MIS which has been developed in the house will provide hands-on experience to all the stakeholders who on realizing the benefits of e-Governance will demand for similar MIS applications in future projects as well. It has helped in functional IT literacy as well, with the users understanding the difference between offline and online, drill down reports, creating signed pdf files, e Stores management, and the like. Since the data entry is largely from Block level, it has also helped in vertical learning of these concepts.

Impacts of Resilience Building

The outcomes have been quantified in terms of safer houses built, better builders developed, number of trained engineers, and empowered homeowners:

- The new houses are better and provide more attractive living places, with improved indoor comfort environment for the residents

because of the project's inputs. Out of the target of 93% of the houses in the state are now earthquake resilient houses.
- The number of builders and contractors who were trained and were involved in the earthquake-resistant construction practices. A total of 1000 masons and their assistants received hands-on training under this project and were actively involved in the earthquake-resistant house construction.
- Trained engineers include local engineers, architects, and other construction professionals employed and mentored by the RM&D Department. More than 300 engineers got trained in earthquake-resistant house construction techniques.
- Empowered homeowners include homeowners who have been involved in driving the process of house construction. About 8000 homeowners comprising 40,000 individuals have gotten empowered by the homeowner-driven construction strategy.
- A set of guidelines which is state-specific have been made for the benefit of the locals such as Operational Guidelines (47 pages) framed for the project, Guidelines for management of Block Level Stores framed, Guidelines for Joint Implementation Model framed, Inspection report format of State Level Monitors notified, Guidelines for Self-purchase Model framed.

Developing Understanding on Ecosystem Approach

Several other projects have also come up in the state for the mitigation and risk reduction of the disaster effects. The project "Capacity Building strategies for managing Complex Disasters in the face on Climate Change" sponsored by NMHS-MoEF and CC, aims to assess the nature, vulnerability, and capacity of the communities to cope with complex disasters in the face of climate change. The project also aims to scrutinize and identify modes of development that suit local requirements for a sustainable future. The project objectives include:

- Develop a clear understanding of hazards, vulnerabilities, and capacities to cope with complex disasters in the current development patterns in the face of climate change.
- To formulate and test developmental strategies with key local stakeholders to cope with complex disasters for a sustainable future.

- Identifying key policy interventions required for redesigning development for a sustainable future.
- Disseminating & mainstreaming sustainable development practices with local communities and policy-level stakeholders.

The project adopts a bottom-up approach focussing on multiple stakeholders at all levels including government officials, PRI representatives, school teachers, and community. The project has focussed on sixteen model GPUs for on-field activities and undertakes intensive community interventions for building their capacity to manage day-to-day shocks and stresses. Annual trainings for government officials and PRI members are being carried out to capacitate local government and decentralize decision-making till village level.

COMMUNITY RISK REGISTER (CRR)

Community Risk Register (CRR) is a public document prepared by the local government which provides an overview of the potential risks in the community which can lead to a disaster. It provides information on the emergencies that can happen in the community, together with an assessment of how likely they are to happen and the impacts if they do. It is designed to inform people about the risks that could occur where they live, so they can think about what they can do to be better prepared in their homes, communities, and businesses. The register also serves as a knowledge base for development planning works.

Looking at all of the risks together can also help emergency services, local authorities, and other organizations plan their joint response. The CRR aims to help these agencies make decisions on emergency planning work and will help them develop better relationships while considering their resources and capacities.

The register has been published in response to the mandates given under Chapter 6 of the Disaster Management Act, 2005, which mandates local authority to take measures as necessary for disaster management. Further information can be accessed through the Sikkim State Disaster Management Authority (SSDMA) website.

The tools like community risk register are empowering people to assess their own and integrate the same in development planning projects enabling community-based risk-informed development. The climate lab established in school as a pilot project is playing a pivotal role in shaping the interest of younger generations towards environment-sensitive development. This project has also provided a common platform for the active engagement of government with the community through live demonstration in community fair. The project focusses on disseminating complex knowledge to the community in a much simpler interactive form, e.g., the issues of non-structural mitigation and the associated solution is explained to the community in Maghe Mela through a shake table demonstration where people can experience how the earthquake affects their home and what are the simple steps to avoid the loss to life and property.

Climate School

A climate school as a concept works towards sensitizing the school children towards climate change in a practical manner. The objective of the exercise is to sensitize the school students about the effects of climate parameters and to instil a curiosity in the young minds to know about the various facets of climate science.

As Climate has a huge influence on complex disasters, measuring of climatic parameters and establishing their linkages with disasters can be done in order to sharpen the knowledge of complex disasters. The climate school aims to record daily weather data through the students for six parameters. These parameters include maximum and minimum temperature, humidity, wind direction, wind speed, rainfall, and atmospheric pressure.

The school selected for this pilot project was the Govt. Junior High School, Upper Syari, Deorali, Gangtok. The school is located in the main city and the proximity to the amenities is more. A training session with seventh grade students was conducted for awareness of school students about climate change and weather instruments. The various parameters for monitoring weather were discussed with the students and the operation of the instruments was shown and explained to them. A group of six students was selected to record weather data from the instruments for a period of one month. After that another group of six students would be selected from the class to record the data. This was planned such that each student gets accustomed to use the instruments.

After that the selected group of six students was taught on how to operate the instruments and take the readings. The student practised and took reading from the instruments and recorded in the register. A weather information board by the name of "Weather Watch" was also put up at the school which displays daily weather data and monthly average weather data for the last month for the recorded parameters.

A teacher was nominated by the school to supervise this activity and act as in-charge of the data recording session. The teacher also acts as a link between the project and the students. They are responsible for maintaining the register of daily recordings.

As a means to generating awareness, the climate school demonstrates the actual variation in the weather conditions by measuring the local weather parameters of the area where the school is situated. In this manner the students get a quantitative idea of how the weather varies during seasons. The study does not use the data recorded by the students for any research purpose as the objective of the exercise is to make children better understand the parameters that affect the weather of their city in the backdrop of complex disasters.

Maghey Mela

Jorethang Maghey Mela is one of the largest Mela in Sikkim celebrated in the month of January every year and is one of the state-level events. Countless tourists from every corner of the globe gather at this festival and are part of it. The varied cultural programmes, ethnicity, traditional dance, cuisines, arts, and handicrafts of Sikkim are showcased at the Mela. Project "Capacity Building Strategies for Managing Complex Disasters in the face of Climate change" funded by National Mission on Himalayan Studies-Ministry of Environment Forest and Climate Change, Government of India (NMHS-MoEF&CC, GoI), led by Indian Institute of Public Administration (IIPA) and SEEDS Technical Services (STS) in collaboration with Sikkim State Disaster Management Authority(SSDMA) also represented at the events with a stall where Climate and Disasters related games, Shake table for earthquake demonstration were given to the public.

School Risk Register (SRR)

School Risk Register provides information on the emergencies that can happen in and around the school, together with an assessment of how likely they are to happen and the impacts if they do. It is designed to inform school authority about the risks that could occur, so they can think about what they can do to be better prepared. The register also serves as a knowledge base for development planning works of the school.

Looking at the risks together can also help in response planning for emergency. The School Risk Register aims to help school authority make decisions on emergency planning work, and will help them develop better relationships while considering their resources and capacities.

The school risk assessment committee is responsible for preparation of School Risk Register. The School Risk Assessment Committee convenes for a meeting at regular intervals as decided by them to prepare/revise the School Risk Register (https://www.climatesmartgovernance.com/projects.php).

Future Pathway for Risk Reduction and Resilience Building

The huge reconstruction exercise after the 2011 was inclusive and comprehensive. It empowered the local people to build their own homes but in a sustainable and safe manner. Following this the state has had many projects undertaking the safety and resilient feature of the structures and infrastructure of the state, as well as resilience building across various hazards. This has put focus on the subject and affected the political will power making safer liveable communities as their priority. The chief minister, in a state conference, on 11th September 2018 announced the following showing a strong political will towards building back better.

1. Felicitation of all individuals/NGOs/SHGs involved in disaster management on the occasion of Republic Day on 26th January 2019.
2. To make Sikkim a model State in disaster management by the year 2020.
3. Introduction of Disaster Management as a subject at the Primary level school curriculum from the next academic session.
4. All infrastructural constructions like construction of buildings, electricity lines, water supply, roads, etc., should be made earthquake resistant.

Conclusion

Reconstruction process should be determined by the "Build Back Better" concept. It ensures the safety of the residents and promotes sustainability and instils it in the residents' lifestyle culturally. It focusses on resilience in the face of all future threats from disasters, climate change impacts, and developmental stresses. It does so by enabling communities and ensuring that the local people and the homeowners are firmly in the driving seat.

In situ rehabilitation is always preferable with relocation being the last resort; safety from all future hazards, including climate change impacts needs to be ensured; sustainability needs to be achieved through appropriate materials and technologies; there needs to be cultural appropriateness in design; the processes need to take the now established owner-driven approach; and monitoring should ideally be done through local bodies but using smart systems and software.

This in situ approach eventually translates into a non-disruptive development and risk reduction pattern, wherein the effort is to build capacity with what exists, and to make it stronger rather than trying to replace it with imported concepts.

Acknowledgements I thankfully acknowledge the Rural Management and Development Department (RMDD), Government of Sikkim for sharing their reports as the entire reconstruction was done by RMDD officers in total transparency and people's participation under the guidance of Hon'ble Chief Minister of Sikkim State. Thanks are due to Dr. Shyamli Singh and Dr. Anshu Sharma (SEEDS India) for helping me in the preparation of this chapter.

References

Barenstein, J. D. (2010). India: From a culture of housing to a philosophy of reconstruction. In T. S. M. Lyons (Ed.), *Building back better: Delivering people-centred housing reconstruction at scale* (pp. 163–188). Practical Action, London.

Freeman, P. K. (2004). Allocation of post-disaster reconstruction financing to housing. *Building Research & Information*, 427–437.

Hidayat, B. (2010). A literature review of the role of project management in post-disaster. In *26th Annual ARCOM Conference* (pp. 1269–1278). Association of Researchers in Construction Management, Leeds, UK.

Mallik, D. (2014). *End poverty in South Asia.* Retrieved 10 March 2018, from The World Bank: http://blogs.worldbank.org/endpovertyinsouthasia/i-will-construct-my-house-myself

NDMA. (2011). *Annual Report 2011.* National Disaster Management Authority, New Delhi.

Sandeep Tambe, S. P. (2018). Post earthquake housing reconstruction in the Sikkim Himalaya: approaches, challenges, and lessons learnt. *Development in Practice*, 647–660.

Sharma, V. K. (2018). Building back better: Focus on resilience and participation. In R. Shaw, T. Izumi, & K. Shiwaku (Eds.), *Science and technology in disaster risk reduction in Asia* (pp. 395–408). Academic Press.

PART IV

Recovery

CHAPTER 15

Post-Disaster Recoveries in Indonesia and Japan: Building Back Better

Minako Sakai

INTRODUCTION

Currently, development goals play an important role in shaping international frameworks. These international frameworks are exemplified in general terms by prominent goals such as the Millennium Development Goals (MDGs) and subsequent replaced by the Sustainable Development Goals (SDGs) in 2016. Both are international development goals led by the United Nations as a global effort to reduce poverty (UNDP, 2020). In terms of post-disaster recovery, the current policy consensus is that the Building Back Better (BBB) framework should be used to formulate the targets of post-disaster recovery processes.

Building Back Better (BBB) emerged as a key concept in disaster management and development discourse, when the international community responded to the impacts of the Indian Ocean Tsunami in 2004.

M. Sakai (✉)
School of Humanities and Social Sciences, The University of New South Wales, Canberra, Australia
e-mail: m.sakai@unsw.edu.au

The UN Special Envoy, Bill Clinton, produced a report on the tsunami recovery in 2006 that highlighted ten key lessons that should be learned from the experience and for better handling of similar situations in the future. The lessons focused on the role of government, donors and aid agencies to take a lead. The concept of BBB reflects the understanding that post-disaster recovery is not simply about returning a state to its pre-disaster condition, but that disasters can be used as a catalyst to build back a society that better meets the needs of the affected community (James & Paton, 2015). BBB gained further attention from policymakers after the Tohoku earthquakes and tsunami that hit Northern Japan in 2011. The Sendai Framework adopted at the Third UN World Conference on Disaster Risk Reduction in Sendai, Japan, on 18 March 2015 reinforced the role of BBB in recovery, rehabilitation and reconstruction (RR & R). It is fair to conclude that state as well as local government agencies have received a mandate to lead the BBB initiatives to mitigate future risks of disasters by following this framework increasing preparedness and strengthening disaster prevention governance. In some disaster-prone countries like Indonesia, the government has established a new specialised agency to strengthen their capacity to manage disasters.

However, alongside the heavy focus on top-down government and donors' roles in taking a lead in BBB initiatives, scholars have increasingly emphasised the importance of civil society in fostering preparedness and leading bottom-up recovery processes (Aldrich, 2017; Andharia, 2019; Kage, 2011; Sakai et al., 2014). The main arguments of these scholars suggest that mobilisation of local resources, including civil society, and how social capital, such as social networks and trust, can enhance the recovery processes. In short, social capital facilitates bottom-up disaster recovery.

Emerging research drawing from a case study of the recovery from Hurricane Katerina in the USA shows that entrepreneurs can also act as agents of change to address the community needs to facilitate BBB (Storr et al., 2015). These research findings indicate that swift disaster recovery requires coordinated partnerships across multiple agencies, rather than giving responsibility to one particular type of enterprise, or association along with state agencies.

Fernandez and Ahmed (2019) have stated future BBB research should identify factors that promote success or failure within local contexts. For example, the concept of BBB was applied to design anti-disaster housing when rebuilding in Aceh, Indonesia, but local needs were not appropriately accommodated in the new housing designs, forcing changes to the traditional way of life (Rahmayati, 2016). Concurring with Fernadez and Ahmed's call to identify factors leading to local success, this chapter highlights the relevance of the embedded economy—social relations and cultural norms that affect the way economic action is conducted (Granovetter, 1985)—and how it influences the way the concept of BBB is imagined and implemented in local contexts.

BBB involves a combination of community resilience and a diverse range of projects for rebuilding physical infrastructure. Businesses and civil society must also play a part so that reconstruction projects progress swiftly. In particular, disaster entrepreneurship is receiving scholarly attention and is a key factor in facilitating the recovery process (Aldrich, 2018; Storr et al., 2015). In this light, mobilisation of resources to undertake projects led by civil society groups to start new projects are expected to play an important role in supporting bottom-up recovery efforts. This article explores how socio-cultural contexts have affected the trajectories of post-disaster recovery processes in two different societies, Indonesia and Japan. The focus of my analysis is on how economic embeddedness has affected recovery efforts and mobilisation of resources from the community for post-disaster recoveries in different socio-cultural contexts.

Raising funds and resources from the community takes a wide range of community resource mobilisation effort, traditionally in-person donations have been the focus but there has been a gradual shift to utilising fintech to mobilise resources online. In this article, I use crowdfunding to refer to resources mobilisation of small sums of funds raised from the community both online and offline (Gras et al., 2017). Crowdfunding is emerging as one of the key methods of raising funds to respond to a local community's needs and to address social problems including through post-disaster recovery initiatives. Crowdfunding includes lending-based, equity-based, reward-based and donation-based crowdfunding (Simons et al., 2019, p. 114). This chapter argues that similar financial or social schemes of crowdfunding can produce different outcomes, subject to the influence of the embeddedness of the perception of the concept of giving and what it entails as a specific cultural practice.

The first section of this chapter will analyse embedded cultures to show the different trajectories of giving and expected returns on funds and resources given. The second section will analyse two case studies, of

Indonesia and Japan, followed by a discussion that explores how such embedded giving has affected the ways people can mobilise funds from the community for post-disaster recovery projects. The final section of the chapter will highlight the ramifications of developing the concept of Building Back Better (BBB) in different socio-cultural contexts as future policy develops.

Raising Resources from the Community

An emerging global trend to support victims of disasters is to donate to disaster relief organisations (Donaldson, 2020). Currently, TV and media can clearly communicate graphic devastation of disaster-affected areas to a wide audience. Seeing the magnitude of such devastation and associated humanitarian crises unfolding compels people to take immediate action. Depending on the size of the disaster, local, national and international community members have been found to donate generously. People can donate to existing charities or set up funds to channel their donations to those in need. As the use of social media and the internet has become popular, people can choose to donate instantly. However, using social media donation channels in the immediate aftermath of the crisis is a challenging way for recipient of raising funds and resources from the local community for the intended targets of those funds. For example, celebrities such as a comedian Celeste Barber raised 51 million dollars to the 2020 bush fires in Australia established an appeal for donations to support NSW RFS to which her followers and community members joined to channel their funds to. However, the pledge to donate to RFS did not mean that the raised funds were all directly going to be distributed to the affected local bush fire victims. This is because donations to RFS are support the operations of RFS, not involving the recovery of victims, although the donors were not fully aware of the rules limiting the beneficiaries of their donations (Mckinell, 2020).

One solution that encourages the utilisation of community resources is to crowdfund specific projects to assist in a rapid recovery. The proposal could contain a plan which is assessed by a third party for endorsement. The platform for crowdfunding originated in the USA and it is often used to raise funds to support startups or specific arts and culture projects (Cho & Kim, 2017; Kemmelmeier et al., 2006). However, often the expected returns from donations and the associated outcomes are influenced by the socio-cultural contexts of the donors and recipients, which in turn impacts on the effectiveness of BBB.

What motivates people to give and what they see as a return varies depending on their social context. While US data show a correlation between giving and religious practice, the Australian data do not indicate a strong correlation (Saunders, 2012). However, a strong tradition of doing good work and tithing, a practice of gifting ten per cent of one's income to a local church, is prevalent among many Christian communities (Bornstein, 2005; Clarke, 2011).

The popularity and range of models for online and offline crowdfunding are growing across the globe because the platform enables people in need to seek funding from their community. With the spread of digital media, these projects are often selected and promoted by a third-party online site if they are convinced of the viability of the proposal. This third party then advertises these projects to the wider community but subtracts management fees to fund their site and pay staff members. While entrepreneurship receives attention in the process of rebuilding the society in line with BBB, it is important to examine how the practice of crowdfunding is being developed by reflecting embeddedness associated with the practice of giving, value placed on the return on the gift and entrepreneurship.

GIVING IN INDONESIA

In general, donors in Indonesia are motivated by their religious obligations to help the disadvantaged in the community. In the majority Muslim population, this is advocated by the concept of *zakat*, and the religious minority groups, accounting for around ten per cent of the entire population, Christians engage in tithing and Buddhists in almsgiving (Sakai 2012). In Indonesia, the participation of religious organisations and their supporters is common in post-disaster recovery, as doing good is seen as an act of devotion (Latief, 2010). People donate extra funds or even volunteer to assist the victims. The uniqueness of these organisations is that they are entirely self-funded, supported by donations. Muslim communities in Indonesia also tend to give generously, as encouraged by their religious obligations (*zakat*) to the poor, and recently institutions have used the concept of *zakat* to mobilise support for social development programs, including disaster relief and poverty reduction (Fauzia,

2013; Latief, 2016). This is because in Indonesia where the state social security safety net is limited, religious institutions are heavily involved in appealing to their congregations to donate to support their charitable activities. In 2019, estimated *zakat* collection was 10.07 trillion Rupiah, an increase of collected *zakat* funds of 9 trillion Rupiah in 2018 (Media Indonesia, 2019); the 2019 figure amounting to around AUD100 million dollars.

As a result of their involvement, social program activities funded by churches, mosques and temples in Indonesia have led to institutionalisation of these programs (Hadiwinata, 2003). These donations also support post-disaster recovery efforts (Nurdin, 2018). Further to this, as religious identity becomes increasingly important for the urban middle-class in contemporary Indonesia (Sakai & Fauzia, 2014a), the amount of Muslim almsgiving is also on the rise. During the recent Covid-19 pandemic in 2020, Indonesian Muslims have continued to donate their *zakat* to assist the disadvantaged (Fauzia, 2020). These organisations offer social assistance programs to people who have lost their jobs due to the economic shutdown, such as transport drivers. The way community members are keen to help each other in times of crisis and difficulty reflects a longstanding tradition of mutual assistance known as *gotong royong* (Bowen, 1986).

Generally speaking, online crowdfunding has become a handy tool among middle-class Indonesians (Anoraga, 2019). This is a method of enhancing the traditional social practice of offering mutual assistance to people in need including the victims of natural disasters as this chapter illustrates. Religiously motivated donations, such as obligatory Muslim almsgiving, are also listed in popular online crowdfunding programs on Kitabisa.com (Anoraga, 2019). The motivation of donors is strongly driven by almsgiving obligations, aiming to assist individuals experiencing hardships such as illness and disasters. My engagement with the Dompet Dhuafa Foundation in 2014 revealed that most of the donors want to pay almsgivings to make social impact but they are too busy to take action themselves. They prefer donations to *zakat* foundations so that their religious obligation has been taken care of. Donors also prefer donations to multiple agencies so that their donations are shared to assist *zakat* organisations.

This religiously connected sense of giving has made inter-faith mutual assistance controversial. During the colonial period in Indonesia some regions, such as North Sumatra, converted to Christianity after the arrival of Christian missionaries. Consequently, Christian organisations tried their best to be discreet with their sponsorship of public aid projects, instead referring to it as a humanitarian group effort free from religious affiliation. Muslim organisations on the other hand used recovery efforts to display their efforts, ensuring their logos are visible on the projects' banners or billboards as sponsors.

In contemporary Indonesia, the mutual assistance concept of *gotong royong* has been institutionalised into national tertiary education. Since 1973, it has been obligatory for all university students to undertake community service known as Kuliah Kerja Nyata (KKN) or Student Service Learning. The aim of KKN is to share professional knowledge obtained by university students with the community in need to bolster welfare in the society, but in practice the students, who self-funding their community engagement tasks, face difficulties due to the lack of bottom-up approaches to community development projects, coupled with limited guidance from the university (Windred, 2017). Reflecting on this challenge, since 2016, the Indonesian government's Ministry of Religious Affairs, which supervises all Islamic educational institutions, has chosen a theme of community engagement for their annual international conference (Kemenag, 2018). The conference held at the State Islamic University, Malang in 2018, organised Community Service Expos and Clinics along with presentations of academic papers on the issue of community service with a focus on various programs representing community engagement activities. I was among the invited speakers at this conference and while visiting the displays in the expo, students explained the KKN program was valuable because they could see that their community service is strongly needed in under-developed communities. Some of them started fundraising campaigns to donate funds to their KKN site. I argue that the act of giving in the Indonesian context is deeply rooted in their obligations and expectations that they will assist both members of their religious community and fellow citizens in times of difficulty.

Giving in Japan

Contrary to the thriving religion-based charitable programs in Indonesia, social assistance programs of organised religions in Japan are less common. In fact, the volume of donations from the Japanese community remains relatively low in comparison with Western countries. According to Suzuki (2017), the average donation per person in Japan was Y27,013

(USD 245) in 2016, one-fifth of the average donation amount in the USA (Suzuki, 2017). This is despite the 2011 Tohoku disasters motivating people in Japan to donate more. The vast majority of volunteers and support for civil society activities do not come directly from religious organisations or congregations. People who feel connected and compassionate express 'unconscious religiosity' to offer mutual assistance to support long-term recovery (Inaba, 2011). It is common for Japanese to believe in '*en*' or a sense of connection based on the idea that everyone's well-being is assisted by others and the provision of assistance is deemed successful if the beneficiary is capable of providing their assistance in turn to the others in need (Sakai & Inaba, 2014).

The profiles of typical donors in Japan can be classified into three types: (1) people who donate on a regular basis, depending on their wealth, to support and improve society; (2) people who volunteer to assist disaster victims on a regular basis; and (3) community members, including parents, who offer mutual assistance for the betterment of the local community (Japan Fundraising Association 2017). However, the majority of the people who donate to charities in Japan belong to the third category. Some organisations assist in the running of community festivals, school fetes and fundraise through schools, examples of these organisation include Akaihane Kyodobokin or the Red Feather Community Chest. These organisations were established in 1947 to support the post-war community recovery and have chapters in every administrative prefecture in Japan to raise donations. Fundraising takes place between October and March across Japan, and local community groups and schools involve students and parents in these activities. 70% of the funds raised are used to support projects that address both local problems and the disadvantaged community, while the remaining 30% of the funds are used to work towards disaster prevention, and broader projects (Akaihane, n.d.). This is one of the rare examples of a long-standing community organisation being supported by its established position in the Japanese community. Other smaller organisations are struggling to raise donations from the community.

One of the exceptions is a long-term disaster relief NGO, Hisaichikyodo NGO Senta, which was established in response to the Kobe earthquake in 1995. They supported themselves by utilising community resources, particularly the volunteers who wanted to take action to assist. They partnered with volunteer university students to run income generating activities, such as regular educational seminars, to make themselves financially viable. Their innovative income generating activities offered new livelihoods (making soft toys called Makenaizo for sale for instance) for the victims, and the profit of the sales funded the organisation (Sakai & Inaba, 2014). This organisation also undertook a new initiative to sell slightly damaged vegetables to consumers as a way to create a new market for farmers whose fields were affected by the ash of a volcano eruption in 2011 (Sakai and Inaba 2014). As the next section of this chapter shows, new forms of BBB crowdfunding have recently emerged in Japan with the aim of assisting the local businesses and entrepreneurship to thrive over a long-term period. The act of giving in Japan through crowdfunding resonates with the pioneer examples shown by Hisaichi Kyodo Senta, and is oriented towards projects that revive lost livelihoods.

Case Studies

The two cases examined in this chapter draw data from two disasters, one in Indonesia and the other in Japan. The Indonesian case study focuses on the recovery effort following the volcanic eruption of Mount Merapi, located near Yogyakarta city, on the island of Java. The volcano erupts regularly and the focus for this chapter is the major eruptions which took place in 2010. The data for the Merapi disaster derive from internet and desk-based research coupled with empirical research conducted in partnership with Gadjah Mada University between 2012 and 2014. The field research involved the victims of the 2010 Merapi eruptions, including two resettlement areas at Kuwang, consisting of 297 households and Gondang, consisting of 414 households both located in the Sleman District of Central Java Province, approximately 30 km away from Yogyakarta City. Prior to the volcano eruptions, the farming was the main livelihood for people in these areas. Non-government organisations, the Dompet Dhuafa Foundation and Gereja Kristen Indonesia, an Indonesian Christian Church, established post-disaster economic recovery initiatives, and also shared their experiences in post-disaster recovery.

The Japanese case study site is Kesennuma City, located in Miyagi Prefecture of Northern Japan, which was damaged by the Tohoku Earthquakes and Tsunami disasters in 2011. The local economy of this small town was stagnant due to its declining population and difficulties in accessing the community of Sendai, a major town in Miyagi. The data for the Japanese cases are predominantly derived from desk-based

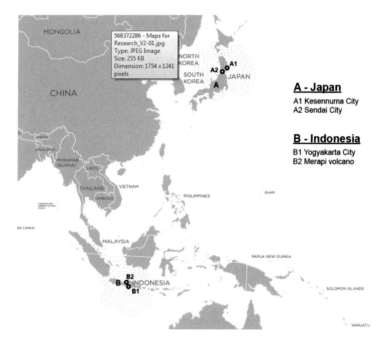

Fig. 15.1 Map of case study sites

research following my observations of NGOs and civil society organisations involved in disaster recovery in Japan since 2011, and my attendance at two major events in 2015: the Japan Fundraising Association Annual Conference, and the Kesennuma City disaster recovery event (Fig. 15.1).

CASE OF THE MOUNT MERAPI ERUPTIONS IN 2010

The Merapi volcano is located in the Special Province of Yogyakarta, in Central Java, Indonesia, and is among the most active volcanoes in the world Mt Merapi erupts regularly every 10–15 years with major eruptions in 1006, 1786, 1822, 1872 and 1930 (Reliefweb, 2006). Prior to the major 2010 eruptions, in 2006 there were continuous small eruptions over several months. The ashes from previous eruptions provide fertile soil for farming and this is the main reason that residents live on the slopes of Mt Merapi. The slopes of Mt Merapi extend into four administrative subdistricts, Sleman, Magelang, Boyolali and Klaten (Sulistiyanto, 2014). The eruptions of October 2010 caused 61,154 people to evacuate, the loss of 341 lives, and estimated total damage valued at 4.23 trillion rupiahs (Handayani et al., 2016, p. 276). Mt Merapi is seen as a double-edge sword, providing a source of livelihood but also exposing residents to extreme danger. Community members believe that it is possible to maintain harmony with Mt Merapi by praying to the guardian (*juru kunci*) of Mt Merapi, Mbah Marijan, a local resident who was responsible for holding back eruptions and thereby safeguarding residents in the region (Sulitiyanto, 2014, p. 122). He was killed in the 2010 eruptions as he did not evacuate in time, and the position of guardianship was subsequently inherited by one of his sons, Mbah Asih (Maula, 2019).

At the time of the Merapi eruptions in 2010, volunteers and donations flooded into the city from all over Java, including Yogyakarta. Religious organisations, both Islamic and Christian, coordinated volunteers and sent them to evacuation shelters. Yogyakarta has more than 40 universities including a top research university, Gadjah Mada University. These institutions could also be mobilised in addition to the support offered by the faith-based organisations. Given this context, it may be assumed that resources from the community could be easily mobilised to assist in the recovery, but in reality mobilisation of resources proved quite difficult and this was due to the following factors. Firstly, fundraising campaigns to assist victims were established immediately after the Mount Merapi eruptions through religious institutions. Because of the historical religious tension, however, Christian-based organisations had to act carefully not to be perceived as being motivated by the possibility of converting Muslim victims to Christianity by offering them assistance. Even though Yogyakarta has an active inter-faith forum known as FBUB involving 12 religious organisations and leaders, suspicion emerged that Christian organisations were offering assistance to Muslim residents in order to convert them. (Sakai & Fauzia, 2014b, p. 46).

Such tension has affected the ways in which resources have been mobilised from community members. For example, when a leading Muslim *zakat* collection organisation, Dompet Dhuafa Foundation launched a program to reconstruct damaged houses on the slopes of Mt Merapi, they invited the Vice President to attend the ceremony and publicised their role in distributing the community funds to the victims. The supported project was easily identified because a foundation stone was laid that was engraved with the name of the project's sponsoring foundation (pictured). These public events and the foundation stone reflect the efforts of the sponsoring foundation to be accountable and to respond to the generosity of donors (Korf, 2006). The public recognition of the distribution of community funds clearly indicated to the donors that their funds had been used to assist the Merapi victims, with the long-term goal of attracting support from these same donors in the future. Projects funded by Christian-based organisations, however, rarely displayed the names of the founders, in order to avoid potential religious tension and conflict in the Merapi region. Religious tension has also affected the participation of volunteers, particularly if the volunteers are not Muslim. In summary, as illustrated here, giving in the form of donations and volunteering is strongly perceived as a devotional act in contemporary Indonesia, and comes with the risk of increasing community tensions among the inter-religious context of relief operations.

Another complicating factor was that university students' Community Learning Service (KKN), that provided assistance to the disaster relief, is not always present at a location near where disasters occur, or do not remain there longer term. For example, students from Gadjah Mada University, located nearby Mt Merapi initially sent students to assist in the Merapi volcanic disaster-affected communities but the purpose of the KKN scheme is to send students to new areas so that other regions can benefit from students' presence in the community. This made it difficult for the community to receive volunteers on a regular basis to assist the community needs in an ongoing way (Ismalina & Sakai, 2013) (Fig. 15.2).

STAGNATED ECONOMIC RECOVERY IN THE MERAPI REGION

As a result of the major volcanic eruptions in 2010, the Indonesian government-designated exclusion zones deemed hazardous for residents and attempted to relocate villages from within these zones. Residents whose villages had been buried by lava had no option but to accept the government's resettlement offers.

The affected residents faced a wide range of problems in terms of their economic recovery. One difficulty was that the regions affected by lava flows were spread across four different administrative units and each

Fig. 15.2 Foundation Stone, an example funded by the Dompet Dhuafa Foundation in the Merapi Slopes, listing the projects sponsored by the foundation

administrative unit had its own policies. Furthermore, affected community members were divided into three groups; the relocated villages, and villages located within the zones deemed disaster prone that were encouraged to relocate, and villages which remained on their original sites with some communal facilities damaged.

As the sites identified for the relocation of villages forced to move lacked enough land for farming, or gaining access to feed for animals was difficult, and so approximately half of the residents discontinued farming after their relocation. Along with this economic change, women, who are usually the secondary earners in Indonesian families, had to try to help make ends meet at the relocation site. They were keen to learn from snack-making training programs provided by government agencies and NGOs after the disaster. Yogyakarta and Central Java are renowned for delicious snacks, including deep fried fruits and vegetables (*keripik*). However, securing a designated production site was difficult due to the lack of communal space in the new location, and the women also had trouble branding their products for marketing because they did not have prior marketing experience. Establishing a cooperative was a logical progression for their business development, but the task was very daunting. In general, cooperative movements in Indonesia are unsuccessful and unpopular (Sugarda, 2016) because of mismanagement of cooperatives during the Suharto period, which led to the erosion of the commodity market (Linebaugh, 1998). Therefore, in Indonesia, it is commonly thought that cooperatives do not safeguard the interest of producers effectively enough. Furthermore, the current Indonesian legal framework (Law No. 17/2012) requires impractical administrative loads, resulting in a third of cooperatives in Indonesia remaining inactive (Sugarda, 2016). In 2020 a concerned Indonesian government is looking into reducing administrative loads to revive the popularity of cooperatives (Rahman, 21 July 2020). In addition, business capital from NGOs and the government was made available only to groups with an aim to develop a cooperative in the future. This was a difficult condition to impose on relatively inexperienced and uneducated victims just trying to make ends meet.

In the main, the Merapi community lacked leaders or figures with personal connections in neighbouring regions or with relevant government agencies. Most residents were farmers with little formal education so they found it difficult to articulate their vision for the future in the official language of Indonesian, and farming on the slopes of Mt Merapi left them with little time to pursue other ventures. When the Merapi volcanic eruptions took place in 2010, online shopping was not widely available. Securing a supply deal with supermarkets or commercial outlets required certification to a production standard and a competent agency to negotiate the deal so that the interests of the community could be promoted (Isbah, 2016). As a result, even motivated individuals found it overwhelming to continue small entrepreneurial businesses because the expected responsibility on behalf of the group, as well as the expectations to set up a cooperative was not represented in the sharing of the workload or profits (Islmalina & Sakai, 2013).

The lack of trans-Merapi initiatives led to each village or community acting independently of each other. Because the area is scenic, with Mt Merapi towering above, and it is also close to Indonesia's cultural heartland of Yogyakarta, tourism has become a popular economic driver. Volcano lava tours involve hiring a jeep with a local guide/driver and these have been attracting tourists in partnership with other businesses. However, tours drive through the exclusion zones close to the top of Mt Merapi. As the tours are only allowed to operate when Mt Merapi is deemed to be safe, the livelihoods of the tour coordinators depend on Mt Merapi's activity.

Rural Tourism Initiatives

As the initial efforts of the Merapi community to develop economic activity largely failed, village tourism has been identified as another way to develop an income stream. The concept of village tourism or *desa wisata* (village tourism) emerged in 2007 as the government decided it should promote Indonesia as a tourist destination (Prafitri & Damayanti, 2016). Tourism that enables travellers to experience home-stays in rural environments is seen as a key part of developing a sustainable tourism industry (Inskeep, 1991) and also an effective way to diversify rural livelihoods.

The difficulty in the Merapi region is that even though some villages are located in disaster-prone areas, they are promoted as village tourism destinations because of their scenic rural views. An example is Desa Turgo, in the Sleman District. Even though the residents of this village were evacuated during the Mt Merapi eruptions, villagers promote their village as a farming education site as part of the village tourism initiatives (Kompasina, 2013).

The Merapi Museum (http://mgm.slemankab.go.id/)in the Sleman District was opened in 2009, just prior to the 2010 eruptions. It provides information about the geology of the Merapi volcano. The museum is frequently visited by school tours and the hall is also rented out for cultural festivals, conferences and wedding receptions. However, this business is not directly aimed at the economic recovery of the Merapi regions affected by the 2010 eruptions.

As the use of internet and social media have spread across Indonesia, several online crowdfunding platforms have come into existence. Launched in 2013, Kitabisa.com ('We can do it'—https://kitabisa.com/) is the largest crowdfunding platform in Indonesia. To date in 2020, the site kitabisa.com listed three projects related to the Merapi community; one was a project to tutor children of poor Merapi residents, which did not succeed in raising the targeted amount, and two projects were designed to raise funds for the purchase of essential tools for chocolate farmers in the Merapi region. Members of the resettlement community were eager to find investors from outside, and to explore and revive the previous KKN contact, but the transient nature of the human connections made it difficult to translate contacts into business opportunities. Offline

Fig. 15.3 Banner of a new snack (*keripik*) business placed along a major roadside

traditional crowdfunding, such as rotatory credit, known as *arisan*, did not offer a solution because it was not seen as an opportunity to raise funds together and it was not possible for donors to engage in marketing activities, including through social media networks. Marketing for them was closely associated with being able to display a banner on a busy street in a traditional way (Fig. 15.3).

CASE OF KESENNUMA CITY, JAPAN

Kesennuma is a small port city in north-east Japan. Its economy was severely damaged in 2011 by the Tohoku earthquake and tsunami disasters which caused over 1,300 deaths, accounting for approximately two per cent of the city's population (Sugawara, 2015). Immediately after the disaster struck, volunteers gathered in Kesennuma to assist the local community with the clean-up.

The post-disaster recovery of Kesennuma posed a complex challenge, principally because the city's population was in decline. It had decreased from 73,489 in 2010 to 61,889 in 2020 (Kesennuma, 2020).

The focus of the post-recovery strategy included the commitment of the people of Kesennuma to BBB by transforming a declining port town into an attractive rural tourism spot (Sugawara, 2015). This section of the chapter discusses how the people of Kesennuma's strategy involved mobilising resources, ideas and funds from the community under the strong and steady leadership of the city's mayor and its business communities. Mobilising crowdfunding and sharing the experience of BBB has been a successful feature of the recovery.

Vision for Kesennuma

Following the 2011 earthquake and tsunami, the reconstruction of Kesennuma using the BBB approach was based on the shared and long-standing practice that businesses and civil society both need to be involved in the rebuilding (Kage, 2011). The mayor of Kesennuma, Mr Shigeru Sugawara, became mayor in 2010 and is serving his third term at the time of writing in 2020. Sugawara majored in marine science and fisheries at Tokyo Suisan University (Tokyo University of Marine Science and Technology, formerly Tokyo University of Fisheries) and worked in a large and successful trading company. He had a posting to the Netherlands in the 1990s before he returned to Kesennuma to work in his family's fishery business. His international business experience has given him a global business outlook. Mayor Sugawara has strongly promoted the idea of reviving Kesennuma as a hometown not only for Kesennuma out-migrants, but also those who feel close and connected to the city.

The rebuilding of Kesennuma involved a drastic economic development policy to position Kesennuma as a slow city as opposed to a fast (food) city. As the population of the town declined, shops along the main street closed permanently with the street becoming known as 'shutter street'. Mayor Sugawara had begun to contemplate a new strategy to revive the town before it was devastated by the Tohoku Disaster (Ishii, 2019).

Visitors were attracted to the experience of slow food, walks around the town, and enjoying the relaxed pace. Their stay would last a few days in order to have time to relax and appreciate Kesennuma. However, clever branding of the town was needed as the Japanese word, *inaka*, meaning a rural town, had negative connotations.

In order to promote the city's new image, in 2013 the city applied to be recognised as the first Japanese member of the Slow Cities League (Cittaslow International). This movement began in a small town in Tuscany Italy and placed Kesennuma within a distinctive global 'Slow City' movement (as of July 2020, the Slow City Movement has successfully expanded its membership and recognition to include over 250 cities, including in China, Australia and North America). Mayor Sugawara stated that Kesennuma could not be urban, and it remained as a small rural town. It would not compete with Sendai, an urban centre in Miyagi Prefecture. The key for reviving Kesennuma was to promote it as a slow city, with its unique produce, such as seafood and Japanese sake, including a national brand—Otokoyama (Sugawara, 2015).

Seeking Donations Through the Hometown Tax System

Kesennuma city's revival plans have been strongly supported by the city's businesses and the mayor's office. They have undertaken a number of innovative initiatives to continue to link Kesennuma with people to keep them connected with the city. Crowdfunding schemes have been strategically used to keep these human connections.

There are at least two types of taxes payable in Japan, a national tax (*kokuzei*) and a residence tax (chihozei), which are obligatory for all citizens. National taxes are collected by the state as revenue for state-run infrastructure and other provisions. The residence tax is used to support local services such as recycling, education, public facilities such as sports facilities and libraries, and aged care. As such, all residents are expected to benefit from the services this tax funds. However, as urbanisation has progressed in Japan, the majority of people have left their hometowns to work in urban areas and consequently the revenue flow from these taxes to smaller towns has declined. Thus, a new tax scheme was introduced, called the hometown tax (*furusato nozei*). In this scheme, remittances of taxes to one's hometown are able to be used as a deduction to offset the residence tax. Furthermore, income tax can be paid to administrative units outside the hometown if the resident chooses to do so. The scheme was introduced nationally in 2008 and has gained popularity as a way to boost local revenue. The government states this tax payment has three main aims: (1) to give choice to individual taxpayers, (2) to enable individuals to support the regions they feel are their home or that they feel connected to and (3) to give an opportunity to better plan the future of Japan (Somusho, n.d. the Ministry of Internal Affairs and Communications, Japan). These funds enable administrative units to promote their own projects, such as supporting local agriculture or tourism, together with other schemes that address the needs of the local community. Indeed it is popular for the hometown tax to be used to support local produce businesses and hometown taxpayers are commonly given a token of thanks for their gift.

Kesennuma City utilised hometown tax schemes to promote their Slow City food and tourism. The city administration has been working closely with local fishermen, agriculture and commerce associations and cooperatives with the aim of boosting the local economy. Kesennuma is renowned for seafood and in partnership with the city's chamber of commerce they have raised a significant amount of hometown tax donations. In 2010, the city received Yen 2,104,000 from 68 donations through the hometown tax scheme, and in 2019 the city received donations from 8598 donors and raised Yen 199,650,110 (AU$2.66 million) (Kesennuma City, 2019a). Kesennuma promotes local produce, particularly seafood, as a return on the gift of hometown taxpayers and also seeks donations to support local civil society groups which are undertaking post-disaster recovery projects within the city (for more information on hometown tax schemes to support Kesennuma, see Kesennuma City, 2019b). For example, in July 2020, the most popular item on the hometown tax homepage from Kesennuma was donations; with one unit costing $37,000 (AU$513) resulting in a gift of 300 grams of local shark fin dishes. Shark fins are among the most expensive items popular among Japanese consumers.

In the immediate aftermath of a major natural disaster in Japan, the government established the hometown tax schemes to raise funds for post-disaster recovery efforts, something akin to a government-endorsed crowdfunding scheme. When southern Japan was inundated with heavy rain in July 2020, the government launched a crowdfunding donation scheme as part of the hometown tax schemes for this disaster, which raised close to 400 million yen in two weeks. It is worth mentioning that in 2019 the government raised almost 1 billion yen from 46,232 donations through this scheme to assist the recovery of regions damaged by two major typhoons. In this circumstance taxpayers are able to designate specific areas damaged by the disaster as the destination of their support, and did not expect to receive a tangible gift in return. The residence tax, thus, provides an opportunity for taxpayers to give according to their vision for a better Japan.

Bolstering Connections for Building Back Better

One of the important elements of BBB is that it recognises that post-disaster recovery does not lie solely in the physical reconstruction of housing and infrastructure. After the 2011 disaster a large number of

Fig. 15.4 Kesennuma City Mascot, Hoya Boya the Ocean Boy

volunteers came to Kesennuma from far away to support the post-disaster recovery efforts. These included communal kitchen hands (*takidashi*), medical assistance teams and general cleanup teams. Although some were volunteers from Tokyo and other urban areas, others were originally from Kesennuma who had relocated to urban areas. In order to connect the volunteers with the supporters of Kesennuma, the city launched informal support groups Riasu Kesennuma, using Facebook and other social media. The group organises recovery events with catchy titles such as "Kesennuma wo genkini suru kai", a gathering to energise Kesennuma with a focus on food. To help give a friendly face to Kesennuma City that people could connect with, a mascot character, Hoya Boya the Ocean Boy was launched (Fig. 15.4) and it is used in all activities and on social media sites.

The Kesennuma wo genkini suru kai provides opportunities for people to receive updates on progress of the Building Back Better program in terms of physical reconstruction and economic development. It also aims to reconnect locals, including the Mayor Sugawara and business owners and supporters, with former volunteers and business contacts who live outside Kesennuma. The Tokyo meeting attended by the author in February 2015 commenced with an update on the post-recovery progress. The highlight of the meeting was a buffet lunch featuring local produce from Kesennuma with Powerpoint slides and a brochure. After lunch, participants took turns in giving a short speech to promote their business in Kesennuma or Tokyo, which has some links to Kesennuma.

To illustrate, some participants were Tokyo residents originally from Kesennuma and others had an emotional attachment to local produce and wanted to order or eat the local produce or cuisine. The event organisers were volunteers including university students who had some connection with Kesennuma through marine science research. A speech to support Kesennuma was delivered by the Meguro Pacific Saury annual festival chair. Pacific saury is seafood which Kesennuma also boasts as its local produce. While Pacific saury is oily and inexpensive, if grilled over charcoal to remove the fat, it makes an appetising dish. Canned Pacific saury is considered to be a cheap but tasty food and has become part of everyday Japanese home cuisine.

Pacific saury also features in a well-known Japanese oral culture comic story of *rakugo*. As the town of Meguro has no direct access to the sea, Pacific saury is not local produce, but ironically the town is best known for providing the best grilled Pacific saury. Based on this comic story, in 1995 Meguro city initiated an annual Pacific saury festival to attract visitors to the area. In 2010, Kesennuma and Meguro City made a sister city arrangement and Kesennuma continues to supply their fresh catch of the Pacific saury to the annual Meguro festival, usually attracting 20,000 to 30,000 visitors every year (Shinagawa kanko, n.d.). As a result, Kesennuma produce is widely promoted through the annual Meguro festival, resulting in connections being forged between Pacific saury producers and consumers around Meguro.

Social connections have also been used to mobilise funds through crowdfunding projects by Kesennuma local community members and the city government. For example, Readyfor is one of the largest crowdfunding platforms in Japan and was established in 2011. Since the 2011 Tohoku disasters, 88 projects involving Kesennuma have been proposed on this site. Such proposals include projects initiated by local high school students to produce sweets using local produce, university students working with the local community in recovery projects and former volunteers continue to support Kesennuma.

Thus, Kunio Ida sought to raise Yen 600,000 for a project to launch a fireworks display in Kesennuma. He had no immediate connection to Kesennuma but came to Kesennuma in April 2011 as a volunteer to run a communal kitchen, and felt compelled to help the recovery of the region further. He made several visits to assist in the recovery program but was not certain what he could do to help as an individual. However, during one visit he was told that community members wanted to watch spectacular fireworks. In Japan, fireworks are usually launched in summer to appease deceased spirits and to energise and support family members left behind. Kunio Ida decided to raise funds for fireworks through Readyfor, in memory of those who died in the disaster. His deceased father was a firework master and he found personal '*en*', to Kesennuma through this project. The fireworks display went ahead in August 2017 (Iida, 2017).

In 2019 Mayor Sugawara launched a crowdfunding project on Readyfor to raise Yen 20 million to construct a memorial monument in the city in the shape of sail. This was intended to assist in the construction of the memorial in partnership with long-standing supporters. He updated the recovery of Kesennuma on a website with video and sought further support from community members. He also posted a thanks video as an acknowledgement of the donors, in addition to sending individuals thank you letters. In the video he commented that the majority of supporters had previously assisted in the recovery of Kesennuma and he invited people to return when the park construction was completed (see https://readyfor.jp/projects/kesennumapark).

Discussion

The two cases explored in this chapter demonstrate how existing embedded culture has affected the way disaster recoveries were perceived, and also responded to in light of the realisation of the concept of Building Back Better (BBB).

Embedded Culture in Development Practices in Indonesia

The recovery initiatives and assistance after the Mount Merapi eruption in 2010 mirrored top-down development practices common in Indonesia at that time. The state has been the main driver of poverty reduction and rural development since independence in 1949, with the aim of making Indonesian citizens prosper (Hadiwinata, 2003). Indonesia's independence was aimed at creating a prosperous nation and encouraging economic development led by state agencies is strongly linked to the sovereignty and pride of the nation. This was used to justify Suharto's style of governance (Emmerson, 1999; Hill, 1994). As a result, rural development and poverty reduction programs were implemented as a top-down development until the Asian financial crisis of the late 1990s, the fall of the dictator Suharto and the establishment of democracy in the early 2000s (Perdana & Maxwell, 2011).

State partnerships with civil society groups, such as NGOs, with the aim of welfare provision have been limited (Sakai, 2012; Thornton et al., 2012). In fact, as tax payments to the state are under-developed in

Indonesia, religious donations are seen as competing against the state tax collection system (Fauzia, 2013). Religious NGOs play a role in redevelopment by offering immediate assistance to the disaster victims, but their scope and resources are limited. NGOs were not always able to implement a bottom-up approach, as NGO workers were often seen as external to the local community and they tended to achieve what external development organisations perceived as successful outcomes from their project (MacRae & Hodgin, 2011; Nurdin, 2018).

Since 2004, the Indonesian government has been trying to implement bottom-up community development projects such as National Community Driven Programs known as PNPM (McCarthy et al., 2017) and BUMDes (village-owned enterprises) to enable each community to manage its own affairs. This is not an isolated case. For example, a similar practice took place for the implementation of the post-2004 Boxing Day Tsunami reconstruction in Aceh which involved significant resources from external international agencies (Clarke et al., 2010). Reconstruction projects in Aceh were mostly undertaken based on the perception of success held by the donors and 'their interpretation of the recipient public' (Fanany, 2010, p. 116).

Donors from the civil society who assisted immediately after the disaster struck appear to be compelled by their religious obligations. Communities in need of disaster assistance naturally hold expectations that assistance will be provided by the government agencies and civil society organisations, but the lack of community leadership, as the Merapi case illustrated, makes it difficult to identify a key mechanism to implement a bottom-up approach for a long-term recovery project. The university students' involvement also remains fragmented because the KKN program is not intended to assist a particular community over a long-term period until it has had a full socio-economic recovery.

Another complexity is the nascent stage of entrepreneurship in Indonesia. Since the Indonesian government has led development projects and mutual support for community members has been focused on charitable giving for immediate mutual help. As the Merapi disaster case has demonstrated, giving by the community has not fully translated into business development opportunities as it is not specifically intended for economic recoveries. Startups and businesses are relatively new in the Indonesian community. The Widodo government has been pushing entrepreneurship as a part of essential education in Indonesia. The goal is that Indonesians will learn to create jobs rather than applying for jobs, with the aim of reducing unemployment and poverty. In 2019, Nadiem Makarim was appointed education minister. He founded the highly successful digital startup, GoJek. With the rise of digital communications and social media in Indonesia, entrepreneurship has become a buzzword in contemporary Indonesia. However, the effectiveness of addressing social needs, such as disaster recovery, by creating financially sustainable businesses through entrepreneurship is yet to be proven.

Embedded Economy in Kesennuma, Japan

Four factors have assisted in the successful mobilisation of funding and resources which has supported a wide range of BBB projects in Kesennuma. Firstly, while the practice of crowdfunding was relatively new when the Tohoku disaster struck Japan in 2011, awareness and participation by the community in disaster recovery was already well established. This is because Japan has had a long history of involving civil society groups in dealing with disasters (Aldrich, 2012). This focus on disaster prevention and recovery by civil society and the community was further articulated after the Kobe earthquakes in 1995. In this case, the state acknowledged the role of volunteers as an important part of post-disaster recovery by amending the Disaster Prevention Law (Saigai taisaku kihon ho). The Kobe earthquake drew more than 1.38 million volunteers to the area over the 12 months after the disaster (see https://www.kobe-np.co.jp/rentoku/sinsai/graph/p6.shtml).

This legal acknowledgement paved the way to legislate the Non-for-Profit Organisations (NPO) law in 1998 which enabled citizens to establish NPOs to address the needs of the community, including post-disaster recovery projects (Sakai and Inaba 2014). The government also offers resources to run workshops and seminars to promote civil societies' disaster prevention effort and to address communities' socio-economic needs. For example, Shakyo and Volunteer Centre has chapters to offer resources to interested community members and their service is funded by the state and local government.

Secondly, cooperatives and farmers' associations have long been established as trustworthy organisations for Japanese consumers. One of the major cooperatives is the Japanese Consumers' Co-operative Union (JCCU), founded in 1951. Its members are spread widely across the nation and they support the consumption of fresh produce through home delivery (online) packages, which are also widely available through supermarket outlets. Another major cooperative association, Pal System published monthly magazines Nonbiru, and currently Waiwai, to promote ideas to support local producers hit by disasters. For example, Nonbiru Vol.56 (June) 2011, three months after the Tohoku disasters, launched a special edition titled "Shopping to support the disabled and disaster-stricken areas". Thus, the practice of buying local produce directly from producers, whether from supermarkets or farmers' associations is a familiar concept for Japanese consumers.

Thirdly, the concept of *en*, that is social relations or association with others, is considered to be most important to safeguard the well-being of individuals and the community. In other words, bolstering *en* is a significant obligation for the Japanese. The BBB projects in Kesennuma have utilised this concept to mobilise resources widely for local business support and this has proven to be a creative use of available resources for post-disaster recovery.

Lastly, in Japan an increasing number of university graduates aspire to make a social impact through their businesses and startups. These students develop their experience first-hand as volunteers assisting in disaster areas where they promote their business. For example, the founding members of Readyfor include elite university graduates who once worked for Dentsu Inc., World No. 6, and the largest Japanese business communication company. Some of the founding members remarked at the time of the annual convention for Fund Raising Japan (14–15 February 2015) that moving up the corporate ladder in Dentsu Inc. did not guarantee job security despite the demanding working hours and lifestyle. Instead, the motivation to startup Readyfor was because they felt it more worthwhile to make a social impact by assisting people through a crowdfunding platform as a startup business· As the Japanese economy stagnated after the GFC in 2008, job security in large business enterprises was not as stable as before. This realisation became widely accepted even among top university graduates, and some of them have been drawn to starting up NPOs or social businesses to make a social impact in Japan through crowdfunding. For example, another crowdfunding platform growing popularity is FAAVO by Campfire, initiated by Ryuta Saito in 2012 with a specific aim to revive hometowns, deserted by young people who move out of their hometown for education and work (see https://camp-fire.jp/faavo). The common theme engendered by crowdfundraising is a notion of a token of thanks through a tangible or intangible gift, which continues to sustain the human relations of *en*. This token of thanks can even be a letter of appreciation when the project has been completed. As hometown tax products have shown, donors can also expect a token of thanks in the form of local produce.

In summary, the relationship should continue in a form to sustain *en*, that is in a form of giving back a completed product, which could foster a startup business. Thus, in Japan the embedded culture of business practice and loosely connected volunteering has facilitated the growth of crowdfunding as a sustainable and effective way to support the BBB initiatives.

Conclusion

This chapter has explored how economic embeddedness involving the concept of giving as part of post-disaster assistance and recovery differs between Indonesia and Japan, and how economic embeddedness has affected post-disaster recovery projects following the principle of BBB. The chapter has demonstrated that local factors need to be taken into account when post-disaster recovery initiatives are implemented if bottom-up post-disaster recovery projects are to be successful. The two cases covered in this chapter, the Mount Merapi eruptions in Indonesia, and the 2011 Tohoku earthquakes and Tsunami disaster in Kesennuma, a rural town in Northern Japan, demonstrate that the practice of giving, expected returns and entrepreneurship strongly reflect the existing socio-cultural and economic norms underpinning these societies. Both cases involved mobilisation of local community resources to assist in the post-disaster recovery efforts, including the use of crowdfunding. However, the analysis in this chapter demonstrates that the same scheme for community resource mobilisation to assist with BBB did not achieve the same outcome due to the different types of economic embeddedness in the two countries.

In Indonesia, the concept of almsgiving and mutual obligation, drives the need to help people in a time of crisis. The expectation of a return on one's gift is generally long term, and because anyone may be struck by crisis people must be prepared to help each other when the need arises. Cooperatives and other economic recovery initiatives did not progress smoothly in the Indonesian example because of the previous failed experiences and lack of local mediators and networks that could mobilise local resources on a continuous basis. On the other hand, in Japan, post-disaster recovery is closely associated with local entrepreneurship and business opportunities, both of which have been a driving forces in economic development and the disaster recovery initiatives of Kesennuma and other disaster-prone regions. Reflecting the economic embeddedness, the affected community leaders and supporters make efforts to maintain social connections of *en* through giving and returning. Returns in Japan are closely linked with ongoing social and business relations, and community recovery, both of which indicate to the supporters that post-disaster recovery is progressing. These differences are not only derived from the economic development of each country, but also the embedded culture surrounding the practice of giving to assist community members in need.

These findings highlight the need to identify key local factors that will assist in disaster recovery. As BBB has become a guiding principle of disaster recovery, it is necessary not to focus too much on identifying a certain project or scheme as of the exclusive way to implement BBB globally. Rather, the best practice of BBB should adequately reflect locally specific schemes incorporating the cultural economic embeddedness in partnership with effective social organisations to fulfil the expectations and needs of the local community.

References

Akaihane. (n.d.). *Akaihane Kyodobokin nitsuite* [About Red Feather Community Chest movement]. Retrieved 10 July 2020 from https://www.akaihane.or.jp/bokin/how/

Aldrich, D. P. (2012). *Building resilience: Social capital in post-disaster recovery.* The University of Chicago Press.

Aldrich, D. P. (2018). A research agenda for disaster entrepreneurship. *Review of Austrian Economics, 31*(4), 457–465. https://doi.org/10.1007/s11138-017-0393-0

Aldrich, D. P. (2017). The importance of social capital in building community resilience. In W. Yan & W. Galloway (Eds.), *Rethinking resilience, adaptation and transformation in a time of change* (pp. 357–364). Springer. https://doi.org/10.1007/978-3-319-50171-0_23

Andharia, J. (2019). *Disaster studies: Exploring intersectionalities in disaster discourse.* Springer.

Anoraga, B. (2019, July). *Kitabisa crowdfunding platform.* Conference presentation, Antropologi Indonesia Conference, Gadjah Mada University.

Bowen, J. R. (1986). On the political construction of tradition: Gotong royong in Indonesia. *The Journal of Asian Studies, 45*(3), 545–561. https://doi.org/10.2307/2056530

Bornstein, E. (2005). *The spirit of development: Protestant NGOs, morality, and economics in Zimbabwe*. Stanford University Press; Eurospan [distributor].
Clarke, M., Ismet, F., & Kenny, S. (2010). *Post-disaster reconstruction: Lessons from Aceh*. Earthscan.
Clarke, M. (2011). *Mission and development: God's work or good works?* Continuum.
Cho, M., & Kim, G. (2017). A cross-cultural comparative analysis of crowdfunding projects in the United States and South Korea. *Computers in Human Behaviour, 72*, 312–320.
Donaldson, C. (2020). *How to get shareholders on board with corporate philanthropy UNSW Newsroom*. Retrieved 21 September 2020 from https://newsroom.unsw.edu.au/news/business-law/how-get-shareholders-board-corporate-philanthropy
Emmerson, D. K. (1999). *Indonesia beyond Suharto: Polity, economy, society, transition*. M.E. Sharpe, Armonk.
Fanany, I. (2010). *Towards a model of constructive interaction between aid donors and recipients in a disaster context: The case of Lampuuk*.
Fauzia, A. (2013). *Faith and the state: A history of Islamic philanthropy in Indonesia*. Brill.
Fauzia, A. (2020). *Covid-19 and the blessings of online Zakat in Indonesia* (NUS Research Report). Retrieved 10 July 2020 from https://ari.nus.edu.sg/20331-16/
Fernandez, G., & Ahmed, I. (2019). "Build back better" approach to disaster recovery: Research trends since 2006. *Progress in Disaster Science, 1*, 100003. https://doi.org/10.1016/j.pdisas.2019.100003
FRJ (Fund Raising Japan). (2015). FRJ Annual Conference Proceedings.
Granovetter, M. (1985). Economic action and social structure: The problem of embeddedness. *American Journal of Sociology, 91*(3), 481–510. https://doi.org/10.1086/228311
Gras, D., Nason, R. S., Lerman, M., & Stellini, M. (2017). Going offline: Broadening crowdfunding research beyond the online context. *Venture Capital, 19*(3), 217–237. https://doi.org/10.1080/13691066.2017.1302061
Hadiwinata, B. (2003). *The politics of NGOs in Indonesia: Developing democracy and managing a movement*. Routledge.
Handayani, D. M., Herliansyah, K., Hartono, B., & Maya Sopha, B. (2016). Community behavior during the evacuation of Mount Merapi eruption disaster. In *IEEE International Conference on Industrial Engineering and Engineering Management (IEEM)*, 276–280. IEEE. https://doi.org/10.1109/IEEM.2016.7797880.
Hill, H. (1994). *Indonesia's new order: The dynamics of socio-economic transformation*. Allen & Unwin.

Iida, K. (2017). *Kesennumani hanabiwo uchiagetai* (I want to launch fireworks full of hope in the sky of Kesennuma!!). Retrieved 19 July 2020 from https://readyfor.jp/projects/mekke2011

Inaba, K. (2011). *Ritashugi to shukyo.* Kobundo.

Inskeep, E. (1991). *Tourism planning: An integrated and sustainable development approach.* Van Nostrand Reinhold.

Isbah, M. F. (2016). *Examining the socio-economic role of Islamic boarding schools (Pesantren) in Indonesia* (PhD thesis). The University of New South Wales, Canberra.

Ishii, K. (2019). *The 12th Kesennuma city, Miyagi prefecture the current location of town development in the 8th year since 3.11.* Retrieved from https://project.nikkeibp.co.jp/atclppp/PPP/030700028/041200018

Ismalina, P., & Sakai, M. (2013). *Building community resilience after the Merapi volcano disaster: A case study of state and private schemes for economic livelihood recovery initiatives in Central Java.* Research Report, Indonesian Development Research Network.

James, H., & Paton, D. (2015). Social capital and the cultural contexts of disaster recovery outcomes in Myanmar and Taiwan. *Global Change, Peace & Security, 27*(2), 207–228. https://doi.org/10.1080/14781158.2015.1030380

Kage, R. (2011). *Civic engagement in Postwar Japan: The revival of a defeated society.* Cambridge University Press.

Kemenag. (2018, October 8–10). *The Third International Conference for University Community Engagement.* International Conference at UIN Malang. http://diktis.kemenag.go.id/icon-uce/

Kemmelmeier, M., Jambor, E. E., & Letner, J. (2006). Individualism and good works: Cultural variation in giving and volunteering across the United States. *Journal of Cross-Cultural Psychology, 37*(3), 327–344.

Kesennuma, (2020). https://www.kesennuma.miyagi.jp/sec/s021/010/020/H28-9/20161014163117.html

Kesennuma City. (2019a). *Kifunojokyo or status of donations.* Retrieved from 19 July 2020. https://www.kesennuma.miyagi.jp/sec/s020/030/010/010/050/1288575677493.html

Kesennuma City. (2019b). *Information on Kesennuma town development support donation (hometown tax payment).* Retrieved 19 July 2020 from https://www.kesennuma.miyagi.jp/sec/s020/030/010/010/180/20161114191521.html

Kompasina. (2013). *Desa wisata Turgo, Petualangan di kaki Gunung Merapi* (Turgo tourism village, Adventure at the Mt Merapi). Retrieved 13 July 2020 from https://www.kompasiana.com/cyberboypower/5528c46d6ea83426408b458b/desa-wisata-turgo-petualangan-di-kaki-gunung-merapi

Korf, B. (2006). Commentary on the special section on the Indian Ocean Tsunami—Disasters, generosity and the other. *Geographical Journal, 172*, 245–247.

Latief, H. (2010). *Melayani umat: Filantropi Islam dan ideologi, sejahteraan kaum modernis* [Serving the community: Islamic philanthropy and social wellbeing for modernist Islam]. Gramedia Pustaka Utama.

Latief, H. (2016). Philanthropy and "Muslim citizenship" in Post-Suharto Indonesia. *Southeast Asian Studies, 5*(2), 269–286. https://doi.org/10.20495/seas.5.2_269

Linebaugh, K. (1998). Indonesian clove cartel still holds Reins despite deal. Editorial. *Asian Wall Street Journal*. Retrieved from http://search.proquest.com/docview/315580357/

MacRae, G., & Hodgkin, D. (2011). Half full or half empty? Shelter after the Jogjakarta earthquake. *Disasters, 35*(1), 243–267. https://doi.org/10.1111/j.1467-7717.2010.01202.x

Maula, F. (2019). *Mengenal Mbah Asih, Jiru kunci Merapi pengganti Mbah Maridjan* (Getting to know Mbak Asih, the Merapi guardian who has replaced Mbah Maridjan). Retrieved 20 July 2020 from https://www.brilio.net/sosok/mengenal-mbah-asih-juru-kunci-merapi-pengganti-mbah-maridjan-1910171.html

McCarthy, J., Steenbergen, D., Warren, C., Acciaioli, G., Baker, G., Lucas, A., & Rambe, V. (2017). Community driven development and structural disadvantage: Interrogating the social turn in development programming in Indonesia. *The Journal of Development Studies, 53*(12), 1988–2004. https://doi.org/10.1080/00220388.2016.1262024

Mckinell, J. (2020, May 25). Celeste Barber's $51 million bushfire money can't be distributed to other charities. *ABC News*. Retrieved from https://www.abc.net.au/news/2020-05-25/celeste-barber-bushfire-fundraiser-money-only-for-rfs/12282016

Media Indonesia. (2019). *2019 Zakat collection exceeds the target*. Retrieved 17 July 2020 from https://mediaindonesia.com/humaniora/280014/pengumpulan-zakat-2019-lampaui-target

Nurdin, M. R. (2018). *Religion and social capital: Civil society organisations in disaster recovery in Indonesia* (PhD Thesis). The University of New South Wales, Canberra.

Perdana, A., & Maxwell, J. (2011). The evolution of poverty alleviation policies: Ideas, issues and actors. In C. Manning & S. Sudarno (Eds.), *Employment, living standards and poverty in contemporary Indonesia* (pp. 273–290). ISEAS Publishing.

Prafitri, G. R., & Damayanti, M. (2016). Kapasitas kelembagaan dalam pengebangan desa wisata (Studi kasus: Desa wisata Ketenger, Banyumas). *Jurnal Pengembangan Kota, 41*, 76–86. https://doi.org/10.14710/jpk.4.1.76-86

Rahman, D. F. (2020, 21 July). Omnibus bill to relax requirements to establish cooperatives: Government. *The Jakarta Post*. Retrieved from https://www.thejakartapost.com/news/2020/07/21/omnibus-bill-to-relax-requirements-to-establish-cooperatives-government.html

Rahmayati, Y. (2016). Reframing "building back better" for post-disaster housing design: A community perspective. *International Journal of Disaster Resilience in the Built Environment*, 7(4), 344–360. https://doi.org/10.1108/IJDRBE-05-2015-0029

Reliefweb. (2006, April 25). *Factbox: Five facts about Indonesia's Merapi Volcano*. Retrieved 20 July 2020 from https://reliefweb.int/report/indonesia/factbox-five-facts-indonesias-merapi-volcano

Sakai, M. (2012). Building a partnership for social service delivery in Indonesia: State and faith-based organisations. *Australian Journal of Social Issues*, 47(3), 373–388.

Sakai, M., & Fauzia, A. (2014a). Islamic orientations in contemporary Indonesia: Islamism on the rise? *Asian Ethnicity*, 15(1), 41–61. https://doi.org/10.1080/14631369.2013.784513

Sakai, M., & Fauzia, A. (2014b). Key factors for capacity-building of disaster relief operations: Indonesian examples. In M. Sakai (Ed.), *Disaster relief in the Asia Pacific* (pp. 33–51). Routledge.

Sakai, M., & Inaba, K. (2014). Fostering civil society organization for disaster relief in Japan. In M. Sakai (Ed.), *Disaster Relief in the Asia Pacific* (pp. 52–66). Routledge.

Sakai, M., Jurriëns, E., Zhang, J., & Thornton, A. (2014). *Disaster relief in the Asia Pacific: Agency and resilience*. N.Y. Routledge.

Saunders, P. (2012). Religiosity, citizenship and attitudes to social policy issues. *Australian Journal of Social Issues*, 47(3), 335–352. https://doi.org/10.1002/j.1839-4655.2012.tb00252.x.

Shinagawa, Kanko. (n.d.). *The 24th Meguro pacific saury festival*. Retrieved 3 July 2020 from https://shinagawa-kanko.or.jp/event/meguronosanmamatsuri

Simons, A., Kaiser, L. F., & vom Brocke, J. (2019). Enterprise crowdfunding: Foundations, applications, and research findings. *Business & Information Systems Engineering: The International Journal of WIRTSCHAFTSINFORMATIK*, 61(1), 113–121.

Somusho. (n.d.). *Furusato Nozei no shikumi* (How hometown tax works). Retrieved 26 October from 2020 https://www.soumu.go.jp/main_sosiki/jichi_zeisei/czaisei/czaisei_seido/furusato/mechanism/deduction.html

Storr, V. H., Haeffele-Balch, S., & Grube, L. E. (2015). *Community revival in the wake of disaster: Lessons in local entrepreneurship*. Palgrave Macmillan.

Sugarda, P. (2016). Cooperatives: Indonesia's sleeping giant or a total failure? A legal perspective. *Social Sciences (Pakistan)*, 11(18), 4388–4392.

Sugawara, S. (2015, February 11). *Mayor's remarks at Kennumawo genkini surukai, Tokyo.*

Sulistiyanto, P., (2014). The politics of the Mount Merapi eruptions in Central Java. In M. Sakai et.al (Eds), *Disaster relief in the Asia Pacific* (pp. 119–131). Routledge.

Suzuki, D. (2017). *Nihonjin wa kifuga kirai? Kifunobunka ganai?* (Japanese people dislike donations? Do they have a culture of donations?). Retrieved 10 July 2020 from https://kifunavi.jp/donation/jp-history/

Thornton, A., Sakai, M., & Hassall, G. (2012). Givers and governance: The potential of faith-based development in the Asia Pacific. *Development in Practice: Religion and Development*, 22(5–6), 779–791. https://doi.org/10.1080/09614524.2012.685864

UNDP. (2020). *Sustainable Development Goals.* United Nations Development Program. Retrieved 17 September, 2020 from https://www.undp.org/content/undp/en/home/sustainable-development-goals/background.html

Windred, S. (2017). Fighting apathy, seeking engagement. *Inside Indonesia.* Retrieved from https://www.insideindonesia.org/fighting-apathy-seeking-engagement

CHAPTER 16

Housing Continuum: Key Determinants Linking Post-Disaster Reconstruction to Resilience in the Long Term

Mittul Vahanvati

INTRODUCTION

Home constitutes the most basic human need in most societies. At a micro-scale, a house is one of the basic human rights and forms the foundation for a safe, comfortable, healthy and prosperous life. For that reason, people invest a large portion of their earnings in their home making it the most expensive asset they possess. At a macro-scale, the earth is the only home known to humans and non-humans, which sustains us through its ecosystem services like freshwater, air and fertile land. However, there is increasing friction in the interaction between the natural system and the human system (housing and the built environment), resulting in disasters.

M. Vahanvati (✉)
RMIT University, Melbourne, VIC, Australia
e-mail: mittul.vahanvati@rmit.edu.au

© The Author(s), under exclusive license to Springer Nature Singapore Pte Ltd. 2022
H. James et al. (eds.), *Disaster Risk Reduction in Asia Pacific*, Disaster Risk, Resilience, Reconstruction and Recovery,
https://doi.org/10.1007/978-981-16-4811-3_16

Disasters are not 'natural'. Human society is equally (if not more) responsible for disaster occurrence. Scholars (e.g. Blaikie et al., 1994) argue that disasters occur at the intersection of the human system and the natural system (i.e. hazards). Human society, especially the built environment, has and continues to use and abuse natural resources (like earth, water, wood and fuel) beyond its replenishing capacity, leaving piles of waste and emitting between 37 and 49% of total greenhouse gases (UN-Habitat, 2019). Such an abusive relationship has not only contributed to an increase in global temperature and climate change (i.e. the health of our planet) but has also made us more vulnerable to disaster impacts. Disasters results in loss of lives, economy and psychological trauma. Since the 1970s the number, magnitude and complexity of rapid onset disasters have increased at a steady pace and so has associated economic loss (CRED EM-DAT, 2009). There are broad categories of disasters— (i) rapid onset, which arrives without much warning (e.g. earthquakes, floods, landslide, avalanche) and (ii) slow onset (e.g. climate change-related sea-level rise, desertification, famine). Rapid onset disasters are also termed as sudden shocks and slow onset as chronic stresses.

Additionally, disasters are not 'neutral' either. They disproportionately impact people living in the least developed countries (LDCs). Data confirm that over the last 20 years (1996–2016), people living in LDCs bore the brunt of disaster mortality, "almost five times more than the average toll in high-income countries" (CRED EM-DAT, 2016). This quantitative data confirms a direct co-relationship between disaster and development level. Societal development relies on population, policy frameworks, land-use zoning, construction standards for housing and the built environment, passive design, equal distribution of resources for poverty alleviation and cultural rootedness without creating social divisions. Changing the development trajectory requires a multi-pronged approach and investment in pre-disaster preparedness or adaptation efforts, which rarely happens in developing countries due to limited resources. The only hope to bring such change is in the long-term success of post-disaster reconstruction efforts. This research focuses on identifying key determinants in terms of policies, practices and participation approaches during post-disaster housing and settlement reconstruction projects that have helped bring such long-term changes.

The chapter first outlines a review of international discourse on housing reconstruction to highlight what is already known about its long-term effectiveness, in terms of strengthening disaster resilience of affected communities. This is followed by the development of a conceptual framework and discussion of case study research methodology. Findings in terms of processes that enabled building resilience at the macro (government), meso (practitioner) and micro (community) scales are discussed and organised in a new framework. The chapter finishes with concluding notes on this research's contribution to existing knowledge and its global implications.

HOUSING RECONSTRUCTION AND ENHANCING SOCIETY'S RESILIENCE

Post-Disaster Reconstruction

Following the Sendai Framework for Disaster Risk Reduction 2015–2030, it is broadly accepted that post-disaster reconstruction offers an opportunity to build back better (BBB) or provide safer housing as well as reorient our societies' development trajectory towards a resilient one. However, our understanding of theoretical concepts such as resilience and practice of post-disaster reconstruction have changed over time.

In the 1900s, the post-disaster response was seen as charity work in response to disasters being considered as acts of God. In the 1960s following World War II, the idea of supporting people after disaster entered the public discourse for the first time. This was evident in the early documented efforts that received external funding as shown by the 1970s avalanche and earthquake in Yungay, Peru (Oliver-Smith, 1979), the 1970 earthquake in Turkey (Ganapati & Ganapati, 2009), the 1976 earthquake in Guatemala and Mexico (Davis, 1978) and the 1977 cyclone in Andhra Pradesh, India (Winchester, 1979). These scholars and a few others (Chambers, 1983; Cuny, 1978; Davis, 1978; Turner, 1976) at the time emphasised the importance of participatory processes as much as the housing product and drew linkages between disaster and development. Apart from emphasis on community participatory reconstruction, there was also a growing emphasis on ecological sustainability. This shift was about a move away from ecosystem 'control' towards the capacity for coexistence—an attribute of resilience.

Until the introduction of the concepts of risk and resilience in the early 1990s, post-disaster efforts and research remained fairly siloed in various fields of studies. Disaster risk was proposed by a multi-disciplinary team of scholars (Blaikie et al., 1994) and represented in a formula as, disaster risk = hazard x exposure x vulnerability/capacities (Blaikie et al., 1994; UNISDR, 2004). Disaster risk is defined as "the potential loss of life, injury, or destroyed or damaged assets which could occur to a system, society or a community in a specific period of time, determined probabilistically as a function of hazard, exposure, vulnerability and capacity" (UNISDR, 2017, 14). This definition suggests that risk is a 'perceived threat' and is 'continuously present' at a spatial and temporal scale. It also highlights that while hazards *cannot* be reduced, exposure and vulnerability *can* be reduced and capacities strengthened—an attribute of resilience.

The Concept of Resilience
A few scholars claim that the resilience perspective "enhances the likelihood of sustaining desirable pathways for development in changing environments where the future is unpredictable" (Folke, 2006, 254; Handmer & Dovers, 1996; Walker & Salt, 2006).

The concept of resilience has gained traction in disaster reconstruction and recovery management since its introduction in the 1990s (Resilience Alliance, 1999) and lately, in climate change adaption. Its origin lies in the Latin verb *resilire* meaning 'to rebound or recoil' (Holling, 1973; IFRC, 2004). In the context of disasters, the concept introduces the inter-relationship between human and natural systems, that is, coupled socio-ecological system (SES). SES resilience to disasters is defined as "*the ability of a system, community or society exposed to hazards to resist, absorb, accommodate, adapt to, transform and recover from the effects of a hazard in a timely and efficient manner, including through the preservation and restoration of its essential basic structures and functions through risk management*" (UNISDR, 2017, 22).

The definition of resilience highlights the few abilities of a system needed for recovery, as shown in Table 16.1. These abilities can be categorised into three typologies: (i) to resist change (engineering resilience), (ii) to absorb or accommodate change (ecosystem or social resilience) and iii) to adapt or transform (coupled socio-ecological systems resilience). The framing of the resilience concept determines the goal of housing reconstruction. Like the concept's definition, varied characteristics and dimensions of SES resilience are identified by a few scholars as listed in Table 16.2. As shown in the table, the four characteristics of SES resilience are: (1) robustness (or resistance), (2) redundancy, (3) resourcefulness and (4) rapidity (or timeliness) (Bevc, 2013; Kapucu et al., 2013). These

Table 16.1 Various meanings of the resilience concept—from the narrow to an integrated socio-ecological systems' interpretation

Various concepts	Focus on and characteristics	States and scales	Natural hazards as	Timing	Related literature
Engineering resilience	Cope/Resist change Constancy Rapidity/Timely recovery Efficiency	One stable-state Linear Cause and effect	External shock	Post-disaster	(Bosher, 2008; Folke, 2006; Haigh & Amaratunga, 2011; IFRC, 2012; Tobin, 1999)
Social or Ecological resilience	Absorb change Robustness Persistence/Absorb change Maintain functioning People-place connection Eliminate redundancy System memory	Multiple stable states Non-linearity	On-going disturbance	Pre-& post-disaster	(Holling, 1973; IFRC, 2012; Jha et al., 2010; Mulligan, 2012)
Coupled Socio-ecological systems (SES) resilience	Adapt or Transform Attain an alternative system Renewal cycles	Feedback loops Context-specific Non-linearity Cross-scale dynamic interactions Nested scale	On-going process	Pre- & post-disaster	(Berkes & Ross, 2013; Berkes et al., 1998; Folke, 2006; Gunderson, 2010; Lizarralde et al., 2015; Walker & Salt, 2006)

Source Adapted from Vahanvati (2017, p. 53)

Table 16.2 Characteristics and dimensions of disaster resilience from a socio-ecological systems (SES) perspective

Authors	Resilience of what	Characteristics	Dimensions of resilience (system of systems)
Gunderson et al. (2002)	Socio-ecological system (SES)	Renewal Reorganisation Development	
Holling & Walker (2003) ecologist	SES	Maintenance of function Self-organisation/change Buffer capacity Adaptive capacity	Structures & processes Human, social, ecological, economic
Folke (2006) ecological economist	SES	Adaptive capacity Transformability Learning/embedded memory Innovation (contains non-linear dynamics, thresholds, reciprocal feedbacks, cross-scale interactions across temporal & spatial scales)	Ecological, social and economic domains
Smit and Wandel (2006)	SES	Contextual derivation Pertinent conditions or exposures Community sensitivities Adaptive strategies	Local (e.g. kinship networks) General social, cultural, political, institutional Economic system Technological Management
Twigg (2009)	SES	Adaptation or resistance Maintenance of basic functions Recovery or 'bouncing back'	Institutional, environmental (risk assessment) Culture (knowledge) Social (health, wellbeing) Financial (livelihood) Physical, technical

(continued)

Table 16.2 (continued)

Authors	Resilience of what	Characteristics	Dimensions of resilience (system of systems)
IFRC (2012)	Community	Robustness Diversity Equity Redundancy (loss) Being well-located (capacity to learn, adapt and be resourceful)	Human (knowledge, health) Social (organised) Political Physical (housing, etc.) Economic opportunity Environmental assets
Bevc in Kapucu et al. (2013)	SES	Robustness Redundancy Resourcefulness Rapidity of recovery (contains loss, feedback loops, interactions)	Technical, organisational, societal Economic Multiple scales
Kruse et al. (2017) EMBRACE framework	Community	Resources and capacities Action (at multiple scales) Learning	Natural or place-based Socio-political Financial Physical Human Political

Source Vahanvati (2017, p. 53)

characteristics fit squarely within a traditional engineering resilience, but, when combined with a fifth characteristic: (5) adaptive/transformative capacity including learning, embedded memory, place-based or contextual derivations, diversity, relate to SES resilience. Central to the concept of socio-ecological systems (SES) resilience is a systems' approach (multi-disciplinary, multi-sectoral), which has many dimensions: multi-scalar (nested or cross-scalar interactions), spatial (context-specific), temporal (time-specific, or evident pre-, during- and long-time after a disaster) and feedback loops between them.

Such varying interpretations of resilience combined with the complexities of the post-disaster context makes the task of operationalising it complicated. Bond (2017, pp. 5–19) and others have proposed frameworks for operationalising resilience. However, empirical evidence supporting whether reconstruction programs/projects have succeeded at enhancing resilience in the long term remains sparse.

Housing at the Centre of Reconstruction and Resilience

Housing stock constitutes the majority of the building stock, globally. The New Urban Agenda (UN-Habitat, 2012) has identified housing to play a central role in efforts to change the development trajectory from vulnerability to resilience. However, cities across the world have a lot of catching up to do. It would require consideration of housing from a whole-of-life and systems approach, which includes consideration for hard assets (e.g. land-use planning, building standards, services and infrastructure, insurance mechanism), soft assets (people-centred) and dynamic assets (nature, climate, disasters). As per the disaster management cycle, a change in the human system needs to be considered as an ongoing process, with pre-disaster preparedness and mitigation efforts as a continuation to post-disaster recovery efforts. Likewise, housing would have to be viewed as a continuum, from—housing production, maintenance to end of life to reconstruction—and beyond.

Since the 'future' environment is changing and unpredictable, it is challenging to prepare for the same. Besides, most LDCs and many cities within developed countries with limited resources struggle to invest in preparedness efforts. Moreover, the majority of international funding is allocated to post-disaster relief and recovery efforts, which provides an opportunity to strengthen resilience. However, there is limited research to substantiate claims about reconstruction's links to building resilience. Nonetheless, there is some emerging scholarship linking reconstruction to SES resilience (e.g. Lyons et al., 2010; Murphy et al., 2018; Wisner, 2017). Limited research on the long-term implications of reconstruction hinders our ability to understand key determinants that serve to build society's resilience. This research seeks to provide an answer to the research question: how does post-disaster housing reconstruction serve to enhance society's resilience in the long term?

Research Methodology

To answer the research question, this research adopts a predominantly qualitative and multi-disciplinary case study method. Four good practice reconstruction projects have been selected from India (for case study selection criteria, see Vahanvati & Beza, 2017). Two case studies are from the state of Gujarat post-2001 earthquake and the other two from Bihar post-2008-Kosi river floods. India is selected because it is one of the transitioning economies, the second-highest populous country in the world, among the top ten countries at high risk of disasters (NIDM, 2001) and has been at the forefront of successful disaster management since the 1990s.

The research methodology incorporates multiple disciplines, multiple scales and longer timeframe, pre-requisites for analysing resilience outcomes. Housing reconstruction is investigated through a longer timeframe or life cycle, including during-, post- and long-term after construction completion (CAPAM, 2004; Lizarralde, 2002). The following four stages of housing are related to the ones proposed by log-frame or LFA—a tool widely used for evaluating development projects (NONIE, 2009):

   i. inputs (planning—resolving land rights issues, settlement layout, house design, building standards revision),
  ii. activities (construction, skills training, monitoring),
 iii. outputs (project closeout, hand-over) and
  iv. Long-term impacts (intended and unintended outcomes).

The disciplines of architecture and sociology are combined with the development and disaster studies. Each stage is investigated from the three dimensions, physical, social and financial, within an ecological context to investigate whether the resilience characteristics are attained in the longer term. A conceptual framework (Fig. 16.1) is derived to represent these three dimensions and their linkages to resilience in the long term (Vahanvati, 2017).

An analytical framework is derived from the conceptual framework and logical framework for analysis (LFA) (for the analytical framework, see Vahanvati & Mulligan, 2017). Data collection is done by combining the method of the social sciences as semi-structured interviews and focus group discussions, and architecture as visual documentation. A total of

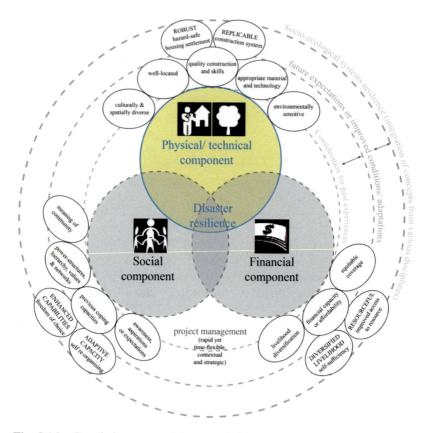

Fig. 16.1 Detailed conceptual framework for post-disaster reconstruction and recovery projects in a spatial and temporal systems' context, with feedback (and feed-forward), loops between past experiences and future expectations. (*Source* Vahanvati 2017)

80 in-depth semi-structured interviews are conducted with three sample groups: (i) 37 beneficiaries; (ii) nine non-beneficiaries and (iii) 34 stakeholders involved in the reconstruction project (government authorities, civil society organisation [CSO], social workers). To be representative of all people and for the purpose of triangulation, these three sample groups are identified purposively based on gender, socio-economic variations and housing condition. Primary empirical data obtained on-site is

complimented by secondary data such as CSO or government reports and other documentation produced at the time of reconstruction. Thematic content analysis is used for the analysis of qualitative data.

FINDINGS: COMPARING THE 2001 GUJARAT EARTHQUAKE WITH THE 2008 BIHAR FLOODS

The Impact of the 2001 Gujarat Earthquake

On 26th January 2001—the Indian Republic national holiday—the Western state of Gujarat was hit by an earthquake of 7.9 magnitude, claiming nearly 20,000 lives (UNDP, 2001) and destroying over one million homes (GoI & UNDP, 2011). The earthquake was declared to be the second largest recorded in Indian history (UNDP, 2009). The two case study sites—Hodko and Patanka settlements—were located at the epicentre of the earthquake and a little further away, respectively. Consequently, Hodko suffered 85% of all assets lost (UNDP, 2009) while in Patanka, 60% (Gupta & Shaw, 2003).

The Impact of the 2008 Kosi River Floods, Bihar

In August 2008, heavy monsoonal rains combined with the rupture of the embankment on the River Kosi had devastating impacts (GoB, World Bank, & GFDRR, 2010). The devastation was massive because of the change in the river's natural course, inundating regions that had not experienced floods since 1963. The floods affected over three million people (PiC, 2010), damaged more than 200,000 homes (GoB & ODRC, 2008a) and devastated livelihoods (cattle and crops). The 2008 flood was declared a national calamity. The two case study sites—Orlaha and Puraini—were in close proximity to the embankment that burst and a bit further away, respectively. Consequently, Orlaha suffered 95% of assets lost while Puraini suffered approximately 60% (GoB & ODRC, 2008b).

POST-DISASTER RECONSTRUCTION PROGRAMS IN INDIAN CASE STUDY SITES

The reconstruction and recovery program development (at a macro-scale by government authorities) and on-ground activities (at a meso-scale undertaken by the civil society organisations and a micro-scale by communities) are outlined in Table 16.3 for all the four settlement reconstruction projects. The key differences in case study projects are highlighted in Tables 16.3, 16.4, and 16.5.

At a macro-scale, since the government of Gujarat had adopted an owner-driven reconstruction (ODR) program for the first time and at-scale, the program was in its infancy. This is implicit in the focus of financial assistance was mainly on housing and infrastructure recovery, which can be termed as the narrow framing or engineering resilience perspective (Table 16.3). However, the government was rewarded for successful recovery due to the rapidity of the recovery (CAPAM, 2004). On the contrary, the government of Bihar had developed a highly sophisticated ODR policy informed by prior experiences of and in collaboration with the consortium termed Owner Driven Reconstruction Collaborative (ODRC). In Bihar the financial assistance was allocated for multiple recoveries—housing, infrastructure, access to water, lighting, sanitation, landscaping and loss of livelihoods. Moreover, they had adopted an agile approach to tailor the program to community needs and were set up for decentralised governance (Vahanvati, 2018). Thus, their program framing was broader or from a systems resilience perspective. Despite such a mature program, the government took 10 years (from 2008 to 2018) to complete reconstruction. As per the success metrics of the World Bank (2015)—timely, efficient and fit for purpose—Bihar's recovery program was claimed to be a partial success (Table 16.4). Nonetheless, the World Bank had taken the responsibility of strengthening government capacity for recovery, Kosi river basin management and livelihood recovery (GoB, World Bank, & GFDRR, 2010).

At meso-scale, from 2001 to 2008, the role of CSOs in India got alleviated from mere housing reconstruction implementers to enablers (Table 16.3). While in 2001, in Gujarat, through public–private partnerships a space was created for the civil society organisations (CSOs) to operate freely in the post-disaster context; in 2008, in Bihar, the government involved CSOs from early days as policy advocates. Subsequently, the responsibility for recovery management transferred from CSOs to the state government from 2001 to 2008.

As much as it is admirable for the state government of Bihar to take the initiative, they needed hand-holding support from ODRC—who had vast on-the-ground reconstruction experience. It was evident that when ODRC managed the implementation of housing reconstruction in pilot

Table 16.3 A summary of multi-scalar reconstruction efforts post-2001 and 2008 disasters

Disaster	Roles at different scales	Case-study sites			
		Hodko, post-2001 Gujarat earthquake	Patanka, post-2001 Gujarat earthquake	Orlaha, post-2008 Bihar floods	Puraini, post-2008 Bihar floods
	Hazard exposure	Earthquake, drought, sandstorms		Floods, cyclone/storm surge, earthquake	
Input and Activities	Governance setup and policy framework at the state level	A nodal agency setup for disaster management (GSDMA 2001a)		✓	
		Top-down and centralised government setup		Decentralised governance setup	
		An owner-driven reconstruction (ODR) policy adopted for the first time in India Allowed for public-private partnerships The state created space for CSOs to operate		A highly sophisticated ODR policy adopted (GoB and ODRC 2008b) A collaborative approach from early days The state took responsibility of recovery	
		Beneficiaries identified by the government			
		Building standards upgraded collaboratively			
		Financial assistance non-uniform package For housing recovery only (narrow framing of engineering resilience) The government encouraged CSOs to top-up funding		Financial assistance uniform package for housing, toilets, solar lighting, and livelihood (systems framing of resilience) Pilot project funded by CSOs Government-funded up-scaling	
		Money transferred directly into the survivors' bank account (in joint name of man and women) and disbursed in three instalments (completion of foundation, walls and entire house)			
	Civil society organisations (CSOs)	Implementation role Selected settlements for reconstruction after signing an MOU with the government		Enabling role Worked on building government capacity through pilot projects in 2 settlements	
		Informal 'Setu Kendras' or shelter hubs established	Ample time given to build trust	Formalised and institutionalised 'Kosi Setu Kendras' setup	
		Brought entire funding	Topped up government funding	Brought entire funding for piloting	Brought entire funding for piloting
		Made minor modifications to government selected beneficiary list			
		Core houses designed with community	Core house design recommended		
		One construction technology proposed		Multiple construction technologies proposed	
		Material banks established		✗	✗

(continued)

Table 16.3 (continued)

		Mason skills training	✓	✓	✓
		Employed local + nonlocal masons	✗	✗	✗
		Provided supervision, monitoring and hand-holding support			
	Community	✗	Built emergency shelter for future		
		Played an active role throughout the recovery process (defining policy, managing housing reconstruction)			
		Collectively resolved land title issues, settlement layout and house location with CSO support			
		✗	Designed own house	✓	✓
		✗	Sourced some materials	Sourced all construction materials	
		A few participated in skills training	The majority participated in skills training		
		Worked as labourers + employed labourers for their own house building			
		Supervised construction with hand-holding support from CSOs			

Source Author

settlements of Bihar, the process went smoothly and led to multiple outcomes (e.g. robust housing, resourcefulness); however, when in hands of the government who had limited experience, the outcomes were not so desirable.

At a micro-scale, 13 years after the earthquake in Gujarat, minimal behavioural changes are witnessed among the residents and the construction sector in Gujarat's Hodko and Patanka settlements. Hodko residents have incrementally discontinued the use of proposed resilience construction technology, while half of Patanka residents continue to replicate it. Having said that, there is an increase in livelihoods (resourcefulness) in both the settlements of Gujarat, evident in their active investment in a better future (e.g. safe house extensions, children's education) and continual adaptation (e.g. investment in diversifying livelihoods).

On the contrary, in Bihar, 7 years post-floods reveal some successes, especially in the construction sector. For example, a majority of residents in Orlaha and Puraini are replicating one of the few proposed multi-hazard resilient technologies (Vahanvati, 2018; Vahanvati & Mulligan, 2017). However, very few residents have managed to increase or diversify their livelihoods. Potentially, it is early days to determine the project's

Table 16.4 Short-term outcomes post-2001 and 2008 reconstruction efforts

Roles at different scales		Case-study sites			
		Hodko, post 2001 Gujarat earthquake	Patanka, post 2001 Gujarat earthquake	Orlaha, post 2008 Bihar floods	Puraini, post 2008 Bihar floods
Short term outcomes + continued capacity building efforts	Government	Awarded UN Sasakawa award in 2003 (GSDMA 2005) and a Commonwealth award (CAPAM 2004)	Mentioned as good practice in IFRC (2004)	x	x
		Partnered with training institutions to provide international level certification to masons (GSDMA 2001b, 2001a)		x	x
	Community	High community satisfaction with every aspect of reconstruction			
		Houses survived the test of the 2006 earthquake measuring 5.6 on the Richter scale (Price and Bhatt 2009)		Houses withstood the test of the 2010 flood and cyclone	
		Lack of access to resources e.g. mud brick machines	Good access to skilled masons for house extensions	Good access to few choices of materials, construction technology and skilled labour	
		Some resentment about equitability of financial package			
	Civil Society Organisation	130 core houses rebuilt	300 core houses rebuilt	41 core houses rebuilt	89 core houses rebuilt
		Continued work beyond for region's development (Kutch Nav Nirman Abhiyan 2013)	Continued work beyond to develop a model village (Gupta and Shaw 2003)	x	x
		x	Mobilised trained masons to form group and link to livelihood	x	x

Source Author

outcomes in terms of behavioural change and adaptive capacities of the residents of Bihar.

Discussion

Nine similar patterns (which are noted as valuable processes/deliverables) are found in all the four case studies, which act as determinants in post-disaster housing reconstruction projects initiating long-lasting change. Out of the nine similar patterns, four are the most significant.

Table 16.5 Long-term impacts of post-disaster reconstruction projects after 2001 and 2008 disasters, from SES resilience perspective

		Case-study sites			
		Hodko, Gujarat	Patanka, Gujarat	Orlaha, Bihar	Puraini, Bihar
Long-term outcomes	Housing robustness & technology replication	x	~	✓	✓
	Redundancy	x	x	✓	✓
	Resourcefulness	✓ Diversified livelihood	~ Increase in the livelihood of all trained masons	x	~ Increase in some trained mason's livelihood
	Rapidity of project	✓	✓	Reconstruction continued for over 9 years (World Bank 2015)	
	The adaptive capacity of society	~ Self-organised in self-help groups; moderate awareness of changing risk, people felt empowered and were capable of investing in a better future	~ Moderate awareness of changing risk	~ Moderate awareness of changing risks, some self-help groups are operational	
				People are continuously improvising their housing, livelihood and challenging the social norms; but, challenges with access to basic needs (e.g. toilets, clean drinking water, roads) is compromising their ability to adapt and forward plan	

Source Author

First, the most significant process was systems design based reconstruction policy formulation, to allow addressing local deep-rooted vulnerabilities. For example, in Bihar, the reconstruction policy was formulated to fund not only housing, but also other systemic issues related to poverty e.g. access to electricity, land titles, loss of livelihood during own house rebuilding. To tailor a localised program, the government and ODRC consortium adopted an agile approach—implementing reconstruction strategy in pilot settlements for improvising (1.3 in Table 16.6). Thus, in Bihar piloting was done before policy formulation which is also considered a safe-to-fail or agile approach.

The second most significant process that ensured social mobilisation and long-term success of housing reconstruction was the set-up of *Setu Kendra (SK)*—meaning bridging centres—shelter and facilitation hubs as one-stop-shop for shelter. SKs were set up during the input stage in both states—Gujarat and Bihar. Each SK comprised of a team that worked in a transdisciplinary manner, including local community members, social workers, built environment professionals (architects, engineers), lawyers

Table 16.6 A novel framework for ODHR projects to enhance the disaster resilience of communities in the long term

PROJECT COMPONENT	PROJECT COMPONENT GOAL (IMPACT)	VALUE DELIVERABLES	ACTIVITIES (INPUTS) BASED ON BEST-PRACTICE CASE-STUDIES & THE KNOWLEDGE GAINED BY TWO INDIAN AGENCIES OVER SEVEN YEARS
1. SYSTEMS DESIGN	To design a contextually appropriate & equitable reconstruction project/ program of projects for reconstruction to have impact beyond robust housing	1.1 Secure government goodwill	i. Determine institutional setup for Disaster Management & governance ii. Advocate for ODR policy where possible iii. Build public-private partnership
		1.2 Define project scope	iv. Incorporate context-specific socio-ecological systems issues (risks and capacities) v. Formulate shared project vision vi. Establish beneficiary selection criteria
		1.3 Test project scope	vii. Refine project scope, technological modifications, financial package and facilitation mode e.g. build model houses; shake-table tests
2. SOCIAL MOBILISATION	To gain and maintain community trust for equitability and enhanced ownership – a foundation for ODHR	2.1 Gain community trust for effective engagement	viii. Understand local meaning of community ix. Assess community needs, priorities and aspirations for housing and settlement x. Learn from communities past coping strategies
		2.2 Mobilise community	xi. Motivate residents to act for themselves and make informed decisions to build back better xii. Raise awareness and maintain transparency about resident's rights and entitlements
3. TECHNICAL MODIFICATION	To improve multi-hazard resilience of construction system for ensuring pertinence, effectiveness and quality of construction in rebuilt houses	3.1 Provide multiple technological choices	xiii. Design multi-hazard resilient housing for demonstration xiv. Develop and disseminate technical guidelines in locally appropriate manner xv. Legalize local, rural and low-cost technology xvi. Establish or not to establish material banks
		3.2 Up-skill local artisans to rebuild robust houses	xvii. Assess local mason's existing skills xviii. Provide skills training and employment to locals (masons, labourers, engineers) for building and supervision
4. CAPACITY BUILDING	To enhance disaster resilience of system for sustaining robustness, redundancy, rapidity resourcefulness and adaptive capacities	4.1 Improve residents' access to resources	xix. Provide continued support to trained masons after completion of reconstruction e.g. skills certification and employment
		4.2 Initiate other projects for improved quality of life	xx. Allow ample time to hand-over (to local partner or government); or to continue onto other projects for addressing systems issues and capacity building xxi. Knowledge transition to inform systems analysis of next project in a continuous spiral

Source Vahanvati (2018) and Vahanvati and Mulligan (2017)

and financial experts. The SKs provided a conduit for two-way transfer of information and communication between the government and the disaster survivors. It must be noted that the SKs were set up informally in Gujarat and were successful. Hence, they were formalised and replicated in Bihar. It is noteworthy that such a transdisciplinary set-up allowed for gaining community trust, mobilising them and improved engagement, in a way that maintains their dignity—thus being promoted internationally as a key to innovation (Vahanvati & Beza, 2015, 2017). However, the value of a formalised and institutional setup of SKs remains to be examined in the longer term.

The third most significant process was providing households with multiple technical choices. The disaster-affected people in Bihar and some in Gujarat were given the freedom to choose for their settlement layout, house design, material and technology selection, along with adequate skills training, social support and financial support. With such a combination of support, the people felt empowered to make the right decisions—at that time, bearing in mind its longer term implications. These processes were done during the input and activity stages. This process is not just participatory but enabling!

The fourth most significant process was continued capacity development efforts beyond housing reconstruction, which typically lasted more than 7 years post-disaster, or until the communities were self-reliant, resourceful and resilient. These practitioners and policymakers due to their mindfulness of each settlement-based communities' varying needs and capacities were best equipped to translate the community capacities into livelihoods on an on-going basis to link with development.

All these nine processes are grouped into four project components, as (i) systems design (1 in Table 16.6), (ii) social mobilisation (2 in Table 16.6), (iii) technical modification (3 in Table 16.6) and (iv) capacity building (4 in Table 16.6). These findings are organised in a new framework, where they are represented as project components in a table format (Table 16.6) as well as a spiral framework (Vahanvati, 2018; Vahanvati & Mulligan, 2017).

Conclusion and Global Implications

In this research, the author set out to identify key determinants that linked housing reconstruction after the disaster to building the resilience of societies long term in the future. Reconstruction projects as case studies were selected from India as the Indian government has been successfully formulating and implementing owner-driven reconstruction programs, at-scale since the 1990s. Comparative analysis of case studies was conducted from a multi-disciplinary and whole-of-life cycle approach. Findings were derived from empirical evidence gathered from the highly experienced Indian CSOs, government officials, and communities or housing beneficiaries as well as secondary data like organisational reports. Similarities in terms of nine processes or deliverables were identified from the four case studies. Four out of nine deliverables were highlighted as the most significant processes that help in changing the development trajectory and strengthening SES resilience of communities. These four identified processes were (i) formulating a localised, strategic and an owner-driven reconstruction program through agility and flexibility in recovery time, (ii) setting up of transdisciplinary shelter hubs for coordination between government and community giving people political voice, (iii) providing the community with a freedom to choose (as it goes beyond community participation) and (iv) sustaining capacity building efforts beyond housing reconstruction completion for capacity development.

It is noteworthy that freedom of choice or 'human capabilities' coined by Nobel laureate Amartya Sen (1997, 1998) for human development context, proved equally important for the long-term success of reconstruction efforts. Yet, the concept is not mentioned in disasters scholarship. The research also confirms that CSOs played an important role in linking micro-scale (community needs) with macro-scale (government mandates, climate change, or systems thinking). Besides, when CSOs had advocacy role (e.g. involved with the government in program formulation and capacity building in Bihar), the program was mature, and the state did well. Likewise, when CSOs had an implementation role, community satisfaction with the process and rebuilt housing outcome was also high (e.g. Gujarat). Thus, an active role for CSOs is important through all stage of reconstruction, alongside the state, as partners.

All findings are grouped into four project components—systems design, social mobilisation, technical modifications and capacity building, to propose a novel framework.

The most important contribution to knowledge is the proposal of a novel framework that links reconstruction to SES resilience. The framework intends to inform practitioners in a field where lessons from the past have been narrowly documented and long-term project outcomes have largely remained unexamined (Vahanvati, 2018). The framework is intentionally kept abstract to allow for required adaptation to suit a context. The author urges donors, policymakers and practitioners to use the framework as key ingredients rather than a step-by-step recipe; draw from an array of disciplinary expertise to encourage community capabilities during-reconstruction; and sustain capacity building efforts beyond-reconstruction completion, for housing reconstruction to facilitate reorienting the development trajectory towards a resilient one long time into the future.

Acknowledgements Dr. Mittul Vahanvati acknowledges the support she received from the RMIT University's Higher Degree by Research Publication Grant, which supported her efforts in producing this research output.

References

Berkes, F., Folke, C., & Colding, J. (Eds.). (1998). *Linking social and ecological systems: Management practices and social mechanisms for building resilience.* Cambridge University Press.

Berkes, F., & Ross, H. (2013). Community resilience: Toward an integrated approach. *Society & Natural Resources, 26*(1), 5–20. https://doi.org/10.1080/08941920.2012.736605

Bevc, C. (2013). Introduction to conceptual insights and applications of resilience. In N. Kapucu, C. V. Hawkins & F.I. Rivera (Eds.), *Disaster resiliency* (pp. 15–20). Routledge.

Blaikie, P., Cannon, T., Davis, I., & Wisner, B. (1994). *At risk: Natural hazards, people's vulnerability and disasters.* Routledge.

Bond, C. A. (2017). *Resilience dividend valuation model: Framework development and initial case studies.* Rand Corporation.

Bosher, L. (2008). *Hazards and the built environment: Attaining built-in resilience.* Taylor & Francis.

CAPAM. (2004). *CAPAM International Innovations Awards Programme 1998–2004.* Commonwealth Association for Public Administration and Management.

Chambers, R. (1983). *Rural development: Putting the last first.* Taylor and Francis.

CRED EM-DAT. (2009). Disaster Classification. CRED, Emergency Events Database (EM-DAT), Belgium.

Cuny, F. (1978). Disasters and the small dwelling: The state of the art. *Disasters, 2*(2–3), 118–124.

Davis, I. (1978). *Shelter after disaster.* Oxford Polytechnic Press.

Em-Dat, C. R. E. D. (2016). *Poverty & death: Disaster mortality, 1996–2015.* CREDCrunch.

Folke, C. (2006). Resilience: The emergence of a perspective for social–ecological systems analyses. *Global Environmental Change, 16*(3), 253–267. https://doi.org/10.1016/j.gloenvcha.2006.04.002

Ganapati, N. E., & Ganapati, S. (2009). Enabling participatory planning after disasters: A case study of the World Bank's housing reconstruction in Turkey. *Journal of the American Planning Association, 75*(1), 41–59.

GoB, & ODRC. (2008a). *Reconstruction and rehabilitation of Kosi flood affected regions in Kosi division: Memorandum of understanding (MOU).* GoB, ODRC, Patna, India.

GoB, & ODRC. (2008b). *Workshop on owner driven reconstruction and rehabilitation for Kosi flood affected regions. Government of Bihar—Department of planning and development.* Owner Driven Reconstruction Collaborative, Patna, India.

GoB, World Bank, & GFDRR (2010). *Bihar Kosi Flood (2008) Needs Assessment Report.* World Bank, Geneva, Switzerland.

GoI, & UNDP. (2011). *Disaster Management in India.* edited by Government of India Ministry of Home Affairs. Nation Centre for Disaster Management, New Delhi, India.

GSDMA. (2001a). *About Gujarat State Disaster Management Authority (GSDMA).* Government of Gujarat. Retrieved 10 March 2015 from www.gsdma.org/about-us/introduction.aspx

GSDMA. (2001b). *Masons training/certification programme.* Government of Gujarat. Retrieved 10 March 2015 from www.gsdma.org/key-projects-programmes/masons-training.aspx

GSDMA. (2005). *Grit and grace: The story of reconstruction Gandhinagar.* GSDMA, Gujarat.

Gunderson, L. (2010). Ecological and human community resilience in response to natural disasters. *Ecology and Society, 15*(2), 18. https://doi.org/10.5751/ES-03381-150218

Gunderson, L., et al. (2002). In Memory of mavericks. *Conservation Ecology, 6*(2). https://doi.org/10.5751/ES-00423-060219

Gupta, M., & Shaw, R. (2003). PNY report. In *Patanka Navjivan Yojana: Towards sustainable community recovery.* Sustainable Environment and Ecological Development (SEEDS), Patan, India.

Haigh, R., & Amaratunga, D. (2011). *Post-disaster reconstruction of the built environment rebuilding for resilience.* Wiley-Blackwell.

Handmer, J. W., & Dovers, S. (1996). A typology of resilience: Rethinking institutions for sustainable development. *Industrial & Environmental Crisis Quarterly, 9*(4), 482–511. https://doi.org/10.1177/108602669600900403

Holling, C. (1973). Resilience and stability of ecological systems. *Annual Review of Ecology and Systematics, 41*(1), 1–23. https://doi.org/10.1146/annurev.es.04.110173.000245

Holing, C., & Walker, B. (2003). Resilence defined. Internet encylopedia of ecological economics. *International Society for Ecological Economics.* http://isecoeco.org/pdf/resilience.pdf

IFRC. (2004). *World Disasters Report 2004—From risk to resilience—Helping communities cope with crisis.* International Federation of Red Cross & Red Crescent Societies (IFRC), Geneva.

IFRC. (2012). *Understanding community resilience and program factors that strengthen them: A comprehensive study of Red Cross and Red Crescent Societies Tsunami Operation.* International Federation of Red Cross & Red Crescent Societies (IFRC), Geneva.

Jha, A. K., Barenstein, J. D., Phelps, P. M., Pittet, D., & Sena, S. (2010). *Safer homes, stronger communities: A handbook for reconstructing after natural disasters.* World Bank.

Kapucu, N., Hawkins, C. V., & Rivera, F. I. (2013). *Disaster resiliency* (pp. 15–20). Routledge.

Kruse, S., Abeling, T., Deeming, H., Fordham, M., Forrester, J., Jülich, S., Karanci, A., Kuhlicke, C., Pelling, M., Pedoth, L., & Schneiderbauer, S. (2017). Conceptualizing community resilience to natural hazards—The emBRACE framework. *Natural Hazards and Earth System Sciences, 17*(12), 2321–2333. https://doi.org/10.5194/nhess-17-2321-2017

Kutch Nav Nirman Abhiyan. (2013). *About us.* Retrieved 23 January 2015 from www.kutchabhiyan.org/about-us.html

Lizarralde, G. (2002). Organizational design, performance and evaluation of post-disaster reconstruction projects. In *Proceedings of conference on improving post-disaster reconstruction in developing countries.* Montreal.

Lizarralde, G., Valladares, A., Olivera, A., Bornstein, L., Gould, K., & Barenstein, J. D. (2015). A systems approach to resilience in the built environment: The case of Cuba. *Disasters, 39*(s1), s76–s95. https://doi.org/10.1111/disa.12109

Lyons, M., Schilderman, T., & Boano, C. (2010). *Building back better: Delivering people-centred housing reconstruction at scale.* Practical Action.

Mulligan, M. (2012). Rebuilding communities after diasters: Lessons from the tsunami diaster in Sri Lanka. *Global Policy, 4*(3), 278–287. https://doi.org/10.1111/17585899.12038

Murphy, R., Pelling, M., Adams, H., Di Vicenz, S., & Visman, E. (2018). Survivor-led response: Local recommendations to operationalise building back better. *International Journal of Disaster Risk Reduction, 31,* 135–142. https://doi.org/10.1016/j.ijdrr.2018.04.009

NIDM. (2001). *The report of high powered committee on disaster management.* National Centre for Disaster Management New Delhi.

NONIE. (2009). *Impact evaluations and development: NONIE guidance on impact evaluation. The network of impact evaluation (NONIE).*

Oliver-Smith, A. (1979). The Yungay Avalanche of 1970: Anthropological perspectives on disaster and social change. *Disasters, 3*(1), 95–101. https://doi.org/10.1111/j.1467-7717.1979.tb00205.x

PiC. (2010). Kosi Reconstruction and Rehabilitation Project. In *People in Centre Consulting* (Ed.). Owner Driven Reconstruction Collaborative, Ahmedabad, India.

Price, G., & Bhatt, M. (2009). *The role of the affected state in humanitarian action: A case study on India.* Overseas Development Institute (ODI)/Humanitarian Policy Group (HPG).

Resilience Alliance. (1999). *About Resilience Alliance.* Retrieved 14 October from https://www.resalliance.org/about

Sen, A. (1997). Human capital and human capability (Editorial). *World Development, 25*(12), 1959.

Sen, A. (1998). Human development and financial conservatism. *World Development, 26*(4), 733–742. https://doi.org/10.1016/S0305-750X(98)00002-3

Smit, B., & Wandel, J. (2006). Adaptation, adaptive capacity and vulnerability. *Global Environmental Change, 16*(3), 282. https://doi.org/10.1016/j.gloenvcha.2006.03.008

Tobin, G. A. (1999). Sustainability and community resilience: The holy grail of hazards planning? *Global Environmental Change b: Environmental Hazards, 1*(1), 13–25. https://doi.org/10.1016/S1464-2867(99)00002-9

Turner, J. (1976). *Housing by people: Towards autonomy in building environments.* Marion Boyars.

Twigg, J. (2009). *Characteristics of a disaster resilient community.* University College London.

UN-Habitat. (2012). *Housing at the centre of the New Urban Agenda.* UN-Habitat. Retrieved 20 March 2019 from https://unhabitat.org/housing-at-the-centre-of-the-new-urban-agenda

UN-Habitat. (2019). *Planners for climate action: Call for course manuals.* UN-Habitat. Retrieved 20 March 2019 from https://www.planners4climate.org/courses-repository

UNDP. (2001). *From relief to recovery: The Gujarat experience.* United Nations Development Programme.

UNDP. (2009). *Kosi Floods 2008: How we coped! What we need? Perception survey on impact and recovery strategies.* United Nations Development Programme.

UNISDR. (2004). *Living with risk: A global review of disaster reduction initiatives.* United Nations International Strategy for Disaster Reduction Secretariat (UNISDR).

UNISDR. (2017). Report of the open-ended intergovernmental expert working group on indicators and terminology relating to disaster risk reduction. In *UNISDR Sustainable Development: Disaster Risk Reduction*. UNISDR.

Vahanvati, M. (2017). *Owner-driven housing reconstruction as a means of enhancing disaster resilience of at-risk communities in India* (Doctor of Philosophy Thesis). RMIT University.

Vahanvati, M. (2018). A novel framework for owner driven reconstruction projects to enhance disaster resilience in the long term. *Disaster Prevention and Management, 27*(4), 421–446. https://doi.org/10.1108/DPM-11-2017-0285

Vahanvati, M., & Beza, B. (2015, July 15–17). Owner-driven reconstruction in India: A case-study of Kosi river floods in Bihar. In *5th International Conference on Building Resilience*. Newcastle, Australia.

Vahanvati, M., & Beza, B. (2017). An owner-driven reconstruction in Bihar. *International Journal of Disaster Resilience in the Built Environment, 8*(3), 306–319. https://doi.org/10.1108/IJDRBE-10-2015-0051

Vahanvati, M., & Mulligan, M. (2017). A new model for effective post-disaster housing reconstruction: Lessons from Gujarat and Bihar in India. *International Journal of Project Management, 35*(5), 802–817. https://doi.org/10.1016/j.ijproman.2017.02.002

Walker, B., & Salt, D. (2006). *Resilience thinking: Sustaining ecosystems and people in a changing world*. Island Press.

Winchester, P. (1979). Disaster relief operations in Andhra Pradesh, Southern India, following the cyclone in November 1977. *Disasters, 3*(2), 173–177. https://doi.org/10.1111/j.1467-7717.1979.tb00222.x

Wisner, B. (2017). "Build back better"? The challenge of Goma and beyond. *International Journal of Disaster Risk Reduction, 26*, 101–105. https://doi.org/10.1016/j.ijdrr.2017.09.027

World Bank. (2015). *Bihar Kosi Flood Recovery Project*. World Bank, Bihar, India.

CHAPTER 17

Disaster Risk Reduction and Recovery in Samoa

Tautala Mauala

Introduction

Samoa is a country at risk of disasters. Her geographic location and physical environment makes the country prone to a number of natural hazards, including earthquakes, volcanic eruptions, cyclones, storm surges, floods, drought, tsunamis and landslides. Samoa is located alongside the "Pacific Ring of Fire", where the continental plates collide causing periodic earthquakes. Samoa is also located where it is regularly visited by tropical cyclones, which can cause secondary hazards such as floods and storm surges. Because of the frequency of their occurrences and the magnitude of their impacts on the national economy, tropical cyclones and floods are considered the major causes of disasters in Samoa (Fakhruddin et al., 2015).

On 29 September 2009, a tsunami hit the south-east coast of Samoa leaving behind a ghastly scene of death and destruction. The tsunami took everyone unprepared. The loss of property and the unprecedented

T. Mauala (✉)
Samoa Red Cross Society (SRCS), Apia, Samoa

loss of life alerted many Samoans to the realization that such an event could happen in their own backyard. This tragedy also highlighted the critical need to assist communities to ready themselves for future events and to help them recognize the need to consciously reduce risks.

This chapter explains the disaster risk management frameworks and infrastructure in Samoa and is largely based on the knowledge and experiences of the Samoa Red Cross Society (SRCS).

Samoa Government Priorities in (Disaster Risk Management) DRM

The Government of Samoa has taken steps to strengthen Disaster Risk Management (DRM). The Disaster & Emergency Management Act, 2007 *(Samoa)* lays down the structure for DRM, which includes the establishment of the Disaster Management Office (DMO) and a Disaster Management Plan (DMP) to be prepared and implemented at national and community levels, for effective planning and risk reduction, response and recovery procedures and promotion of coordination among the response agencies. The provisions of the Act also clearly indicate a shift from the erstwhile relief-oriented approach to a more comprehensive risk management approach. This is a significant progress in terms of providing an overall framework for future DRM intervention at all levels.

The National Disaster Management Plan (NDMP) 2017–2020, provides a policy framework that promotes a whole-of-country and multi-sectoral approach to DRM at the local, national, and regional level. The NDMP has worked towards the expectation that communities are protected from hazards, and where emergency situations occur, communities will be well served by effective response, relief and recovery arrangements. A holistic approach to DRM aims at:

- reducing impacts of and increasing Samoa's resilience to natural and human-induced hazards;
- improving DRM through effective public leadership, coordination, development and implementation;
- mainstreaming DRM across all sectors including economic, social and infrastructure and from national level to the village communities;
- promoting sustainability by raising public awareness of DRM including a focus on a vulnerable population.

The National Action Plan (NAP) 2017–2021, is an operational document, providing a day-to-day guide for operations and a monitoring, evaluation and learning framework to assess performance and advance accountability of the National Disaster Management Office (NDMO), in conjunction with the NDMP 2017–2020. The NAP highlights the imperative to mainstream DRM across all 14 sectors[1] of government and addresses all stages of DRM at the sector level. Mainstreaming DRM is through shared responsibilities in decision-making with key stakeholders from government, communities, the private sector, development partners and civil societies such as the SRCS. It is only through coordinated and sustained collaboration with all the stakeholders that DRM challenges can be mitigated and resolved.

Samoa participated in two Hyogo Framework for Action National Progress reviews, developed Coastal Infrastructure Management Plans, installed an Early Warning System along the south east of the country and developed a comprehensive Community Disaster and Climate Risk Management (CDCRM) program. The government has embraced the Sendai Framework for Disaster Risk Reduction 2015–2030; the World Humanitarian Summit Outcome 2016; the implementation of the SIDS Accelerated Modalities of Actions (SAMOA) Pathway, the United Nations Sustainable Development Goals (SDGs) and other relevant frameworks and agreements such as the Framework for Resilient Development in the Pacific (FRDP) 2017–2030, an integrated approach to address Climate Change and DRM and strengthen efforts towards building resilience, at the local level.

Strategically, the outcomes and outputs articulated in the NAP, align to the National Strategy for the Development of Samoa, the National Environment Sector Plan, and are reflective of Samoa's *Disaster and Emergency Act 2007*. The NAP reflects global and regional priorities articulated in the above international agreements (Pacific Community, 2016; UN General Assembly, 2014, 2015; UNISDR, 2015). It is further informed by lessons learnt from the 2009 tsunami, the 2012 Tropical Cyclone Evan and 2018 Tropical Cyclone Gita operations in Samoa. All of these disasters highlighted Samoa's strengths in DRM and operational challenges requiring further attention.

However, the priorities laid out for Samoa post-2015 are to improve the quality of health education, and strengthen health promotion techniques. This chapter further highlights potential measures that could be used to address the increasing issue of non-communicable diseases as part of the post-2015 health framework in Samoa, with measures including the implementation of targeted programs.

Guiding Principles in DRM

Risk reduction, disaster preparedness, response and recovery are the responsibility of all sectors at all levels.

Risk reduction, disaster preparedness, response and recovery are part of the development process. Building the capacity of sectors in order to reduce the risks from and respond to emergencies requires strong and long-term commitment and sound managerial and technical programs. Use knowledge innovation and education to build a culture of safety and resilience (Government of Samoa, 2017b, pp. 10–11).

An all-hazard approach is essential. Planning processes, risk assessment and other tools necessary for *disaster preparedness, mitigation and response* are similar regardless of the nature of the hazard.

The capacity of the sectors must be enhanced to face all types of major risks, from epidemics, to natural disasters to technological accidents, well known risks to new or emerging threats. All sectors must build on existing expertise and capacity in all relevant departments and programs as well as outside guidance.

At the national level the ministries are the lead agencies which includes among others, the SRCS, non-governmental organizations, private sector, communities and development partners.

All phases of DRM require a multi-sectoral approach. At the national and local levels, reducing the impact of emergencies, disasters and other crises requires a multi-sectoral outlook. Proper land use management and design of housing or new health facilities may, for instance, contribute most to decreasing mortality and morbidity. The provision of public health services and medical care, for example, is dependent on the preparedness of other sectors such as: law and order, transport and communications, lifeline services (water and electricity) and public works, search and rescue, fire services, social services, housing etc.

At the international level, Samoa seeks the collaboration of international agencies, especially those with a specific mandate in managing the risks and promoting disaster preparedness at multi-sectoral level such as the United Nations' Development Programme, Office for the Coordination of Humanitarian Affairs, UNICEF, International Strategy for Disaster Reduction, the international and regional financial institutions donors, the International Federation of Red Cross and Red Crescent (IFRC) and relevant non-governmental organizations.

A tailored governance structure, which is consistent with whole-of-government governance policy, lays a solid foundation for management oversight by focussing capability and effort to efficiently and effectively implement programs and services in Samoa. Such support includes the development of strategies, norms and standards, advocacy and awareness building, capacity building and transfer of knowledge and management skills as well as the provision of technical advice. The structure should also be sufficiently flexible to enable timely responses to new responsibilities and challenges.

Sectoral Approach to DRM

Sectoral approach to DRM aimed at creating coherent and inclusive practices by mobilizing government agencies, civil societies, private sector, development partners and the community with common interests in a strategic manner.

Under the NDMO coordination role, the sector framework encourages communication and information sharing across agencies through each sector's coordination unit. The NDMO ensures sectors execute objectives and responsibilities to implement DRM according to plan.

The scope of activities proposed by each of the fourteen sectors was determined by issues and gaps, identified during the national situation analysis and consultation workshops with stakeholders and are considered priority issues for actions under the four phases of DRM.

To fulfil its obligations to the Sendai Framework for Disaster Risk Reduction 2015–2030 (UNISDR, 2015, p. 13), the Samoan Government strongly encouraged its agencies and organizations to:

- undertake DRM and climate change Capability Assessment to identify skills, tools, training and resources required in the areas of DRM and climate change adaptation
- identify measures leading to the strengthening of capacity in resilience;
- develop a risk-based multi-criteria assessment tool to assist the prioritization of DRR and CCA within and between sectors;

- develop DRM policies, plans, regulations, strategies and guidelines and submit to the NDMO for inclusion in the NDMP and other related policy documents;
- ensure incorporation of DRM measures in all their development policies;
- strengthen institutional, systemic and individual capacity and adequate skills development, succession planning and knowledge sharing to ensure continuity, and skills level are maintained for emergency and resilience planning;
- support sector coordinators to actively participate in DRM activities, coordinated by the NDMO;
- take part in ongoing DRM activities coordinated by the NDMO;
- mainstream DRM, CCA and other cross-cutting issues into sector planning;
- integrate DRM considerations in budgetary allocations and human resourcing;
- foster networks and cooperation between agencies to integrate DRM and CCA by sharing information, technology and professional expertise;
- plan and monitor DRM activities with national monitoring and evaluation tool.

The need to provide a strong coordination mechanism is to strengthen the institutional framework for collaboration and sharing of resources, expertise and tools, for effective DRM through *risk reduction, preparedness, response and recovery* (Table 17.1).

Whatever the scale of hazards, it is the local community that either suffers the brunt of, or survives from hazards' devastating effects. The population in affected communities is almost always the first responders, who manage the emergencies at the household and community level. By managing emergencies well, it prevents the escalation of these emergencies into disasters. This is acknowledged in the National Disaster Management Plan (Government of Samoa, 2017a, p. 20) where the role of the village in the plan is described below:

> The Village Council and village organisations are responsible for co-ordinating disaster mitigation and preparedness programs and activities at the community level, and for coordinating village response activities for specific threats. This role includes:

Table 17.1 Stakeholders' roles in prevention and preparedness

Stakeholders	Roles and responsibilities
National Disaster Council (Cabinet)	– High level oversight, policy and strategic guidance and direction for DRM implementation and institutional strengthening
Disaster Advisory Committee (DAC)	– Policy and planning oversight including the NDMP, DRM NAP and supporting documents, for approval of the NDC and Cabinet – Accountable for identification, implementation and Monitoring and Evaluation of DRM programs and activities
National Disaster Management Office (NDMO)	– Acts as secretariat for DRM and facilitate regular DAC meetings; – Convener of the National DRM Platform; – Follow up on NDMP implementation with stakeholders; – Facilitate reporting to NDC, DAC and development partners; – Provide technical guidance and direction for DRM and support in developing capacity; – Implement disaster prevention and preparedness programs in collaboration with response agencies, sectors, villages, private sector, NGOs and other stakeholders
Climate change division	– policy guidance and direction for CCA and capacity building; – works closely with NDMO to ensure mainstreaming of CCA into sector planning and budget systems

(continued)

I. Initiating Community Response;
II. Information Dissemination;
III. Shelter Management;
IV. Damage Assessment;
V. Relief Co-Ordination.

Table 17.1 (continued)

Stakeholders	Roles and responsibilities
Ministries, Agencies and local partners	– Ministries and agencies: Lead and facilitate the integration of NDMP and actions into Corporate Plans and budgets systems; – Local partners: Facilitate integration of NDMP actions into respective planning and budget systems; – Facilitate implementation of NDMP in coordination with DAC; – Ensure progress reporting on NDMP implementation through the National Monitoring and Evaluation framework; – Advocate for CCA, DRM and resilience
Community	– Support Framework implementation; – Participate in DRM and CCA decision-making; – Implementation of community disaster and climate risk reduction and preparedness measures; – Support the dissemination of public awareness on disaster resilience information; – Provide feedback to assist monitoring and evaluation to further improve DRM arrangements, systems, processes and programs
Development partners and donors	– All regional and international development partners and donors to liaise with NDMO, DAC, local stakeholders in support of the implementation of NDMP through DRM NAP activities and recommended DRM actions for each of the sectors to strengthen resilience

It is the role of the Ministry of Women, Community and Social Development (MWCSD), to support, monitor and liaise with Village Councils and organisations as they implement disaster management activities, and to keep the DAC informed of the level of village preparedness.

Moreover, it is the local community who are required to take measures to manage risk long before a hazard strikes.

Disasters are increasingly recognized as a threat to sustainable development, poverty reduction, achievement of the Millennium Development Goals and the implementation of the Sustainable Development Goals. Through its ongoing work with vulnerable urban households communities, the Samoa Red Cross has found that poor households are particularly vulnerable to negative shocks arising from disaster events for a number of reasons: The poor own fewer productive assets; are more likely to reside in hazardous locations and in substandard housing; and are primarily dependent on their own labour to meet their livelihood needs. Such risk profiles give them fewer options to cope with and recover from the loss of assets, or the death or disability of household members in the event of a disaster. It has been the experience of the Samoan Red Cross that in such situations, poor households may use sub-optimal or even harmful coping strategies such as reducing consumption expenditures on food, health and education or trying to increase incomes by sending children to work. This can have long-term implications in the form of negative human development impacts and lower future income streams, and thus poverty traps.

The importance of community-based participatory approaches is now generally recognized in the fields of disaster preparedness, mitigation and, increasingly, also in disaster response and recovery. The rationale for using participative approaches in disaster reduction is well known:

- Local communities are the first responders when a disaster happens. In the hours following a disaster search and rescue and provision of immediate assistance to the injured and homeless are almost entirely carried out by family members, relatives and neighbours. In the case of small-scale events, communities may be left entirely to their own devices, as there may be no external assistance available at all.
- Top-down disaster risk reduction programs often fail to address the specific vulnerabilities, needs and demands of at risk communities. These vulnerabilities and needs can only be identified through a process of direct consultation and dialogue with communities concerned, because communities understand local realities and contexts better than outsiders.
- Even the most vulnerable communities possess skills, knowledge, resources (materials, labour) and capacities. These assets are often overlooked and underutilized and, in some cases, even undermined by external actors.

It is therefore crucial that at risk communities are actively involved in the identification and analysis of the risks they are faced with and participate directly in the planning, design, implementation, monitoring and evaluation of disaster and climate risk activities.

Samoa has a very high number of climate risk related projects underway, focussing on reducing vulnerability to the impacts of climate change, particularly in the areas of forestry and agriculture, water, health, climate forecasting and meteorology. Greater attention is also given to addressing coastal resource management, fisheries and disaster risk reduction concerns (Beca International Consultants, 2001).

Gender equity has been considered a prominent component of any current adaptation project or proposed strategy (UN LDC Group 2015). The primary responses to managing the health risks of climate change are mitigation, reduction of human influence on the climate system, adaptation activities through designed projects for prevention, risk reduction and recovery. The morbidity profile of the population is tending towards non-communicable diseases, where strong primary health care, health education and nutrition programs have an important preventative role to play, as there is increasing concern surrounding high levels of non-communicable diseases and related health issues in the country, and the costs involved with addressing these problems (Table 17.2).

The NDMP is based on the innovative utilization of resources and effective coordination of government agencies, civil societies, villages, private sector and development partners in support of DRM. Key stakeholders include: government ministries and agencies which have been allocated management related roles and responsibilities; community government representatives (village mayors, women and youth representatives) in conjunction with the MWCSD; village disaster and climate committees and emergency response teams; NGOs and Samoa Red Cross Society (SRCS); the private sector and overseas Missions, development partners and organizations which are engaged in rendering assistance to the Government of Samoa when a disaster situation arises.

It is also recognized that the most vulnerable people in disasters are often women, children, the elderly and people with disabilities that are most severely affected (IFRC, 2021), and are drawing attention of the humanitarian sector to providing them appropriate assistance according to their immediate needs being identified in the outcomes of initial disaster assessments (IDA).

Table 17.2 Stakeholders' roles in response and recovery

Health and medical

Response function	Lead agency	Roles and responsibilities
First Aid	SRCS	Provide first aid training and first aid services to injured people
Transport & movement of casualties	NHS	Provide ambulance, medical triage and evacuation teams
Medical treatment	NHS	Provide medical therapy, treatments, medical team members and resources. Ensure hospitals & health services are in operation and resourced
Public health	MoH	Coordinate PH response, advise and resources into the control of the spread of diseases
Management of deceased victims	MoP	Manage identification and handling transportation of deceased victims personal effects, reconciliation and notify next of kin
Mortuary services	MJCA	Provide mortuary services
Counselling and support	NHS	Provide PSS services to those affected by emergency and disasters
Search and rescue		
Land search	MoP	Coordinate search for the missing people on land; provide needs and resources
Land rescue (e.g. structural collapse and accidents)	FESA	Coordinate rescue of People. Provide needs and resources
Maritime search/rescue (vessels & air craft in sea)	MWTI, Maritime SPA	Provide "On Scene Commander" and Coordinate maritime rescue activities
Evacuation		
Evacuation of people	MNRE NDMO MoP	Determine if evacuation is required; give warning to trigger evacuation by activating siren system

(continued)

Table 17.2 (continued)

Health and medical

Response function	Lead agency	Roles and responsibilities
	MoP FESA Village ERT	Evacuate areas required for public safety and at risk areas within villages
Community welfare		
Registration evacuees	NEOC logistics unit	Identify and record information on affected people by the disaster
Temporary shelter	NEOC logistics unit	Establish shelters for the Evacuees
Disaster food	NEOC logistics unit	Coordinate and provide emergency food supply for affected population
Disaster clothing	NEOC logistics unit	Coordinate emergency clothing supplies to affected population
Animal welfare	APS	Provide facilities, supplies for wellbeing of animals affected by disasters
Finances		
Disaster finances	MoF	Coordinate collection, allocation and provision of monetary aid to those affected by the disaster
Logistics supplies		
Incoming resources	NEOC logistics unit	Coordinate and prioritize resources (human and physical) required in response to the situations; – procurement payment, – access, staging; – distribution and return of resources if necessary
Information management		
Public information	NEOC	Provide information to Public on ER & actions they must take to: – disseminate warnings to alert and monitor agencies – appoint spokespeople for emergency events

(continued)

Table 17.2 (continued)

Health and medical

Response function	Lead agency	Roles and responsibilities
Communication Between response agencies and Sectors	MNRE (NDMO)	Ensure communication systems are in place for communication purpose Create communication protocols and reporting processes
Impact assessment		
Reconnaissance and needs assessment	NEOC	Coordinate reconnaissance of affected areas and disseminate information to response agencies. Identify assessment teams and provide necessary support, tools equipment and systems
Building safety evaluations	MWTI building structure	Coordinate assessment of damaged structures if they can be fixed, to ensure safety to occupy
Building health assessment	MoH	Coordinate assessment of structures against health problems if they are to be reoccupied
Utility services impacts	NEOC	Assess damage to utility services. Take actions to quickly restore services
Access impacts - roads	MWTI - Roads	Assess damage to road networks and quickly restore transportation
Access restoration - air	SAA	Assess damage to air transport networks and quickly restore services
Access restoration - marine	MWTI Maritime	Assess damage to Marine transportation networks and quickly restore facilities and services
Environmental impact	MNRE	Coordinate assessment of impacts on air, coastal land, water and report to NDC/DAC

(continued)

Table 17.2 (continued)

Health and medical		
Response function	Lead agency	Roles and responsibilities
Agriculture impact	MAF	Coordinate assessment of impacts on agriculture, fisheries & resources, to identify food needs of affected people Liaise with food safety cluster
Impact on education	MESC	Coordinate, lead initial assessment on schools and education Provide tools, equipment and assessment teams and liaise with Education Sector partners

ROLE OF THE SAMOA RED CROSS SOCIETY IN DRM

SRCS is a major player in DRM in Samoa. It has been mandated for this role in an MoU signed with the Government of Samoa (GoS) in 1983, officially recognizing it as a voluntary relief society, auxiliary to the public authorities in the humanitarian field, and as the only Red Cross Society operating in Samoa. This means that the SRCS has a legal status and distinctive relationship with the government by mobilizing and organizing civilian populations to work with the authorities in a neutral and impartial manner to alleviate human suffering in emergencies and situations of particular vulnerability.

This provision further elaborates the independence and autonomous nature of the SRCS in order to respond immediately when an emergency or disaster arise. The ongoing implementation of the SRCS Disaster Preparedness program and its immediate response when disasters strike Samoa has earned for itself the respect and confidence of government, the International Red Cross and Red Crescent Movement and the International Donor Community.

Disaster Risk Reduction

Disasters occur when natural or technological hazards have an impact on human beings and their environment. We have experienced that, those who have more resources, often have a greater capacity to withstand effects of a hazard than the poorer members of a society (IFRC, 2000). Rapid population growth, urban migration, inequitable patterns of land ownership, lack of education and awareness and subsistence agriculture on lease-hold lands lead to vulnerable conditions such as unsafe siting of buildings and settlements, overcrowded homes, unhealthy environment, malnutrition, deforestation, unemployment and illiteracy (IFRC, 2000).

SRCS's approach to planning risk reduction and emergency response measures, always starts by understanding the nature and probability of occurrences of hazards our people face, through assessing societal elements at risk (people, structures, services and activities) due to these hazards, if and when they occur. Engagement with villagers has allowed SRCS to have a solid grasp of communities' specific vulnerabilities and capacities, which help them to effectively choose and design meaningful risk reduction measures that best utilize and build on communities' strengths further, while reducing their vulnerabilities. This way, communities understand how they perceive the identified risks and what importance they place, on reduction of specific risks.

Where literacy and access to the media and other sources of information are limited, people lack knowledge and/or awareness of the hazards that threaten them. Loss of traditional knowledge of local threats can also reduce hazard awareness over time. On the other hand, our village people found it difficult to understand the technical knowledge involved in media awareness and weather bulletins. The SRCS has provided assistance to our communities, by simply translating the technical information in local language, so they can easily learn the concepts of our awareness messages, and understand the literature beyond being able to respond more effectively when emergencies and disasters arise.

The basic objective of the National Building Code of Samoa is to ensure acceptable standards of structural sufficiency, fire safety, health, amenity and response to the impacts of climate change, are provided so that buildings facilities and sites are constructed, maintained and demolished in a safe and environmentally responsible manner.

International Disaster Response Law (IDRL)—What is often overlooked, is the area of legal preparedness. Without the appropriate legal instruments to deal with disaster response, authorities can be overwhelmed by relief operations and vital aid can be delayed from reaching the vulnerable people who need it most. The chances of small island nations requiring international assistance in the aftermath of a disaster is very high, they are small, isolated states, susceptible to climate change, sea level rise, natural and environmental disasters with limited capacities. Managing such assistance can be extremely challenging. Unintended red tapes can tie aid efforts in knots, with urgently needed goods stuck behind "business as usual" procedures. On the other hand, gaps in national oversight over international efforts in the chaotic atmosphere after a disaster can result in poor quality, poor coordination and poor accountability. Very often, we see both types of problems in the same operation.

Disaster Preparedness

Knowing what to do and having appropriate skills, supplies and equipment to do it with, increase the chance of survival and limit damage when disasters arise. In many widespread disasters, people may need two weeks of supplies to get by till water, electricity and telecommunications are turned back on. If there are serious physical injuries, help will probably not arrive in time, unless people have some basic first aid skills on how to stop bleeding, clean a wound, or prevent a collapse due to poor or weakened health conditions. These preparedness knowledge and skills, need to be practised time and time again, through well-structured emergency and disaster programs, including regular drill exercises.

The extent of the SRCS relief program depends on the magnitude of the disaster, the needs already covered by others and the responsibilities delegated by the government or by the national relief plan. SRCS aims to respond to disasters more effectively by mobilizing appropriate resources (volunteers, funds and relief supplies etc.), and using its community-based network in a coordinated manner so that initial hazardous effects are countered and immediate needs of affected communities are met.

SRCS also endeavours to obtain from government an exemption from all taxes and custom duties concerning, the entry into and transit through the country, of funds and relief supplies intended for the victims of disasters. It further seeks to obtain travel facilities and quick granting of travel visas for RCRC personnel entering to assist in the relief operation. The IFRC also continues to work with all our 192 governments to recognise the International Disaster Response Law (IDRL) guidelines they helped create, to help improve delayed responses to the most affected population.

Disaster Response

SRCS in its endeavour to prevent and alleviate human suffering, considers it a fundamental right of all people to both offer and receive humanitarian assistance. Hence it has a fundamental duty to provide relief to all disaster victims and assistance to those most vulnerable to future disasters.

SRCS recognizes that in helping disaster victims to survive, relief programs must look to the future and ensure that people are not be left more vulnerable to the future disasters. Relief programs should attempt to build upon the capacities of those being assisted, involve them in the management and implementation of program activities and act with a sense of accountability towards the beneficiaries.

Red Cross assistance to victims is given without any distinction as to sex, nationality, race, religion, social condition or political opinion. It is made available solely on the basis of the relative importance or urgency of individual needs. Its relief is administered with economy, efficiency and effectiveness as in reporting, audited accounts of income and expenditure reflecting a true and fair view of the operation.

Disaster Recovery

Many Samoan families who have lived along the coastal areas of the country, are now moving inland because their homes have been either lost or damaged from impacts of climate change and natural disasters such as storm surges and river flows. Others are faced with water and sanitation needs, lost livelihoods and experienced food shortages. SRCS helps to train members of the vulnerable communities and households on appropriate life skills they must possess in order to cope with similar problems affecting their health, livelihoods and environment.

DRR also encompasses food security, and SRCS community-based volunteers assist to teach community members on agricultural skills and provide materials to establish vegetable gardens to help supplement their healthy diets and boost their income through selling surplus produce at local markets.

Rainwater Harvesting (RWH), is a simple technique that offers many benefits. It uses basic technology at an affordable cost, which is applicable at small scale with a minimum specific expertise and knowledge. Rainwater is collected on the house roof and transported with gutters through an attached "first flush" system into a water tank storage where it collects relatively clean water for households' healthy consumption.

Ventilated Improved Pit (VIP) latrines, offer improved sanitation by eliminating flies and smell through air circulation exiting from air vents and further advancement made to the rest of the system. The implementation involved the installation of VIP latrine super structures including, dug pits with straight sides and flat bases and the super structure; with the attached hand-wash device.

Time and again we have seen how the chaotic atmosphere after a disaster can result in poor hygiene conditions having the potential for diseases outbreaks, but recovery phase through various means of assistance can provide the best to achieve DRM purposes, alleviate human suffering and save lives.

Priority Actions

Improving local capacity to respond to disasters and public health emergencies.

In future disasters, the NEOC is responsible for signalling the shift from one operational mode to another as the situation unfolds. Inter-sector and multi-sectoral coordination will continue to be provided by the DAC members according to the NDMP. Rapid assessments will be conducted within the first 72 hours as an inter-sectoral exercise involving a mix of specialists, and according to the severity of a disaster and the damage done, to ensure security and safety of the responding team members. Community trained ERT members, will be in immediate action, according to their respective roles and responsibilities, and when it is safe to do so. Outcomes of the rapid assessments will identify the sources and consequences of the situation that will assist in determining if response strategies are to be mounted.

Scaling up actions with vulnerable communities in health promotion, disease prevention and disaster risk reduction.

Efforts to strengthen mainstreaming of DRR across sectors, include systematic and visible integration of commitments to gender equality and women's empowerment, disability, human rights, building on the existing body of knowledge concerning recommendation, guidelines and best practices for sector specific gender mainstreaming. For "gender", each sector plan will elaborate on specific cross-cutting actions as such in their respective areas through gender-sensitive policymaking, monitoring and evaluation and integrating gender in vulnerability, risk and capacity assessments, to also consider female participation and leadership in disaster management and promoting systematic collection and use of sex and age disaggregated data and gender analysis.

Renewing and increasing programming and advocacy on priority humanitarian issues, especially fighting intolerance, stigma and discrimination and promoting DRR.

Risks and Challenges

The numbers and diversity of international responders have continued to challenge the ability of affected island nations to effectively facilitate and regulate aids. Therefore, the need for legal preparedness to address these challenges and ensure swift and effective aid to affected communities is as high as ever.

Risks

- frequent and severe disasters;
- frequent quakes in the region may activate dormant volcano in years;
- great DRM systems not usually practised by several stakeholders;
- several sector coordination units are not proactive enough in DRM;
- non-traditional actors, new to disaster response have entered the field in disasters and created frustrations among local actors;
- ongoing developing infrastructure.
- over regulations in some areas lead to unnecessary bureaucratic bottlenecks slowing entry and distribution of relief for those in urgent need;
- disproportionate allocations of financial resources among DRM stakeholders;
- great communication and technology could not withstand hazard impacts;
- totally new change of leadership in the NDMO and several government offices.

Conclusions and Recommendations

Conclusions

As with all issues related to disaster preparedness, it can be difficult to prioritize the strengthening of laws and procedures for future, hypothetical events, particularly in countries that have not recently experienced major disasters or significant complications around international assistance in the past. However, for anyone who thought that the world would never see an event as devastating as the 2004 Indian Ocean tsunami, or an international response as large and as challenging as the one following that calamity, these have supplied some powerful rejoinders. The Haiti earthquake has clearly demonstrated the life-saving benefits and significant difficulties of enormous international response operations. The 2009 tsunami in Samoa; the Japan earthquake, tsunami and the nuclear emergency, has further shown the potential for even the world's most prepared countries both to require outside assistance and to be challenged to manage an abundance of offers. Many other disasters on all five continents have likewise proven that all states have a stake in making themselves prepared.

With the adoption of the Sendai Framework for DRR in 2015 and in view of the pending entry into force of the Paris Agreement in 2020, the IFRC's Disaster Law Program has also received an increasing number of requests from States to provide recommendations to facilitate integration between wider governance arrangements in normative frameworks, e.g. the National Adaptation Plan (NAP) processes of the Paris Agreement and the risk reduction strategy process of the Sendai Framework (Target E). In this regard, it was proposed that the IFRC International Conference adopt a resolution on climate smart disaster laws and policies that leave no one behind. The resolution will encourage States to strengthen legal and policy frameworks for disaster preparedness and response with support from their National Societies such as the SRCS, as appropriate. It will also call for recognition of:—the importance of integrating the protection and inclusion of vulnerable groups into relevant disaster laws and policies in order to ensure that no one is left behind,—the advantages of a joined-up approach in policy and institutional arrangements for DRM and climate change adaptation,—the new "Checklist on law and disaster preparedness and response" as a useful nonbinding tool for analysis (IFRC, 2019).

Yet ensuring the protection and security of the most vulnerable, at risk and disaster-affected populations is crucial to effective DRM. Therefore, innovative guidance and recommendations are needed to provide support to States to address the main protection gaps and challenges in disaster law and policies.

REFERENCES

Beca International Consultants Ltd. (2001). *Coastal infrastructure management project: CIM strategy*. Prepared for Government of Samoa. https://www.sprep.org/att/IRC/eCOPIES/countries/samoa/56.pdf

Disaster and Emergency Management Act (2007) (Samoa). https://www.ifrc.org/Docs/idrl/678EN.pdf

Fakhruddin, S. H. M., Babel, M. S., & Kawasaki, A. (2015). Assessing the vulnerability of infrastructure to climate change on the Islands of Samoa. *Natural Hazards Earth System Science, 15*, 1343–1356. https://doi.org/10.5194/nhess-15-1343-2015

Geneva Convention Act. (2015) (Samoa). https://www.palemene.ws/wp-content/uploads/01.Acts/Acts%202015/Geneva-Conventions-Act-2015-Eng.pdf

Government of Samoa. (2017a). *National disaster management plan, 2017–2020*. https://samoa-data.sprep.org/system/files/Samoa-national-disaster-management-plan-2017-2020-final-web.pdf

Government of Samoa. (2017b). *National action plan for disaster risk management, 2017–2021*. https://samoa-data.sprep.org/system/files/Samoa-national-action-plan-for-DRM-2017-2021-final-web.pdf

IFRC. (2000). *Introduction to disaster preparedness*. Disaster Preparedness Training Program, Participant Resource & Learning Module. https://www.ifrc.org/Global/Publications/disasters/all.pdf

IFRC. (2019). *Disaster laws and policies that leave no one behind—Resolution 7*. 33rd International Conference of the Red Cross and Red Crescent, Geneva, Switzerland, 9–12 December. https://rcrcconference.org/app/uploads/2019/12/33IC_R7-Disaster-Law-resolution-adopted-EN-1.pdf

IFRC. (2020) *The fundamental principles of the red cross and red crescent Movement*. https://www.icrc.org/en/fundamental-principles

IFRC. (2021). *What is vulnerability?* https://www.ifrc.org/en/what-we-do/disaster-management/about-disasters/what-is-a-disaster/what-is-vulnerability/

Pacific Community. (2016). *Framework for resilient development in the pacific, 2017–2030*. Voluntary Guidelines for the Pacific Islands Region. Retrieved from http://tep-a.org/wp-content/uploads/2017/05/FRDP_2016_finalResilient_Dev_pacific.pdf

Samoa Red Cross Act. (1993). (Samoa). http://www.paclii.org/ws/legis/con sol_act/srca1993158/

UN. (2005). *Hyogo Framework for Action 2005–2015: Building the resilience of nations and communities to disasters*, 22 January 2005, A/CONF.206/6. Retrieved 5 January 2021 from https://www.refworld.org/docid/42b98a 704.html

UN General Assembly. (2014). *SIDS Accelerated Modalities of Action (SAMOA) Pathway*. Retrieved 5 January 2021 from https://sustainabledevelopment.un. org/samoapathway.html

UN General Assembly. (2015). *Transforming our world: The 2030 agenda for sustainable development*. https://sustainabledevelopment.un.org/post2015/ transformingourworld/publication

UNISDR. (2015). *Sendai framework for disaster risk reduction 2015–2030*. Retrieved 5 January 2021 from https://www.undrr.org/publication/sendai-framework-disaster-risk-reduction-2015-2030

CHAPTER 18

Towards a Resilient Asia Pacific Region

*Vinod Sharma, Helen James, Rajib Shaw,
and Anna Lukasiewicz*

Introduction

Disaster risk reduction is getting priority in most countries since the signing of the Sendai Framework for Disaster Risk Reduction (SFDRR) in 2015. As most of the Sustainable Development Goals, signed by these countries, lead to DRR, the subject is getting more importance in development planning. It is a known fact that mortality has declined considerably after SFDRR and thus one of the main objectives is being met. However, economic losses have increased because of the frequency of hazards and their magnitude. Naturally triggered disasters are closely

---

V. Sharma
Indian Institute of Public Administration, New Delhi, India

H. James · A. Lukasiewicz (✉)
Australian National University, Canberra, ACT, Australia
e-mail: anna.lukasiewicz@anu.edu.au

R. Shaw
Keio University, Tokyo, Japan
e-mail: shaw@sfc.keio.ac.jp

related with development. In developing countries, if development is not well planned, it is an invitation to disasters. Nature cannot be cruel to mankind and gives us enough resources to survive and grow, but human greed converts it into calamity. Mahatma Gandhi stated that *'Nature has enough for everybody's need but not for their greed'*. It is known that the geographical setting of Asia and the Pacific makes the region highly vulnerable for disasters. The other two factors, poverty and population, add in to increasing vulnerability of the region. Few other parameters such as low literacy rate, gender engagement and empowerment, and poor governance also increase the vulnerability for disasters. There is considerable growth in urban areas in Asia, which is unplanned and unsafe, which has increased vulnerability of most of the cities. In India, every monsoon season, most of the cities face flash floods, and landslides in hilly towns.

The IDNDR from 1990 to 2000 was eye opener for all developed and developing countries. In most of the Asian countries, where disaster management was relief centric, there is a paradigm shift towards disaster preparedness and mitigation was required to save human life loss, their economies and environmental damage. In some countries the losses from disasters were more than 2–3% of their GDP. Hyogo Framework gave momentum to making national and local level plans and gave disaster preparedness and mitigation as one of the main priorities. The third International Conference on Disaster Management in Sendai resulted in the Sendai Framework with goals, priorities and targets on which more than 197 countries are working. Though most of the countries developed national level plans, but local level plans are still not there as adequately functional and effective. These countries are working to mainstream DRR in development process. Climate change is another big factor which increased vulnerability to Hydro-meteorological hazards throughout the world. The unprecedented weather events made most cities vulnerable to flash floods and related disasters. Climate change has more impact on small island countries. The impact is visible in all developed and developing countries. The Sendai Framework, SDGs and Paris Agreement, if properly analyzed, give lots of overlapping inputs and raise the need to make an 'Integrated Disaster Risk Reduction Plan'. Similar plans at local level can be more effective for sustainable growth and DRR. In the context of climate change and global pandemic 'Covid-19' disaster expert should work on complex and multiple disasters. The concept of disaster preparedness and response should be seen in the worst-case scenario, as the world is facing today. There were number of big events in South

East Asia during this period. A number of cyclones, floods, flash floods and droughts gave another challenge to the DRR experts in working on multiple and complex disasters. Many countries are still facing forest fires and the pandemic at the same time. Multi-hazard preparedness, disaster education, capacity building, use of science and technology and post disaster recovery are the main aspects covered in the book.

Book Structure

The book has four parts and 18 chapters including an Introduction and Conclusion, written by well-known experts working in the area of Disaster Risk Reduction (DRR). The book is dedicated to one of the champions of DRR and renowned scientist and researcher, Prof. Helen James, who organized an international conference in 2018 at Australian National University and invited more than 100 experts and researchers to contribute to the event. Few selected people were asked to contribute chapters which are incorporated in the book.

The four parts of the book are more or less as per the priorities of the Sendai Framework. The first part on Risk Governance is crucial as Government is the main stakeholder in DRR. Knowing risk and mainstreaming it into development is very much required. Risk governance is required at every level (regional, national, provincial and local). Understanding the underlying causes of disaster vulnerability and concept of risk is important to build 'Risk Reduction' in day to day governance.

Governance

As environment and disasters do not recognize political boundaries, regional cooperation is very important. Initiatives by ASEAN and SAARC countries in regional cooperation are good examples but their sustenance is possible only if all member countries recognize the importance of DRR. The ASEAN countries are progressing well, whereas SAARC cooperation in DRR is not that effective because risk reduction requires similar understanding, proper funding and due investments from all partner countries. Similarly, non-governmental organizations (NGOs) and other civil society players also play an important role in DRR. The civil society and private sectors should be inducted in all DRR initiatives. The national plans prepared by most countries should be linked with provincial, city, village level DRR plan.

Most of the developed countries are going up to family and individual level plans. Earlier, local community and volunteers had a very prominent role in providing early warning even in response, and this should be encouraged in disaster prone countries and should get proper recognition in the system. There is a need to revise the plans on regular basis and develop capacity for proper implementation. In case there are different plans for DRR, Climate Change, implementation of SDGs, developmental schemes, then all the plans can be merged into one integrated plan. The national plans should be linked with sub national (provincial) and local level plans for their effectiveness.

Most of the time the top down approach is there in development and DRR but experts find that the bottom up approach is more sustainable and effective (Chapter 2). The involvement of indigenous community in planning gave much better results in New Zealand (Chapter 3). They developed 'Maori Disaster Management' theory and implementation of disaster preparedness and response by participation of indigenous community and local government. Similar observations in Australia, where Aboriginal governance and disaster management plans for fire and other disaster were more effective (Chapter 5). Integrated approach in disaster preparedness, mitigation, response and recovery, where all stakeholders, public, private, civil, army, police, civil defence, work together will give much better results in domestic and offshore disasters (Chapter 4). In DRR involvement and participation of all stakeholders and their coordination assists administration to face any kind of calamity. Indigenous knowledge and past practices should be documented and part of disaster planning.

EDUCATION AND CAPACITY

DRR education and capacity building are pillars of effective Disaster Resilience. DRR education can be started from primary education and continue up to higher and technical education. In India, a school safety program was launched for all the states of the country with two objectives, assessing school vulnerability for natural hazards and giving disaster education to the students. They should understand their risk and think of risk reduction. The program got momentum throughout the country and some of the states are spending money and extended the program to all schools of the state for risk reduction and to educate children, teachers and parents about DRR. This kind of national programs are very good way to educate the community and involve them in the process. There is responsibility of school teachers and principals before, during and after disaster.

In Chapter 8, an analysis is made of the role of educators in various situations in the post-disaster phase. The study is very interesting as their role get changed in changing situations of disasters. Similarly, identification and capacity building of various stakeholders is important for effective management. This can also be started from the foundation courses of the civil administrators and should be part of in-service training as well. As dimensions of disaster risk are changing every day, every season and every year, updated knowledge and innovative practices are required by the DRR practitioners. Community is one of the most important stakeholders. Public awareness and regular mock drills are an important component of capacity building. Empowering people by educating them that if they live in harmony with nature, it will lead to disaster resilience for the villages and towns will provide them a sustainable habitat (Chapter 6).

Public awareness with socio-cultural media and art can be very effective way for education in most of the countries (Chapter 7). Folk songs and art work are still used in flood and cyclone prone states in India. The traditional way of understanding disaster vulnerability and risk is a simple and acceptable method of building capacity of the affected community. Media has a very important role in DRR throughout the globe. Now social media commands more attention from the younger generation and is available to most people. In recent disasters in Asia, use of social media like Facebook, WhatsApp groups and Twitter was widely applied in providing relief, shelter, and even in rescuing people. Social media is being widely used in giving weather forecasts, early warning, giving helpline numbers during emergencies and even in response. Thus social media is a very good means of public education and training to volunteers working in DRR.

In higher studies, disaster risk reduction is included in a number of universities throughout the world. In India and Philippines, new MBA courses are launched where focus is not only on finance, accounting, human resource management etc., but also on disaster risk, risk analysis, risk reduction, risk transfer, risk management, economics of disasters, cost benefit analysis and change management. Chapter 10 is a case study of such a course in the Philippines. In India, all the technical institutions and medical colleges are giving disaster education after 2005 and this will give long term advantage to the country. There are number of universities giving master's degree in disaster management. Even all research institutions of science and technology is giving emphasis of DRR. Though, first aid training was started by Red Cross long back but even knowledge of other medical emergencies and mental health is required for all stakeholders. During Covid-19, people suffered from the virus but equal number of people suffered from mental health issues such as acute depression.

SCIENCE AND TECHNOLOGY

Science and technology application in DRR also gained momentum after the Sendai Framework. The UN started the UN Science Technology Academia Advisory Group (STAAG) and in Asia, Asia Science Technology and Academia Advisory Group (ASTAAG) contributed a lot in sensitizing countries to the importance of science, technology and innovation in DRR and involved the private sector in the process. The S&T application is required at every stage of Disaster Risk Management from the pre-disaster phase, at the time of disaster and post disaster reconstruction, rehabilitation and recovery. There are a number of examples of countries investing in technology for strengthening early warning system and which could save human lives and economic losses. In cyclone forecasting, warning and giving accurate data about wind speed, direction and accuracy in landfall has saved millions of people in last decade alone. In 2020 two cyclones, Amphan and Nisarg remained as a hazard only and could not turn into disaster because of use of appropriate technology. Similarly, flood forecasting and warning system in most of flood prone countries are most of time 99.9% accurate.

Chapter 12 deals with use of science and technology in flood risk management. If we include social science also, the scope will be much bigger. If DRR is part of the social system, culture of disaster preparedness, culture of mitigation, culture of quick response will get inducted in society's cultural ethos, and disaster risk management will become simpler for the authorities dealing with DRR (Chapter 13). The combination of science and technology and people's participation is the key of success in DRR. In case local traditional wisdom is also included, it will help address long term recovery of the affected community in a self-driven way. Chapter 14 discusses the case study of a small northern state of India,

Sikkim. Here post disaster reconstruction and rehabilitation were taken as an opportunity for building disaster resilience in the state.

Recovery

Post disaster recovery should include some important aspects of disaster preparedness and mitigation. If the process is participatory and transparent, the recovery process takes less time. Reconstruction is a good means of educating people about safe construction and principles of disaster resilience. The forth priority of the Sendai Framework is to strengthen preparedness for response and 'Build Back Better', which is discussed in chapters 14 and 16. There are policies, plans, techno-legal regime, but their implementation is possible if there is ownership and acceptance by the community. This is only possible in disaster recovery phase. The concept of post disaster recovery is a very big subject and comparatively new in many countries but this is getting place in national plans as frequency of disasters are increasing because of climate change and unplanned growth in urban and rural areas. Each disaster provides a unique opportunity for sustainable development and to make resilient infrastructure. India is advocating for a resilient infrastructure fund that may be created on regional basis as part of regional cooperation in DRR. Japan is a unique example of post disaster reconstruction and investing in mitigation programs. In Chapter 15, lessons learned from Japan and Indonesia in disaster recovery are discussed. There are many things other countries can learn from them. Chapter 16 is on 'owner driven approach' in disaster reconstruction which is accepted widely but takes a long time in implementation. Chapter 17 is a detailed case study of disaster recovery in Samoa after a Tsunami in 2009 in which various aspects of coordination between different stakeholders and community are discussed.

Concluding Remark

South East Asia is a living laboratory for natural disasters. Each year people face a number of big disasters. In case we have proper documentation of each such disaster and share the lessons learned, each country can benefit. Data sharing, use of new scientific knowledge, academic course contents developed by various universities and technical institutions, training modules developed for various disasters and different stakeholders, innovations in early warning systems, new construction technology, setting up of a common research fund for disaster research in Asia are a few suggestions for regional cooperation in DRR. In case there is proper mainstreaming of DRR in different sectors of governance such as agriculture, forestry, environmental management, livestock management, and DRR is part of all development schemes, it can save human lives and economic losses. Keeping the Sendai Framework as a central point in national and sub national schemes, highly vulnerable countries can become disaster resilient in a span of 10–20 years. Each disaster is specific and people, their perceptions, experiences, governance, scientific knowledge, education, preparedness level and response cannot be the same. This is a learning opportunity for the community and all stakeholders. There is always need of scientific literature on natural disasters, their origin, impact and community recovery.

Index

A
adaptive capacity
  assessment, 194, 195
  institutional, 197
adaptive leadership, 62
Afghanistan, 58
agriculture, 177, 308, 309, 356, 360, 361, 376
all-hazards approach, 8, 56, 183, 350
altruism, 254
anxiety, 129, 176
arts, 123, 124, 142, 143, 285, 294
  Indigenous, 78, 82, 110, 136, 285
  painting, 101, 103, 110, 131, 132
  performing, 4, 140, 152
  song, 10, 49, 124–126, 373
  visual, 10, 130, 131, 133, 138, 140
Asia Pacific, 2, 3
Australia, 20, 32, 33, 56–59, 63–65, 67, 71, 74, 130, 131, 133, 156, 178, 180, 182, 294, 295, 307, 372
  Aboriginal communities, 72, 86, 88
  disaster policy, 20, 31, 183
  emergency management, 24, 38, 175–180
  Indigenous peoples, 107–109, 143

B
beliefs, 10, 98, 99, 101, 103, 110, 113, 117, 118, 124, 125, 131, 132, 135, 138, 139, 142, 217
Bourdieu, P., 46, 261, 262, 265
Build Back Better, 7, 13, 274, 279, 286, 287, 291, 294, 309, 310, 312, 325, 375

C
Canada, 38, 63, 236
capability, 47, 58, 60, 62, 113, 180
  of communities, 217
  of government, 64, 351
  of Indigenous communities, 89
  planning, 180–182
capacity, 4
  adaptive, 114, 191, 198, 328, 329

building, 5, 8, 13, 281, 283, 341, 342, 350, 351, 371–373
community, 87, 131, 133, 140, 179, 182, 224, 282
coping, 191, 195, 197–199
emergency services, 86
government, 7, 57, 66
local, 87, 88, 182, 364
operational, 24
climate change adaptation, 2, 190, 193, 195, 351, 366
collaborative disaster management, 43–45
collective efficacy, 141
commons, 257, 264
communitas, 12, 251–255, 258, 259, 263
community
  participation, 4, 6, 141, 314, 341
community based disaster management, 254
community engagement, 76, 86, 138, 139, 223, 241, 297
community resources, 218, 294, 298, 316
Community Risk Register, 283
complex operations, 58, 60
corrosive communities, 252, 259, 264
cosmology, 75, 99, 100, 108, 113
COVID-19, 2, 7, 8, 257, 296, 370, 374
crisis, 56, 255, 296
  ecological, 115
  existential, 100
  financial, 312
  management, 57
  mental health, 167
  planning, 67
  response, 9, 56, 57, 60, 66
crowdfunding, 293–296, 299, 305, 307–309, 311, 312, 314–316
cultural capital, 217, 265

cultural disconnection, 142
cultural diversity, 51, 140
cultural norms, 76, 293
cultural practices, 40
cultural reconnection, 142
cultural regeneration, 134, 140
cultural reintegration, 130, 143
cultural values, 40, 109
culture
  tribal, 41, 134, 135
  Western, 98, 100–103, 113, 117

D
digitisation, 59, 62
disaster
  catastrophic, 11, 45, 47, 148, 175–178, 180–182, 237, 244
  humanitarian, 55
  law, 3, 361, 363, 366, 367
  policy, 9, 20, 21, 30
disaster housing, 292
disaster recovery processes, 133, 138, 293
disaster risk reduction, 2
  education, 4
  health sector, 8
  policies, 214
disciplinary silos, 12, 244
disempower, 98, 103, 104, 117

E
earthquakes, 130, 132, 134, 161, 176, 178, 187, 201, 219, 238, 256, 264, 274, 292, 324, 347
  Canterbury, 39, 40, 45, 147, 148, 153, 179, 260
  Kobe, 314
economic capital, 217, 265
ecosystem approach, 282
education
  Indigenous, 111

INDEX 379

embedded economy, 293, 314, 316, 317
emotion/emotional, 110, 112, 125, 157, 165, 310
  catharsis, 141
  crisis, 103, 117
  impacts, 127, 128150
  needs, 150
  recovery, 151
  support, 254
  wellbeing, 133, 162, 167
empowerment, 10, 87, 99, 107, 110, 112, 118, 127, 256, 265, 279, 281–283, 286, 340, 364, 370, 373
entrepreneurship, 189, 205, 293, 295, 299, 313, 316
environmental capital, 218
environmental hazards, 124, 142
ethnomusicology, 140
extreme floods, 234–237, 239

F
farming, 299, 300, 303–305
fatalism, 127, 129, 130, 138
fire, 5, 32, 33, 38, 76, 77, 85, 126, 127, 133, 161, 168, 177, 178, 182, 294, 350, 361, 372
  Aboriginal management, 10, 72, 75, 79, 85, 89
  management, 23, 27, 76, 77
forestry, 356, 376

H
harmony, 10, 98, 99, 107–113, 116, 118, 301, 373
health, 8, 30, 31, 112, 113, 117, 167, 177, 259, 265, 324, 328, 349, 350, 355–364, 374
helping, 11, 58, 65, 129, 164, 168, 261, 262, 265, 363

higher education, 4, 11, 188, 189, 193, 204
historical hydrology, 240, 241, 243
housing affordability, 30, 265
housing reconstruction, 273
human capital, 38, 58, 62

I
identity, 46, 48, 50, 88, 106, 112, 130, 135, 296
India, 13, 239, 271, 273, 274, 285, 325, 331, 333, 334, 341, 370, 372–375
Indigenous knowledge, 82, 114, 372
Indonesia, 13, 236, 292–297, 299, 300, 302–305, 312, 313, 316, 375
inter-faith relations, 296, 301
international conflict response, 58
Iwi Management Plans, 41, 42

J
Japan, 3, 4, 13, 148, 152–154, 156, 157, 161, 164, 166, 177, 204, 292–294, 297–299, 306–309, 311, 314–316, 366, 375
  Great East Japan Earthquake, 4, 262, 263
joined-up government, 59, 67

L
leadership, 59–61, 65, 77
  effective, 59, 348
  Indigenous, 77, 79
  strategic, 67
  training, 46
  transformational, 130
lessons analysis, 59

M

Māori, 9, 37, 39, 40, 43–51, 142
mass-casualty disasters, 56
Master of Business Administration, 189, 200
Merapi, 221
  disaster, 299, 301, 302
  eruptions, 300, 301, 305, 316
  recovery, 302, 304, 305, 312, 313
  volcano, 221, 299, 300
Millennium Development Goals, 291, 355
mitigation, 2, 3, 6, 20, 30, 46, 77, 131, 149, 150, 191, 195, 198, 205, 215, 223, 254, 282, 284, 330, 350, 355, 356, 370, 372, 374, 375
mutual aid, 179, 252, 254

N

national security, 60, 63, 64, 66, 67
nature, 10, 98, 100–104, 108–110, 112, 113, 116–118, 135, 137, 141, 241, 330, 370, 373
Nepal, 148, 152, 153, 158, 166, 271, 277, 281
New Zealand, 9, 37–39, 41, 43, 45–49, 51, 63, 142, 147, 153–155, 157, 158, 161, 164, 166, 167, 177, 182, 372
non-government organisations, 20, 25, 46, 77, 197–199, 234, 286, 299, 300, 303, 304, 312, 353, 356, 371
Northern Territory, 73, 74, 76, 77, 86, 89, 177

P

Paiwanese, 134–136, 143
palaeoflood, 236, 239–243
participation
  Indigenous, 41, 42, 47, 73, 80, 86, 89, 90, 372
  public, 13, 271, 274, 374
Philippines, 3, 6, 11, 187–190, 192, 200, 204, 207, 236, 373
policy integration, 29, 31, 63
policy learning, 19, 21, 22, 25–29, 31, 32, 34
  forms of, 22, 23, 25
  levels of, 9, 22, 26
policy problem, 24, 28, 29
political capital, 218
post-disaster housing, 324, 330
post-disaster recovery, 6, 13, 292, 296, 299, 309, 316, 330, 371, 375
post-earthquake assessment, 274
post-earthquake reconstruction, 273
power, 23, 47, 48, 81, 83, 88, 98, 104, 115, 118, 136, 218, 234, 254, 255, 257, 260, 286
preparedness, 2, 3, 6, 9–12, 56, 60, 61, 67, 77, 124, 130, 133, 138, 139, 148, 149, 151, 176, 180, 183, 191, 195, 198, 214, 219, 254, 271, 273, 274, 292, 324, 330, 350, 352–355, 360–362, 366, 370, 372, 374–376

R

reconstruction
  cultural, 136
  disaster, 134
  housing, 276, 279, 286, 309, 326, 331, 334, 338, 340, 341
  outcomes, 334, 337, 338, 341
  post-disaster, 273, 275, 276, 307, 325, 333, 338, 374, 375
  processes, 13
  projects, 273, 293, 331, 334, 337
recovery, 2, 56, 126, 129
  community-based, 142

eco-centric, 7
recovery outcomes, 141
recovery planning, 131, 133, 165
recovery processes, 125, 151, 291, 292
Red Cross, 160, 167, 351, 360, 363, 374
relocation, 134, 136, 141, 142, 164, 167, 287, 303
resilience, 9, 126, 129, 130, 136, 138, 192, 216, 221–223, 226, 256, 261, 287, 325–331, 334, 336, 338, 341, 350, 354
  building, 2, 7, 13, 44, 72, 78, 88, 188, 192, 218, 264, 281, 286, 330, 340, 349, 351, 375
  community, 12, 86, 87, 89, 150, 214, 217, 218, 222, 293
  measurement, 221, 224, 226
  national, 3, 6, 76
  planning, 352
  science, 214
response strategies, 178, 273, 364
risk, 4, 8, 25, 52, 67, 87, 88, 98, 100, 117, 124, 131, 134, 141, 175, 178, 182, 188, 190, 194, 201, 206, 214–216, 219, 233, 245, 251, 259, 262–264, 325, 328, 331, 347, 358, 365, 367, 373, 374
  appetite, 182
  assessment, 8, 9, 12, 149, 218, 224, 226, 234, 237, 241, 243
  communication, 4, 124, 143
  governance, 2, 3, 5, 45, 234
  management, 8, 11, 26, 66, 179, 189, 191, 192, 200, 201, 203–206, 326, 348
  mitigation, 132
  reduction, 1, 4–8, 12, 13, 19, 20, 31, 45, 52, 56–58, 67, 113, 123, 169, 192, 193, 214, 227, 254, 258, 272, 273, 286, 287, 348, 352, 355, 364, 369, 372
  understanding of, 149, 233, 241
risk acceptance, 126

S
Samoa, 13, 148, 153, 155, 158, 160, 161, 164, 166, 348–351, 356, 361, 363, 366, 375
Samoa Red Cross Society, 14, 348, 355, 356, 360
School Risk Register, 285, 286
schools, 4, 11, 142, 148, 150–152, 157, 160–169, 203, 218, 273, 298, 360, 372
  principals, 153, 157, 158, 166
  students, 158–160
  teachers, 156, 162, 167
science technology, 2, 5, 9, 12, 374
scientific knowledge, 13, 84, 102, 272, 375, 376
security challenges, 56, 59
Sendai Framework, 5, 8, 21, 45, 190, 192, 201, 274, 292, 325, 349, 351, 366, 369–371, 374–376
social capital, 7, 39, 46, 87, 197, 200, 218, 251–253, 260, 263–265, 292
social constructionism, 99, 104, 105, 107, 117, 213
social ecology, 258
social energy, 255, 256
social infrastructure, 13, 252, 256, 258–260, 263–265
socialisation, 99, 116
social media, 139, 258, 265, 294, 305, 310, 314, 373
social support, 139, 141, 151
solidarity, 253, 258
  social, 254
song lyrics, 124–126, 130, 138, 139
spirituality, 115, 116, 135, 136

sustainable development, 4, 11, 21, 189, 193, 206, 283, 375
Sustainable Development Goals, 8, 20, 21, 190, 193, 201, 291, 349, 355, 369
symbolic capital, 262, 265
symbolic interactionism, 105

T

Taiwan, 130, 131, 134, 136, 140, 143
taxes, 265, 308, 309, 312, 316, 362
tiger teams, 65, 66
Timor-Leste, 58, 236
Tohoku, 153, 262
  disaster, 263, 292, 298, 299, 306, 307, 311, 314–316
toxic disasters, 252, 259, 263, 264
transformative education, 112, 114–116, 118
transformative learning, 113–115
transformative pedagogies, 98
travel, 108, 305, 362
tribal recovery, 135
tsunami, 13, 126, 148, 153, 161, 164, 177, 178, 187, 262, 292, 307, 347, 349, 366, 375
  Indian Ocean Tsunami, 3, 177, 257, 273, 291, 313, 366
Typhoon Morakot, 134, 135, 141

U

United Kingdom, 38, 59, 63, 65, 66
United States, 12, 38, 63, 183, 214, 219–223, 295

V

Vanuatu, 148, 153, 157, 161, 166, 167
victimology, 259

victims, 7, 11, 87, 156, 166, 168, 273, 294–296, 298, 299, 301, 304, 313, 357, 362, 363
volunteers, 5, 32, 84, 160, 168, 179, 257, 298, 301, 302, 306, 310, 311, 314, 315, 362, 363, 372, 373
vulnerability, 2, 12, 20, 21, 25, 29, 30, 34, 149, 188, 191, 192, 214–216, 219, 221, 223, 224, 226, 234, 241, 269, 282, 326, 330, 342, 356, 360, 365, 370–373
  assessment, 219, 221, 224

W

war, 55, 258, 325
warnings, 10, 124, 126, 127, 130, 138, 139, 262
wellbeing, 11, 37, 38, 40, 100, 103, 108, 112, 162, 167, 168, 255, 315, 328, 358
Western
  education, 102, 103, 116
  science, 111, 112
whole-of-government, 30, 31, 56, 58, 60, 63, 64, 351
worldviews, 99
  dysfunctional, 107
  Indigenous, 10, 88, 99, 107, 113, 117
  nature-based, 98, 107, 110, 110, 117
  rational, 98, 100, 104, 107, 117, 261
  Western, 10, 77, 98, 100–104, 107, 113, 114, 117, 118

Y

young people, 75, 79, 81, 150, 165, 315

Printed in the United States
by Baker & Taylor Publisher Services